PROPERTY RIGHTS

PROPERTY RIGHTS

Edited by

**Ellen Frankel Paul, Fred D. Miller, Jr.,
and Jeffrey Paul**

CAMBRIDGE
UNIVERSITY PRESS

Published by the Press Syndicate of the University of Cambridge
The Pitt Building, Trumpington Street, Cambridge CB2 1RP, England
40 West 20th Street, New York, NY 10011, USA
10 Stamford Road, Oakleigh, Melbourne, Victoria 3166, Australia

First published 1994

Printed in the United States of America

Library of Congress Cataloging-in-Publication Data

Property rights / edited by Ellen Frankel Paul,
Fred D. Miller, Jr., and Jeffrey Paul.   p.   cm.
Includes bibliographical references and index.
ISBN 0-521-46739-X (pbk.)
1. Right of property—Economic aspects.   2. Right of property—
Moral and ethical aspects.
I. Paul, Ellen Frankel.   II. Miller, Fred Dycus, 1944–
III. Paul, Jeffrey.
HB711.P734   1994
333.3–dc20   94-17506
CIP

ISBN 0-521-46739-X paperback

The essays in this book have also been published,
without introduction and index, in the semiannual journal
Social Philosophy & Policy, Volume 11, Number 2,
which is available by subscription.

CONTENTS

INTRODUCTION

A system of property rights places limits on the actions of individuals and governments, affects the distribution and use of resources, and invokes legal sanctions to remedy rights violations. Thus, any comprehensive discussion of property must draw on a range of disciplines: philosophy, politics, economics, and legal theory. It must address a number of fundamental questions: What is the nature of ownership, and should there be limits on the rights that attend it? Should property be held privately or in common, or should some combination of these two types of ownership prevail? To what extent does the legitimacy of a system of property depend on considerations of economic efficiency or distributive justice?

The essays in this volume examine these questions, as well as other important issues, from a variety of perspectives. Some explore the theory of original acquisition, asking how it is possible for people to acquire rights to previously unowned resources. Others deal with the concept of self-ownership, analyzing its relationship to other kinds of ownership or discussing the limits of the freedom of individuals to make decisions regarding the use of their own bodies. Still others look at legal or constitutional issues, attempting to determine what laws and constitutional provisions are needed to defend property rights, or what property regimes best promote stability of expectations and the ability of people to plan their futures.

In the opening essay, "A Positive Account of Property Rights," David Friedman notes that there are significant similarities among three types of rights: those that libertarian philosophers perceive as just, those that can be shown to be economically efficient, and those that are actually recognized and protected in Western societies. He attempts to explain these similarities by setting out an account of property rights which does not appeal to moral sentiments or legal sanctions—an account which is framed, instead, in terms of strategic, self-interested behavior, and which is designed to show why people are willing to defend certain rights of their own and respect certain rights of others. The key to Friedman's analysis is the Schelling point: a possible outcome of strategic conflict that is a particularly good candidate for resolving such conflict because of its perceived uniqueness. An example of a simple Schelling point is the decision by two people to solve a dispute over some resource by dividing it fifty-fifty. A vastly more complex Schelling point, according to Friedman, is civil society itself: a set of institutions which establish mutual expectations about what rights the members of the society are committed to defending. On this account, the Schelling point of existing Western societies has come about through self-enforcing contracts established between pairs or among small groups of contractors, and through the gradual evolution of norms. Contracting begins with natural property—things one party can control at a much lower cost than others—and natural property includes the right to one's own body, a right that seems just to libertarians. These facts, Friedman notes, help to explain significant areas of correspondence between existing rights and rights libertarian philosophers view as just. Moreover, the fact that evolved norms tend to be economically efficient helps to explain the similarities between existing rights and efficient rights.

Like Friedman, Richard A. Epstein is interested in assessing, and accounting for, the justice and efficiency of existing systems of property rights. In "On the Optimal Mix of Private and Common Property," Epstein focuses on the mixed system of rights that has evolved in English and American law, arguing that property rules must be tailored to the kinds of resources whose use they are to govern. He thus rejects both the extreme libertarian position that all property should be private, and the extreme socialist position that all private property should be abolished in favor of some system of common ownership. On Epstein's view, the decision about whether some resource should be moved from the commons into private hands is to be made on grounds of economic efficiency: privatization is to proceed if, and only if, the incremental gains from privatization exceed the incremental costs. If we apply this test, Epstein argues, we are likely to find that land, labor, and moveable goods are best governed by private property rules, while resources such as roads and bodies of water may be handled more efficiently as common property. Still other resources, such as the broadcast spectrum, may be treated as common property in some respects and private property in others: the airwaves are common in the sense that landowners are not permitted to exclude stations from broadcasting "into" or "through" their property, yet transmissions are private in the sense that a station owner may exclude others from broadcasting at his assigned frequency. Moreover, on this view, the status of a resource may change with the development of new technologies—as happened with water rights in the nineteenth century, when the use of mills for power led to more extensive private rights in rivers. Epstein concludes that there is no final answer to the question of whether a particular resource should be common or private property: our systems of property should coevolve with our understanding of resources and their uses.

The legitimacy of transferring property from common use to private ownership is also the focus of David Schmidtz's contribution to this volume, "The Institution of Property." Schmidtz begins with John Locke's famous argument, according to which one may acquire a previously unowned resource by mixing one's labor with it—for example, by tilling a plot of land. Locke claimed that such acquisition was legitimate so long as certain conditions were met, most importantly the proviso that "enough, and as good" be left in common for others.[1] Schmidtz notes that a number of later theorists have challenged Locke's argument for original acquisition on the ground that this proviso can never be met, since every act of privatization leaves less for those that come along later. Yet Schmidtz argues that private ownership offers a far better means of preserving resources than does common ownership. Resources held in common tend to be overused, since no individual has an incentive to preserve them, while everyone has an incentive to use as much of the resource as he can before it is depleted. Private ownership, by contrast, can lead to the husbanding of resources and hence to the preservation of their value over time. Moreover, private ownership leads to increases in productivity that vastly improve the conditions of life for future generations. Like Epstein, however, Schmidtz acknowledges that some systems of common ownership—those that carefully regulate access and use—can facilitate production and commerce as well as private ownership can. Thus, societies are likely to evolve a complex mix of common and private property as they attempt to find ways of using scarce resources most efficiently.

A. John Simmons explores the issue of original acquisition further in his contribution, "Original-Acquisition Justifications of Private Property." Simmons examines Locke's argument—as well as those of Samuel Pufendorf and Robert Nozick—in an effort to deal with certain real and alleged problems faced by all theories that attempt to justify property by appealing to historical or conjectural accounts of its origin. Such theories meet with a number of standard objections: Most acts of original acquisition are said to have taken place in the remote past, and it is difficult to see how such acts could justify the holdings that actually exist today. Original-acquisition arguments offer at best a partial justification of private property, since they fail to show that nonprivate forms of property could not yield the same advantages. Moreover, original-acquisition theories posit an unfamiliar and counterintuitive power: the power of individuals to create, by unilateral action, onerous moral obligations on the part of others. Simmons responds to each of these objections in detail, basing his responses on a careful analysis of the nature of justification—an analysis which distinguishes between justifications that purport to demonstrate private property's *permissibility* and those that purport to demonstrate its *optimality*. He concludes that demands for more-stringent optimality justifications are unreasonable, but that permissibility justifications can have a great deal of force and ought to be taken seriously in contemporary property theory.

---

[1] John Locke, *Two Treatises of Government*, ed. Peter Laslett (New York: Mentor, 1960), *Second Treatise*, section 27.

Both Schmidtz and Simmons work with the assumption that, if a system of property is to be just, the initial holdings under that system must be just; hence the importance of justifying original acquisition. Other theorists, however, have challenged this view. In "The Advantages and Difficulties of the Humean Theory of Property," Jeremy Waldron explores the position of one such theorist, David Hume. Hume held that we should not concern ourselves with the origin or distribution of initial holdings; instead, we should accept any distribution which promises stability, in order to reduce the level of conflict brought about by disagreements over holdings, and to bring about the gains made possible by market exchange. On this view, the initial assignment of property rights is the outcome of an agreement, based on mutual advantage, to ratify existing possessions, even when those possessions were established arbitrarily or through coercion. Waldron considers the advantages that theories like Hume's have over their more moralistic counterparts, such as the theories of Locke and Jean-Jacques Rousseau, and argues that Humean theories would be far easier to implement in practice than the others. He also examines some of the difficulties involved in the proposition that a Humean model is all one needs for a theory of justice, focusing on the model recently put forward by economist James Buchanan. Finally, he criticizes arguments recently set out by David Gauthier and others who attempt to reconcile the structure of such a model with a substantive commitment to distributive fairness or equality. He concludes that it might be possible to defend a modified Humean model, on the basis of its ability to avoid the disruptive effects of intractable disagreements over justice.

While Waldron addresses the legitimacy of initial holdings, Jules L. Coleman is concerned with broader questions of justice in the distribution of property rights. In his essay "Corrective Justice and Property Rights," Coleman examines the workings of corrective justice within property regimes that are not themselves fully just. Under such regimes, by hypothesis, some individuals have more property than they are entitled to, while others have less. It is possible that wrongful losses imposed, by theft or fraud, upon those who have more, might result in a distribution of property that is more just overall. Should such losses be sustained by law? Or should they be rectified through compensation, even when the payment of compensation would result in a return to a distribution that is less just? Coleman responds to these questions by setting out a conception of corrective justice based on the concepts of "loss," "wrongfulness," and "responsibility." He argues that duties of compensation for losses could arise under such a conception even when the enforcement of such duties would help perpetuate unjust distributions. The key to his argument is the idea that corrective justice helps promote individual well-being and autonomy. Duties of compensation, he believes, are essential to the establishment of a framework within which individuals can formulate meaningful projects and plans and rationally invest in their implementation.

Any effort to assess the legitimacy of a particular distribution of property presupposes standards of judgment and proof, and these standards are the focus of Gary Lawson's contribution to this volume, "Proving Ownership." In order to prove propositions about property rights, Lawson notes, one needs to know what counts as evidence for the truth of a proposition, how much that evidence counts, and how much evidence is needed to justify a claim. Thus, the justification of any ownership claim requires all three of these elements: standards of admissibility, of significance, and of proof. Yet Lawson contends that legal theorists have given too little thought to the selection of these standards, especially standards of proof. He believes that the American legal system implicitly recognizes a relatively weak standard: the principle that the law should adopt the "best available" theory of property rights and the "best available" legal rules that can be derived from the chosen theory. More demanding standards—such as proof "by a preponderance of the evidence" or "beyond a reasonable doubt"—are often used in establishing matters of fact, but are not brought to bear in evaluating matters of law. Lawson explores the likely consequences of adopting more demanding standards for the proof of legal propositions, and addresses concerns that various standards provoke. On the one hand, employing a weak standard can lead to an atmosphere of excessive coercion, as the law intervenes in more and more disputes over property. On the other hand, employing a strong standard can lead to an increase in lawlessness, as individuals, faced with an unresponsive legal system, turn to settling their own disputes. Lawson concludes with the suggestion that a strong standard of proof might be useful if it were tempered by adjustments in the standards of admissibility and significance.

Like Lawson, James Tully is concerned with the legal standards for settling disputes over ownership. In "Aboriginal Property and Western Theory: Recovering a Middle Ground," Tully examines a specific, long-standing dispute: the conflict over rights to land between the Aboriginal peoples of North America and the governments of the United States and Canada. The central question in this conflict is whether there can be a theoretical justification for the establishment of non-Aboriginal systems of property in North America. Contemporary Western theories of property, Tully notes, generally presuppose one of three starting points: individuals in a state of nature or behind a veil of ignorance prior to the establishment of a system of property; individuals within a set of shared traditions and institutions derived from European history; or a community bound together by a set of shared traditions and institutions. None of these views is equipped to deal with the clash of competing traditions, and thus none can accommodate the existence of Aboriginal governments and property regimes that were already well developed at the time when European settlers arrived in the New World. Tully argues that a theory of non-Aboriginal property in North America can be just only if it recognizes the prior existence of Aboriginal systems. He proposes a cross-cultural "Aboriginal and common law" system which would allow for the coexistence of various traditions. Under such a system, negotiations between two rival traditions would recognize the equal standing of the traditions, would respect the forms of argumentation and negotiation of each culture, and would lead to treaty relations based on consent rather than on force or deceit.

Tully's discussion of Aboriginal and Western property regimes illustrates that the resolution of disputes and the protection of property rights require the construction of a just legal system. In "Property Rights, Innovation, and Constitutional Structure," Jonathan R. Macey explores the issues confronting those who seek to construct such a system, focusing on the problems faced by the Framers of the U.S. Constitution. Macey begins with a discussion of the meaning of "property" and of the relationship between morals and property rights. He argues that property rights, conceived as rights to command resources, can be obtained either through mutually beneficial market transactions, or through amorally redistributive, coerced governmental transfers of wealth. Market transactions, he believes, increase societal wealth, while governmental transfers reduce it. Thus, when individuals set about designing a legal system, they have strong incentives to create constitutional rules that encourage market transactions and discourage the process of seeking coerced governmental transfers (known as "rent-seeking"). Macey explains that the Framers of the U.S. Constitution understood the wealth-creation/rent-seeking dichotomy very well, and shows how they employed a number of strategies to address it. These strategies included the establishment of a bicameral legislature, a presidential veto power, and an independent judiciary, all of which were designed to make rent-seeking more difficult and costly. Macey concludes by examining the erosion of property rights under the American legal system, arguing that a number of factors, including innovations in the organization of Congress, have made it possible for politicians and interest groups to overcome protections for property rights embodied in the Constitution.

Macey's discussion relies on the conception of a property right as a right to command resources—that is, a freedom to use and dispose of such resources as one sees fit—and indeed, many prominent theorists have conceived of rights in just this way. Yet what precisely is the relationship between property and freedom, and how far should the right to control resources extend? Gerald F. Gaus addresses these questions in his essay "Property, Rights, and Freedom." Gaus focuses on a classical-liberal view of ownership and freedom, in which having an ownership right over some resource involves four elements: the right to use the resource, the right to exclude others from its use, the right to demand compensation if others use or damage the resource, and the right to transfer all these rights. On the basis of this view, Gaus argues that at least some rights—including, e.g., rights to bodily integrity and freedom of religion—are not classical-liberal property rights, since they lack one or more of these four elements. Moreover, property rights are not merely rights to freedom, since they involve two elements that simple freedom rights are generally thought to lack: powers of transfer and claims to demand noninterference on the part of others. Thus, there can be no straightforward reduction of freedom rights to property rights, or vice versa. Nevertheless, Gaus contends, freedom and property are related, in the sense that property rights, to one's body and to external resources, involve a kind of "moral space": a sphere of activity within which one is largely free to act. To say that this freedom of action is not always complete sovereignty in a classical-liberal or libertarian sense, is not to deny the important link between freedom and property.

The right to control one's body, an issue Gaus touches on briefly, is the subject of the final two essays of this collection. In "Self-Ownership, Autonomy, and Property Rights," Alan Ryan argues that talk of self-ownership plays no necessary role in the defense of liberal politics and, in fact, fails to illuminate the kind of autonomy that liberal political theorists wish to promote. Some theorists have held that ownership of one's body entitles one to use and dispose of it as one wishes, given the usual constraints against violating the rights of others; but Ryan argues that, historically, this view of self-ownership has not been the norm. In Locke's political theory, for instance, each individual has "a *Property* in his own *Person*,"[2] yet this property brings with it duties of self-preservation and the preservation of mankind. Ryan provides a detailed discussion of the concept of self-ownership in Locke's writings and in the writings of Immanuel Kant and G. W. F. Hegel, and offers a critique of the concept's use by modern theorists such as Robert Nozick. He maintains that a certain conception of self-ownership—one that stresses responsibility toward oneself and others—might be a useful element in a social or political theory that emphasizes our ties to one another rather than our rights against one another. He concludes with the suggestion that skepticism about talk of self-ownership need not detract from the liberal theorist's conviction that autonomy and private property are crucial to the defense of a free society.

A special case of self-ownership—the right to sell parts of one's body—is the focus of Stephen R. Munzer's contribution to this volume, "An Uneasy Case against Property Rights in Body Parts." Munzer notes that most countries legally permit only the donation of body parts, not their sale, and that such restrictions lead to shortages and to long waiting peri-

---

[2] Locke, *Second Treatise*, section 27.

ods for patients needing organ transplants. Calls for the legalization of sales of body parts, however, face strong opposition from those who object to the treatment of body parts as "commodities," fearing that such treatment would offend human dignity. Munzer believes that a market in body parts should not be prohibited altogether; nevertheless, he argues that it is morally objectionable for an individual to sell one of his body parts if the sale would diminish his dignity. Such a diminution would occur if a body part were transferred for a reason that was not strong enough in light of the nature of the part sold. On this view, sales of replenishable parts such as hair, blood, and sperm are the least objectionable, while sales of unreplenishable organs such as kidneys or corneas are far more worrisome. Munzer's discussion touches on a range of topics: the nature of dignity and the various ways of offending dignity; the difference between dignity-value and market-value; and the moral implications of participating in a market for body parts as a buyer, seller, or broker. He concludes by considering how the language of the market — "property," "commodity," "money," "price" — can affect the ways in which people view themselves and others.

Rights to property are at the center of a number of crucial debates in political and legal theory. The discussions of the nature and limits of property contained in these twelve essays represent important contributions to those debates.

ACKNOWLEDGMENTS

This volume could not have been produced without the help of a number of individuals at the Social Philosophy and Policy Center, Bowling Green State University. Among them are Mary Dilsaver, Terrie Weaver, and Carrie-Ann Lynch.

The editors would like to extend special thanks to Executive Manager Kory Swanson, for offering invaluable administrative support; to Publication Specialist Tamara Sharp, for attending to innumerable day-to-day details of the book's preparation; and to Managing Editor Harry Dolan, for providing dedicated assistance throughout the editorial and production processes.

CONTRIBUTORS

David Friedman is currently Visiting Professor at Cornell Law School. He received his Ph.D. in 1971 from the University of Chicago, and has taught economics at Virginia Polytechnic Institute, the University of California at Irvine, the University of California at Los Angeles, Tulane University, and the University of Chicago. From 1986 to 1993, he was an Olin Fellow in law and economics at University of Chicago Law School. He is the author of *The Machinery of Freedom: Guide to a Radical Capitalism* (1971, 1978, 1989), *Price Theory: An Intermediate Text* (1986, 1990), and numerous articles.

Richard A. Epstein is James Parker Hall Distinguished Service Professor of Law at the University of Chicago. He is the author of *Takings: Private Property and the Power of Eminent Domain* (1985), *Forbidden Grounds: The Case against Employment Discrimination Laws* (1992), and *Bargaining with the State* (1993). He is an editor of the *Journal of Law and Economics* and a member of the American Academy of Arts and Sciences.

David Schmidtz is Associate Professor of Philosophy at Yale University. He is the author of *The Limits of Government: An Essay on the Public Goods Argument* (1991) and *Rational Choice and Moral Agency* (1994). He is a previous contributor to *Social Philosophy & Policy*, and his essays have also appeared in the *Journal of Philosophy* and *Ethics*.

A. John Simmons is Professor of Philosophy at the University of Virginia, where he has taught since 1976, specializing in political, moral, and legal philosophy. He received his Ph.D. in philosophy from Cornell University in 1977. His works include *Moral Principles and Political Obligations* (1979), *The Lockean Theory of Rights* (1992), *On the Edge of Anarchy* (1993), and many articles in philosophy, law, and politics journals and in philosophical encyclopedias. He is an editor of the journal *Philosophy & Public Affairs* and is currently writing a new book on political obligation.

Jeremy Waldron is Professor of Law and Associate Dean at Boalt Hall, and Chair of the Jurisprudence and Social Policy Program, University of California at Berkeley. He has taught at the University of Otago in New Zealand, at Oxford University, and at the University of Edinburgh, and he recently held a visiting appointment in the Ethics and Public Life Program at Cornell University. He has published numerous articles on rights, property, and liberalism, many of which have been collected in *Liberal Rights: Collected Papers 1981–91* (1993). He is the editor of *Theories of Rights* (1984) and *Nonsense upon Stilts: Bentham, Burke, and Marx on the Rights of Man* (1987), and the author of *The Right to Private Property* (1988) and *The*

Law (1990). His current research is on the philosophical conceptualization of poverty, need, and homelessness.

Jules L. Coleman is John A. Garver Professor of Jurisprudence and Philosophy at Yale Law School. He is the author of numerous articles and several books, including *Markets, Morals, and the Law* (1988) and *Risks and Wrongs* (1992). He is presently completing an edited collection of five volumes of outstanding essays in legal philosophy to be published by Garland Press in a series edited by Robert Nozick. His current interests include problems relating metaphysical and epistemic objectivity to the nature of legal authority.

Gary Lawson is Associate Professor at Northwestern University School of Law, where he has taught since 1988. He has been a John M. Olin Research Fellow at Yale Law School, a law clerk to Justice Antonin Scalia, an Attorney-Adviser at the Office of Legal Counsel in the United States Department of Justice, and an attorney in private practice. He received his J.D. from Yale Law School in 1983.

James Tully is Professor of Philosophy at McGill University in Montreal, Quebec. He is the author of numerous publications on modern political philosophy and its complex history. He specializes in using studies of the history of political philosophy to throw critical light on assumptions and problems in contemporary political philosophy. Among his recent books are *An Approach to Political Philosophy: Locke in Contexts* (1993) and his critical edition of Samuel Pufendorf's *On the Duty of Man and Citizen* (1991). He is also the editor of *Philosophy in a Pluralistic Age: Critical Perspectives on the Philosophy of Charles Taylor* (1994).

Jonathan R. Macey is J. DuPratt White Professor of Law and Director of the John M. Olin Program in Law and Economics at Cornell University. A graduate of Harvard College and Yale Law School, he served as a law clerk to the Honorable Henry J. Friendly of the U.S. Court of Appeals for the Second Circuit. His research interests lie in the fields of public choice, law and economics, banking, and corporate and securities law. In addition to his teaching at Cornell, he has taught at the University of Chicago, Emory University School of Law, the Stockholm School of Economics, the University of Tokyo, the University of Toronto, and the University of Virginia.

Gerald F. Gaus is Professor of Philosophy and Political Science at the University of Minnesota, Duluth. He was formerly Research Fellow in Philosophy in the Research School of Social Sciences of the Australian National University, and has been Visiting Research Fellow at the University of New England and Visiting Scholar at the Social Philosophy and

Policy Center. He is the author of *The Modern Liberal Theory of Man* (1983) and *Value and Justification* (1990), and the coeditor, with Stanley Benn, of *Public and Private in Social Life* (1983). He is currently completing a book entitled *Justificatory Liberalism*.

Alan Ryan is Professor of Politics at Princeton University. He was until 1988 Fellow and Tutor in Politics and Reader in Politics at New College, Oxford University. He is the author of *Property and Political Theory* (1984), *Property* (1987), and *Bertrand Russell: A Political Life* (1988), and has just finished a study of John Dewey's contribution to twentieth-century liberalism.

Stephen R. Munzer is Professor of Law at the University of California at Los Angeles. After graduating from the University of Kansas in 1966, he completed a B.Phil. in philosophy at Oxford University in 1969 and received a J.D. degree from Yale Law School in 1972, where he was executive editor of the *Yale Law Journal*. He has practiced law at Covington & Burling in Washington, D.C., taught philosophy at Rutgers University, and taught law at the University of Minnesota. He is the author of *A Theory of Property* (1990).

A POSITIVE ACCOUNT OF PROPERTY RIGHTS

By David Friedman

In thinking and talking about rights, including property rights, it seems natural to put the argument in either moral or legal terms. From the former viewpoint, rights are part of a description of what actions are right or wrong. The fact that I have a right to do something is an argument, although not necessarily a sufficient argument, that someone who prevents me from doing it is acting wrongly.[1]

From the legal standpoint, rights are a description either of what the law says or of how it is enforced. On the latter interpretation, "I have a right to do X" translates as something like "If I do X the police will not arrest me; if someone tries to stop me from doing X the police will arrest him."[2] From this standpoint, one might claim that people in Holland have the right to buy marijuana and that people in America have the right to drive five miles per hour over the speed limit, even though both are illegal.

Both of these approaches have serious difficulties if our goal is to understand the phenomenon of rights, and associated phenomena, as they actually exist in the real world. We frequently observe behavior which looks like the claiming of rights and the recognition of rights in contexts where neither a moral nor a legal account seems relevant.

Consider, for example, Great Britain's "right" to control Hong Kong, Kowloon, and the New Territories. It is difficult to explain Communist China's willingness to respect that right on moral grounds, given that, from the Maoist standpoint, neither the government of Britain nor previous, non-Communist Chinese governments with which Britain had signed agreements were entities entitled to any moral respect. It seems equally difficult to explain it on legal grounds, given the general weakness of international law and the fact that for part of the period in question, Great Britain (as a member state of the United Nations) was at war with China. An alternative explanation—that the Chinese government believed that British occupation of Hong Kong was in its own interest— seems inconsistent with the Chinese failure to renew the lease on the New Territories, due to expire in 1997.

A second example is presented by the 1982 Falklands war. On the face of it, the clash looks like an attempted trespass repelled. Moral and legal

---

[1] For a sophisticated discussion of rights from the standpoint of moral philosophy, see Judith Jarvis Thomson, *The Realm of Rights* (Cambridge: Harvard University Press, 1990).

[2] Or the equivalent in civil rather than criminal terms.

accounts seem irrelevant, given the attitude of Argentina toward the British claim. Yet the willingness of Britain to accept costs far out of proportion to the value of the prize being fought over is difficult to explain except on the theory that the British felt they were defending their property, which raises the question of what that concept means in such a context.

A further difficulty with moral accounts of rights, in particular of property rights, is the degree to which the property rights that people actually respect seem to depend on facts that are morally irrelevant. This difficulty presents itself in libertarian accounts of property as the problem of initial acquisition. It is far from clear even in principle how unowned resources such as land can become private property. Even if one accepts an account, such as that of Locke, of how initial acquisition might justly have occurred, that account provides little justification for the existing pattern of property rights, given the high probability that any piece of property has been unjustly seized at least once since it was first cleared. Yet billions of people, now and in the past, base much of their behavior on respect for property claims that seem either morally arbitrary or clearly unjust.

A further difficulty with legal accounts of rights is that they are to some degree circular. We observe that police will act in certain ways and that their actions (and related actions by judges, juries, etc.) imply that certain people have certain rights. But the behavior of police is itself in part a consequence of rights — such as the right of the state to collect taxes and pay them to the police as wages, and the property right that the police then have over the money they receive.

For all of these reasons, I believe it is worth attempting a positive account of rights — an account which is both amoral and alegal. In Section I of this essay, I present such an account — one in which rights, in particular property rights, are a consequence of strategic behavior and may exist with no moral or legal support.[3] The account is presented both

---

[3] The approach presented here is an extension of arguments made in my review of *Further Explorations in the Theory of Anarchy*, ed. Gordon Tullock (Blacksburg: University Publications, 1974), published in *Public Choice*, vol. 25 (1976), pp. 101–4. Elements of the argument have also appeared in David Friedman, "Many, Few, One — Social Harmony and the Shrunken Choice Set," *American Economic Review*, vol. 70, no. 1 (March 1980), pp. 225–32. A very similar approach is presented in Robert Sugden, *The Economics of Rights, Co-operation, and Welfare* (Oxford: Blackwell, 1986). The chief difference between Sugden's discussion and mine is that his argument is put primarily in terms of evolutionarily stable strategies, where mine is put in terms of Schelling points. Sugden also provides interesting examples of the same general line of argument in the work of eighteenth-century writers, in particular David Hume.

Throughout most of this essay, I present the argument as the working out of my own ideas. Readers familiar with the literature may feel, with some justice, that I fail to acknowledge how much of it has been said before by other people, often in somewhat different terms. I have presented it in this form in part because I am trying to work out the logic of a set of related ideas, not their history, and in part because that is how it in fact developed; most of the material in Section I of this essay was first written down, and some of it first published, more than fifteen years ago. I am grateful to the editors of this volume for providing an opportunity and incentive to compile and expand it.

as an explanation of how rights could arise in a Hobbesian anarchy and as an explanation of the nature of rights as we observe them around us. In Section II, I suggest ways in which something like the present structure of rights might have developed.

One puzzling feature of rights as we observe them is the degree to which the same conclusions seem to follow from very different assumptions. Thus, roughly similar structures of rights can be and are deduced by libertarian philosophers trying to show what set of natural rights is just and by economists trying to show what set of legal rules would be efficient. And the structures of rights that they deduce seem similar to those observed in human behavior and embodied in the common law. In Section III, I try to suggest at least partial explanations for this triple coincidence—the apparent similarity among what is, what is just, and what is efficient.

I. Schelling Points, Self-Enforcing Contracts, and the Paradox of Order

Several writers have tried to analyze the transition from a Hobbesian state of nature to a state of civil order in terms of a set of hypothetical contracts establishing an initial distribution of property rights based on a pre-existing distribution of power.[4] One difficulty with this approach is that in the initial situation there are no institutions to enforce contracts. How can people in that situation change it by making contracts which are unenforceable and thus of no effect?[5]

The same problem can be seen from the other side by asking in what sense our society, or any society, is ever *out* of a Hobbesian state of nature. What do we have, what have we created, that does not exist in the Hobbesian jungle? Civil order is not defined by the existence of physical objects—court rooms, police uniforms, law books. We can easily enough imagine a Hobbesian jungle—in the middle of a war, say—coexisting with all the physical appurtenances of civil society; and primitive peoples, without court rooms or law books, nonetheless live in a state of civil order.

Nor does it suffice to say that we are in a state of civil order because we have judges to interpret our laws and police to enforce them. Why do those people act in that way? Presumably because it is in their private interest to do so—just as potential criminals obey the law for the same reason. But that is how people act in the Hobbesian jungle. There too, one man may happen to enforce a rule, and another happen to obey it,

---

[4] I would like to thank James Buchanan for bringing Schelling points to my attention and Gordon Tullock for provoking me into exploring them further. See especially Winston Bush, "Individual Welfare in Anarchy," in *Explorations in the Theory of Anarchy*, ed. Gordon Tullock (Blacksburg: University Publications, 1973).

[5] This point is made by Gordon Tullock in "Corruption and Anarchy," in Tullock, ed., *Further Explorations*.

because each finds it in his own interest to do so. What is it that we have and the Hobbesian jungle does not have that makes it in the interest of people to behave in a law-abiding and peaceful manner? To say that the answer is "police, courts, government" only throws the question back a step; if civil order is enforced by men with guns, what controls them?

There are two sorts of answers to these questions. One is that the difference is a moral one. People somehow accept an obligation, agree *not* to behave according to simple self-interest, feel themselves bound by that agreement, and alter their actions accordingly.

There are difficulties with this sort of explanation. First, there is the empirical observation that people do not feel themselves bound to obey laws; many, perhaps most, people feel free to violate those laws (speed limits, drinking laws, customs regulations) which they disagree with and believe they can get away with breaking. Second, to the extent that people do feel a moral obligation to obey social rules, it is hard to derive that feeling from any variant of social-contract theory. The traditional variants encounter the difficulty eloquently described by Lysander Spooner:[6] since we ourselves did not sign the contract, we are not bound by it.

The difficulties with deriving moral obligation from the sort of pairwise social contract suggested by Winston Bush[7] are equally great. Even if we consider that each of us is, at every instant, in an implicit contract with each of his neighbors to respect some agreed-upon set of rights, still that contract, in Bush's model, is based on the threat of coercion. It has no more moral legitimacy, according to conventional moral ideas, than the obligation to pay off a protection racket.

It may be possible to explain the difference between a Hobbesian state of nature and civil society as a moral difference, but I prefer the alternative explanation—that the essential difference is not in the motivation of the players but in the strategic situation they face. This raises the question of how making an agreement—in a society with no mechanisms for enforcing agreements—can change anything, the strategic situation included.

A. The tool: Schelling points[8]

2,5,9,25,69,73,82,96,100,126,150

Two people are separately confronted with the list of numbers shown above and offered a reward if they independently choose the same num-

---

[6] Lysander Spooner, *No Treason: No. VI, The Constitution of No Authority* (1870; reprint, Larkspur, CO: Pine Tree Press, 1966).

[7] Bush, "Individual Welfare in Anarchy."

[8] Thomas C. Schelling, *The Strategy of Conflict* (Oxford: Oxford University Press, 1960), ch. 3. While I am using Schelling's concept, my analysis of it, in particular my grounds for applying it to games with communication, is somewhat different from his.

ber. If the two are mathematicians, it is likely that they will both choose 2 — the only even prime. Nonmathematicians are likely to choose 100 — a number which seems, to the mathematicians, no more unique than the other two exact squares. Illiterates might agree on 69, because of its peculiar symmetry — as would, for a different reason, those whose interest in numbers is more prurient than mathematical.

There are three things worth noting about this simple problem in coordination without communication. The first is that each pair of players is looking for a number that is in some way unique. To a mathematician, all three squares are special numbers, as are the three primes. But if they try to coordinate on a square or a prime, they have only one chance in three of success — and besides, one may be trying primes and the other squares. The number 2 is unique. If the set of numbers did not contain 2 but did contain only one prime (or only one square, or one perfect number) they would choose that.

The second thing to note is that there is no single right answer; the number chosen by one player, and hence the number that ought to be chosen by the other, depends on the categories that the person choosing uses to classify the alternatives. The right strategy is to find some classification in terms of which there is a unique number, then choose that number — a strategy whose implementation depends on the particular classifications that pair of players uses. Thus, the right answer depends on subjective characteristics of the players.

The third point, which follows from this, is that it is possible to succeed in the game because of, not in spite of, the bounded rationality of the players. To a mind of sufficient scope every number is unique.[9] It is only because the players are limited to a small number of the possible classification schemes for numbers, and because the two players may be limited to the same schemes, that a correct choice may exist. In this respect the theory of this game is radically different from conventional game theory, which assumes players with unlimited ability to examine alternatives and thus abstracts away from all subjective characteristics of the players except those embodied in their utility functions.[10]

Consider now two players playing the game called bilateral monopoly. They have a dollar to divide between them, provided they can agree on

[9] There is a semi-serious theorem according to which all integers are interesting. The proof is by induction. If some positive integers are uninteresting, then there must be a smallest positive uninteresting integer. But this unique characteristic makes that number interesting. So there can be no smallest uninteresting positive integer, so there can be no uninteresting positive integers. Similarly, *mutatis mutandis*, for negative integers.

[10] In practice, game theory sometimes smuggles subjective characteristics back into the argument in the process of choosing a particular strategy set. A famous example of this problem is the analysis of oligopoly. The assumption that the firm's strategy is defined as a choice of quantity and the assumption that it is defined as a choice of price lead to very different conclusions. See David Friedman, *Price Theory: An Intermediate Text* (Cincinnati: South-Western Publishing Co., 1990), ch. 11.

how to divide it. Superficially, there is no resemblance between this game and the one discussed above; the players are free to talk with each other as much as they want.

But while they can talk freely, there is a sense in which they cannot communicate at all. It is in my interest to persuade you that I will only be satisfied with a large fraction of the dollar; if I am really unwilling to accept anything less than ninety cents, you are better off agreeing to accept ten cents than holding out for more and getting nothing. Since it is in the interest of each of us to persuade the other of his resolve, all statements to that effect can be ignored; they would be made whether true or not. What each player has to do is to guess what the other's real demand is, what the fraction of the dollar is without which he will refuse to agree. That cannot be communicated, simply because it pays each player to lie about it. The situation is therefore similar to that in the previous game; the players must coordinate their demands (so that they add up to a dollar) without communication. It seems likely that they will do so by agreeing to split the dollar fifty-fifty.

The same points made about the previous game apply here, although less obviously. The players are looking for a unique solution; if I decide that the natural split is one-third/two-thirds, and you agree, both of us reasoning from a mystic belief in the significance of the number three, there is still the risk that each will decide he is entitled to the two-thirds.

To see that the solution depends on the particular categories used by the players, imagine that both have been brought up to believe that utility, not money, is the relevant payoff, and suppose further that both believe the marginal utility of a dollar to be inversely proportional to the recipient's income. In that case, the solution to the game is not a fifty-fifty split of money but a fifty-fifty split of utility—implying a division of the dollar into shares proportional to the two players' incomes.[11]

Such an outcome, chosen because of its uniqueness, is called a Schelling point, after Thomas Schelling who originated the idea. It provides a possible solution to the problem of coordination without communication. As this example shows, it is relevant both to situations where communication is physically impossible and to situations where communication is impossible because there is no way that either party can provide the other with a reason to believe that what he says is true.

Even if it is impossible for the players in such a game to communicate their real demands, it may still be possible for them to affect the outcome by what they say. They could do so, not by directly communicating their own strategies (any such statement will be disbelieved), but by altering the other player's categories, the ways in which he organizes the alterna-

---

[11] I have discussed this point, and the game of bilateral monopoly, at greater length in David Friedman, "Bilateral Monopoly: A Solution," Fels Discussion Paper No. 52, University of Pennsylvania, March 1974 (unpublished, available from the author).

tives of the game, and thus changing the Schelling points which depend on those categories.

In the case just discussed, for example, one player (presumably the richer) might remind the other of their shared belief in the importance of utility in order to make sure the equi-utility Schelling point would be chosen. If, in the first game I described, the players were allowed to talk before seeing the numbers, a conversation on the interesting properties of primes or the special uniqueness of the lowest of a series of numbers might well alter the Schelling point, and thus the result of the game. One can interpret a good deal of bargaining behavior in this light — as an attempt by one party to make the other see the situation in a particular way, so as to generate a Schelling point favorable to the first party.

A slightly different way in which one may conceptualize the process of agreement on a Schelling point is in terms of bargaining costs in a context of continuous bargaining.[12] Consider a situation in which the number of possible outcomes is very large. Suppose the process of bargaining is itself costly, either because it consumes time or because each player bears costs (such as staying out on strike) in trying to validate his threats. As long as the players are faced with a choice among a large number of comparable alternatives, each proposal by one player is likely to call forth a competing proposal from another, slanted a little more toward his own interest.

But suppose there is one outcome that is seen as unique. A player who proposes that outcome may be perceived as offering, not a choice between that outcome, another slightly different, another different still, . . . but a choice between that outcome and continued bargaining. A player who says that he insists on the unique outcome and will not settle for anything less may be believable, where a similar statement about a different outcome would not be. He can convincingly argue that he will stand by his proposed outcome because, once he gives it up, he has no idea where he will end up or how high the costs of getting there will be.

In order for a Schelling point to provide a peaceful resolution to a conflict of interest, both parties must conceptualize the alternatives in similar ways — similar enough so that they can agree about which possible outcomes are unique, and thus attractive as potential Schelling points. So one interesting implication of the argument is that violent conflict is especially likely to occur on the boundary between cultures, where people with very different ways of viewing the world interact.

B. Up from Hobbes

Two people are living in a Hobbesian state of nature. Each can injure or steal from the other, at some cost, and each can spend resources on his

---

[12] This approach is discussed in Friedman, "Many, Few, One" (*supra* note 3).

own defense. Since conflict consumes resources, both could benefit by agreeing on what each owns and thereafter each respecting the other's property. The joint benefit might be divided in different ways, according to the particular set of property rights they agree on—what property belongs to whom, and whether either has a property right in tribute from the other. This is a special case of the game—bilateral monopoly—described above.

Each player, of course, will threaten to refuse to make any such agreement unless he gets the division he wants. Each will disbelieve most of the other's threats. If their ability to coerce and defend is roughly equal, and if there is some natural division of contested property (such as a stream running between their farms), it is likely that they will find a Schelling point in the form of an agreement to accept that division, respect each other's rights, and pay no tribute.

If one (being, perhaps, slightly more powerful) tries to insist on a small tribute, arguing that it will still leave the other better off than continued conflict, the other may believably refuse, arguing that once he concedes any tribute there is no natural limit to what the other can demand. Agreeing to tribute costs the victim not only the tribute but the only available Schelling point. The expected cost to him of such an agreement includes both the possible cost of paying higher tribute in the future and the risk of future conflicts if in the future he rejects demands for higher tribute. That cost may be high enough to establish the credibility of his insistence that he will choose continued conflict over the payment of even a small tribute.

So far we have considered the Schelling point that generates an agreement. But the agreement itself, whether generated by a Schelling point or in some other way, is thereafter itself a Schelling point. It is a unique outcome of which both players are conscious. Once it has been made, a policy of "if you do not abide by the agreement, I will revert to the use of force, even if the violation is small compared to the cost of conflict" is believable for precisely the same reason the refusal to pay tribute, or any insistence by a bargainer on a Schelling point, is believable. The signing of a contract establishes a new Schelling point and thereby alters the strategic situation. The contract enforces itself.

This applies not only to the initial pairwise social contract but to subsequent contracts as well. Suppose you have an orchard and I have an axe. After agreeing on our mutual property rights, you offer me a bushel of apples to cut down a tree that is shading your orchard. I cut down the tree as agreed, but you refuse to give me the apples. What happens?

So far as our physical situation is concerned, I am no more able to compel you to pay me a bushel of apples now than I was before you made the offer and I cut down the tree—our material resources, our ability to hurt each other and defend ourselves, are the same as they were. Yet my threat to cut down your orchard unless you pay up is more credible than it would have been before, both because I have more reason to carry through on it and because you have less reason to resist it. Before, the attempt to get a bushel of apples from you would have been an attempt to move you away from the Schelling point established by the initial contract. Now it is an attempt to restore the Schelling point established by our subsequent agreement.

A more conventional explanation of this is that the reason it is in your interest to deliver the apples once you have agreed to do so is that you wish to establish a reputation for keeping promises, and that the reason it is in my interest to punish you if you do not deliver the apples is because I wish to establish a reputation for enforcing contracts made with me. While this may be true, there are two reasons why it cannot be a complete explanation. First, it depends on a particular perception of consistent behavior—in pure logic, there is no more reason to think of "always enforce" as more consistent than "back down the first, third, fifth, . . . time and fight the second, fourth, sixth, . . . time." Each describes a single possible strategy. The important difference between them is that the former is a Schelling point and the latter is not—a fact not about the strategies but about the way we classify them.

A second and related problem with the conventional account is that I might equally well wish to establish a reputation as a consistent extortionist. We need some way of explaining why I cut down the shade tree first, instead of simply committing myself to demand your apples. If the former pattern creates a Schelling point of contract fulfillment and the latter does not, that provides a possible explanation.

I believe I have now resolved the apparent paradox of contracting out of the Hobbesian jungle. The process of contracting changes the situation because it establishes new Schelling points, which in turn affect the strategic situation and its outcome. The same analysis can be used from the other side to explain what constitutes civil society. The laws and customs of civil society are an elaborate network of Schelling points. If my neighbor annoys me by growing ugly flowers, I do nothing. If he dumps his garbage on my lawn, I retaliate—possibly in kind. If he threatens to dump garbage on my lawn, or play a trumpet fanfare at 3 A.M. every morning, unless I pay him a modest tribute, I refuse—even if I am convinced that the available legal defenses would cost more than the tribute he is demanding.

If a policeman arrests me—even for a crime I did not commit—I go along peacefully. If he tries to rob my house, I fight, even if the cost of doing so is more than the direct cost of letting him rob me. Each of us knows what behavior by everyone else is within the rules and what behavior implies unlimited demands, the violation of the Schelling point, and the ultimate return to the Hobbesian jungle. The latter behavior is prevented by the threat of conflict even if (as in the British defense of the Falklands) the direct costs of surrender are much lower than the direct costs of conflict.

One question this raises is how we succeed in committing ourselves not to back down in such situations. One answer has been suggested already. It is in my long-run interest not to back down because if I do I can expect further demands: "[I]f once you have paid him the danegeld/You never get rid of the Dane."[13]

This explanation is not entirely adequate. In some situations, the aggressor may be able to commit himself to keeping your surrender secret and limiting his own demands. In others, the short-run costs of resistance may be larger than the long-run costs of surrender.

People (and nations) do sometimes surrender to such demands. If they do so less often than a simple calculation of costs and benefits might predict, the explanation may be found in a class of arguments made by Robert Frank and others.[14]

The central insight of such arguments is that even if surrender is sometimes in my private interest, being the sort of person who will surrender when it is in his interest to do so may not be, since if it is known that I will not back down, there is no point in making the initial demand.[15] My first best option is to pretend to be tough, in the hope that the demand will not be made, while reserving the option of surrendering if my bluff is called. If, however, humans are imperfectly able to lie to each other about what sort of people they are—as seems to be the case—then the best available option may be to really be tough, despite the risk that I will occasionally find myself forced to fight when I would be better off surrendering.

None of this argument depends on moral sanctions. I may (indeed do) believe that the tax collector is morally equivalent to the robber. I accept one and fight the other because of my beliefs about other people's behavior—what they will or will not fight for—and because there are beliefs about my behavior which I wish others to hold. We are bound together by a set of mutually reinforcing strategic expectations.

II. TWO ROUTES FROM HOBBES TO HERE

My argument so far has dealt with two ends of an extended process. I started with an explanation of how it was possible, in a two-person world, to take the first steps toward bargaining out of a Hobbesian state

[13] Rudyard Kipling, "Danegeld," in *Rudyard Kipling's Verse: Definitive Edition* (Garden City: Doubleday, 1940), pp. 716–17.

[14] Robert Frank, *Passions within Reason: The Strategic Role of the Emotions* (New York: Norton, 1988). See also the discussion in Friedman, *Price Theory*, pp. 288–90, which deals with the same strategy seen from the standpoint of the aggressor, the bully committing himself to carry through his threats even if doing so is not in his immediate interest.

[15] Danegeld as it actually existed did not entirely fit the pattern of behavior I am discussing here. The initial Danish invasions were for land and loot. In agreeing to be bought off, the invading armies may have been giving up an opportunity to do something they in fact wanted to do.

of nature. I ended with an explanation of how the same logic maintains civil order as we know it. Missing is any explanation of the intermediate steps by which the complicated and functional order in which we live might have been constructed.

One possibility is legislation. If an important part of the way in which individuals classify actions is "legal/illegal," then the fact of legal change, whether by a king, legislature, or court system, changes the way in which they classify the alternatives, which in turn changes the set of Schelling points. If the court has recognized property rights in water but not in air, I classify pollution of my section of the river as aggression and fight it, by legal, social, or even illegal means. I classify pollution of my air by my neighbor's soap factory as an inconvenient nuisance and either put up with it or try to buy him off. Under these circumstances legislation is, to a considerable degree, self-enforcing; the pattern of property rights might well survive even if the enforcement arm of the state vanished or became impotent.

While this may be part of the explanation for civil order, it cannot be all of it, for at least three reasons. First, some rights have no legal rules associated with them—the right not to have someone cut ahead of me in a line, for example. Second, many, perhaps most, people are selective about which legal rules they take seriously—as can easily be observed on any U.S. highway. And finally, there are well-documented situations in which property rights exist and are respected even though they are inconsistent with the relevant legal rights.

This final point brings up a second possible explanation of how the pattern of expectations might have come into existence—that it is due not to the creation of laws but to the evolution of norms. Robert Ellickson, in a recent book, describes how relations among neighbors function in Shasta County, California.[16] One of his most striking observations is that in many cases, including conflicts over trespass by animals and the allocation of the cost of building fences between neighbors, the inhabitants ignore the relevant laws and act instead according to well-understood nonlegal norms. Ellickson offers no adequate account of how such norms develop or of why they provide, in some contexts but not in all, at least approximately efficient rules. A possible answer to that puzzle brings us back to the two-person social contract discussed in the previous section.[17]

One might try to explain functional norms by evolution. Perhaps, over time, societies with better norms conquer, absorb, or are imitated by societies with worse norms, producing a world of well-designed societies. The problem with that explanation is that such a process should take centuries, if not millennia—which does not fit the facts as Ellickson reports

---

[16] Robert Ellickson, *Order without Law* (Cambridge: Harvard University Press, 1991).

[17] See my review of Ellickson: David Friedman, "Less Law than Meets the Eye," *Michigan Law Review*, vol. 90, no. 6 (May 1992), pp. 1444–52.

them. Whaling norms in the nineteenth century, for example, seem to have adjusted rapidly to changes in the species being hunted.

Perhaps what is happening is evolution, but evolution involving groups much smaller and more fluid than entire societies. Consider a norm, such as honesty, that can profitably be followed by small groups within a society, applicable only within the group. Groups with efficient norms will prosper and grow by recruitment. Others will imitate them. Groups with similar norms will tend to fuse, in order to obtain the same benefits on a larger scale. If one system of norms works better than its competitors, it will eventually spread through the entire society. When circumstances change and new problems arise, the process can repeat itself on a smaller scale, generating modified norms to deal with the new problems. In effect, what we have is the pairwise contracting out of the Hobbesian state of nature, repeated many times between pairs and within small groups.

This conjecture about how norms arise and change suggests a prediction: Even if a norm is efficient, it will not arise if its benefits depend on its being generally adopted. Suppose we define a norm as *locally efficient* if, with regard to any two individuals following the norm, there is no different norm such that at least one would be better off and the other no worse off if they both switched to it. A norm is *globally efficient* if there is no different norm such that at least one person would be better off and nobody worse off if everyone switched to it.[18]

Consider the whaling norms that Ellickson discusses. It is in the interest of any pair of captains to agree in advance to an efficient rule for dealing with whales that one ship harpoons and another one brings in, just as it is in the interest of a pair of individuals to agree to be honest with each other. But a rule for holding down the total number of whales killed so as to preserve the population of whales is useful only if almost everyone follows it. The former type of norm existed, the latter did not—with the result that nineteenth-century whalers did an efficient job of hunting one species after another to near-extinction.[19]

---

[18] I apologize to mathematicians and my fellow economists for using "local" and "global" in senses that may seem inconsistent with their usual usage in classifying maxima; I will be happy to consider suggestions for alternative terminology. To make my usage of the terms seem less idiosyncratic, think of a change in norms involving only two people as a small change and one involving many as a large change, and think of an "improvement" as a change to a situation that is Pareto superior for those who are changing. Then a locally efficient set of norms, like a local optimum, is one that cannot be improved by a small change.

For a more mathematically elaborate approach to defining small and large changes and using them to analyze the evolution of rules in a population, see Friedman, "Bilateral Monopoly" (*supra* note 11).

[19] A slightly different way of putting this argument is in terms of what Richard Dawkins has described as the evolution of "memes": ideas evolving in an environment consisting of the minds of humans. See Richard Dawkins, *The Selfish Gene* (New York: Oxford University Press, 1976), pp. 203–15. One reason a meme—such as the belief that "one ought to be honest toward honest people"—will spread is that those holding it are observed to be more successful as a result. But in order for the process to get past the early stage, when the meme

The evolution of norms, then, provides a second possible account of how we get from Hobbes to here. Where the recognition of rights between two people, such as neighbors, or within a small group, provides mutual benefits, it is in the interest of the parties concerned to recognize such rights.[20] By doing so they change the pattern of Schelling points that determines the equilibrium of their interaction, in a way which provides (some) protection for the rights in question. Over a long period of time, the result is to create a set of consistent mutual expectations, and one that tends to be locally, although not necessarily globally, efficient.

III. Law, Justice, and Efficiency

In thinking about issues of rights, I find myself playing two quite different roles. As a human being and (like all human beings) an amateur philosopher, I have moral intuitions; from that standpoint, the question I ask is "Why ought one not to steal?" and the answer is "Because it is wicked." As an economist, I ask and answer different questions. One is "What are the consequences of people being free to steal?" Much of the economic analysis of law is devoted to answering questions of that sort. Another is "Why do people (often) not steal?"

This essay is an attempt to answer that final sort of question. I have tried to answer the economist's question about rights rather than the philosopher's, not because economics is more important than moral philosophy, but because I am more confident in my ability to use economics to produce answers.[21] I have been encouraged in this policy by a curious and convenient coincidence: in most cases, the rules I conclude to be efficient are also the rules I believe to be just.

It is not a double but a triple coincidence. The rules I believe to be efficient and just are also, to a significant degree, the rules enforced by the laws and norms of the society I live in.[22] In this essay, I have sketched some ideas about the nature of those rules and how they have evolved.

---

is still rare in the population, it must be useful to hold the meme even when most other people do not. This works for memes representing norms such as honesty, but it does not work for a meme for conservation of whales. It is accordingly puzzling that memes in favor of conservation have spread so rapidly in the current U.S. population—to the point where belief in conservation has become very nearly the secular equivalent of a state religion.

[20] To put the argument in something closer to conventional-game-theory terms, I am combining a familiar concept of dominance in multiplayer games with the idea of transaction costs. Outcome A dominates outcome B if there is some set of people who together can produce A and who all prefer A to B. A small number of people can produce a change—such as the adoption of a norm among themselves—that only involves changing their own behavior. A large group, because of transaction costs, cannot.

[21] This point is discussed in David Friedman, *The Machinery of Freedom*, 2d ed. (La Salle, IL: Open Court, 1989), chs. 41–43.

[22] The correspondence is not perfect; it would be in some ways closer if I were writing this essay a century ago. A particular form of the correspondence—the claim that the common law tends to be economically efficient—has been a central element of the work of Judge Richard Posner, one of the leading scholars in the law-and-economics tradition. See Richard Posner, *Economic Analysis of Law*, 4th ed. (Boston: Little Brown, 1992).

This raises the question of why, if my account is correct, the rules produced in this way resemble those that I deduce to be efficient and intuit to be just.

In trying to answer that question, I find it useful to start by considering a class of property which underlies all other property and exists even in a Hobbesian state of nature.

I can control the motions of my body by a simple act of will. You can control its motions by imposing overwhelming force, by making believable threats to which I will yield, or in various other ways. Controlling it may be possible for both of us, but it is much cheaper and easier for me. In this sense, we may describe my body as my natural property. The same description applies to my gun—because I know where I hid it and you do not. Even land may be natural property to some extent if my detailed knowledge of the terrain makes it easier for me to use or defend it. Such property is natural inasmuch as my possession of it exists in the state of nature and is independent of social convention. The fact that I can control certain things more cheaply than you can is technology, not law or morals.

Natural property is a useful starting point for explaining the similarities among what is, what should be, and what would be efficient, because it is relevant to all three.

If the account I have offered is correct, our actual civil order is the result of extended bargaining, based ultimately on natural property. It was my control over my body that made the initial steps out of the state of nature possible. So natural property is relevant to what is—to the existing pattern of laws and norms.

In a world of no transaction costs, any initial allocation of property rights is efficient.[23] In a world with positive transaction costs, the basis for choosing among alternative allocations is the cost of enforcing and changing them. A set of rules in which I own my body and you own yours is superior to one in which each owns the other's body, or each has a half interest in each body, in part because it is so much easier to enforce. So we have a Coasian argument for the relevance of natural property to what is efficient.

This argument also provides a second connection between natural property and what is. My earlier arguments suggest that the evolution of rules tends to move in a direction that is at least locally efficient. If so, and if rules that allocate natural property to its natural owner are efficient, we would expect to observe such rules. Put differently, the argument for local efficiency of evolved norms provides a reason for some similarity between the rules we observe and the rules that are efficient.[24]

---

[23] Ronald Coase, "The Problem of Social Cost," *Journal of Law and Economics*, vol. 3 (1960), pp. 1–44.

[24] I am not claiming here that slavery is never observed or that it is never efficient. One can imagine circumstances in which the self-enforcing element of contracts would be too weak to enforce the contract that would be superior to slavery. An example is the prisoner

What, if anything, does natural property have to do with what ought to be? That depends on what normative account one accepts. For those of us who accept a libertarian account, in which the underlying right is my right to own myself and whatever I have obtained by voluntary agreement with others who own it, the connection is immediate. Self-ownership is both a moral axiom and a technological fact. Voluntary exchange is both a morally legitimate way of altering the pattern of ownership and, if my account of bargaining from the state of nature is correct, a technologically possible way (although not necessarily the only such) of altering a Schelling point and thus an equilibrium.

We now have the beginning of an explanation of the similarity among actual rules, efficient rules, and just rules. The status of this explanation, and of the fact being explained, is not, however, the same for the relation between the first two as it is for the relation of either to the third.

The existence of rules can be observed and the efficiency of rules can be deduced, at least in principle, from observed technologies and economic theory. Thus, the claim that there is some correspondence between what exists and what is efficient is a positive rather than a normative claim.[25]

What ought to be, on the other hand, is, at least in this essay, simply a description of my moral intuitions. If I conclude that the rules that would be just are similar to both the rules that exist and the rules that would be efficient, that may simply be evidence that my moral judgments are *ex post* rationalizations of the world I live in or the conclusions of my economic analysis.

One further similarity between the ethics and the social order that I have been discussing is worth mentioning. Both are essentially decentralized. The ethical position makes no attempt to evaluate individuals from above — in terms of their worth in the eyes of God. It consists rather of a description of what obligations each individual has to each other individual.[26] The social order, to the extent that it is evolved rather than legis-

---

of war who is confined because there is no other way of enforcing his agreement to pay for his freedom. A counterexample is the institution of parole, as it in fact developed. See Bruno S. Frey and Heinz Buhofer, "Prisoners and Property Rights," *Journal of Law and Economics*, vol. 31 (April 1988), pp. 19–46.

The argument given here provides a possible explanation for the Posnerian thesis that common law tends to be economically efficient. Common law presumably originated as a set of (locally efficient) norms converted over time into legally enforceable rules. If this interpretation is correct, we would expect common law to have become less efficient over time, since the mechanism that generates the efficiency of norms would not apply to legal rules defined and interpreted by a third party.

[25] The obvious example of such a claim is Posner's thesis that the common law tends to be economically efficient. Testing that conjecture is an extraordinarily difficult and complicated project, but it is in principle a positive one. See Posner, *Economic Analysis of Law*.

[26] This point is discussed at greater length in David Friedman, "Should the Characteristics of Victims and Criminals Count? *Payne v. Tennessee* and Two Views of Efficient Punishment," *Boston College Law Review*, vol. 34, no. 4 (July 1993).

lated, is a set of rules that exist because it was in the interest of pairs of individuals to abide by them, not because it was decided by someone that they would promote the general good of society.[27]

IV. CONCLUSIONS

The central project of this essay has been to give an account of rights, especially property rights, that is both amoral and alegal—an account that would explain the sort of behavior we associate with rights even in a world lacking law, law enforcement, and feelings of moral obligation.[28] I have tried first to explain how, with no legal system to enforce contracts, it might still be possible to contract out of a Hobbesian state of nature, and then to show how the same analysis can be used to understand in what sense a civil order, such as our own society, is different from a Hobbesian state of nature. Having offered answers to those questions, I then tried to show how we might get from the state of nature to something like the present society, and tried to use the analysis to partially explain the puzzling similarity between actual rules, just rules, and efficient rules.

If my analysis is correct, civil order is an elaborate Schelling point, maintained by the same forces that maintain simpler Schelling points in a state of nature. Property ownership[29] is alterable by contract because Schelling points are altered by the making of contracts. Legal rules are in large part a superstructure erected upon an underlying structure of self-enforcing rights.

Law and Economics, Cornell Law School

---

[27] Which is not to imply that legislated rules necessarily are designed for the good of society, but only that they might be.

[28] This is not the only way in which a positive account of rights might be developed. Sugden pursues a similar project in a framework where conventions develop as players of a multiplayer game learn by experience and alter their behavior accordingly; see Sugden, *Economics of Rights, Co-operation, and Welfare* (*supra* note 3). Another alternative would be a sociobiological explanation, in which respect for property is an inherited behavior pattern that evolved because it resulted in increased fitness—which is to say, reproductive success.

It is unclear to what extent these are really competing explanations, rather than different views of the same elephant. The sociobiological account may be seen as Sugden's repeated game, repeated through many generations, or as my account in a world where humans' ability to alter property rights by contract simply reflects the richer set of Schelling points available to them. My sketchy account of the development of norms and Sugden's more detailed account of the development of conventions are the same, save that he emphasizes anonymous adaptation where I emphasize explicit contracts among small subgroups. His account of the underlying games takes the available strategy set as given, where mine takes it as a subjective fact about the players that may, under some circumstances, be alterable. The similarities among the explanations are close; it is unclear whether the differences are sufficiently great to lead to significant differences in their implications.

[29] By "property ownership" I mean the ability to control things, not the legal right to do so.

ON THE OPTIMAL MIX OF PRIVATE
AND COMMON PROPERTY*

By Richard A. Epstein

I. Two Philosophical Extremes

A broad range of intellectual perspectives may be brought to bear on any important social institution. To this general rule, the institution of private property is no exception. The desirability of private property has been endlessly debated across the disciplines: philosophical, historical, economic, and legal. Yet there is very little consensus over its proper social role and limitations. Is it possible to find a unique solution to questions of property and private ownership, good for all resources and for all times? The famous defense of private property that is found in chapter 5 of John Locke's *Second Treatise of Government* answers this question in the affirmative, for Locke writes as though all property was given to mankind in common, and then seeks to find the quickest and most expeditious way to convert all common property into private property. His implicit, but undefended, assumption is that common forms of property are both undesirable and unstable, while private forms of ownership are always just the opposite. Yet his preferred method for moving from a commons to a regime of private property—the unilateral decision to appropriate by each actor—is one that has been frequently condemned as a sop to unbridled egotism, even though it is subject to two constraints: the first against waste, and the second requiring the appropriator to leave "enough, and as good" for others.[1]

The charges of Locke's egotism are overblown. But it hardly follows that his system is beyond reproach. A moment's reflection shows that neither of these two constraints can effectively police the transition from a regime of common property to private property. The constraint against waste does not inhibit the unwelcome egotistical actions of any individual. So long as the individual who removes something from the commons must pay some positive cost (whether in labor, uncertainty, or money) in making resources private, he will not commit waste, for in so doing he would leave himself worse off than he would have been if he had done nothing at all. Wholly without regard to any legal side-

---

* I would like to thank Jay Wright for his usual thorough and able research assistance.

[1] See John Locke, *Two Treatises of Government*, ed. Peter Laslett (New York: Mentor, 1960), *Second Treatise* [1690], ch. 5, section 27 (for the "enough, and as good" proviso) and section 31 (against waste).

constraint on waste, he will only convert common property to private property when his gains exceed his costs. By confining himself to those actions, he can beat back any charge of waste even if he ignores the interests of others. If the commons defines the proper initial position, then Locke's constraint against waste is too weak to impose sufficient restrictions against excessive privatization, for losses to other individuals may still be systematically ignored even though the constraint is satisfied.

On the other side, Locke's second constraint, the insistence that "enough, and as good" be left over for others, is *too* restrictive of private appropriation. If just as much and as good must always be left available to others, then *all* takings will be prohibited no matter how large the private gains, so long as resources are in any measure scarce in a state of nature. Once the initial appropriator removes anything from the commons, how can there be as much left as before? And if he takes, as self-interest dictates, the best that is available, then how can what remains be as good as what has been taken? If Locke had weakened this condition to some form of a balancing test—e.g., take when private gains exceed losses to others—then often *almost* as much and as good would be left over. But in his effort to avoid this slippery slope, Locke takes a categorical position that is both clear and incorrect. His first constraint does not bind at all; his second constraint binds too tightly.

This reference to a "balancing" approach indicates a better way to satisfy Locke's sound intuitions that *some* restraints should be imposed on the ability of individuals to remove property from the commons. The proper approach to removal of goods from the commons, however, is always to make the appropriate *marginal* adjustments. In each case the proper question is whether the additional gains from privatizing the commons are greater or less than the incremental costs from privatizing. If the gains are greater, then the actions should be allowed; if not, then they should be prohibited. Thinking in these marginal terms was not congenial to Locke or his times, and the formal apparatus for understanding economics at the margin only developed toward the end of the nineteenth century in the work of Alfred Marshall. But the point here is not to criticize Locke for his failure to anticipate the future. It is to understand the intellectual limitations of his position. Because of his failure to consider adjustments at the margin, Locke's two constraints drive us away from all such intermediate positions: either everything must be left behind (because of the second constraint), or everything may be taken (in spite of the first).

It is not surprising that actual social mechanisms for dealing with transitions between the commons and private property avoid any all-or-nothing response and seek to accommodate some appropriate mix of private and common property. The point becomes clear in Locke's own treatment of water rights, where Locke cleverly writes as though the current law satisfied the constraints of his system, when in fact the opposite was, and is, true.[2] In addition, his arguments for property seem to support the privatization of all roads, parks, and open spaces, when again common practice from the earliest times has gone the other way. Implicitly, his argument regards common ownership as leaving resources in an unstable state of the world. Private ownership is the preferred end-state for all resources.

This preference for one uniform regime for natural resources is not confined to the uncompromising champions of private property. The socialist tradition, starting with Marx and Engels in *The Communist Manifesto*, called strongly for the abolition of all private property rights in land, and for a similar abolition of all rights of inheritance.[3] The insistence on this polar opposite is also not without its intellectual antecedents. The famous condemnation of private property in Jean-Jacques Rousseau's *Discourse on Inequality* captures the mood well: "The first person who, having fenced off a plot of ground, took it into his head to say *this is mine* and found people simple enough to believe him, was the true founder of civil society."[4] The implication to be drawn from this observation was that this transition, far from being inevitable, was wholly unwelcome. While Locke sought to contrive ways to remove natural resources from the commons, Rousseau did all in his power to keep them there, proclaiming "the fruits belong to all and the earth to no one."[5] The rhetorical force of this passage stems from the losses borne by those who are excluded when property rights over any land vest in a single individual. Rousseau treats private property not as a functional system justified by long use, but as an egotistical, destructive, and impulsive arrangement—created, as it was, by one who took it into his head—that is not capable of rational defense. Ah, but who eats which fruits?

II. Finding a Middle Position

These two strong philosophical positions are clearly belied by the historical evolution of property, even within the framework of classical legal

---

[2] See the discussion of water rights in Section III below.

[3] Karl Marx and Friedrich Engels, *The Communist Manifesto*, in *Karl Marx: Selected Writings*, ed. David McLellan (Oxford: Oxford University Press, 1977), pp. 232, 237.

[4] Jean-Jacques Rousseau, *Discourse on the Origins and the Foundations of Inequality among Men* [1755], in *The First and Second Discourses*, ed. Roger D. Masters (New York: St. Martin's Press, 1964), pp. 141–42.

[5] *Ibid.*, p. 142. To fill in the blanks, the full sentence reads:

What crimes, wars, murders, what miseries and horrors would the human race have been spared by someone who, uprooting the stakes or filling in the ditch, had shouted to his fellow-men: Beware of listening to this impostor: you are lost if you forget that the fruits belong to all and the earth to no one!

systems. Thus, the Roman system of property law is normally celebrated for its insistence on the absolute nature of individual *dominium* over particular assets, but its actual operation recognized that both common and private property were permanent and indispensable parts of the total system. A similar distribution of property rights between private and common is characteristic of modern legal systems, even those which feature strong and vibrant capitalist economies. The persistent theoretical question is why a mixed solution should dominate either of the two extremes. Analytically, the only way in which a middle position can be defined and justified is to identify at least two divergent tendencies that must be reconciled in order to reach the optimal solution: otherwise, we should prefer one or the other corner position. Once the advantages of private and common ownership are isolated, they can be traded off against each other in individual cases. As a matter of abstract principle, either extreme position may be defended, and so too may any middle position. But no matter how shrill the rhetoric on either side, any responsible search for a sound system of property rights searches for the net social advantage by minimizing the sum of the rival inconveniences.

The first concern is the loss imposed on strangers by any practice of exclusion. It is just that loss that Rousseau and the latter-day champions of socialism are quick to spot. The flip side of private ownership is the correlative obligation on *all others* to forbear from entry or use of the property belonging to another, or from using force or deception to block its disposition to a third party. Recall William Blackstone's famous aphorism that treats the right of property "as that sole and despotic dominion which one man claims and exercises over the external things of the world, in total exclusion of the right of any other individual in the universe,"[6] where the unmistakable implication of the last three words is that everyone, but everyone, else is out.[7] This inherent limitation necessarily imposes costs on third parties by restricting their freedom of action, so it is fruitless to pretend that the institution of private property represents all gain and no pain.

Any satisfactory justification of private property cannot pretend that these external losses do not occur. It must claim instead that some compensating advantage makes these losses well worth bearing. Sometimes, at least, they are not. For example, where the cooperation of a large number of individuals is necessary in order for any individual to obtain private gain, private property can often create problems of mutual blockade

---

[6] William Blackstone, *Commentaries on the Laws of England* (Chicago and London: University of Chicago Press, 1979), p. 2.

[7] Note, for what it is worth, that the use of the phrase "in the universe" is inconsistent with the positivist notion that property rights are good only in the jurisdiction that confers them. Here it appears that all are equally bound, whether or not they are subjects of the sovereign of the place where the property is located.

that prevent all persons from achieving their desired end. Just think of what would happen if the law required the consent of all landowners before airplanes could fly high in the skies or before broadcasters could transmit their signals.[8] The problems of negotiation are large if rights of exclusion are allowed; yet the interference with other productive uses of the land is minor when overflight and transmission are routinely allowed. By the same token, however, the existence of private rights *between broadcasters* (who are confined to specific frequencies) and *between airlines* (whose planes must travel in designated corridors) shows that the principle of exclusion is not vanquished solely because landowners must tolerate some invasion of their airspace. Instead, a different configuration of private rights is chosen, congenial to the nature of the resource in question.[9]

Any complete analysis of property rights, however, cannot overlook the substantial costs of administering systems of common property. In some instances the problems are scant, because there is food there for the taking. Rousseau's image of the "fruits of the earth" makes it appear that the major function of a system of property is to divide the spoils that nature provides. Yet even where fruit just grows on trees, someone has to decide who gets the fruits from the lower branches, and who must climb somewhat higher. A system that allows the first taker to keep the fruit is as egotistical with respect to fruit as a system of private property in land is with respect to the earth and the trees that grow on it. In good temperate climates, however, crops do not just grow trees. Cultivation is also required. Given that constraint, a system of common ownership may well create an obstacle to effective use of the land. First, someone (it is not clear who) has to coordinate the activities of the various claimants to the common pool. Where use of the resource is open to all, coordination may be frustrated by the arrival of a single willful latecomer. Two rival and inconsistent plans cannot both be implemented with respect to a single piece of land.

In addition, incentives for productive labor must be created when the natural fruits of the earth are not there for the taking. The earlier writers on private property loved the saying that no one should be allowed "to reap where he has not sown." Coming from temperate regions, they knew whereof they spoke. Crops from the earth were not the result of natural abundance, but depended on large inputs of human labor. If *Y*

---

[8] See *Burnham v. Beverly Airways, Inc.*, 42 N.E.2d 575 (Mass. 1942), noting that low-level interference with land use is a very different matter. On the broadcast spectrum, see Jonathan W. Emord, *Freedom, Technology, and the First Amendment* (San Francisco: Pacific Research Institute, 1991), ch. 11, noting that the question of wrongful harm caused by use of radio frequencies was always to other frequency users. Harm to landowners was not an issue.

[9] For a further discussion of these issues, see Richard A. Epstein, "Property as a Civil Right," *California Western Law Review*, 1992, pp. 187–207.

could gather the crops X planted, then X came out worse off than if he had done nothing at all.[10] Protecting the harvest induced the original planting, and outsiders could gain from a strong system of property rights that allowed the harvested fruits to be bartered or sold.[11] In their concern with the negative externalities from exclusion, the opponents of private property tend to forget the *positive externalities* that are the unintended but welcome side effect of voluntary trade: the increased wealth creates additional opportunities for third persons to enter into win/win contracts of their own. Institutions of common property impose costs of coordination and may dull the incentives for production and trade that a system of private property nurtures.

The question then is which of the two sets of costs—coordination or exclusion—is likely to prove larger. The question here cannot be answered in the abstract, but depends heavily on the nature of the resource in question and the technology that is available to exploit it: so much the examples of the spectrum and overflight should demonstrate. It follows, therefore, that the constant trade-off of the gains and losses of exclusion will vary across different settings, leading to different social arrangements. Indeed, the range of solutions is not confined to a simple choice between property open to all and property closed to all but a single owner. In practice and in theory, it is possible to articulate a wide set of workable intermediate solutions. The paradigmatic case of private property involves ownership by one person—"private" itself comes from the Latin meaning single or sole. But the system of private property also allows the creation of concurrent ownership (the joint tenancies and tenancies in common of the common law) among small groups of individuals by means of voluntary agreement. It should not, however, be supposed that all forms of common ownership have to be created

---

[10] Blackstone, *Commentaries*, p. 7:

> And the art of agriculture, by a regular connexion and consequence, introduced and established the idea of a more permanent property in the soil, than had hitherto been received or adopted. It was clear that the earth would not produce her fruits in sufficient quantities, without the assistance of tillage: but who would be at the pains of tilling it, if another might watch an opportunity to seise upon and enjoy the product of his industry, art, and labour?

Blackstone had similar views with respect to chattels and construction:

> But no man would be at the trouble to provide either [habitations or raiments], so long as he had only a usufructuary property in them, which was to cease the instant that he quitted possession;—if, as soon as he walked out of his tent, or pulled off his garment, the next stranger who came by would have a right to inhabit the one, and to wear the other. (*Ibid.*, p. 4)

[11] This is a point that Locke clearly recognized; see his *Second Treatise*, section 34 (one "ought not to meddle with what was already improved by another's Labour"); and section 37 ("he who appropriates land to himself by his labour, does not lessen but increase the common stock of mankind").

through a voluntary recombination of strong private rights. It is also possible to have *closed* systems of communal rights, as with riparian rights — those rights in water belonging to the adjacent landowners. Finally, there are systems that fall in between, as with the medieval villages in which access to the commons was allowed uniformly to the members, but where outsiders were excluded.[12]

In determining which property regime is best for a given resource, the claims for the dominance of private property, as opposed to common property, need not necessarily prevail. Sometimes the recognition and protection of certain public rights does a far better job in adjusting the conflicts of interest between the claimants of exclusive property rights and their opponents. It is important therefore to set out the boundaries between these various regimes with some degree of particularity in order to be able to decide whether a certain resource should be held privately or in common. Overclaiming either way has the same devastating consequences that it has in other areas of intellectual discourse: the defense of counterintuitive or outrageous positions discredits the core cases that are worth preserving. It is for just this reason that the extreme forms of libertarianism, which exclude any possibility of taxation at all, face a set of massive challenges that are better met by classical-liberal theories of limited government that concede — indeed insist — that some forms of taxation are legitimate, and then direct their fire to the abuses of selective (e.g., taxes on a single commodity such as gasoline or hotels), regressive, or progressive taxation, all the while insisting on the dominance of freedom of contract in competitive markets. A strong defense of private property, then, must rest on a theory that accounts for different forms of public property, and it must draw the lines between them.

III. SOME HISTORICAL EVIDENCE

The specification of a complete model of property rights thus leads to the conclusion that no single regime of property rights will be good for all times and for all occasions. The choice of regimes will be rich and varied, but it should *not* be supposed for that reason that choosing one system of property rights in preference to another is simply a matter of convention, such that, so long as the rules of the game are clear at the outset, their content is of no concern. To follow David Hume, these rights

---

[12] See, e.g., Glenn G. Stevenson, *Common Property Economics* (Cambridge: Cambridge University Press, 1991), ch. 3, for a discussion of the difference between unlimited open access and common property. Locke himself understood the point, for he notes that enclosure of land cannot be made when the land is held in common by compact, that is, by a small group of individuals who have agreed to keep it open by contract. See Locke, *Second Treatise*, ch. 5, section 35. In essence, he has described a closed commons, different from that which exists in the state of nature.

may be artificial, in the sense that they are set by human convention, but they are not arbitrary, in the sense that one set is as good as another.[13]

In legal practice the lines between common and private property have long been recognized in the most traditional and orthodox treatments of the subject. Here it is instructive to look at the classification of "Things" found in *The Institutes of Justinian*, which provides a brief and powerful statement of the conventional classification on the subject, adopted first in the Roman system, and subsequently carried over quite comfortably into the English common-law systems. At the outset, Justinian aligns himself with neither class of philosophical purists. Instead, in his *first* sentence on the matter he divides property into public and private:

> Of these, some admit of private ownership, while others, it is held, cannot belong to individuals; for some things are by natural law common to all, some are public, some belong to a society or corporation, and some belong to no one. But most things belong to individuals, being acquired by various titles as will appear from what follows.[14]

The list of Justinian thus contains three separate categories. The first, those things belonging to all, include "the air, running water, the sea, and consequently, the sea-shore." The second, those things belonging to a society or a corporation, include public buildings, and more ominously, city walls, which are not only public but "sanctioned" by divine law, "because any sanction against them is visited with capital punishment." Justinian is thus careful to distinguish, as we are sometimes wont to forget, between property which is left in the commons, and that which is held by the state which reserves the right to exclude its own citizens. The third category, private property, includes everything else, whether acquired by occupation or by transfer from other individuals, again in accordance with the dictates of natural law.[15]

The tripartite scheme propounded by Justinian's *Institutes* may make a good deal of practical sense, but this famous text lacks any rigorous justification for the result, for Justinian is most disinclined to give any functional account of the foundations of property law. For Justinian, "natural law" (or "natural reason"—the terms were used interchangeably) was the universal solvent by which legal truths were tested, and was chosen

---

[13] See David Hume, *A Treatise of Human Nature*, ed. L. A. Selby-Bigge (Oxford: Clarendon Press, 1888), Book 3.

[14] *The Institutes of Justinian*, 5th ed., trans. J. B. Moyle (Oxford: Clarendon Press, 1913), Book 2, Title 1, pr. The reference to various titles, i.e., ways of acquiring ownership of private property, forms the basis for Blackstone's treatment of the subject in his *Commentaries*. See Blackstone, *Commentaries*, chs. 14–19.

[15] *Institutes of Justinian*, Book 3, Title 1, 11–48.

because of its reliance on rational processes of inference alone.[16] Natural reason is often Delphic in the way in which its speaks, but for Justinian and others in the Roman tradition, natural law contained two components. First, it was the law that was common to all nations regardless of the variations in local culture and local laws.[17] Second, it was the kind of law that endured; it was immutable and not subject to variation and volatility.[18] Neither of these tests *explain* why the rules that are ordained by natural law should be followed. Instead, they operate only as proxies of the sort: "If every one has done it for a long time, then whatever has been done cannot be all bad, even if we do not quite understand why it is good." What was lacking in Justinian, and in the classical writers who followed him (Joseph Glanvil, Henry de Bracton, Hugo Grotius, Samuel Pufendorf, John Locke, David Hume, William Blackstone), was any overt *justificatory* apparatus for the classification that he announced, or the decision to place given forms of property in any particular class.

In order to create the apparatus, it is necessary to demystify the law of property, and to ask how the institution in question relates to the human ends that it is designed to serve. In dealing with this issue, it is clear that long-held widely established customs should, in principle, be entitled to some respect, just as Justinian urged. The customs in question typically apply to recurrent situations in any society. The participants to the immediate dispute have strong and clashing interests in the outcome of the particular case. Viewed in isolation, these interests tend to cancel each other out, for what the one side gains, the other side loses. Nonetheless, the dispute is resolved not by the participants themselves, but by disinterested third parties who have no stake in the outcome of the case, but a large stake in the long-term operation of the system as a whole.[19]

---

[16] Richard Hooker's characterization of the law of reason captures the matter well: "Law rational therefore, which men commonly use to call the law of nature, meaning thereby the law which human nature knoweth itself in reason universally bound unto, which also for that cause may be termed most fitly the law of reason." Quoted in Hadley Arkes, "Natural Law and the Law: An Exchange," *First Things*, no. 23 (May 1992), p. 46.

[17] *Institutes of Justinian*, Book 1, Title 2, 1: "[T]hose rules prescribed by natural reason for all men are observed by all peoples alike, and are called the law of nations."

[18] *Ibid.*, Book 1, Title 2, 11: "But the laws of nature, which are observed by all nations alike, are established, as it were, by divine providence, and remain ever fixed and immutable; but the municipal laws of each individual state are subject to frequent change, either by the tacit consent of the people, or by the subsequent enactment of another statute."

[19] The impartial spectator is, of course, Adam Smith's contribution to the overall issue. See his *Theory of Moral Sentiments*, ed. A. L. Macfie and D. D. Raphael (Indianapolis: Liberty Classics, 1982), and also his *Lectures on Jurisprudence*, ed. R. L. Meek, D. D. Raphael, and P. G. Stein (Indianapolis: Liberty Classics, 1982). See, e.g., his discussion of the role of the impartial spectator in justifying the rules of occupation as they existed in both Roman and common law, in Smith, *Lectures on Jurisprudence*, p. 17:

> From the system I have already explain'd, you will remember that I told you we may conceive an injury was done one when an impartial spectator would be of the opin-

To the extent that one party wishes to advance a ruinous rule for some business or profession, he will face two major constraints. First, he will have to persuade independent observers that the ruinous rule is one that they should adopt for the system as a whole. If the judges are experienced in the trade or business in which the case arises, then their own knowledge, bolstered by arguments from the other side, will incline them in the opposite direction, toward the preservation of whatever (nonruinous) principle currently governs the business. Second, the individual player has a strong private incentive to concede defeat in a particular case if the preservation of the current principle in fact works for his long-term advantage. Quite simply, the maintenance of the current principle for that person is just too valuable. Thus, if the amount in dispute is $100, and the value of the current principle to the litigant is $1,000 in terms of long-term future relationships, then it is in his interest to sacrifice the case for the sake of preserving the current principle, and to come out $900 ahead. That calculation will not be disturbed even if the other party to the litigation wins on both the facts and the principle, and comes out, say, $1,100 ahead. In situations like this, it is common for there to be no litigation at all. Instead (if the facts are not in issue), the party in the wrong may tender the money instead, and demand in exchange only an assurance that the applicable principle will be applied uniformly in future disputes when roles are reversed, so that he will share in its advantages.

Mechanisms of this sort work best in certain trades or businesses, where the level of repeat play within a closed community is great, where technological innovation is low or unimportant, and where the same persons are likely to assume all the roles in a given set of transactions, as by being a buyer in one case and a seller in the next.[20] The extrapolation from those customs of close-knit groups to the general rules of mankind, however, is something of a leap, given that the same mechanisms of repeat interaction are likely to prove less effective.[21] To understand why Justinian's tripartite division works as well as it does requires a more systematic look at the costs and benefits of these various rules, as applied to different settings. The easiest way to do that, moreover, is to ask the question "What would the world look like, if the rules were in some sense reversed?" Consider, then, his three categories of property.

---

ion he was injured, and would join him in his concern and go along with him when he defended the subject in his possession against any violent attack, or used force to recover what had been thus wrongfully wrested out of his hands.

[20] For elaboration, see Richard A. Epstein, "The Path to *The T. J. Hooper*: The Theory and History of Custom in the Law of Tort," *Journal of Legal Studies*, vol. 21 (1992), pp. 1–38.

[21] Just this contrast is stressed in Robert C. Ellickson, "Property in Land," *Yale Law Journal*, vol. 102 (1993), pp. 1315, 1320, where he defends the efficiency thesis, which "asserts that *land rules within a close-knit group evolve so as to minimize its members' costs*" (italics in original).

Common property. To see the sense of common property, suppose the law allowed anyone to claim individual ownership over the seas, or that city walls could be divided and ripped down. While consequentialist systems of most stripes are frequently attacked on the ground that their outcomes are indeterminate, that objection will not work for the fundamental categories at issue here, even if it might explain why it is so difficult, say, to choose between different liability rules, such as negligence and strict liability for harms inflicted on a stranger.[22]

Start with water rights over the high seas and the rivers, and assume that these could be made private. The question of who is entitled to assume the preferred position as private owner is not easily answered, for it is hard to know who was the first user of an ocean or river, or any part thereof; and metes and bounds are not easily established over bodies of water. But the key point here is not whether exclusive possession could be implemented in practice if allowed in theory. It is whether that exclusive possession should be allowed. Consider the relative costs of exclusion and coordination: the critical point is that the exclusive possession claimed by one is likely to impose very high costs on all nonowners, relative to the gains obtained by the holder of property. Today, the oceans and rivers may be used for transportation, for recreation, for fishing, and for trade. The thought that one nation or one person could block travel on the high seas, or impose tolls for their use, is an unpleasant specter. The costs of coordination are in general low, for it is possible to develop, as were in fact developed, rules of the road which allow ships to pass each other by in peace and safety even as they ply common waters on separate missions. It was, and is, possible to organize these rules of the road without supervising the composition of the traffic.[23] The owner of each vessel may have to coordinate any particular trip with others that his ships make, and may have to struggle to be sure that perishables reach port in time for sale, and that durables are safely stored and protected. A sound system of rules of the road need not take any of these coordination problems into account.

The situation with seas and rivers, therefore, is very different from that of a toll road, where private ownership is often needed to create the

---

[22] The literature on this issue is huge. For my early full-throated defense of strict liability in stranger cases, see Richard A. Epstein, "A Theory of Strict Liability," *Journal of Legal Studies*, vol. 2 (1973), pp. 151–204. For my later, more cautious views in the same direction, see Richard A. Epstein, "Causation—In Context: An Afterword," *Chicago-Kent Law Review*, vol. 63 (1987), pp. 653–80.

[23] This was the mistake made with the spectrum when Justice Felix Frankfurter, having noted the need to prevent interference, held that the charge of the Federal Communications Commission to determine the public interest, convenience, and necessity also allowed it to determine the composition of the traffic. See *NBC v. United States*, 319 U.S. 190, 215–16 (1943). It almost goes without saying that the problem of scarcity could be relieved by a price system, without the need for administrative determination of who is entitled to use what frequency. And, never forget, R. H. Coase, "The Federal Communications Commission," *Journal of Law and Economics*, vol. 2, (1959), pp. 1–40.

improvement in the first place; nor is there any need to allow one person to reap in order that he might have an incentive to sow. It is rather a situation in which the privatization of the public waters creates all sorts of transactional barriers without making any correlative improvements in the underlying resource. No one has to maintain the Mediterranean Sea. And it hardly makes sense for one person to own a river, or some portion of it, if the price of that ownership is to exclude access to its waters by all riparians, and travel and recreation along the river by the public at large. These are cases where the costs of exclusion are high relative to the benefits that it generates. Open regimes with universal access are better.

Yet even here the analysis is not at an end, for while the primary values in the use of seas and rivers are preserved when they are held in common, further improvement is possible if some limited conversion of water to private use is tolerated. The underlying instinct shows the importance of making marginal adjustments to fundamental institutions. In principle, the formal problem to be solved (though Justinian and the Romans would scarcely have put it this way) is how to take a body of water, which has value in multiple uses simultaneously, and devise a system of rights which maximizes the value from the sum of its common *and* private uses. Any solution that keeps all water in rivers and seas is one that implicitly says that the first drop of water diverted from the system produces losses to the common that are greater than the private gains produced from such diversions. Where water is plentiful, and rivers and seas are high, this extreme position looks to be wrong on its face. To be sure, any diversion means that there is not "enough, and as good" found inside the commons as before, so if the Lockean Proviso had been rigorously applied in earlier times, no diversion could have been tolerated. But if the inquiry is made on marginal terms, then an initial low-level set of diversions should, at least under some circumstances, produce private gains that exceed the losses to the commons.

The Romans had an intuitive sense of the relative values at stake, because they in fact adopted an intermediate solution that left the commons dominant, but nonetheless allowed some diversion from it. Thus, it was routinely held that each of the riparians had a "usufructuary" interest in the water which allowed them to make limited diversions for domestic uses — some damage to the commons was tolerated, but unlimited use was prohibited.[24] In essence, the rule is a crude effort to reach the kind of intermediate position that is uncongenial to defenders of pure public or pure private property regimes. The riparians' interest, moreover, was not defined in terms of any strict amount of flow. When the waters in the commons were low, the amount that could be taken from it was reduced in proportion as well, which is what we should expect if

[24] See *Institutes of Justinian*, Book 2, Title 1.

the purpose of the system is to maximize the values of the sum of the private and collective uses.

However functional this system may have been, the doctrinal solution was conceptually a tricky one for the Romans as well. The model for the usufructuary interest in water was the usufruct in land—an interest analogous to the life estate under English law, save that it was not transferable without the consent of the owner of the underlying property.[25] With land, the usufruct was created by grant from the owner of the underlying property and allowed the usufructuary to use the land and to gather the fruits. There was typically a single usufructuary and a single owner of the land, so typically *all* the fruits could be gathered and consumed. In contrast, the usufruct in water was not created by a single owner of the commons; nor was there any fruit that was capable of collection, for the drop of water that was taken from the common pool was indistinguishable from the one that remained. Nor did the language of tilling the land have any obvious analogy with water. Finally, there was no obvious explanation as to why someone who did not have title to the water could make some portion of it his own by unilateral act: why was his conduct not an illegal conversion?

The gaps between the usufruct in land and that in water cannot be bridged in doctrinal terms. The question, then, is why it survives, and to that query the only answer is that the social gains from the practice were so large as to make its survival worthwhile. The Romans borrowed private-law conceptions applicable to land, and, with some tugging here and hauling there, invoked them to establish a mixed regime in water that proved stable not only in Roman times, but also for long periods of English law, where riparians likewise were said to have a usufructuary interest in water.

The proof here is in the pudding. Locke himself resorts to just this body of law in justifying his rule of acquisition:

> Though the Water running in the Fountain be every ones, yet who can doubt, but that in the Pitcher is his only who drew it out? His *labour* hath taken it out of the hands of Nature, where it was common, and belong'd equally to all her Children, and *hath* thereby *appropriated* it to himself.[26]

Clearly, something serious is amiss here. Locke uses the labor theory of value to account for property rights in both land and water, but is help-

---

[25] See, e.g., *The Institutes of Gaius*, trans. F. de Zulueta (Oxford: Clarendon Press, 1946), II, 30, where a purported conveyance to a third party is ineffective, even if all forms are observed.

[26] Locke, *Second Treatise*, section 29.

less to explain how two so divergent sets of property rights can be accounted for by a single variable—the extent of labor. Locke's attachment to the labor theory is so strong that he misses the correct rationalization for a sound set of social practices, which asks what set of rules will create the incentives for the optimal value of the contested resource. With water, systems of unlimited acquisition by private act do very badly, yet the labor theory of value gives no clue as to what intermediate measure could determine how much water can be removed or why: if one pitcher could be removed, why not an entire swimming pool? Locke's views suggest that the rules of acquisition that are suitable for fountains will work for rivers as well, and do so for all time.[27] An ounce of labor gets a river full of water: no wonder socialists and communitarians have a field day with Locke and the unearned increment![28]

The alternative account that I have urged here stresses the contingent nature of social judgments about property. The strength of that account is revealed by the subsequent evolution of water law. Technology—more specifically, the use of mills for power—changed the relative value of various water uses during the early nineteenth century.[29] Not without pain, the system of property rights changed with it, for the dominantly defensive position of the older system of water rights gave way to alternative systems that allowed more extensive private use of rivers. While the relative proportions of private and common use had changed, the legal system evolved, if only by fits and starts, to a new position-that had the same generic feature as the older system of common law: it maximized the value of the sum of all relevant uses, at least to the extent that imperfect human institutions can do so. As the exploitation of water moved west in the United States, the in-stream uses were of scarcely any value at all, as the rough waters were ill-suited for either transportation or fishing; and the system of prior appropriation placed enormous preference with the private use of water by nearby landowners. Even here, there was no special reason to give preference to riparians, who as often as not were located on some barren cliff far above the running water. The first appropriator—the first party who was prepared to make extensive private

[27] For my further criticisms of the labor theory of value, see Richard A. Epstein, "Possession as the Root of Title," *Georgia Law Review*, vol. 13 (1979), pp. 1221–43; and Richard A. Epstein, "Luck," *Social Philosophy & Policy*, vol. 6, no. 1 (1988), pp. 17–38.

[28] Or for that matter, with efforts to justify the acquisition of property on a theory of desert. See John Christman, "Entrepreneurs, Profits, and Deserving Market Shares," *Social Philosophy & Policy*, vol. 6, no. 1 (1988), pp. 1–16. The mistake in Christman's elegant analysis is that he thinks he destroys the Lockean theory by undermining a theory of individual desert. But he fails to come to grips with the full range of efficiency arguments that can be used to defend the institution—or indeed to make the strongest arguments against the desert theory itself.

[29] For a splendid account of the transformation, see Carol M. Rose, "Energy and Efficiency in the Realignment of Common-Law Water Rights," *Journal of Legal Studies*, vol. 19 (1990), pp. 261–96.

investments in the water — was given the dominant right. If one thinks that these variations were fortuitous, then one must explain why property rights in water did not evolve in the opposite direction.

The contrast between rights in water and in land is useful from a historical perspective because it puts into nice perspective Blackstone's image of the despot presiding over private property.[30] Blackstone's image is quite plausible for land, at least before overflights and spectrum use became valuable. But it is, and was even in Blackstone's time, a very bad statement of the right of property as it applies across the board: water law shows the dominance of common property over private property, and of a mixed property regime over both. The fact that the common law could have entertained two such different systems at the same time is a tribute both to its good common sense and to its avoidance of dangerous philosophical generalizations. It is not a sign of any fatal intellectual ambivalence or inconsistency.

The soundness of the Roman and English views of water rights, as just explicated, is only reinforced within the transaction-cost framework, first made central to the analysis of property rights by Ronald Coase.[31] Coase's central insight was that for efficiency purposes, any initial allocation of property rights will do, so long as the cost of correcting initial allocative mistakes made by the positive law is zero. But once transaction costs are high, the initial allocation stands a good chance of becoming the final allocation; therefore, the legal system, whether through custom or positive law, should seek to make initial assignments that approximate the end-state ideal. If one were to allow waters to be taken by first possession, the rest of mankind could presumably band together and purchase those waters for the public domain. But the ability to coordinate the efforts of thousands of separate individuals, many of whom are not yet in being, in order to arrange for that reassignment, are so great that it could not happen, even by extraordinary efforts and with good fortune. So it is better to keep the rights in the public domain in the first place.

Publicly owned property. As noted above, Justinian's system also had a second form of public property: those public structures, most notably the city walls, that were held and controlled by the state. One could conceive of these as jointly owned by citizens, and capable of partition in the ways applicable to ordinary forms of joint property: one owner could take his share, or insist that the whole be sold and the proceeds divided. Nevertheless, partition might be sensible for the family ranch, but it is an invitation to evident disaster with respect to fortifications that are a critical public good — a good whose value is preserved only if the integrity of its

[30] See note 6 above.

[31] Ronald H. Coase, "The Problem of Social Cost," *Journal of Law and Economics*, vol. 3 (1960), pp. 1–44.

structures is maintained. Whatever the rules for the ordinary family farm, partition and alienation should not be attributable to these forms of property, again because the external costs dwarf the potential private gains.

Similarly, the city walls could have been treated as an open commons, accessible to all who were prepared to obey the rules of the road. But city walls, like national borders, were critical for security, and security was only maintainable when access was restricted. The walls could not have been entrusted to any single private actor, so the state had to assume strong central control over them, to act as an owner to maintain and to protect them. But the possibilities of gains from trade were nonexistent, and hence the prohibition on partition or sale. A third form of ownership was needed, and was developed, to handle the unique problems of the operation of necessarily public structures.

Private property. The treatment of common property is a subject to which little space is devoted in the Roman materials. For Justinian, the private side of the line receives more attention, because it is the area in which individual persons may engage in voluntary actions to obtain and transfer property rights. The sheer volume of transactions thus gives this area a practical importance for lawyers that makes it seem somewhat more important in the overall system of rights than it actually is. For Justinian, the major principle of organization is one that classifies private property by the mode through which the individual owner obtains title.

Justinian's system of title has an enormous staying power in the law, and sets the framework by which Blackstone in his *Commentaries* organizes his discussion of private property.[32] Within this general framework, Justinian's discussion begins with the modes of original acquisition, which are so critical precisely because land and animals are regarded as owned by no one in the initial position.[33] The legal system, however, abhors any kind of vacuum, and thus encourages simple and unilateral private actions to give each thing an owner: occupation of land and capture of animals, for example. Thereafter, the rules of voluntary transfer — sale, gift, bequest, and perhaps inheritance — take over to allow for the transfer of rights by consensual means.[34] Of equal importance to the

---

[32] Blackstone, *Commentaries*, chs. 14–19. The titles that he discusses are Title by Descent, Title by Purchase, Title by Escheat, Title by Occupancy, Title by Prescription, Title by Forfeiture, and Title by Alienation. Only the last has to do with consensual arrangements.

[33] *Institutes of Justinian*, Book 2, Title 1, 12.

[34] The "perhaps" before inheritance is deliberate. Blackstone was generally of the opinion that inheritance was not a natural right of property but was one that could be given or withheld by the state. See Blackstone, *Commentaries*, chs. 10–13. From the point of view of the analysis here, this concession clearly seems to be a mistake, for it leaves open two possibilities neither of which are conducive to overall creation of wealth. One is that the property reverts back to its unowned state, so that the first occupier after death can control it. This institution which celebrates the "general occupant" was rejected as a general matter in English law. The *assize mort d'ancestor* was designed in the reign of Henry II to allow the heir to bring suit to recover land which was entered by a stranger after the death of an ancestor. For particulars, see F. W. Maitland, *The Forms of Action at Common Law*, ed. A.

Romans, and indeed to any civilization in which title to property is insecure because of political turmoil or war, is a set of rules that establishes property rights when land is illegally taken from its owner and transferred to another person. To govern these situations of improper transfer of title, it is necessary to develop at great length the rules of adverse possession, prescription, and disposition of property by nonowners.[35] These rules are always messy and uncertain, as anyone familiar with the question of restitution of property in Eastern Europe is aware. There is a strong tendency to invoke the principle that no one should ever profit from his own wrong, which is offset by the need for stability in future transactions notwithstanding the injustice of past transactions.

The rules of original possession and voluntary transfer do have a great degree of intrinsic stability. Indeed, Justinian regards them as universal and immutable under his familiar natural-rights approach. But again, he does not attempt any assessment of the costs and benefits of the regime he defends. If that were done, the voluntary forms of transfer would come out quite well today. If A has rights over X, then the transfer of those rights to B should work to the mutual benefit of both parties. In ordinary cases these transfers create few or no disadvantages to third parties, who have the option of trading with either A or B, depending on

---

Chaytnor and W. J. Whittaker (Cambridge: Cambridge University Press, 1936), pp. 19–40. The second possibility is that the concession allows for extensive taxation of the property by the state as a precondition to its passage to the next generation. Blackstone was doubtless aware that the English kings had long levied taxes and imposed burdens on succession at death, and doubtless did not want to announce a doctrine of private property law that was so subversive of the then-common practice. It is also worth noting that the constitutionality of death taxes in the U.S. has rested in large measure on the proposition that "[t]he right to take property by devise or descent is the creature of the law, and not a natural right—a privilege, and therefore the authority which confers it may impose conditions on it." *Magoun v. Illinois Trust & Savings Bank*, 170 U.S. 283, 288 (1898) (sustaining state inheritance tax). See also *Knowlton v. United States*, 178 U.S. 41 (1899) (sustaining federal inheritance tax).

[35] "Adverse possession" refers to the body of rules that determines when a party in possession of real property loses the right to recover it from someone who has occupied it "adverse" to his interest. "Prescription" is a more general term that refers to the creation of rights by conduct that is inconsistent with the ownership of another: thus, an easement is acquired by prescription if one person openly and notoriously uses a path across the land of another. The problem of disposition by nonowners arises whenever X sells or otherwise disposes of O's property without O's authorization or consent.

This last topic was one of vast importance in the ancient law because of the high volume of theft and the want of any system of recordation. The orthodox legal theory of all legal systems presupposed that no one could convey a better title than he had; but that position placed the good-faith purchaser at risk even when the original owner was the "cheaper cost-avoider" with respect to the common risk, often illegal sale by a bailee or a thief. By allowing the good-faith purchaser to claim clear title, the basic legal rule created incentives for the original owner to be careful in his selection of bailee or to better guard his property. Although there were many local variations, the pragmatic instinct generally won out over the theoretical impulse to protect the original owner from the loss of title without consent and without the commission of any wrong. For discussion of the Roman rules, see *Institutes of Justinian*, Book 2, Title 1, 25–34; see also Saul X. Levmore, "Variety and Uniformity in the Treatment of Good Faith Purchasers," *Journal of Legal Studies*, vol. 16 (1987), pp. 43–65, for a wide comparative discussion.

who owns the goods in question.[36] However, the rule of initial acquisition that allows for capture of wild animals would not appear nearly so immutable or so sound as the natural-law tradition has it. To be sure, in ancient times, the common-pool problems of overfishing and the like might not have been serious, given the smaller population base; or these practices might have been regulated by a set of implicit customs that bound local communities. But these customs tend to have a shadowy, unwritten existence that never quite makes it into the law reports or legal treatises.

The costs of the occupation rule for establishing property rights, moreover, need not be constant across time. Harold Demsetz's powerful analysis of the capture rule for wild animals, made over a generation ago, still rings true today.[37] Where the hunting and fishing are done for the internal consumption of a tribe or community, the yields that are taken are likely to be sustainable. But the moment the catch is coveted by some large external market, the demand for it can easily become so great that the negative welfare consequences of the "immutable rule" of capture become quickly apparent. At this point the original rule of capture will usually give way to some alternative regime that will allow (when nonmigratory animals cooperate)[38] exclusive hunting rights to specific groups for specific territories. Now that one party owns both the stock and the yield, as is the case for animals with fixed territories, incentives for long-term conservation of resources create gains that justify the increased costs of defining and policing the territorial boundaries. The new set of property rights does a better job of balancing external costs against internal gains: for while there are surely losers from the creation of hunting territories, the risk of the wholesale destruction of valuable forms of game and fish is substantially diminished.

Unfortunately, Locke missed the full complexity of the relationship between capture and exchange. In his view the possibility of exchange, as measured by the introduction of *"a little piece of yellow Metal,"*[39] obvi-

[36] The same result applies to contracts for the sale of labor. If A has promised his services to B, and C desires them, it is possible for C to purchase the right to use them from B. That transaction is far clumsier than the purchase of goods, and it is therefore more common for individual persons to reserve the right to redeploy their labor when that option is an important one. But where the contract for labor involves the transfer of information, or the development of transaction-specific capital, long-term contracts may be preferred in order to protect B from being held up by A midway through the project. Often covenants not to compete are part of the original agreement.

[37] Harold Demsetz, "Toward a Theory of Property Rights," *American Economic Review*, vol. 57 (Papers & Proceedings, 1967).

[38] The system of territories does not work for migratory animals and birds. There the temptation of any single landowner is to capture the animals while they are on his territory, no matter what their state of maturity. Some comprehensive treaty across territories is needed, which is no easy matter to obtain. Think of the difficulties in finding some international accommodation on whaling that keeps the Norwegians, Japanese, and Americans happy.

[39] Locke, *Second Treatise*, section 37.

ated the need to place any limitations on what could be withdrawn from the commons: "[H]e who appropriates land to himself by his labour, does not lessen but increase the common stock of mankind. For the provisions serving to the support of humane life, produced by one acre of inclosed and cultivated land, are (to speak much within compasse) ten times more, than those, which are yeilded by an acre of Land, of an equal richnesse, lyeing wast in common."[40] The clear implication of this proposition is that outsiders gain ample compensation for what they have lost by way of acquisition by virtue of their enhanced possibilities of gain through trade. Using territories for hunting has the same result, but sticking with the rule of capture of individual animals (which Locke himself had endorsed)[41] is ruinous, as the Demsetz example on territorial boundary creation shows. Water rights are subject to the same analysis, for the right of alienation creates additional reasons to limit the right of capture. In order to prevent the excessive depletion of the common pool, standard rules of English property law refused to allow the riparian to alienate water as a commodity separate from the land.[42]

The theoretical implication should be clear. The labor theory of acquisition does not give any information on the question of whether alienation of the property should be allowed after acquisition. Instead, the decisive inquiry is whether the alienation leads to the destruction of the commons or whether it does not. If it does, then any gains from trade are likely to be dwarfed by the losses to the common pool. If it does not, then the gains from trade are *added* to the gains from increased production that a system of property rights allows. As before, the ultimate judgment does not depend on any immutable system of property rights. Rather, it depends on the relative force of two inconsistent tendencies. In all cases the objective is to maximize the sum of value attributable to both the common stock and its yield, and to adopt the legal rules which achieve that result.

So long as the results of this inquiry are contingent, it follows that transitions between legal regimes will be appropriate when the relative costs shift in systematic ways. In order to complete the picture, therefore, it is necessary to account as well for the costs of transition, and while the issue has been insufficiently studied, it is rare that such transition takes place without genuine political travail or instances of injustice. The English enclosure movement between the sixteenth and eighteenth centuries, for example, converted common lands to private ones. It may well have provided some overall efficiency gains, but the customary claims of poor and marginal groups to the commons were destroyed because they were not

[40] *Ibid.*

[41] *Ibid.*, section 30.

[42] Richard A. Epstein, "Why Restrain Alienation?" *Columbia Law Review*, vol. 85 (1985), pp. 970–90.

documented in writing.[43] Indeed, Locke's famous chapter on property could easily be read in historical context as a disguised defense of the enclosure movement. Similarly, the shift from a system of riparian rights (limited rights in landowners adjacent to rivers and lakes to remove water) to prior appropriation rights (great rights of removal to the first appropriator, even if not a riparian) in the western states of the U.S. during the nineteenth century was often accompanied by political turmoil and private violence.[44] Likewise, the rules that allowed for first possession of minerals, whales, and fish from the public seas have proved to be increasingly unsatisfactory over time, and the effort to rework them by comprehensive treaty has been a prolonged exercise in international frustration.[45]

The difficulties of fashioning suitable rules for the acquisition of rights in water or wild animals, however, need not carry over to labor or to unowned land. For labor, the traditional rule of "acquisition" has been Locke's — every person has property rights in his own person.[46] Similarly, for land, the common-pool problems so evident with wildlife are far less of a concern, so the case for altering the first-possession rule announced by Justinian is far weaker. To be sure, the use of land could always result in external harms to other individuals; but the classical law of nuisance, with its general prohibition against physical invasions and its more limited affirmative obligations of lateral and subjacent support between neighbors, has done a reasonably good job of policing the boundaries.[47] It is possible to eliminate all boundary disputes between neighbors by eliminating boundaries, that is, by having a system of common ownership of property where the allocation decisions are made by some system of governance or vote. Done voluntarily, there is no reason to object to that solution, save to note that it is not likely to be chosen very often: persons who do not get along as neighbors are hardly likely to do better as partners.

Any insistence, however, on mandatory common ownership is a recipe for disaster: co-owners are not chosen but imposed, so the level of

[43] See E. P. Thompson, *Customs in Common* (New York: The New Press, 1991), pp. 97–184.

[44] See *Coffin v. The Left Hand Ditch Co.*, 6 Colo. 443 (1882), an action brought by a prior appropriator against a riparian who destroyed a dam used to secure the diversion of water from the river.

[45] See, e.g., Robert C. Ellickson, *Order without Law: How Neighbors Settle Disputes* (Cambridge: Harvard University Press, 1991).

[46] See Locke, *Second Treatise*, section 27. For a similar broad account of property rights in the person, see James Madison, "Property" [1792], reprinted in *The Founders' Constitution*, ed. P. Kurland and R. Lerner (Chicago and London: University of Chicago Press, 1987), ch. 16.

[47] Lateral support is the support that the land of one owner gives to the land of his neighbor; subjacent support is that which land below gives to land located above it, as with mining claims. The duty of support implies that one person is not allowed to dig on his land to the extent that the land of a neighbor will no longer stay in place. For explication of the various rules governing these matters, see Richard A. Epstein, "Nuisance Law: Corrective Justice and Its Utilitarian Constraints," *Journal of Legal Studies*, vol. 8 (1979), pp. 49–102.

mutual distrust is likely to be high. Disagreement over the common plan of development, or over the division of benefits and burdens, is virtually certain to produce massive forms of paralysis from which there is no escape. A division of the property is ruled out by the inflexible requirement of common ownership; and a sale of the property, or of any interest therein, is not likely to succeed if a suitable purchaser cannot be found — and who wants to buy into a lawsuit or a family dispute? Boundary disputes are the price paid in order to avoid the governance problems that arise from forced associations. But it is far easier to keep a neighbor off your land than it is to prevent a co-owner from using more than his pro rata share of common property, or to force him to contribute his pro rata share of labor to the joint venture.[48]

IV. The Constitutional Aftermath

It is time now briefly to bring this discussion of private and common property into the modern era, for the failure to appreciate the distinctive position of common property in any complete system of property rights has led to a serious incompleteness in the basic American constitutional structure. Initially, it should be noted that the American constitutional plan was alert to creating explicit constitutional protections for private property: "[N]or shall private property be taken for public use, without just compensation."[49] This clause, which has, in my view, been largely frittered away,[50] was designed to allow the state to take property without obtaining consent in the individual case, so long as it left the person whose property was taken no worse off than he was before the taking. Rightly understood, the use of the takings clause works a neat compromise between the Scylla of majority rule and the Charybdis of unanimous consent. The holdout problems of unanimous consent are avoided by allowing political majorities, or supermajorities, to act; but by the same token, the just-compensation clause prevents the expropriation of those who have lost in the political struggle.

The American Constitution, however, is quiet about what should be done with property that is held in common. Must it be left in the original position? Can it be sold or given away? Who should have access to it? In order to answer these questions, a wide range of constitutional doctrines have been proposed, all of which have in common one feature: an insecure mooring in a constitutional text that was not sensitive to the problem at hand. It is useful, therefore, to mention just two of the cases that raise these difficulties before ending this essay.

[48] See Ellickson, "Property in Land" (*supra* note 21), pp. 1327–28.

[49] U.S. Constitution, Amendment 5.

[50] See Richard A. Epstein, *Takings: Private Property and the Power of Eminent Domain* (Cambridge: Harvard University Press, 1985). I will spare the reader the details of the argument here.

The first of the important cases is *Corfield v. Coryell*.[51] It is best remembered today for its stirring declaration of the individual rights protected by the privileges-and-immunities clause of Article IV: "The Citizens of each State shall be entitled to all Privileges and Immunities of Citizens in the several States." *Corfield* is best known for its impressive enumeration of the rights that fell under this clause.[52] But the case itself involved the question of whether the state of New Jersey could prevent citizens of other states from collecting oysters in New Jersey territorial waters. Notwithstanding Justice Bushrod Washington's famous list, New Jersey could use its sovereign power to keep the outsiders from sharing in the oyster harvest. But why? If, as was said, the oysters were unowned, then why shouldn't outsiders be in a position to claim them, for privileges and immunities include the right "to take, hold and dispose of property, either real or personal." If one begins with Justinian's view that the oysters are not owned until reduced to private possession, then outsiders can collect oysters on the same terms as the good citizens of New Jersey.

The analysis takes a very different turn if oysters are regarded as common property, as Justice Washington concluded:

> Where those private rights do not exist to the exclusion of the common right, that of fishing belongs to all the citizens or subjects of the state. It is the property of all; to be enjoyed by them in subordination to the laws which regulate its use. They may be considered as tenants in common of this property; and they are so exclusively entitled to the use of it, that it cannot be enjoyed by others without the tacit consent, or the express permission of the sovereign who has the power to regulate its use.[53]

---

[51] *Corfield v. Coryell*, 6 Fed. Case 546 (Cir. Ct. E. D. Pa. 1823). The decision was handed down by Justice Bushrod Washington while he was riding circuit between Supreme Court terms.

[52] *Ibid.*, pp. 551–52:

What these fundamental principles are, it would perhaps be more tedious than difficult to enumerate. They may, however, be all comprehended under the following general heads: Protection by the government; the enjoyment of life and liberty, with the right to acquire and possess property of every kind, and to pursue and obtain happiness and safety; subject nevertheless to such restraints as the government may justly prescribe for the general good of the whole. The right of a citizen of one state to pass through, or to reside in any other state, for purposes of trade, agriculture, professional pursuits, or otherwise; to claim the benefit of the writ of habeas corpus; to institute and maintain actions of any kind in courts of the state; to take, hold and dispose of property, either real or personal; and an exemption from higher taxes or impositions than are paid by the other citizens of the state; may be mentioned as some of the particular privileges and immunities of citizens, which are clearly embraced by the general description of privileges deemed to be fundamental: to which may be added, the elective franchise, as regulated and established by the laws or constitution of the state in which it is to be exercised.

[53] *Ibid.*, p. 552.

What was once an abstract philosophical dispute has been transformed into an intensely practical issue. Justice Washington started from a Lockean position that all oysters were owned in common. He then accepted that taking possession of the oysters reduced them to private ownership. But his commoners included only the citizens of New Jersey, not the citizens of the world. An issue that had been skirted by all the learned authors — just who had access to the commons — was now settled by the federal structure of the American Constitution. Yet if Justice Washington had followed the classical Roman view that treated wild animals as unowned in a state of nature, then the case would have had to come out the other way: anyone could take.

The questions at stake in *Corfield* were purely distributional. To be sure, excessive gathering of the oysters could prove harmful, and New Jersey, with its eye on "the general good of the whole," could have prescribed limitations on the number of oysters that could be removed from any particular bed. But if all persons were equally entitled to the oysters, then New Jersey could not exclude outsiders from the class of permissible users, even though it could limit their catch just as it could limit that of its citizens. True complications arise, however, if the state decides to auction off limited rights to the oyster beds, as many economists have suggested. If that were done, who would keep the proceeds? Simply to deposit them into New Jersey's treasury would be to allow outsiders to access the beds but not to share in the money collected for their use, as insiders would. Yet finding some way to allow outsiders to share in the proceeds is not easy to do. Better minds will have to work out a just solution.

In the second case, *Geer v. Connecticut*,[54] Connecticut had passed a statute forbidding any person from killing "any woodcock, ruffled grouse or quail for the purpose of conveying the same beyond the limits of the state," or from transporting them out of the state. Since the statute applied to citizens and noncitizens alike, it could not be challenged under the privileges-and-immunities clause of Article IV. But it was challenged as an impermissible exercise of state power under the commerce clause.[55] In rejecting the challenge to the statute, Justice Edward D. White began with a dutiful citation of the Roman authorities, which he promptly misread: "Among other subdivisions, things were classified by the Roman law into public and common. The latter embrace animals *ferae naturae* [wild animals], which, having no owner, were considered as

---

[54] *Geer v. Connecticut*, 161 U.S. 519 (1896).

[55] U.S. Constitution, Article I, section 8: "Congress shall have Power . . . [t]o regulate Commerce with foreign Nations, and among the several States and with the Indian Tribes." The clause reads as though it only confers powers on Congress and imposes no limitations on the states, save where state law is in direct conflict with federal legislation. But the clause has long been read to contain a "negative" or "dormant" power to preclude state regulation that interferes with trade and transportation across state lines even in the absence of congressional legislation.

belonging in common to all the citizens of the State."[56] This passage is
then followed by a quotation from Justinian's *Digest* which stands for the
proposition exactly opposite of that asserted: namely, that to be unowned
is not to be held in common, so that all might take.[57] Even though the
doctrinal argument has shifted, Justinian's *Digest* and the long list of subsequent classical writings were said to resolve a delicate point of federal
jurisdiction. To be sure, Justice Stephen J. Field dissented on the classical ground that the state's power could not be invoked *"where the State has
never had the game in its possession or under its control or use."*[58] And in the
fullness of time Justice Field's dissent became law, for *Geer* was dis-
patched in 1977 — when the Supreme Court reversed its position on this
point of property law by holding that "[a] state does not stand in the
same position as the owner of a private game preserve, and it is pure fan-
tasy to talk of 'owning' wild fish, birds, or animals. Neither the States nor
the Federal Government, any more than a hopeful fisherman or hunter,
has title to these creatures until they are reduced to possession by skill-
ful capture."[59]

V. CONCLUSION

It should be evident that the law of property has followed more or less
consistent lines since the time of Justinian. Nor should that result be
either troubling or surprising, for the borrowing from Roman sources by
English and American law shows that the common roots of these two different legal systems are far more important than any differences between
them on points of detail. The classical categories have proved their staying power in modern settings. On the other hand, the conceptual foundations of the classical system have proved less durable. The classical
scholars had claimed that the rules of property rights were discoverable
by pure reason and were universal in their application. A fuller understanding of the system suggests that the opposite conclusion is true.
Property rights are human inventions and thus respond to technological
changes. Rightly understood, these systems work, albeit imperfectly, to
maximize the total value of the relevant resources, not only for the property owners, but for the population at large.

At first glance, this formulation seems to undercut one of the major virtues of a system of property — the certainty that allows individuals to plan

[56] *Geer v. Connecticut*, p. 522.

[57] Justinian's *Digest*, Book 41, Title 1, 1: "Thus all the animals which can be taken upon
the earth, in the sea, or in the air, that is to say, wild animals, belong to those who take
them . . . [b]ecause that which belongs to nobody is acquired by the natural law by the
person who first possesses it." See *The Digest of Justinian*, ed. Alan Watson (Philadelphia:
University of Pennsylvania Press, 1985).

[58] *Geer v. Connecticut*, p. 539.

[59] *Douglas v. Seacoast Products, Inc.*, 431 U.S. 265, 284 (1977). This passage was cited with
approval in *Hughes v. Oklahoma*, 441 U.S. 322, 334-35 (1979), overruling *Geer v. Connecticut*
and restoring the ancient law of property to its traditional splendor.

their own lives. But in reality it does not. Certainty is one of the virtues that fits into the consequentialist calculus. In some of the most important cases it plays a critical role. For land, labor, and chattels, there is really no reason today to depart from the Roman structure of property law. The strength of that system comes from the endless array of voluntary transformations that issue from the raw building-blocks of labor and property. Sale, mortgage, partnership, lease, bailment, and hire form mighty molecules from the simple atoms of the basic system. They fuel today's engine of production and human well-being. The technological reasons that cry out for novel rules for water, the spectrum, overflights, or computer software, do not apply to garden-variety land uses. Here stability is the dominant virtue, for the longer the time horizons on which individuals can count, the more inventive their private transactions and the lower the necessary rate of return to keep them in any deal.

To be sure, challenges to the traditional legal conceptions will be made on the ground that changed social circumstances always require us to revisit older legal rules. Yet simply because these challenges are advanced does not mean that they should be accepted.[60] The constraints of the theory of value-maximization usually stand as a powerful barrier against efforts to return land, labor, and movable property to a commons, or worse, to put them under direct government control. All the benefits of privatization still remain, and before one rushes headlong to place all land in the commons, several hard questions should be asked: Is it possible to constrain the adverse effects of private use on other individuals by morelimited restrictions on land use, such as those found in the common law of nuisance? Will the proposed restriction of private use actually serve to protect the commons? Are the private losses larger than the social gains that would be obtained? Are there major political abuses when politicians have discretion to define and redefine property rights at will?

To the followers of Justinian, the immutable nature of property avoided these complications: so clear was the bundle of rights in land possessed by a single owner. The categorical nature of a system of natural law has its comfort. But today that older faith and innocence is lost, and even a qualified defense of private property as an institution has to be mounted inch by inch. But private property has coexisted, and should coexist, with systems of common property as well. Finding and keeping the proper line between the two systems is a task that requires hard work and clear thinking throughout the ages. It is easy to say: minimize the sum of the costs of exclusion and coordination. But it is often a delicate task to reach the correct balance.

Law, University of Chicago

---

[60] See Richard A. Epstein, "The Static Conception of the Common Law," *Journal of Legal Studies*, vol. 9 (1980), pp. 253–75.

THE INSTITUTION OF PROPERTY*

By David Schmidtz

I. Original Appropriation: The Problem

The typical method of acquiring a property right involves transfer from a previous owner. But sooner or later, that chain of transfers traces back to the beginning. That is why we have a philosophical problem. How does a thing legitimately become a piece of property *for the first time*?

In this essay, I follow the custom of distinguishing between mere liberties and full-blooded rights.[1] If I have the *liberty* of doing X, then it is permissible for me to do X. But the mere fact that I am at liberty to do X leaves open the possibility that you might be at liberty to interfere with my doing X. Accordingly, liberties are not full-blooded rights, since my having a *right* to do X has the additional implication that others are not at liberty to interfere with my doing X. When it comes to mere liberties, interference is not a violation. You can violate rights, but you cannot violate liberties.

What must I do in order to *stake a claim* to a piece of land? When I stake a claim, I change other people's relation to the land in such a way that they are no longer at liberty to use or dispose of it without my permission. Staking a claim thus involves acting so as to *cancel* other people's liberties, so that they are no longer at liberty to act in ways that interfere with my liberties regarding that piece of land. If I have a right to farm a piece of land, that means two things: (1) It is permissible for me to farm the land—that is, I have a liberty. (2) And in certain ways it is not permissible for others to interfere. To say I have a right to the land is to say other people no longer have liberties with respect to that land, and that I have a claim against anyone who acts as if they do have liberties with respect to it.[2]

The problem regarding land, then, is that there will be a time when no one owns it. At that time, no one has a right that anyone else stay off it.

---

* For helpful comments, I thank Robert Ellickson, Carol Rose, Elizabeth Willott, as well as the editors of, and the other contributors to, this volume. Thanks also to audiences at the Institute for Humane Studies and at the American Philosophical Association (especially commentator George Harris) for lively and useful discussion.

[1] The custom traces back to Wesley Newcomb Hohfeld. See Hohfeld, *Fundamental Legal Conceptions* (New Haven: Yale University Press, 1919). Note that Hohfeld's discussion was about the conceptual analysis of legal rights, whereas this essay is about the moral justification of a particular kind of legal right, namely the right to exclude.

[2] A process of staking a claim need not, however, cancel all of another person's liberties with respect to that piece of land. I return to this point in Section V.

Everyone has the liberty of using it.[3] How do we go from each person having a liberty to someone having an exclusive right to the land? In the most abstract terms, the answer has to be this: The change occurs when some people exercise their liberty in such a way that others cannot interfere without at the same time infringing a right.[4]

People can forbid someone else's appropriation of a resource only when they have rights to that resource, not just liberties. If we are talking about a case of original appropriation, then it is true by hypothesis that the most that anyone else has over that land is a liberty, and liberties are not rights. If other people do have rights to that resource, then the question is how they acquired such rights. If we can answer that question, then that will tell us how original appropriation works. Clearly, people do not acquire rights merely by asserting them. At the same time, to establish a moral claim to unowned land, people do not need to make as strong a case as they would need to make in order to justify confiscating someone else's land, because it is not as if someone already owns it.

Since there is no prior owner in original-appropriation cases, there is no one from whom one can or needs to get consent.[5] What, then, must

---

[3] Given that we seek to explain how an exclusive property right comes into existence, there is no avoiding the assumption that people have liberties. Since we cannot assume that people already have a right to exclude, we must consider situations in which, regarding a certain piece of land, no one yet has the right to exclude. And the situation in which no one has the right to exclude is the situation in which everyone has liberties. Thus, to question the origin of exclusive rights is to presuppose that people have liberties.

[4] In passing, the Lockean approach to justifying particular acts of appropriation involves arguing that when we mix labor with unowned resources, we take something to which we have a right (assuming we have a right to our labor) and annex it to something else to which we have a liberty. (See John Locke, *Two Treatises of Government*, ed. Peter Laslett [New York: Mentor, 1960], *Second Treatise*, ch. 5.) As Robert Nozick asks, though, "why isn't mixing what I own with what I don't own a way of losing what I own rather than a way of gaining what I don't?" (See Nozick, *Anarchy, State, and Utopia* [New York: Basic Books, 1974], pp. 174–75.) Suppose I own a can of tomato juice but decide to pour it into the ocean. Why does that mean I have lost my tomato juice? Why is it not a way of coming to own the ocean by mixing labor (namely, the labor by which I acquired my can of juice) with it?

The Lockean answer is something like this: Labor-mixing creates rights because it involves exercising a liberty in such a way that others cannot interfere with that liberty without also violating a right. That is not what happens, though, when I pour my tomato juice into the ocean. If I own the juice, then I have a right that you not take it from me and drink it yourself, or pour it in the ocean without my permission. But none of those rights are violated by people who use the ocean after I pour the juice into it myself. Therefore, my pouring of juice has no bearing on their liberty to use the ocean. I annexed the ocean to my tomato juice only by severing the connection between the tomato juice and my person. As the story stands, the tomato juice no longer is, or ever can be, integrated into my ongoing projects. Unless there is more to the story than meets the eye—if what seems to be a simple pouring of juice into the ocean is really nothing more than pouring juice in the ocean—I have abandoned my claim to it. Although I do not take the Lockean approach of trying to ground original appropriation in a story about labor-mixing, I admit that the approach is intuitively appealing, and I would say it has the resources to answer Nozick's famous question.

[5] Following Locke (*Second Treatise*, section 25), some might say we hold the earth in common as a gift from God, but holding the earth in common does not imply that we own it. Holding is merely holding. Locke himself (in the passage just cited) distinguishes between the idea of property and the idea of holding the earth in common as a gift from God, as A.

a person do? Locke's idea seems to have been that any residual common (perhaps need-based) claim to the land could be met if a person could appropriate it without prejudice to other people, in other words, if a person could leave enough and as good for others. This so-called Lockean Proviso can be interpreted in many ways, but an adequate interpretation will reflect the fact that this is its point—to license claims to land that can be made without prejudice to others.[6]

We also should consider whether the "others" who are to be left with enough and as good include not just people currently on the scene—one's fellow explorers, perhaps—but latecomers as well, including people not yet born. Most theorists accept the more demanding interpretation.[7] It seems to fit well with Locke's idea that the preservation of mankind (which definitely includes future generations) is the ultimate criterion by which any use of resources is to be assessed. Aside from that, we offer an obviously more compelling defense of an appropriation if we can argue that there was enough left over not just for the appropriator's fellow explorers, but also for generations to come. The following section explores the implications of the supposition that those in a position to appropriate resources from the commons have an obligation to leave enough and as good for future generations.[8]

II. Original Appropriation: A Solution

Philosophers who work on the original-appropriation issue, though, generally conclude that the Lockean Proviso is logically impossible to sat-

---

John Simmons points out. See Simmons, *The Lockean Theory of Rights* (Princeton: Princeton University Press, 1992), p. 232 n. 33. And James Tully points out an interesting ambiguity concerning the rights to goods held in common when he distinguishes between the common right to use and the right to common use. See Tully, *A Discourse on Property* (Cambridge: Cambridge University Press, 1980), p. 97.

[6] See Simmons, *The Lockean Theory of Rights*, p. 283, on nonspoilage and on leaving fair shares for others as inside and outside limits on how much one can appropriate. According to Simmons, a fair share, one that leaves enough and as good for others, is the outside limit on how much a person can appropriate. Within that limit, we are further restricted to taking what we can use before it spoils. (In *Second Treatise*, sections 46ff., Locke argued that introducing money as a durable store of value effectively renders the inside limit inoperative.) This leaves us having to say more about what keeps the outside limit from collapsing in on us and ruling out appropriation altogether, but I still find Simmons's distinction attractive.

[7] As John Sanders asks, "[w]hat possible argument could at the same time require that the present generation have scruples about leaving enough and as good for one another, while shrugging off such concern for future generations?" See Sanders, "Justice and the Initial Acquisition of Private Property," *Harvard Journal of Law and Public Policy*, vol. 10 (1987), p. 377.

[8] If this more demanding test proves impossible to pass, we may be forced to abandon it in favor of something less stringent. For arguments that Locke intended the Proviso as a sufficient but not necessary condition, see Judith Jarvis Thomson, "Property Acquisition," *Journal of Philosophy*, vol. 73 (1976), pp. 664–66; and Jeremy Waldron, "Enough and as Good Left for Others," *Philosophical Quarterly*, vol. 29 (1976), pp. 319–28.

isfy. The way Judith Thomson puts it, if "the first labor-mixer must literally leave as much and as good for others who come along later, then no one can come to own anything, for there are only finitely many things in the world so that every taking leaves less for others."[9] Thomson is hardly alone in taking this position: "The Lockean Proviso, in the contemporary world of overpopulation and scarce resources, can almost never be met."[10] "The condition that there be enough and as good left for others could not of course be literally satisfied by any system of private property rights."[11] "Every acquisition worsens the lot of others — and worsens their lot in relevant ways."[12] And so on. If we take something out of the cookie jar, we *must* be leaving less for others. To many people, this conclusion appears self-evident. It has to be right.

A. *Appropriation is not a zero-sum game*

But it is not right. First, it is by no means impossible — certainly not logically impossible — for one taking to leave as much for others. Surely we can at least imagine a logically possible world of magic cookie jars in which, every time you take out one cookie, more and better cookies take its place.

Second, the logically possible world I just imagined is the sort of world we actually live in. Philosophers who write on the subject of original appropriation tend to speak as if people who arrive first, and thus do all the appropriating, are much luckier than those who come later. The truth is, first appropriators begin the process of resource creation, while latecomers like ourselves get most of the benefits. Consider the Jamestown colony of 1607. Exactly what was it, we should ask, that made their situation so much better than ours? They never had to worry about being overcharged for car repairs. They never awoke in the middle of the night to the sound of noisy refrigerators, or leaky faucets, or flushing toilets. They never had to agonize over the choice of long-distance telephone companies. Are these the things that make us wish we had gotten there first?

Many philosophers say, in effect, that original appropriators got the good stuff. We got ugly leftovers. But in truth, original appropriation benefits latecomers far more than it benefits original appropriators. Original appropriation is a cornucopia of wealth, but mainly for latecomers rather

[9] Judith Jarvis Thomson, *The Realm of Rights* (Cambridge, MA: Harvard University Press, 1990), p. 330.

[10] Virginia Held, introduction to *Property, Profits, and Economic Justice*, ed. V. Held (Belmont: Wadsworth, 1980), p. 6.

[11] Rolf Sartorius, "Persons and Property," *Utility and Rights*, ed. R. G. Frey (Minneapolis: University of Minnesota Press, 1984), p. 210.

[12] J. H. Bogart, "Lockean Provisos and State of Nature Theories," *Ethics*, vol. 95 (1985), p. 834.

than for original appropriators themselves.[13] The original appropriators never dreamt of things we latecomers take for granted. The poorest among us have life expectancies exceeding theirs by several *decades*.

Original appropriation diminishes the stock of what can be originally appropriated,[14] but that is not the same thing as diminishing the stock of what can be owned. On the contrary, in taking control of resources and thereby reducing the stock of what can be originally appropriated, people typically generate massive increases in the stock of what can be owned. The lesson is that appropriation is not a zero-sum game. It is a positive-sum game. As Locke himself stressed, it creates the possibility of mutual benefit on a massive scale.[15]

Thus, the idea that original appropriators have obligations because of what they took away from latecomers is a mistake. Of course, I am not saying that members of later generations have no obligations to each other. No such sweeping (and implausible) claim is implied here. What I am saying, though, is that no obligation on the part of people now living has anything to do with the fact that not everyone had a chance to engage in original appropriation.

B. The commons prior to appropriation is not a zero-sum game either

The second point is that the commons before appropriation is not a zero-sum game either. Typically it is a negative-sum game. Let me tell two stories.[16] The first comes from the coral reefs of the Philippine and Tongan Islands. People once fished those reefs with lures and traps, but have recently caught on to a technique called bleach-fishing, which involves dumping bleach into the reefs. It turns out that fish have trouble breathing sodium hypochlorite. Partially asphyxiated, they float to the surface where they are easy to collect. The problem is, the coral itself is

---

[13] The commerce made possible by original appropriation also creates pollution, of course, and other negative externalities as well. I compare externalities associated with open-access commons to externalities associated with private parcels in Subsection IIB and Section III.

[14] At least, this is so when we are talking about resources like land. With intellectual property, in contrast, it seems that appropriations of ideas expand the horizon for new appropriations, making possible the increasingly rapid rate of new appropriations. See Jonathan R. Macey, "Property Rights, Innovation, and Constitutional Structure," in this volume.

[15] Or, at least, Locke estimates that 99 percent of the value of the products of the earth is attributable to labor inputs (*Second Treatise*, section 40), perhaps even as much as 99.9 percent (section 43). When we conjoin this to the premise (implicit in section 35) that parceling the commons releases labor to multiply the products of the earth, we get the conclusion that, using contemporary terms, appropriation is a positive-sum game.

[16] The first story is lifted from chapter 2 of David Schmidtz, *The Limits of Government* (Boulder: Westview Press, 1991). I thank Kent Jeffreys at the Competitive Enterprise Institute, Jo Kwong at the Atlas Research Foundation, and especially Peggy Fosdick at the National Aquarium for information regarding the second story. Copies of relevant correspondence and legal documents are on file with the author. For the full story, see Sam and Peggy Fosdick, *Last Chance Lost*, forthcoming.

a living animal, or composite thereof. It suffocates along with the fish, and the dead reef is no longer a viable habitat. You might say the fishermen ought to be more responsible. They ought to preserve the reefs for their children. But that misses the point, which is that the fishermen lack the option of saving the coral for their children. The coral is in the commons. Access to it is unrestricted. So long as that is true, the only options the fishermen have are to destroy the reef themselves or leave it to be destroyed by the next person who comes along. The solution is to change the institutional arrangement, removing the coral from the commons by making it accessible only to those who will utilize the resource in a manner that is consistent with its capacity to renew itself.

The second story comes from the Cayman Islands. The Atlantic Green Turtle (*Chelonia Mydas*, known by more than one common name) has long been prized as a source of meat and eggs. Sadly, there are now, by some estimates, only three thousand left in the wild. Commerce in Atlantic Green Turtles has been regulated in various ways since 1973 by the Convention on International Trade in Endangered Species and, in the United States, by the Fish and Wildlife Service, the Department of Commerce, and the Department of the Interior. That sort of protection has proven ineffective. The turtles are a commonly held resource, and poachers continued to harvest that resource by dark of night. In response, a group of entrepreneurs and concerned scientists started a company called Cayman Turtle Farm, staffed it with former poachers, and began raising and selling captive-bred sea turtles. The business was legal because the existing regulations regarding commerce in Atlantic Green Turtles contained (somewhat ambiguous) exemptions allowing commerce in captive-bred animals. In the wild, most new hatchlings are seized by predators before they can crawl from nest to sea. In consequence, as few as a tenth of 1 percent of wild hatchlings survive to adulthood, but Cayman Turtle Farm through trial and error gradually boosted the surviving hatchling rate to something over 50 percent. In doing so, the company became profitable and developed a worldwide market. At the peak of operations, they were rearing in excess of a hundred thousand Atlantic Green Turtles and had begun releasing large numbers of hatchlings and yearlings into the wild.

In 1978, the Atlantic Green Turtle was reclassified under the Endangered Species Act as an endangered species. Cayman Turtle Farm hoped that the restructured act would contain an exemption allowing commerce in captive-bred animals, but in the end it did not. In consequence, Cayman Farm was shut out of American markets. Even worse, the company could no longer ship its products via American ports, which meant it lost the access it had had via Miami to world markets. It exists today only to serve the population of the Cayman Islands themselves. The farm's former employees have gone back to poaching, and the future of the Atlantic Green Turtle is once again hanging by a thread.

What do these stories tell us? While thinking about them, we might pause to wonder why cows and chickens were not wiped out hundreds of years ago. We slaughter them by the millions, and yet they are not endangered. How could that be? The moral of these stories is that an obligation to leave enough and as good for generations to come, if there is such a thing, could sometimes *require* rather than forbid original appropriation.[17] If we treated Atlantic Green Turtles the way we treat cows, that would be a positive-sum game and we would have plenty of turtles. If we treated cows the way we treat Atlantic Green Turtles, that would be a negative-sum game and cows would be an endangered species.

Of course, this is not to say the cornucopia of wealth generated by the appropriation and subsequent mobilization of resources is necessarily an unambiguous benefit. With production comes pollution, for example. I do not claim there is an easy answer to the question of which sort of regime best handles such problems. I explore that question in the following section. The thing to note here, though, is that we do not have to justify preserving the commons in its original, pristine, unappropriated form, because preserving it in its pristine original form is not an option. The commons is not a time capsule. Leaving resources in the commons is not at all like putting resources in a time capsule as a legacy for future generations. Time capsules may be a fine thing. They certainly preserve things. But before you can put something in a time capsule, you have to appropriate it.

Similarly, I do not deny that there may be individuals or groups who attach no value to the increases in life expectancy and other benefits that accompany the appropriation of resources for productive use. Such individuals or groups might genuinely prefer to maintain a steady-state system that indefinitely supports their lifestyles as hunter-gatherers, untainted by the shoes and fishing rods and safety matches of Western culture. If original appropriation forces such people to participate in a culture they would rather have no part of, then from their point of view, original appropriation may cost more than it is worth.

Here is something to keep in mind, though. First, remember that the commons is not a way of preserving the status quo. There may be people whose quality of life drops after appropriation, but the economic pres-

---

[17] I claimed this in chapter 2 of *Limits of Government* as well. As one correspondent asked in response, "if we take the Proviso seriously — and assume it is actually enforced — then why would there be a tragedy of the commons? . . . If the Proviso precluded the taking of the property in the first place, then it doesn't seem as if the resource would be overutilized." My point is that although the Proviso morally precludes bleach-fishing, the practice continues. Any particular fisherman thus operates against a background of Proviso violations. But a moral fisherman still faces the question of how to leave enough and as good for others. The background of violations does not change the question, but it does change the answer. (In particular, as the following section explains, when the burden of common use exceeds the land's carrying capacity, the Proviso comes to require, not merely permit, original appropriation.)

sures that drive appropriation might have compromised their quality of life even more if the appropriated resources had been left in the unregulated commons.

Second, would-be hunter-gatherers may not, as a matter of fact, be forced to participate in Western culture. As far as I know, there are vast areas of land (in northern Canada, say) where the life of a hunter-gatherer remains an option. Moreover, those who opt for lives as hunter-gatherers retain the significant advantage of being able to participate in Western culture on a drop-in basis — during medical emergencies, to trade for supplies, and so on.

Now, I can imagine someone saying, "This shows a shocking lack of foresight. Even if the hunter-gatherer life is an option now, it may not be so in another few years. That option is disappearing as the land is appropriated for other purposes." Suppose we concede that the option really is disappearing. What would that prove? It would prove that, under current real-world conditions, the lifestyle of the hunter-gather cannot be sustained by the unregulated commons. It would show that, if hunter-gatherers want their children to have the option of living as hunter-gatherers, then they too need to do some appropriating. If they want a steady-state civilization, they need to be aware that they will not find it in an unregulated commons. They need to deny that their territory is or ought to be an unregulated commons. They need to argue that they, as rightful owners, have a right to regulate access to it. They need to argue that they have a right to exclude oil companies, for example, which have much to gain by treating northern Canada as an unregulated commons.[18]

Note that there is a distinction between justifying institutions that regulate appropriation and justifying particular acts of appropriation. To draw upon the game metaphor one more time, we may think of original appropriation as a game and particular acts of appropriation as moves within that game. In those terms, my objective is to justify the game rather than particular moves within the game. Particular moves within the game may have nothing to recommend them. Indeed, suppose we say (for argument's sake) that any act of appropriation will appear morally arbitrary when viewed in isolation. Even so, there may be morally compelling reasons to have an institutional framework in which claims to property are recognized on the basis of moves that would carry no moral weight in an institutional vacuum.[19] The question, from this perspective, is not "What justifies original appropriation?" but rather "What gets justified in virtue of helping to secure the preservation of humankind?"

[18] See James Tully, "Aboriginal Property and Western Theory: Recovering a Middle Ground," in this volume.

[19] Common law, in its wisdom, implicitly acknowledges morally weighty reasons for not requiring original appropriators to supply morally weighty reasons for their appropriations. For a discussion of first possession as the root of common-law title, see Carol Rose, "Possession as the Origin of Property," *University of Chicago Law Review*, vol. 52 (1985), pp. 73–88.

Original appropriation is one answer to the latter question. Particular acts of appropriation are justified not because they carry moral weight but rather because they are permitted moves within a game that carries moral weight.

The Proviso calls for a comparative-systems approach. If you say appropriations do not leave enough and as good for others, the reply should be "compared to what?" Compared to the commons as it was? As it is? As it will be? Leaving land in the commons does not leave enough and as good for others. To leave enough and as good for others, you generally need to remove it from the commons. Removing goods from the commons stimulates increases in the stock of what can be owned and limits the losses that occur in tragic commons.[20] Original appropriation replaces a negative-sum game with a positive-sum game. Therein lies a moral justification for social structures that enshrine the right to take resources out of the commons and establish exclusive control over them. We need to take resources out of the commons if we want them to still be there for our children—or anyone else's.

III. What Kind of Property Institution Is Implied?

Because the historical discussion of the original-appropriation problem tends to focus on its implications for the justification of private property, it would be easy to interpret me as having just offered an argument exclusively in support of private property.[21] That is not how the argument works. I do indeed take the institution of private property to be justified as a generally effective way of regulating access to scarce resources. The institution of private property preserves resources under a wide variety of circumstances. It is surely the preeminent vehicle for turning negative-sum commons into positive-sum property regimes. However, it is not the only way. Evidently, it is not even always the best way. From here on, I take a comparative-institutions approach.[22]

---

[20] A tragic commons is an unregulated commons in which a pattern of collective use of an otherwise renewable resource exceeds sustainable yields, yet the individual members of the group have no incentive to individually scale back their own use. The coral reefs of the Philippine and Tongan Islands are paradigmatically tragic commons. See Garrett Hardin, "A Tragedy of the Commons," *Science*, vol. 162 (1968), pp. 1243–48.

[21] An earlier version of the argument was so interpreted by one of the smartest people I know. See Gregory Kavka's review of *Limits of Government* in *Ethics*, vol. 102 (1992), p. 400.

[22] James Grunebaum, seemingly against such an approach, writes: "Any moral justification of a form of ownership grounded upon an original act of appropriation in a state of nature must show not only that the particular form is thus grounded, but also that no other form can be so grounded." Why would Grunebaum think this? He explains a few sentences later:

> If the standard of justification is the production of greater benefit or utility for each [person] than the state of nature commons, then private ownership, private usufruct, and collective cooperative ownership may be morally justified. The problem is that this state of nature justification shows all three to be justified, which means that this state of

If private property is so great and the open-access commons is so horrible, we might ask, then why is it so easy to find examples of property that is more or less open to the public? Public property is not always a product of rapacious governments or mad ideologues. Sometimes it evolves spontaneously as a way of solving real problems. The rest of this essay is devoted to two questions. First, when is original appropriation of resources from the commons required by (my rendition of) the Lockean Proviso? Second, when might public property institutions be justified as an effective way of removing resources from the commons, thereby preserving them against commons tragedies? Fortunately, the literature already contains many examples of the kinds of empirical research one would need to do in order to answer these questions. The remainder of this essay is thus mainly a summary of and application of (together with a bit of commentary upon) evidence gathered by Harold Demsetz, Robert Ellickson, and Carol Rose. Their research illustrates how various property institutions can help to ensure that enough and as good is left for future generations.

An unregulated commons will tend to be perfectly adequate so long as the pattern of utilization remains within the land's carrying capacity, to use Garrett Hardin's term.[23] When the land nears its carrying capacity, though, there will be pressure to shift to a more exclusive regime. As an example of an unregulated commons that evolved into something else when traffic increased to the point of exceeding carrying capacity, consider Harold Demsetz's tale of how property institutions evolved among indigenous tribes of the Labrador peninsula.[24] As Demsetz tells the story, the region's people had for generations treated the land as an open-access commons. The population was small. There was plenty to eat. In that situation, the Proviso was satisfied. Original appropriation would have been permissible, other things equal, but it was by no means required.

With the advent of the fur trade, though, the scale of hunting and trapping activity increased sharply. Suddenly there was scarcity. The population of game animals began to dwindle. The unregulated commons had

---

nature argument cannot be used to decide which of the three is morally preferable. A complete justification would have to show that private ownership and only private ownership fulfills the standard of justification.

See Grunebaum, "Ownership as Theft," *Monist*, vol. 73 (1990), p. 545. To look for what Grunebaum calls a complete justification, then, is to presume that the number of (completely) justifiable forms of property is exactly one. Accordingly, what Grunebaum calls complete justification is not what I am looking for, because I do not presume there is exactly one form of property that can be justified.

[23] A resource's carrying capacity is the size of the population that the resource can sustain indefinitely. See Garrett Hardin, "The Ethical Implications of Carrying Capacity," in *Managing the Commons*, ed. G. Hardin and J. Baden (San Francisco: W. H. Freeman, 1977).

[24] Harold Demsetz, "Toward a Theory of Property Rights," *American Economic Review*, vol. 57 (Papers & Proceedings, 1967), pp. 347–59.

been fine for a while, but now the tribes were heading for the classic trag-edy.[25] So family clans marked out family plots. The game animals in question were small animals like beavers and otters that do not migrate much. Marking out plots of land thus effectively privatized small game as well as the land itself. The tribes converted the commons in nonmigra-tory fur-bearing game to family parcels when the fur trade became lucra-tive enough to spur a rising demand that threatened the land's carrying capacity. When demand began to exceed carrying capacity, that was when the Proviso came not only to permit but to require original appro-priation.

One other interesting nuance of the privatization of fur-bearing game: although the fur was privatized, the meat was not privatized in the same way. As before, there was still plenty of meat to go around, so tribal law allowed trespass on someone else's land in order to hunt for meat. Tres-passers could kill a beaver and take the meat, but they had to leave the pelt displayed in a prominent place to signal that they had been there and had respected the clan's right to the pelt. The new conventions went to the heart of the matter, privatizing what had to be privatized, leaving intact liberties that people had always enjoyed with respect to other resources.

Robert Ellickson, in the process of extending Demsetz's line of research, has come to believe that a broad campaign to abolish either private or common property in land would be ludicrous. Since Ellickson's path-breaking article has only very recently been published, it is not yet widely known, especially outside the field of law. Thus, I think it will be worth-while for me to go into some detail.[26]

Every ownership regime has its own special externality problems (p. 1326). Communal management leads to shirking on maintenance and improvements and to overconsumption, because individuals receive at most a fraction of the value of their labor, and bear at most a fraction of the costs of their consumption. Minimizing these disincentives requires intensive monitoring of people's production and consumption activities. In practice, communal regimes also lead to indiscriminate dumping of wastes, ranging from piles of unwashed dishes on up.[27] A regime of pri-vately managed parcels, in turn, can also lead to indiscriminate dumping

---

[25] See note 20 above.

[26] Robert C. Ellickson, "Property in Land," Yale Law Journal, vol. 102 (1993), pp. 1315–1400. Material from this article is used by permission of the author, the Yale Law Journal, and Fred B. Rothman & Company. While I take little credit for the ideas in the remainder of this section, any errors are presumably mine. Page references to Ellickson's essay will be given parenthetically in the text.

[27] "Group ownership does not necessarily imply government ownership, of course. The sorry environmental records of federal land agencies and Communist regimes are a sharp reminder that governments are often particularly inept managers of large tracts" (Ellickson, "Property in Land," p. 1335).

of wastes and to various other uses that ignore spillover effects on neighbors. One advantage of private property is that owners can buy each other out and reshuffle their holdings in such a way as to minimize the extent to which their activities bother each other. But it does not always work out so nicely, and the reshuffling can be expensive. There are transaction costs. Thus, one plausible goal would be to have a regime that minimizes the sum of transaction costs and the cost of externalities.

Is it best to convert a common holding to smaller parcels or to manage it as a commune with power to exclude nonmembers? It depends on what kind of activities people tend to engage in. Ellickson (p. 1325) separates activities into three categories, according to how widely the effects of those activities are felt: small (like cultivating a tomato plant), medium (like building a small dam to create a pond in a stream), and large (like starting a fire that scatters fumes over a large area). The distinction is not meant to be sharp. It concerns the size of the area over which *external effects*, or spillover effects, are worth worrying about. Ellickson says private regimes are clearly superior as methods for minimizing the costs of small and medium events. With large events, though, there is no easy or sweeping answer to the question of which regime is best.

When land is parceled out, the effects of small events are almost entirely internalized (p. 1327). Ellickson credits that point to Demsetz, and adds that a lot of the internalization process has to do with changing monitoring costs. Private owners need only monitor border-crossings, whereas communal owners need to monitor people's movements in much more elaborate ways. As Ellickson puts it, "detecting the presence of a trespasser is much less demanding than evaluating the conduct of a person who is privileged to be where he is" (p. 1327). Guard dogs and motion detectors can detect trespassers; the detection of shirking is not so easy. Compared to private regimes, monitoring costs associated with small events in communes are prohibitive. It is not that private parcels do not require monitoring—they do. But the cost of monitoring small events is far lower, and the kind of monitoring that has to be done is less intrusive.[28] In short, "when land uses have no spillover effects, individual ownership directly and precisely punishes land misuse and rewards productive labor" (p. 1327).

The effects of medium events are not fully internalized. Nevertheless,

---

[28] One might think Ellickson's claim presumes an ability to compare the cost of a communal regime's single monitor to the cost of private owners' each monitoring their own parcels. But I think we can control for this variable. First, we can compare the cost of a communal regime's central monitoring of general behavior to the cost of central monitoring of border crossings in a private regime. If it were more efficient for private owners to monitor their own fences, then my way of controlling the variables will be biased in favor of the communal regime, but even the biased comparison would, I think, support Ellickson's claim that monitoring would be less expensive and less intrusive in a private regime.

privatization has the advantage of limiting the number of people having to be *consulted* about how to deal with the externality, which reduces transaction costs. Instead of each of twenty-five communal owners being involved as liberty-holders with respect to the affected area, you involve a much smaller number consisting of those owning parcels in the immediate area of the medium event. Thus, when it comes to medium events, a virtue of privatization is that it tends to reduce the extent to which people need to resort to bargaining or coordinated effort with large numbers of people.[29]

Ellickson mentions two further benefits of privatization. First, privatization increases the extent to which interactions are of a repeating character. It tends to put people in long-term, face-to-face, binary relations with neighbors. It thereby increases the extent to which people's dealings are with familiar and friendly faces, which is valuable in its own right and also insofar as it puts the resolution of externality problems from medium events in the hands of persons who are most likely to have ongoing relationships, and thus most likely to be motivated to cooperate (p. 1331). Second, privatization puts decisions in the hands of people most familiar with local circumstances. Privatization tends to leave disputes arising from medium events in the hands of people in the immediate vicinity, who tend to have a better understanding of local conditions and thus are in a better position to devise resolutions without harmful unintended consequences. They are in a better position to appraise the costs and benefits of a medium event like building a dam.

Large events create prospects of holdout and free-rider problems, which are difficulties for any kind of property regime. There is no general answer to the question of which regime is better at dealing with them (p. 1335). Private regimes can respond in a variety of ways, through contract law, tort law, regulatory statutes (nuisance laws, zoning restrictions, etc.) and a matrix of conventions about neighborliness. All of these responses will be imperfect. An alternative is to return the land to the commons, and that too is imperfect.

I think it is worth adding here that large events might fall into one of two categories. Starting a fire that makes a lot of obnoxious smoke might affect people in ways that constitute violations of known legal rights or of settled community norms. Or it might affect people in ways not prohibited by laws or settled norms pertaining to border crossings. Most of the problems regarding large events arise when ensuing disputes over entitlements are not settled by existing customs or laws. That is not a problem with the parceling of land per se, but rather with the fact that things like air and waterways remain in an unregulated commons. The obvious solution, *theoretically*, is to privatize the air and waterways. But there is no foreseeable prospect of being able to privatize the air, at least

---

[29] See also Demsetz, "Toward a Theory of Property Rights," pp. 356–57.

not in the same way that we privatize land. We need to look for something less obvious.

While it is difficult to parcel out air, partly because air would migrate from one parcel to another, it is easier to parcel out the sea, and easier still to parcel out land. Privatization of one form or another often is feasible, but it is important to understand that privatization is a cluster concept. It does, after all, take different forms, and different forms have different incentive properties. Sometimes, simply parceling out land or sea is not enough to stabilize possession of the resources that make the land or sea valuable in the first place. Suppose, for example, that a valued resource, such as fish or game, is known to migrate from one parcel to another. In that case, owners would have an incentive to grab as much of the migrating resource as they can whenever it passes through their own territory. Thus, it is not obvious that simply fencing off parcels of fishing grounds would give fishermen reason not to exceed sustainable yields. It depends in part on the extent to which the sought-after fish would migrate from one parcel to another, and on the conventions that might evolve to help neighbors deal with the inadequacy of their fences.

Another form of privatization that can fail to solve commons problems involves the temporal parceling of, say, time-share condominiums. When people own a Hawaiian condominium for only one month out of the year, they lack the incentive to invest their vacation time in the condominium's ongoing upkeep. Norms of "leaving the place in better shape than it was in when you arrived" might evolve, but temporal parceling hardly ensures the evolution of such norms. The lesson is that not all forms of privatization are equally good at facilitating efficient resource management. Privatization per se is not a panacea, and not all forms of privatization are equal.

In any case, there are obvious difficulties with how private property regimes handle large events. And the extent and nature of the difficulties will depend on the details of the private property regime. Now, as Ellickson stresses, what we need is a comparative-systems approach. So, for purposes of comparison, he looked at how communal regimes handle large events.

The Jamestown Colony was the first permanent English settlement in North America. It began in 1607 as a commune. Half the colony died of disease and starvation that first summer. New shiploads replenished the population, but the winter of 1609 cut the population from five hundred to sixty. By 1611, the colony instituted private vegetable gardens, and systematically converted its land holdings to private parcels in 1619. Why did they go communal in the first place? Are there advantages to communal regimes? Ellickson discusses several, of which I will mention two.

First, communal regimes might be adopted as a form of risk-spreading under conditions where the risks are substantial and where more effective risk-spreading mechanisms, like insurance, are not available. But risk-spreading creates moral hazards in the course of creating a particular form of security.[30] Thus, as communities build up reserves of capital to the point where they can offer private or public insurance, they tend to privatize. Second, a communal regime might be an effective response to economies of scale in the large-scale public works that are crucial in getting a community started. To build a fort, man its walls, dig wells, and so on, a communal economy is an obvious choice as a way of mobilizing the teams of workers needed to execute these urgent tasks. As these tasks are completed and the welfare of the community increasingly comes to depend on small events, the communal regime gives way to private parcels. At Jamestown, Plymouth, and Salt Lake, formerly communal settlers "understandably would switch to private land tenure, the system that most cheaply induces individuals to undertake small and medium events that are socially useful" (pp. 1342–43).

Few communes have stood the test of time. Perhaps the most enduring and successful communes in Western civilization are the agricultural settlements of the Hutterites, dating in Europe back to the sixteenth century. There are now around twenty-eight thousand people living in such communities. Hutterites are deeply committed Anabaptist Protestants and believe in a fairly strict sharing both of land and of products of labor. They forbid the possession of radio or television sets, to give one example of how they strictly control contact with the outside world.[31]

Hutterite communities have three special things going for them. (1) *A population cap*: When a settlement reaches a population of one hundred twenty, a portion of the community must leave to start a new community (p. 1347). The cap helps them retain a close-knit society. (2) *Communal dining and worship*: People congregate several times a day, which facilitates a rapid exchange of information about individual behavior and a ready avenue for supplying feedback to those whose behavior deviates from the norm (p. 1350). (3) *A ban on birth control*: When combined with the dearth of alternative forms of recreation, the ban on birth control leads to the average woman having nine children (p. 1360). This more than offsets the very low rate of emigration.

Ellickson also discusses kibbutzim and other relatively less impressive examples of communal property regimes. But the most pervasive and enduring example of communal ownership in America, Ellickson says, is the family household. American suburbia consists of family communes

---

[30] Insurance schemes create what is called a moral hazard when they shift the cost of risk-taking from risk-takers to other members of the risk-sharing pool, thereby reducing people's incentive to avoid or minimize risks.

[31] There were several Hutterite colonies near Calgary, Alberta, where I grew up. We almost never saw them except on Saturdays, selling chickens and eggs at the farmer's market, where they were conspicuous because of their custom of dressing in loose-fitting black clothing.

nested within a network of open-access roadways (p. 1395). Family homes tacitly recognize limits to how far people can go in converting common holdings to individual parcels. There are some relationships where the costs would swamp the benefits. As an illustration of Ellickson's point, consider your living room. You could fully privatize it, having one household member own it and the others pay user fees. The user fees could then be used to pay family members or outside help to keep it clean. The arrangement would have certain advantages. The average living room, for example, is notably subject to overgrazing and shirking on maintenance. Yet people put up with it. No one charges user fees to household members. As irritating as it might be to let the living room be degraded by communal use, doing so remains better than treating it as one person's exclusive domain.

IV. THE LIMITS OF PRIVATE PROPERTY

Many commons (such as our living rooms) are managed by custom rather than by government, so saying there is a role for common property and saying there is a role for government are two different things. Carol Rose tells of how, in the nineteenth century, there was a kind of property that was thought to be inherently held by society at large. The idea of "inherently public property" was not taken to imply any particular role for formal government over and above whatever enforcement role is implied by private property. Society's right was natural insofar as it was held to precede and supersede any claim to the property that might be made by government. Rose says that "[i]mplicit in these older doctrines is the notion that, even if a property should be open to the public, it does not follow that public rights should necessarily vest in an active governmental manager."[32] Thus, sometimes the rights were understood to be held by the "unorganized public" (Rose, p. 736) rather than by the governmentally organized public.

Custom is a form of management different from exclusive ownership by either individuals or governments. Custom is in part a self-managing system for according property rights (Rose, p. 742). In contrast, we might describe the nation-state as a means of centralizing the management of common concerns. Given that description, Rose's point is that common concerns are often well handled (indeed best handled) by the decentralized, piecemeal, and self-managing mechanisms that arise at the local level.[33] For example, consider how custom informally governs the kind

---

[32] Carol Rose, "The Comedy of the Commons: Custom, Commerce, and Inherently Public Property," *University of Chicago Law Review*, vol. 53 (1986), p. 720. Subsequent references to this essay will be given parenthetically in the text.

[33] I thank Jeremy Waldron for this point.

of rights-claims you establish by taking a place in line at a supermarket checkout counter.

The open-field agricultural practices of medieval times gave peasants exclusive cropping rights to a number of scattered thin strips of arable land in each of the village fields. The strips were private during the growing season, but after the harvest the open fields became a commons for grazing livestock. Thus, ownership of parcels was usufructuary in the sense that once the harvest was in, ownership reverted to the common herdsmen without any negotiation or process of formal transfer. The farmer had an exclusive claim to the land only so long as he was using it for the purpose of bringing in a harvest.

The scattering of strips was a means of diversification, reducing the risk of being ruined by small or medium events: small fires, pest infestations, etc. The post-harvest commons in grazing land exploited economies of scale in fencing and tending a herd. The scattering of thin strips also made it harder for a communal herdsman to maneuver the herd into dropping a disproportionate amount of manure on his own cropland (Ellickson, p. 1390). Customary use of medieval commons was hedged with restrictions limiting depletion of resources. Custom prohibited activities inconsistent with the land's ability to recover (Rose, p. 743). The commons tragedy did not occur, because custom allowed the villagers to own livestock only in proportion to the relative size of their land holdings.

Rose also has interesting things to say on the topic of travel routes. Human welfare depends on commerce, on truck and barter. Truck and barter is a public good of a kind. It opens up new markets and creates new streams of income as it goes, expanding the set of opportunities for everyone. The surprising thing is that this is a basis for a limited argument in favor of public property. Rose points out that common waterways and roadways minimized the cost of the travel needed to engage in commerce, and the encouragement of trade served the general good. Trade is an activity that exhibits certain economies of scale. The more holdouts who can be tempted to enter the market, the more opportunities for mutual gain there are for everyone in the market. The more the merrier, in contrast to tragic commons.

The "service to commerce" rationale does not on its face unequivocally weigh in favor of publicly held travel lanes, however. There are two kinds of response to the need for easy-access travel routes. (1) First, consider that the different elements of the bundle of rights that constitutes a piece of property are often separable. In particular, the right to exclude other people from partaking of one's crops can be separated from the right to exclude other people from crossing one's land en route. Accordingly, a system could parcel out the land in some respects, so that people could have private crops and so on, while at the same time leaving the land in an open-access commons specifically for travel purposes. People could cross the land as they pleased, although they might be guilty of trespass if they were to stop for a picnic. However, notice how this compromises the minimization of monitoring costs. With travel privileges, it is once again behavior rather than mere presence that has to be monitored. Devices like guard dogs and motion detectors would lose their utility (Ellickson, p. 1382). (2) Rather than compromise privatization by allowing people to retain travel privileges over otherwise private property, it really is plausible to hold lanes of travel in common.[34] To secure the benefits of both private land tenure and ready transportation, then, a group is wise to embed its private parcels within a network of public rights-of-way upon which all members are privileged to travel (Ellickson, p. 1382).

Facilitation of commerce, Rose says, historically has been a central rationale for leaving transportation routes in the commons. She adds that it may also have been thought important that inherently public property could enhance the sociability of the members of an otherwise atomized society. Commerce has positive external effects, both as an engine of wealth creation and as an educating and socializing institution (Rose, p. 775). Albert Hirschman[35] talks about how self-interest was once conceived of as a motivation that stood in contrast to more destructive motivations, especially revenge, vainglory, religious fervor, and the like. People from Thomas Hobbes to Adam Smith thought that if people could be induced to truck and barter, that would divert them from the pastime of killing each other in wars of religion or nationalism.[36]

So if commerce is a civilizing influence as well as the engine of wealth creation in human affairs, then "grazing" the marketplace has positive externalities in the same way that grazing a common pasture has negative externalities. We have what Rose calls a comedy of the commons rather than a tragedy. Thus, there is a rationale for public thoroughfares. If they improve access to the market, thereby facilitating the market activities that make people in general better off, public thoroughfares might, on balance, be worth the cost.

If I understand the argument correctly, the idea that commerce gener-

[34] Land held in common qua lane of travel need not be treated as public property for other purposes. In practice, easements are granted for travel along well-defined corridors, such that owners lose the right to close those corridors to travelers, but owners do not necessarily have to put up with people who want to race up and down the corridor as a form of recreation.

[35] See Albert Hirschman, *The Passions and the Interests* (Princeton: Princeton University Press, 1977), pp. 49–66.

[36] See also Stephen Holmes, "The Secret History of Self-Interest," *Beyond Self-Interest*, ed. Jane Mansbridge (Chicago: University of Chicago Press, 1990), pp. 267–86. It was only after Smith, Holmes says, that the concept of self-interest was expanded to the point where theorists began saying that self-interest is the sole human motivation. The reason for this was political. As commerce caught on, the aristocracy still held political power, and resisted the tide of democracy on the grounds that peasants were unfit to express a voice in government. Peasants were not sufficiently high-minded; they were driven by grubby self-interest. But people like Jeremy Bentham came back with the retort, and the new theory to back it up, that every human action was driven by self-interest, so if aristocrats thought they were different from and better than peasants, they were just kidding themselves.

ates positive externalities is crucial. If the benefits of one's trucking and bartering were fully internalized, then efficiency would require that one's decisions accurately reflect all of the activity's costs, including transportation costs. If that were the case, competitively priced travel services would be exactly what would be called for, but Rose concludes that it is not the case. Open-access transportation routes, she believes, provide for a certain equality of opportunity and enhance freedom of travel and assembly (Rose, pp. 767–69), and such things make people in general better off, not just economically, but socially and culturally as well. Ellickson and Rose agree that public rights of way are problematic, but conclude that the least of evils probably consists of putting up with a bit of commons tragedy. The mixed system is probably better than the totally private but compromised system.

V. Open Access versus Maximum Access

The commerce that private property encourages is a central part of the mechanism by which parceling resources leaves enough and as good for others. Indeed, it tends to leave more for others than had originally been there. We would reach the limits of that sort of argument for privatization if we were to reach a point when further privatization would choke off commerce rather than foster it. We want access to commerce to be as convenient as possible.

Yet there is something here that recalls debates regarding patents and copyrights. We want maximum access to technological innovation, too, so why do we protect intellectual property with patent and copyright law? Why not have open access to technological innovations as soon as they appear? The answer is that open-access is not necessarily the same as maximum access. Free access to state-of-the-art technology maximizes access in the short term. Nevertheless, a patent system that (for a time) gives exclusive access to technological innovation might maximize access to innovation in the long run by creating incentives to seek to capture the right to temporarily offer new products at monopoly prices. There is a difficult empirical question here about what arrangements best induce technological innovation.[37] A similar empirical question arises regarding how best to induce the activities that create the travel opportunities that facilitate commerce. There is no necessary connection between open access and maximum access. If maximum access to commerce is the end, then open access has to be evaluated as a means, not to be confused with the end itself.

[37] Demsetz, "Toward a Theory of Property Rights," p. 359, offers a succinct version of the case for property rights in patents and copyrights. For an argument against patent laws, see Tom Palmer, "Intellectual Property: A Non-Posnerian Law and Economics Approach," *Hamline Law Review*, vol. 12 (1989), pp. 261–304.

Perhaps, as Rose and Ellickson seem to think, highways should be free and open to the public. How about air travel lanes? It would seem that the upshot of the argument is that we should want air travel to be maximally accessible as well. Does that mean airlines should be required to give away their seats free of charge? Presumably not. If we were talking about seating on airlines, open access would mean zero access. Rose is not saying that seats on airplanes should be open access, of course. Perhaps air travel *corridors* (as defined by navigational easements) should be open access, free to whatever airlines have the equipment to use them. Similarly, perhaps taxicab licensing, which regulates supply so as to maintain high prices, should be prohibited. The liberty to drive a taxi should, perhaps, be something akin to open-access common property. Such a regime would present itself to drivers as a tragic unregulated commons, because it would force prices down to competitive levels. To customers, though, such a regime would present itself as a fully competitive market, one that maximizes service to commerce.

There is an interesting ambiguity here. Open access for travelers is not the same thing as open access for providers of travel services. Opening access to *providers* of taxi service maximizes service to *travelers*, whereas forcing providers to open access directly to travelers, by mandating free access to the taxis themselves, would obliterate rather than optimize that particular mode of travel. Similarly, government-provided public roads may or may not maximize service to commerce. If selling off all the public roads would produce a competitive market rather than a monopoly, then doing so might make travel more enjoyable than it is now. In any event, the question is empirical in nature. There surely have been times in history when open access was equivalent to maximum access. But that need not always be the case.

VI. CONCLUSIONS

This essay argued that the original appropriation of and subsequent regulation of access to scarce resources is justifiable as a mechanism for preserving opportunities for future generations. In short, when resources are not scarce, the Lockean Proviso permits appropriation; when resources are scarce, the Proviso requires appropriation. It is possible to appropriate without prejudice to future generations. Indeed, when resources are scarce, it is leaving them in the commons that would be prejudicial to future generations.

There are various means of exclusive control, though, and my argument does not presume that there is one form of exclusive control that uniquely serves this purpose. Is private control better than communal control? That can depend in part on what kind of activities are most prevalent in a community at any given time. It also can depend on the extent to which communal control implies control by a distant bureaucracy rather than by local custom. When the preponderance of activity in a community comes to consist of small and medium events, a preponderantly private regime is unequivocally best at creating opportunities for current and future generations to acquire a measure of wealth. Regarding the regulation of large events, there is no unequivocal answer to the question of what sort of regime is best.

Even leaving aside large events, though, it does not follow that a *totally* private regime would be appropriate. This is because people need to truck and barter, and as Ellickson and Rose persuasively argue, service to commerce weighs in favor of travel lanes being set aside as open-access commons. I accepted the spirit of their argument, subject to the following caveat, which I think they would accept. The end is maximum access, not open access. Open access is merely a means, a sometimes effective means, to that end. Thus, for example, the highest quality and quantity of access to commerce might be secured not by open-access freeways but rather by tollways (where the latter might or might not be privately owned). User fees can have a dampening effect on commerce, but by the same token, capital improvements financed by user fees can encourage commerce, and the net effect is sometimes positive.

Mechanisms for regulating access to scarce resources are manifestly justified as a means of preserving resources for future generations. The best kind of property regime is probably one that is mainly but not entirely private and that is free to evolve, becoming more or less private in particular sectors of economic activity as people adapt to changing social and technological circumstances.

Philosophy, Yale University

ORIGINAL-ACQUISITION JUSTIFICATIONS OF PRIVATE PROPERTY*

By A. John Simmons

I. Original Acquisition

My aim in this essay is to explore the nature and force of "original-acquisition" justifications of private property. By "original-acquisition" justifications, I mean those arguments which purport to establish or importantly contribute to the moral defense of private property by: (a) offering a moral/historical account of how legitimate private property rights for persons first arose (i.e., at a time prior to which no such rights existed); (b) offering a hypothetical or conjectural account of how justified private property could arise (or have arisen) from a propertyless condition; or (c) simply defending an account of how an individual can (or did) make private property in some previously unowned thing (where "things" might include not only land, natural resources, and artifacts, but also, e.g., ideas or other individuals). The "original acquisition" to which such justifications centrally refer, then, may be either the first instance(s) of legitimate private property in human history (typically assumed to have been many centuries ago on earth), or only the first legitimate acquisition of some *particular* thing (which might, for instance, have occurred yesterday or occur in the future on Mars). But in either case, the justification will involve or entail the defense of one or more moral principles specifying how unowned (or collectively owned) things can become privately owned[1] — that is, the defense of the kind of principles Robert Nozick has called "principles of justice in acquisition."[2]

Most of the first (i.e., seventeenth-century) generation of sophisticated property theories, of course, were "original-acquisition" (henceforth

* For their helpful comments on an earlier draft of this essay, I am grateful to the other contributors to this volume, to its editors, and to Nancy Schauber.

[1] In other words, arguments of type (a) or (b) will *entail* some argument(s) of type (c).

[2] Robert Nozick, *Anarchy, State, and Utopia* (New York: Basic Books, 1974), pp. 150–53. Jeremy Waldron has recently argued for restricting the notion of principles of justice in acquisition (what he calls "PJAs") to those which specify "that the transition to the private ownership of a resource can be effected by the *unilateral action* of the individual who is to be the owner" (Waldron, *The Right to Private Property* [Oxford: Oxford University Press, 1988], p. 263; my emphasis). I use the notion more broadly here. I see no reason to deny that a principle concerns the process of "just acquisition" simply because it specifies that taking possession requires the permission or cooperation (e.g., in making contracts or establishing conventions) of other persons. I discuss below (in Section IV) Waldron's main argument against "*unilateral* PJAs."

"OA") justifications of private property. Hugo Grotius, Samuel Pufendorf, Richard Cumberland, and John Locke, for example, all tried to defend at least some forms or aspects of private property precisely by presenting historical accounts (or, on some interpretations, conjectural or hypothetical accounts) of the process which created justified private property from a state in which the earth and its resources were all unowned (or only collectively owned). In large part these accounts were just very creative interpretations of the biblical Genesis story; but they relied in part as well on anthropological and economic data and speculation (about, e.g., primitive economies, the origins of money, etc.). Most important, these accounts were taken by their authors to have *moral* weight, to constitute *justifications* of private property by virtue of portraying the historical process in question as morally untarnished, or even obligatory. They were certainly not intended as morally neutral (or condemnatory) histories of a process, such as we might now offer in discussing the origins of practices like sun worship or human slavery.[3]

These and later OA justifications of private property attempted to secure this "moral weight" for their histories by direct or implicit appeal to a wide range of principles, all of which were supposed to evaluate positively the actions and events involved in the historical genesis of private property. Thus, Pufendorf and Grotius appealed to a principle of fidelity, to emphasize the sanctity of the compact or agreement which allowed division of the earth; Thomas Hobbes appealed to the authority (also "contractual" in origin) of the sovereign who makes the laws creating private property; David Hume appealed to the utility of naturally arising conventions; and Locke appealed to the principle that mixing what is yours with what is not yours may add to the quantity of what is yours. Of these seriously historical OA accounts, my discussion will reveal that I take Locke's to be the one most worth discussing. This is true not only because of the more obvious problems with the competing accounts[4] and because of the obvious connections between Locke's and some contemporary OA justifications, but also because of the apparent "natural-

---

[3] Original-acquisition *condemnations* of private property, or at least of certain kinds of private property systems, are, of course, also familiar. Take, as obvious examples, the arguments offered by many of the Levellers and by Jean-Jacques Rousseau in his *Second Discourse*.

[4] Historical compact theories seem both to involve simple fiction (i.e., concerning the occurrence of a genuine and binding historical agreement) and to appeal to an event which could have no binding force for later persons (i.e., the descendants of the historical contractors). Hobbesian positivism seems too "thin" to count as *justifying* much of anything, deriving authority (and the "consent" of subjects) from mere asymmetry of physical power. Humean conventionalism faces obvious problems in the nonmaximizing character of its associated conception of moral virtue, and particularly in its "conventional rule utilitarian" account of the artificial virtues. Indeed, given the possibility that Hume may be trying to justify many stages in the *evolution* of property conventions (and, consequently, shifts in property systems and relations), it may be misleading to describe his account as an attempted OA justification at all. The Lockean account, by contrast, can at least be restated in a theoretically plausible fashion, or so I argue in my book *The Lockean Theory of Rights* (Princeton: Princeton University Press, 1992), ch. 5.

ness" and "timelessness" of the principles to which Locke appeals (and hence their apparent lack of reliance on widely varying conventions and laws concerning property).

Interest in questions about the justificatory force of such OA arguments for private property has been rekindled in the past two decades by Nozick's gestures toward a similar OA approach. Nozick tells no story about the genesis of private property (his is an OA justification falling in my class [c]). Indeed, he notoriously refuses to state or defend any theory of just acquisition at all, leaving us to simply assume that he must have in mind some principle which is at least broadly Lockean.[5] But despite the vagueness of his account, Nozick clearly intends to take full advantage of the same set of compelling intuitions as did his OA predecessors: that private property in some form or under some conditions must be morally acceptable, that such ownership must have a point of origin,[6] but that such ownership cannot arise from nothing, requiring instead a morally interesting human act (or set of acts) as cause.[7]

The current state of play, however, seems to be this. There is a solid consensus among philosophers and legal and political theorists that attempted OA justifications of private property, when presented in any even remotely plausible form, in fact have little or no interesting justificatory force. However compelling their intuitive underpinnings might be, they can justify nothing which helps much in our deliberations about the possible moral defense of private property in contemporary society. Indeed, the standard view now seems to be that OA justifications face insuperable difficulties in even presenting their basic components in a theoretically coherent or morally nonrepugnant fashion.

I will argue in this essay that the familiar recent critique of OA justifications of private property is in fact quite unreasonably overstated. I will contend that OA justifications can (properly presented and defended) be

[5] Nozick, *Anarchy, State, and Utopia*, p. 153. Nozick contents himself with arguing that whatever principle of justice in acquisition is defended, it must incorporate a proper version of the Lockean Proviso (*ibid.*, pp. 175–82) — that is, a proviso specifying that appropriators must leave "enough and as good" to be appropriated by others.

[6] Judith Jarvis Thomson claims that "the following thesis is accepted by most philosophers nowadays: The Ownership-Has-Origins Thesis: X owns a thing if and only if something happened that made X own it" (Thomson, *The Realm of Rights* [Cambridge: Harvard University Press, 1990], p. 323). Thomson argues that the thesis is in fact true (*ibid.*, p. 336).

[7] In Locke, of course, the act is the unilateral extension of prior property in one's person and one's labor into things in the external world. In Grotius and Pufendorf, the act is the multilateral historical compact or agreement. Concern that no human acts could *create* property from nothing has led some contemporary philosophers to reject the "Ownership-Has-Origins Thesis" (see note 6 above), and to claim that property must in some sense have existed all along. See, e.g., Hillel Steiner, "The Natural Right to the Means of Production," *Philosophical Quarterly*, vol. 27, no. 106 (January 1977), esp. pp. 48–49; and Eric Mack's reply to Steiner in "Distributive Justice and the Tensions of Lockeanism," *Social Philosophy & Policy*, vol. 1, no. 1 (Autumn 1983), pp. 140–43. Classically, of course, Robert Filmer's *Patriarcha* supplied the best example of the view that the world was owned from the beginning of the human race (by virtue of God's gift to Adam).

forceful for and of interest in contemporary property theory—that is, that
we (and not just the libertarians among us) must take OA justifications
very seriously in considering viable styles of possible justifications for private property. Showing this will require me to be more careful than is
usual in talking about the idea of justification. We must be clear about just
what an OA argument can justify and in what way or what respect it justifies (the subject of Section II below). I must also try to defuse a set of
powerful and well-known objections to OA justifications (in Sections III
and IV). My object will not be to actually defend (or fully state) some particular OA argument, but only to dampen contemporary skepticism about
the possible justificatory force of such arguments, considered as a class.

II. Justification

Talk of "justifying private property" is, of course, deplorably vague and
ambiguous, however happily such language may be used (without further explanation) in much of the philosophical literature on property. The
"justifications" we actually offer in everyday life for our actions or practices cover a very wide range, from those as weak as merely asserting
some favorable property of a thing (e.g., "it gives people pleasure") to
those as strong as all-things-considered demonstrations of moral flawless-
ness or optimality. I will suggest here that the project of "justifying private property" should be understood as that of meeting or rebutting
certain kinds of fundamental moral objections to that institution: either
"comparative" objections that alternative arrangements are morally preferable, or "noncomparative" objections that the institution of private
property involves or sanctions wrongdoing or vice. The full ambiguity of
the expression "justifying private property," however, springs from at
least two distinct sources. One part of the problem concerns the impre-
cision of the expression with regard to the "level" of justification that is
at issue. A second part concerns the fact that justifications can be either
(what I will call) "*optimality* justifications" or "*permissibility* justifications."
    Let me begin with optimality justifications and try to distinguish the
various "levels" at which they might proceed. Philosophical attempts to
"justify private property" are most often attempts to defend the comparative judgment that private property systems, considered as a *general type*
of institutional (or possibly preinstitutional) arrangement, are morally
superior to alternative types of property systems (as well as to possible
arrangements in which there is no form of property at all).[8] Private property (in this general sense) might thus be portrayed as morally optimal
because it is more conducive than any alternative type of system to the
advancement of the most important moral goals, or because it uniquely

---

[8] See Waldron, *The Right to Private Property*, p. 60. I here use the notion of a "private
property system" in, I think, roughly the way detailed by Waldron (*ibid.*, pp. 31–33, 37–46).

(or most fully) satisfies the most important moral rules (where these goals or rules might concern, e.g., human preservation, human happiness, moral character or its development, individual desert, or self-government or nondependence). Less commonly, but still perfectly intelligibly, "justifying private property" is taken to mean presenting the much more specific demonstration that some *particular kind* of private property system is the best possible property arrangement, where the kind in question is distinguished not only from all kinds of non–private property (or nonproperty) arrangements, but also from alternative kinds of private property systems. These alternative kinds might include, say, systems specifying that different packages of rights constitute private property or that a different range of things are possible objects of private property rights.[9]

But this most basic ambiguity in "level" (between "general-type" justifications and "particular-kind" justifications) is far from being the only problem we face in trying to understand what is meant by claims to "justify private property." For there are both further "levels" at which justifications, still properly so-called, can be aimed, and different kinds of conclusions that count as "justifying." On the first point, we should remember that it is perfectly common in efforts to "justify private property" to be arguing neither for a general type of property system nor for a specific kind of private property system, but rather for a certain actually instantiated system (or range of systems) — namely, our own private property system or the range of such systems currently instantiated in modern (primarily Western) "market economies." Many theorists both understand our proper task in the justificatory enterprise, and interpret classical OA justifications, in terms of justifying our own (or their own) existing private property system(s). The relevant justifications do not concern some general or particular *ideal*; rather, they are conservative "local-kind" justifications, concerned to show that our own private property system is morally optimal (or optimal for us).

Alternatively, it is also easy to find self-described justifications of private property whose actual goal is only to defend as morally optimal a particular class of claim rights *within* existing property systems. Typically, such justifications will try to uphold the claims or holdings of a particular group or economic class within the society in question (e.g., the society's farmers, factory owners, artisans). And it still seems fair to use the label "justifications of private property" even for arguments of such limited scope (which we can call "local-class" justifications), insofar as they,

[9] Waldron contends that "a philosophical argument can determine only, as it were, the general shape of a blueprint for the good society. Even if we find that there are good moral grounds for preferring private property to collective property, we still face the question of what conception of private property to adopt" (*ibid.*, p. 61). But I assume Waldron would happily allow that the more specific demonstration, if successfully completed (contrary to his expectations), would count as a different, and even more powerful, justification of private property.

like the others we have mentioned, are also moral defenses of private property rights, even if they do not involve justifying entire (ideal or local) property systems.

Optimality justifications of private property, then, need not be understood as being all of one sort. But further, "justifications" of private property need not take the form of showing private property to be *the optimal* arrangement at all with respect to some moral goal(s) or principle(s). When I try in my everyday life to morally justify my actions, I do not always do so by arguing that what I did was the very best thing I could have done in the circumstances, by making the comparative claim that it was morally superior to all possible alternatives. Often it is sufficient (i.e., sufficient to constitute a *justification*) to show that what I did was morally *permissible*, or that it was otherwise morally legitimate.[10] All too frequently this is the best that I could even hope to show. My action constituted no wrong to others and exemplified no vice, even if there were other equally justifiable (or even preferable) actions I could have performed instead. There were, in short, no telling moral objections of a noncomparative sort to my conduct.

Similarly, I believe, we should think it sufficient to "justify private property" (in one familiar sense of "justification") if we show that private property (at whatever the relevant "level") is morally permissible or legitimate, even if it is not morally optimal or clearly superior to all alternatives. To show this is to offer a "permissibility justification," an argument that private property does not violate basic moral rules and is not subject to other kinds of basic (noncomparative) moral objections. And permissibility justifications can be aimed at all of the same "levels" as optimality justifications can — at the levels of general types of systems, particular kinds of systems, existing or local systems (or ranges of systems), or classes within existing systems. The familiar attempts to show that private property is the *best possible* (i.e., optimal) property arrangement should be viewed as (attempted) "justifications" of a *stronger* sort, not as justifications of the *only* sort. To justify an ideal private property system or to justify an actual distribution of private property rights, it is enough to show that they fall within the range of the morally acceptable. To suppose otherwise is to accept (mistakenly, in my opinion) the view that at least significant parts of morality must be *maximizing*, that for all possible institutional arrangements there must be top-to-bottom moral rankings within which only the top scores pass. Such a denial of moral *thresholds* requires (to say the least) extensive argument.

One final complication should be mentioned. Moral justifications (and, consequently, moral justifications of private property) need not be even as strong as my characterization of "permissibility justifications" has sug-

---

[10] Most moral theories that admit the distinction, of course, hold that moral optimality entails moral permissibility. I assume such a view in these remarks.

gested. In evaluating actions, we may take them to be morally justified (i.e., optimal or permissible) even if we acknowledge that they were wrong or impermissible *in some respects*. Morally justified actions — actions which are acceptable, right, or best "all things considered" — may harm or even violate the rights of some person(s), provided the actions have some compensating moral properties that make them on balance best or acceptable (i.e., provided their "right-making" characteristics outweigh their "wrong-making" characteristics). So-called "moral dilemmas" can typically be "solved" only by performing actions which are justified in only this minimal sense. I suggest that we remember this sense of "justification" in thinking about the justification of private property. Private property (at whatever level) might be justified "on balance," even if, say, a private property system involved harm to, disadvantage for, or even violation of the rights of some persons living under that system. Showing that some are harmed or disadvantaged by private property, say, does not suffice to show that the institution of private property is impermissible or even suboptimal (i.e., inferior to possible alternatives). On my reading of Locke's arguments, for instance, his belief that governments are justified in "settling" property within their territories[11] is precisely a belief that they may justifiably decide genuinely controversial claims (i.e., those to which there are legitimate moral objections), in whatever fashion is seen by them to be best on balance.[12]

III. ORIGINAL-ACQUISITION JUSTIFICATIONS

Having noted the diversity of possible aims involved in "justifying private property," we can return now to OA justifications. What kinds of justifications *are* OA justifications? What exactly have OA justifications been trying to be justifications of? And, more important, what *could* such arguments justify? Why, if at all, should we today have any interest in OA justifications?

We can begin by thinking about the goals of the classical OA justifications of private property. It is obvious, first, that most of these arguments displayed a strong conservative, local bias — that is, that the "level" of private property justifications their authors attempted was at least in part that of defending the private property systems enforced in their own societies.[13] And it is probably fair to say not only that in that respect the clas-

---

[11] John Locke, *Two Treatises of Government*, ed. Peter Laslett (New York: Mentor, 1960), *Second Treatise*, sections 38, 45. Subsequent references to the *Two Treatises of Government* will be by I or II, followed by section number.

[12] See my *Lockean Theory of Rights*, pp. 307–18.

[13] Thomas Horne argues at some length that Grotius, John Selden, Hobbes, Cumberland, Pufendorf, James Tyrrell, and Locke all "accepted the legitimacy of private property in general and, more specifically, the distribution of property that existed in their society" (Horne, *Property Rights and Poverty* [Chapel Hill: University of North Carolina Press, 1990], pp. 10, 17, 31, 48). I state below my disagreement with this position in the case of Locke.

sical justifications clearly failed, but that all such attempts have clearly been doomed to failure. None of the classical "justifications" was sufficiently fine-grained, imaginative, or forceful to justify all aspects of any imaginable property system, let alone all aspects of the private property systems in legal force at the time their authors conceived them. More generally, however, it seems true that if "justifying private property" is taken to involve justifying in its entirety some actual property system that has been enforced in a prominent modern political society, then no justification of private property is possible. All actual modern property systems have been in many ways manifestly and systematically unjust—both in the acquisitions and transfers they have permitted and in the limits and redistributions they have and have not imposed. But to admit this is only to admit that one sort of justification of private property (a "local-kind" justification) is not and has not in the past been possible; it is not, in my view, to admit that private property cannot be justified, that a defensible system of private property is not achievable.

In the OA justifications of Locke and Pufendorf, we can see the forms, at least, of different and less purely conservative "justifications of private property," of the sorts discussed above. Locke's defense of private property, for instance, while undoubtedly conservative in many respects, was by no means a simple attempt to justify the entire private property system in place in English society in the 1670s and 1680s. It was rather an attempt to portray as clearly unjustified certain of the rights acknowledged within that system—especially those of the very wealthy, idle aristocracy—while presenting as clearly justified certain others—those of the landed gentry (who had rights to the products of the land worked by those they hired) and the commercial classes, as well as the more obvious cases of persons whose rights were in goods with which they had more directly mixed their labor (independent farmers and craftsmen, settlers of overseas wastelands, and so on).[14] Locke's was only a "local-*class*" justification. I will suggest later (in Section IV) that we can plausibly develop such arguments to produce a kind of *presumptive* justification of particular kinds of property claims within property systems that cannot themselves be justified in their entirety. Such selective, presumptive justifications, as we will see, advance admittedly defeasible claims about moral legitimacy (in the sense I will develop in Section IV), but seem to call in the absence of counterargument not for the abandonment of property systems, but for revisions in unjustified practices around the solid center of presumptively justified claims.

Further, however, we can see in the arguments of both Locke and Pufendorf their common conviction that one can sufficiently "justify private property" by showing it to be merely a morally *permissible* (or morally possible) arrangement, even without any demonstration of its moral optimality. In Pufendorf this conviction is transparent. For according to

[14] See my *Lockean Theory of Rights*, pp. 288–306, 317–18.

his OA story, God's gift of "the earth, its products, and its creatures" to humankind came with no specific instructions about the kind of property system that ought to be instituted. On the contrary, "the law of nature approves all conventions which have been introduced about things by men, provided they involve no contradiction or do not overturn society."[15] Private property systems (of various sorts) are justified in the abstract, on Pufendorf's view, by virtue of their being members of that class of permissible systems on which persons might settle. And existing private property systems in actual societies are justified by virtue of their both belonging to that class and being systems on which people have in fact settled. Justifications of both *types* of systems and *existing* systems are "permissibility justifications"; they proceed without any demonstration of moral optimality.

Similarly, despite Locke's apparent argument that private property is in fact also morally optimal (meaning, in this case, that we are morally required to create it),[16] the main burden of Locke's case is *also*, like Pufendorf's, showing that a private property system is morally possible or permissible. This demonstration has, in fact, at least four distinct points, only the last three of which are of much continuing philosophical interest. First, of course, Locke intends to show how private property is morally possible in the face of apparent scriptural assertions of "original community." If God gave the earth to mankind in common, how could it be morally permissible for persons to take portions of the earth (or its resources) as private property? Locke's (not very convincing) answer is that God gave the world to us for our productive *use*, and productive use requires private property.[17]

---

[15] Samuel Pufendorf, *De Jure Naturae et Gentium Libri Octo* (*The Law of Nature and Nations in Eight Books*) [1672], vol. 2, trans. C. H. and W. A. Oldfather (Oxford: Clarendon Press, and London: Humphrey Milford, 1934), bk. 4, ch. 4, section 4:

> Yet it was far from God to prescribe a universal manner of possessing things, which all men were bound to observe. And so things were created neither proper nor common (in positive community) by any express command of God, but these distinctions were later created by men as the peace of human society demanded.

[16] I summarize Locke's argument below and in note 17.

[17] This argument, of course, seems to show not only that private property is morally permissible, but also that it is obligatory to create it. For if (a) we are obligated to preserve ourselves (II, 6), (b) we need the earth's resources to survive, and (c) we can only productively use those resources by privately appropriating them, then it follows that we are obligated to appropriate. Premise (c), of course, is the weak premise in the argument, since productive use of *common* property seems quite possible. Locke's argument runs specifically as follows:

> '[T]is very clear, that God . . . has given the Earth . . . to Mankind in common. But this being supposed, it seems to some a very great difficulty, how any one should ever come to have a *Property* in any thing. . . . God . . . hath also given them reason to make use of [the world and its resources] to the best advantage of Life . . . yet being given for the use of Men, there must of necessity be a means *to appropriate* them some way or other before they can be of any use, or at all beneficial to any particular Man. (II, 25, 26; some italics deleted)

Second, Locke wants to show how it is morally possible for private property in external things to arise (without direct donation from God to individuals) from a condition in which there is no such property at all. The opponent here (again) is Robert Filmer, who argues that the proper way to understand the source of all subsequent private property is in terms of transfers from Adam's original dominion over all the world. If there is *no* original private property in parts of the world, as Locke contends, then (given the absence of any evidence of later donations by God) private property seems miraculously to spring from nothing. Locke's response is that the moral possibility of private property in external things is explained via our prior property in our persons and our labor (II, 27, 39, 44).

Third, Locke tries to show that, quite independent of worries about scripture, taking private property does not necessarily constitute a harm or wrong to other persons. If creating private property in originally unowned things inevitably and wrongfully deprived others of needed goods or fair opportunities, then one could attack private property as morally impermissible and attack existing private property systems as fundamentally and uniformly unjust (as did many of the Levellers writing shortly before Locke). Locke defends the moral permissibility of private property by arguing that in conditions of abundance, one's private appropriations harm no other persons (II, 33, 36), and that even in conditions of greater scarcity, acts of private appropriation need not either treat others unfairly or make anyone worse off than they would have been in the absence of those acts (II, 40–43).

Finally, Locke is attempting to show the moral possibility of meaningful, lasting private property rights by showing how they could arise in nonpolitical, nonlegal, noncontractual contexts. Once he discards the compact theorists' convenient but preposterous fiction of a historical agreement about the division of property, and then discards the Hobbesian, positivist derivation of private property rights from far-too-alterable civil law, Locke seems to face again the impossible task of pulling the private property rabbit from the hat of "the mere corporal act of one person."[18] Locke's strategy is to show that *some* private corporal acts (i.e., those involving purposive labor on unowned nature) are at least as morally significant as contracts between persons or civil laws backed by threat of sanctions.

Throughout these arguments, the *primary* force of Locke's OA justification of private property is to display private property rights as morally possible or permissible, and to articulate the conditions under which this permissibility is sustained. This is true despite Locke's further (unwarranted) conviction that creating private property is also morally *required*. The "permissibility arguments" constitute an attempted *justification* of pri-

[18] Pufendorf, *De Jure Naturae et Gentium*, bk. 4, ch. 4, section 5.

vate property in the sense specified earlier: if successful, they show that private property claims can be legitimate (i.e., morally acceptable), probably were once mostly legitimate, and may still be legitimate in certain (possibly quite widespread) contexts. Showing this, even without demonstrating the moral optimality of private property, would constitute a very significant justificatory achievement. Indeed, simply showing that (and how) private property claims *can* be legitimate under certain physically possible conditions — even when those conditions are now virtually unsatisfiable in most of the world — would still constitute a sort of permissibility justification of private property. The idea of "justification" at work in this most minimal sense of the term is simply the denial of "absolute" (i.e., necessary) wrongness. We might similarly try to give a minimal permissibility justification of, say, slavery, by arguing for its moral permissibility under possible conditions (e.g., dire and otherwise unavoidable societal poverty) that are admitted to be quite unusual or even nonexistent in modern societies. But, as we will see, OA justifications of private property in fact promise to advance well beyond such minimal justifications.

IV. Remoteness Objections

This understanding of the senses in which OA justifications are trying to justify private property can help us to see more clearly why some familiar complaints about OA justifications are considerably less forceful than is often supposed. For instance, probably the most common criticisms of OA justifications emphasize the *distance* between the rights they attempt to justify and any rights we might today be interested in trying to justify. What OA justifications justify is too *remote* from our present concerns to be theoretically or practically important. These complaints take at least three forms.[19] First, it is claimed that the conditions under which OA justifications could actually justify anything are conditions impossibly remote from those in which we live today. OA arguments (at best) justify private property by appeal to the significance of, e.g., labor on, or occupancy of, or compact with respect to unowned goods in an unregulated time of abundance. But nobody deals with unowned goods anymore, since there are none left to deal with. And far from living in an unregulated time of abundance, we live under firmly established laws and conventions governing property and in circumstances of quite real scarcity of many natural resources. OA justifications may justify *something*, the argument goes, but they simply don't "apply" to concerns

[19] One possible form of the complaint that I will not discuss here is that most OA justifications have concerned themselves exclusively or primarily with *tangible* property, where today our concerns about property centrally include such things as intellectual property, equity in companies, etc. I will simply assume here (without argument) that a suitably revised OA justification could deal satisfactorily with nontangible property as well.

about property today, being based on a set of "unrealistic" assumptions.[20]

Second, and even worse (some argue), the conditions and actors imagined in OA histories are probably not even remotely accurate representations of those existing even at the times they concern, nor could we possibly know if they were. As Jeremy Waldron puts it:

> One does not have to be an ethical relativist to see the difficulties here. What were conditions like when resources were first taken into ownership? How well developed was moral consciousness? Were those to whom the principle [of just acquisition] was supposed to apply capable of implementing it properly? Could it conceivably have been a principle which they held and abided by explicitly? Or in any way? If we turn from ancient to modern capabilities, how can *we* make sense *now* of principles whose only direct application was hundreds or perhaps thousands of years ago? If we cannot, does that not deprive such a principle of any right to be regarded as the generating basis of a system of entitlements that is to continue to constrain us today?[21]

Finally, even supposing that we are convinced by some OA justification that legitimate private property actually arose (or could have arisen) in the foggy past, in exactly the way specified in the OA history, it is not clear how this would bear on the property claims made by persons today. Even if original acquisitions of things were legitimate, and even if that property was transferred and exchanged as the theory imagines, our knowledge of the history of the process of acquisition and transfer is so spotty that we could not possibly reach any conclusions about who is entitled to what today. Any property rights that may legitimately have arisen at the time when things were first acquired have been so muddied by force, fraud, and our simple ignorance of the relevant histories that we

---

[20] Virginia Held claims that

> Locke's assumptions concerning the justifiable acquisition of property are, however, seldom plausible in the contemporary world. The unowned wilderness waiting to be appropriated, so central to Locke's argument, no longer exists. Rarely do we simply mix our labor with nature. . . . An even more serious difficulty . . . is that the Lockean proviso, in the contemporary world of overpopulation and scarce resources, can almost never be met. ("Introduction," *Property, Profits, and Economic Justice*, ed. Virginia Held [Belmont: Wadsworth, 1980], pp. 5–6)

See also James O. Grunebaum, *Private Ownership* (London: Routledge & Kegan Paul, 1987), pp. 53, 66–67, 85, and Grunebaum, "Ownership as Theft," *Monist*, vol. 73, no. 4 (October 1990), p. 544; Lawrence Becker, *Property Rights* (London: Routledge & Kegan Paul, 1977), p. 48; and Thomas Mautner, "Locke on Original Appropriation," *American Philosophical Quarterly*, vol. 19, no. 3 (July 1982), pp. 267–68. For a response specifically to concerns about the Lockean Proviso (on which I do not comment here), see David Schmidtz, *The Limits of Government* (Boulder: Westview Press, 1991), pp. 17–27.

[21] Waldron, *The Right to Private Property*, p. 259.

may as well just forget about trying to reconstruct the history of property and accept some nonhistorical conception of property rights.[22]

I hope it is clear by now that much can be said on behalf of OA justifications of private property and against such criticisms. In response to the charge that the conditions of life are now very remote from those appealed to in OA justifications, we can note first that even if true, these charges do not affect at least the most minimal sort of permissibility justification of private property which might be accomplished by an OA argument. OA justifications, by specifying the range of principles and conditions for just original acquisition, can at the very least claim to have shown that legitimate private property is morally possible (i.e., permissible under physically possible conditions), even if it is seldom possible today. But further, the principles appealed to (explicitly or implicitly) in OA histories are not historically relative in any but the most contingent sense. They are not only principles that apply in conditions which are (merely) physically possible, but principles that *can* apply to our circumstances again, today or in the future, should the conditions of human life (or those for some specific group of humans) change in certain (easily imagined) ways.

Indeed, if the OA justification is alleged not to "apply" to contemporary life because of conditions of scarcity and the lack of unowned land and resources, it is possible to reply simply that there *are* vast quantities of unowned (or common) land and resources available to humankind today, both within the territories of existing political societies and external to them (in Antarctica, for instance, or on the moons and other planets of our solar system). The use of resources in these places, and even the colonization of our moon or of Mars, are not such fanciful possibilities that it is not meaningful or interesting to ask what could justly be claimed as private property in such enterprises. If the principles appealed to in some OA justification are valid, they are principles that may well apply again in the future in contexts such as these. While takings of these still-unowned things are, of course, regulated by domestic laws and international agreements, it is well worth considering both whether these laws and treaties are in fact morally *binding* on all of us, and what kinds of claims on things would be morally defensible in the absence of binding laws and treaties of this sort.[23]

---

[22] Mautner argues on these grounds that "a theory of original appropriation is irrelevant to questions concerning contemporary property rights" ("Locke on Original Appropriation," p. 268). See also Loren E. Lomasky, *Persons, Rights, and the Moral Community* (Oxford: Oxford University Press, 1987), pp. 115–16; Will Kymlicka, *Liberalism, Community, and Culture* (Oxford: Oxford University Press, 1989), pp. 158–59; and Schmidtz's reply in *The Limits of Government*, pp. 27–31. For a much earlier version of this style of argument, see Herbert Spencer, *Social Statics* (1851), ch. 9, section 3 (New York: Augustus M. Kelley, 1969), pp. 115–16.

[23] See my *Lockean Theory of Rights*, pp. 235–36. My *Moral Principles and Political Obligations* (Princeton: Princeton University Press, 1979) challenges the moral authority of existing governments or states to enforce such laws and to make treaties or agreements of this sort on our behalf.

Second, to the charge that OA justifications imagine wildly unrealistic (or at least unknowable) conditions for the acquisition of private property, we must first acknowledge that the classical OA accounts (such as those of Grotius, Pufendorf, and Locke) were so concerned with interpreting (or reinterpreting) scripture that their histories will naturally look bizarre to contemporary secular-humanist eyes. We cannot today think of primitive eras as populated with full-blown, self-conscious, socialized, morally aware persons; so we cannot think of these OA histories as accurate accounts of primitive life. But insofar as OA justifications of private property do not concern the first *brute takings by human beings*, but rather the first *creations of property by persons* (where persons are understood to be rational, morally developed, self-conscious, purposive agents), we can reasonably grant OA justifications this much: OA histories, suitably revised, might constitute roughly accurate accounts of the emergence of private property (i.e., moral rights in external things) at whatever period in our actual history persons (or groups of persons) began purposive appropriations. But even if we think that OA arguments have not given us even remotely accurate histories of the origins of property (leaving aside the history of mere brute takings by nonpersons), the *principles* of just acquisition defended in OA justifications of private property may still be defensible and applicable both to well-documented historical contexts (such as those instances of seventeenth- and eighteenth-century wilderness homesteads and settlements that did no harm to native inhabitants) and to contemporary or future contexts (such as the taking of goods in space).

Finally, to the charge that original acquisitions have no traceable relation to current holdings, and so are irrelevant to contemporary evaluations of property arrangements or distributions, consider the following response on behalf of OA justifications. Even if OA justifications cannot provide moral defenses of entire existing property systems and cannot provide proper pedigrees for any current property claims, they can provide *presumptive justifications* of certain classes of private property claims, even within systems that sanction some clear injustices. Take, for example, the central thesis (in my view) of Locke's OA justification: that your purposeful labor (using only what is yours) on what is either unowned or already owned by you, can yield property for you in the product of your labor (including as part of the product that which was labored upon, if it was unowned). This thesis, if defensible, can have real force even within existing property systems that are admitted to be unjust and that leave nothing unowned to be claimed by individual laborers. It can have force, for instance, if we allow that some current legal or conventional property rights — such as modest holdings which neither unfairly deprive nor permit unreasonable control over others — may still be morally defensible, and should be presumed to be so in the absence of evidence to the contrary, even within illegitimate property systems. This can be allowed for reasons similar to those advanced by theorists who allow that an illegitimate *government* may still be morally warranted in administering reasonable legal punishments to rapists and murderers, despite the availability of a sound critique of its overall legitimacy that condemns it for other aspects of its operations. Only an (in my view, unreasonable) insistence that all moral justification of property must be at the level of property *systems* (or, by analogy, governments or political systems) can block the possibility of presumptive justifications of particular claims within unjustified systems.

Suppose, for instance, that we believe that existing private property systems are indefensible because of, say, the inequality and human suffering they permit, or the impotence and lack of autonomy for the unfortunate that they sanction. OA justifications might still establish a presumptive justification of some current private property claims within these systems, provided there is no evidence that those claims are tainted by the problems that taint the system as a whole. If, say, I earn a modest wage as a gardener on another's property, or I sell vegetables grown on a small plot of my own, and I use the money to buy needed clothing and food for myself and my family, one might argue for a presumptive justification of my (or my family's) claim to property in the clothing and food, based squarely on Lockean principles. I am entitled to the products of my labor (using self-acquired skills) — or, in one of our cases, to the wages exchanged (by agreement) for labor on what belongs to another — provided that I do no harm to others in my acquisitions or exchanges. If there is no evidence that the land or resources I employ were wrongfully acquired, and no indication that my possession or use harms or unfairly disadvantages others, we can *presume* either a natural, historical entitlement or a justified institutional entitlement (depending on our theoretical predilections) to the modest holdings I use in my purposive labors. Justice may, of course, demand that I receive, or live under a system which guarantees me, *more* than this modest share. But insofar as my limited claims seem to objectionably disadvantage or harm no others, it is not clear why my claims should be viewed as incapable of moral justification.[24] It is easy to imagine similar moral defenses of claims to many kinds of small holdings, to handcrafts, or to noninstitutional ideas or inventions (provided, at least, that the knowledge employed was fairly acquired). No *further* justification of such claims to private property (e.g., that they are recognized claims within a justified *system* of private property) seems necessary.[25] For these claims are (*ex hypothesi*) not tainted by

[24] Indeed, even Marx and Engels allowed that "we by no means intend to abolish this personal appropriation of the products of labour, an appropriation that is made for the maintenance and reproduction of human life" (*The Communist Manifesto*, in *Karl Marx: Selected Writings*, ed. D. McLellan [Oxford: Oxford University Press, 1977], p. 232). See also Andrew Reeve's remarks on the "pure artisan" and "integrated production" models of productive activity in Reeve, *Property* (Atlantic Highlands: Humanities Press, 1986), pp. 128–29.

[25] Eric Mack argues for what he calls "the Practice theory of private property," claiming that we have a natural right to a justifiable *practice* of private property (Mack, "Self-Ownership and the Right to Property," *Monist*, vol. 73, no. 4 [October 1990], p. 535). That

what taints the system that is in place in the society; and (again, *ex hypothesi*) on the best historical evidence available these claims are consistent with defensible OA principles.

There are at least two very controversial assumptions made here, neither of which I can discuss fully in this essay. The first concerns shifting the burden of proof in the way we think about historical justifications. In the absence of both (a) a complete pedigree for some contemporary holding and (b) any historical or contemporary evidence which might count as a reason for denying entitlement to that holding, we can insist either that (1) we should presume entitlement (my view); (2) we can say nothing about entitlement (which is, I believe, the standard view); or (3) we should presume the holding is unjust, given that "force and fraud have reigned supreme in the history of mankind."[26] Given (among other things) the importance of holdings to persons' projects and life plans and the apparent innocence of the holdings in question, I think the first position takes more seriously than the others the moral considerations at issue.

A second central and very controversial assumption involves my challenge to the most familiar way of distinguishing between historical-entitlement views, which supposedly concentrate on rights to *particular* goods, and "patterned" conceptions of justice, which focus on general rights to just *shares* of social goods. As stated I think the distinction is drawn too sharply. My own view is that any adequate *historical-*entitlement view will still need to refer centrally to (historically justified) rights to "shares"—both in connection with compensation for goods which are, e.g., stolen and then destroyed (where entitlement will then be to an appropriate share of the wrongdoer's goods), and in connection with initially just holdings which must be "downsized" to accommodate increased demands for fair access to the goods in question (where, e.g., the Lockean Proviso, applied now not to takings but to holdings, entitles others to a share of what you were initially entitled to acquire and keep). If genuinely historical entitlements can be to shares of goods (e.g., to shares of goods that were previously held legitimately in their entirety by others), *presumptive* justifications of small holdings, even in the absence of complete pedigrees for those holdings, seem much easier to motivate. For small shares seem likely to be ones which can still be justified after satisfying the historical requirements of "downsizing."

None of this is quite to say, with Gerald Gaus and Loren Lomasky, that the "justificatory embarrassment" of OA stories can only be avoided if we discard their historical trappings, that we should understand them instead as trying to identify or emphasize "the *telos* of property rights,"

---

may seem to amount to an insistence on justification solely at the level of systems of property. But Mack allows as well (as I do here) that certain "vivid instances" of property rights "stand on their own. They need not draw their moral force from their place within any larger normative system" (*ibid.*, p. 529).

[26] Mautner, "Locke on Original Appropriation" (*supra* note 20), p. 267.

or as "fixing the spotlight" on the guiding intuitions of property justifications.[27] For the presumptive justifications imagined above are in a straightforward sense *historical* justifications, and such justifications have obvious historical applications.[28] But my arguments do suggest that insofar as OA principles successfully pick out a set of actions and conditions which generate property claims, they may not only apply within existing systems, but may also supply us with a conception of what the *point* of property systems ought to be (at least in part). Those arrangements that reliably produce distributions of institutional rights which *contradict* defensible OA principles (i.e., which disallow naturally permissible claims or allow naturally impermissible ones) are for that reason morally suspect, even if there may be *other* goals (e.g., distributive ones) which we think property systems should also advance or secure.

V. Partial Justification, Question-Begging, and Unfamiliar Obligations

Even if the "distance" between OA justifications and contemporary concerns is not as much of a problem as many critics of these accounts have alleged, there are two rather different lines of attack on OA justifications that are sufficiently compelling to require a reply here. The first line of attack has been most directly launched by James Grunebaum. OA justifications of private property, he argues, are defective because they are only partial and because they are question-begging. First, a defect shared by all OA justifications is the failure to show that *other*, nonprivate forms of property are not just as defensible as private property under the original conditions imagined in OA stories. OA justifications of private property invariably stress the advantages, in terms of mutual benefit, of private appropriation, making these advantages the centerpiece of their justifications. But in fact private usufruct or collective or social appropriations would yield the same kinds of advantages as private appropriation.

---

[27] Gerald Gaus and Loren Lomasky, "Are Property Rights Problematic?" *Monist*, vol. 73, no. 4 (October 1990), pp. 496–98.

[28] OA justifications of the sort described here are historical in something like Nozick's sense: current justifiability of a particular claim depends (in the Lockean version of the argument) on past labor and on the (presumed) absence of past wrongs or presence of rectifying adjustments or developments in the history of the particular claim in question. There is no appeal to structural or patterned considerations—e.g., to an independent principle of desert or equality. And while the force of OA justifications does *not* turn on the plausibility of any story about the primitive historical origins of property (as Gaus and Lomasky rightly insist in *ibid.*, p. 498), OA justifications do, of course, *apply* to historical circumstances in the same ways they apply to contemporary or future ones (as argued above). In this regard, Gaus and Lomasky are right to compare the use of OA histories in property theory with the use of state-of-nature stories in political philosophy (*ibid.*). The state of nature (in Locke, for instance) can be thought of as a particular relation among persons which may be exemplified at any time, including past, historical times. As such, the state of nature is not the first period, or any particular period, in human history, though it is a relation that has had many historical instantiations. On the state of nature, both as it is used by Locke and as a concept of general interest in political philosophy, see my *On the Edge of Anarchy: Locke, Consent, and the Limits of Society* (Princeton: Princeton University Press, 1993), ch. 1.

The best justification of private property an OA argument could yield, then, would be only "partial."[29] Second, Grunebaum argues, OA justifications are uniformly question-begging. Such justifications specify the conditions for taking unowned goods; but "unowned" can mean many things, depending on which conception of ownership is being assumed. OA theorists mean by "unowned," "not *privately* owned." And this simply begs the question against alternative possible forms of ownership. For what is privately unowned may be owned in some other sense, and thus not available for private appropriation.[30]

To the charge that OA justifications can be at best only "partial," several replies seem possible here, the most important of which has already been suggested above. For one thing, it is not at all clear that different kinds of appropriations *do* all yield the same advantages under the principles by which OA justifications of private property typically proceed. On Locke's argument, for instance, not just mutual advantage in material terms but the facilitation of *self-government* (i.e., nondependence in the widest sense) is a central concern. But it is easy to think of ways in which self-government might be more fully promoted by private appropriations than by social or collective appropriation.[31] "Mutual benefit," understood to *include* the good of self-government, might then be quite differentially served by different forms of appropriation and hence might select private property as uniquely justified or morally optimal.

More important, however, is this. Even if private property is *not* uniquely justifiable within the terms of an OA argument, it is unclear why this should be taken to show that an OA justification of private property is objectionably "partial." As we have seen, demonstrations of moral possibility or permissibility (what I called "permissibility justifications") are perfectly respectable forms of moral justification, even if they are not the strongest possible form. So even if Grunebaum's point about other, nonprivate forms of appropriation is accepted, it seems that we should conclude *not* that private property is not justified by OA arguments, but rather that several forms of property can be so justified.[32] After all, we do not conclude from the fact that many possible acts are all morally permissible or acceptable for me that *no* act I perform can be fully justified. And in any event, the classical OA justifications did *not* typically involve maintaining that usufruct was not justifiable or that *groups* of persons

[29] In Grunebaum, "Ownership as Theft" (*supra* note 20), pp. 545–46, "partial" justifications are contrasted with "complete" ones. In Grunebaum, *Private Ownership*, pp. 57–59, 62–63, 66, the contrast is with "conclusive" justifications. See also Waldron, *The Right to Private Property*, p. 252.

[30] Grunebaum, *Private Ownership*, pp. 53, 74, 80–81, 84–85. Grunebaum's primary target is Nozick, but he generalizes the attack on p. 85.

[31] See my *Lockean Theory of Rights*, pp. 264–65, 275.

[32] The possibility of parallel, equally justified, but quite different property systems (even within the same territory) is discussed by James Tully in the context of his interesting examination of Aboriginal and colonial property in North America. See Tully, "Aboriginal Property and Western Theory: Recovering a Middle Ground," in this volume.

could not collectively appropriate land or resources. Indeed, Pufendorf explicitly discussed original collective appropriation, regarding it as *also* justified (i.e., in addition to justified private appropriation).[33] Perhaps the real worry is that if several forms of appropriation are all equally justified, we cannot tell from any appropriative act(s) which form of property right has been acquired. But if this is the concern, it seems easy to dispel; for acquisition of property rights will always turn centrally on the nature of the intentions and purposes of the appropriating persons. These intentions and purposes could easily prove to be sufficient to determine the form of right acquired, just as they are central in determining the extent and duration of the right acquired.

To Grunebaum's second charge—that OA justifications are question-begging—our reply can be even briefer. When Locke, for example, talks about appropriating goods, he is, as Grunebaum suggests, thinking about "privately unowned" goods. But Locke's arguments in no sense beg the question against alternative conceptions of ownership, for he does not even talk about goods being "unowned" *simpliciter*. Locke does not use this "question-begging" language for the simple reason that he assumes that *common* ownership of the world is the relevant background condition against which private appropriation is to be understood.[34] His arguments concern (1) the conditions under which claims to private property can *override* (or, in Locke's terms, "over-balance" [II, 40] or "exclude" [II, 27]) claims to alternative kinds of property, and (2) the facts that establish the superiority of private to other forms of property. Locke's arguments may fail, but they do not fail by begging the question against private ownership's competition.

The second line of attack on OA justifications of private property that I will discuss here has recently been advanced by Waldron. Typical OA justifications fail, the argument goes, because they involve trying to justify something that none of us on reflection can really regard as justifiable—namely, the deliberate, unilateral imposition by individuals of onerous obligations on all others. OA arguments normally entail that persons can, by their acts of acquisition, deliberately create for others universal moral duties of forbearance and noninterference with respect to holdings of possibly scarce resources. Such a power (to create significant moral burdens for others at will) is "radically unfamiliar" and "repugnant" to us, and it is therefore a power of which we should be highly suspicious. Needless to say, we should be equally suspicious of any argument which purports to justify such a power for individuals.[35]

[33] Pufendorf, *De Jure Naturae et Gentium*, bk. 4, ch. 6, sections 3–4.

[34] I have argued elsewhere that Locke's conception of original community is one of *positive* community (*Lockean Theory of Rights*, pp. 236–41, 279–81).

[35] Waldron, *The Right to Private Property*, pp. 265–71. See also Becker, *Property Rights* (*supra* note 20), p. 44; and Allan Gibbard, "Natural Property Rights," in *Readings in Social and Political Philosophy*, ed. R. M. Stewart (New York: Oxford University Press, 1986), pp. 237–38. Waldron argues further that the kinds of principles defended in OA justifications fail the

Gaus and Lomasky have responded to Waldron's argument by maintaining that it is unreasonable to single out for this attack just those principles that purport to justify unilateral acquisition of original private
property rights. *All* claim rights involve correlative moral burdens for others, burdens which may also be onerous. Original property rights in a
thing are no different in this respect from other rights. The claim that
there is a moral burden on others always requires justification, the same
strength of justification for property rights (and their correlative obligations) as for any other rights. And, in any event, Gaus and Lomasky
argue, we are quite familiar with cases of persons having the moral power
to unilaterally and deliberately impose moral burdens on others. For
instance, given the familiar moral obligation to reward desert, one person can pile obligations on others simply by doing things which ground
desert claims.[36]

This response, I think, is inadequate to eliminate the sorts of concerns
that motivate Waldron's attack on OA justifications of private property.
For, in the first place, Waldron is clearly worried not so much by the mere
existence of (or the need for justification of) onerous moral burdens, but
rather by the suggestion that one person might have the right unilaterally to impose such burdens at will on others, deliberately and for the
very purpose of limiting their freedom. And it is certainly not true of all
claim rights that they subject others to that kind of liability. Most of the
claim rights we take for granted (e.g., our "general" rights to noninterference) are not only not imposed unilaterally by anyone's deliberate acts,
but are not imposed at all. They are, rather, part of the moral background
conditions through which each person's moral agency is to be understood. But second, the example Gaus and Lomasky provide of a "familiar" right that is analogous to the right of property acquisition is not a
very persuasive example. The right to be given what we deserve (and the
correlative obligation of others to render to us what we deserve) is not,
I expect, one that many of us take for granted. I doubt that I can find anyone who takes herself to be obligated to reward me for all of my merito-
rious conduct this year. Such rights and obligations only seem at all
familiar in the kinds of institutional contexts Gaus and Lomasky's example actually involves, where, say, a department head is understood by all
to have *agreed* to reward (academic!) merit in her colleagues—and thus

negative test of hypothetical consent (*The Right to Private Property*, pp. 272–78), but he allows
that incorporating a strong Lockean Proviso may permit an OA justification to escape his
attacks (*ibid.*, pp. 281–83). I will not here discuss these additional components of Waldron's
case. I should note here as well that Waldron's argument strikes primarily against Lockean-
style OA justifications. OA justifications which appeal to compacts or agreements, of course,
involve defending no rights of *unilateral* imposition of obligation. But such arguments face
other obvious problems of their own.

[36] Gaus and Lomasky, "Are Property Rights Problematic?" esp. pp. 492–93. For a different style of attack on Waldron's argument, but one which also emphasizes the significance
of desert claims, see Stephen R. Munzer, "The Acquisition of Property Rights," *Notre Dame
Law Review*, vol. 66, no. 3 (1991), pp. 669–78.

has a purely *consensual* obligation to do so, *not* an (onerous?) obligation unilaterally and deliberately imposed at will by another.[37] Finally, of course, if one pursued acts which deserved reward for the very purpose of limiting another's liberty (i.e., in order to burden her with obligations), one's efforts would very likely be self-defeating, such motives seeming, as they do, rather unmeritorious.

None of this is to say, however, that Waldron's complaint about OA justifications is unanswerable. I think, in fact, that Gaus and Lomasky are quite correct in asserting that the kinds of rights and obligations that worry Waldron are more familiar and considerably less repugnant than he suggests (even if the example they employ to illustrate their suggestion is an unpersuasive one). Such rights and obligations arise or are at issue in a wide range of contexts, particularly those involving certain special transactions, competitive situations, and the "activation" of general rights. For instance, I may make a legal will, unilaterally imposing on all others an obligation to respect its terms (which they previously lacked), for the very purpose of limiting others' freedom to dispose of my estate in ways contrary to my wishes. I may occupy a public tennis court to practice my serve, or we may take the softball field in the park for our game, unilaterally imposing on all others obligations to refrain from interference, and do so for the very purpose of enjoying our activities unhindered by such interference. Or I may rush to the patent office and register my invention, unilaterally imposing certain obligations of restraint on all others, for the very purpose of limiting others' freedom to likewise take advantage with their competing inventions. I may buy the rare stamp that many others are busy saving their money to buy, or I may organize a nature walk for children along trails many others use to seek solitude. How different are the rights and obligations involved in these contexts from the right of the original appropriator to take unowned goods, unilaterally imposing obligations of noninterference on all others, for the very purpose of restricting their liberty to impede her free use and enjoyment of the goods? Not, I think, very different. And the rights and obligations I have mentioned are both familiar and widely accepted, regarded by almost nobody as morally repugnant. Indeed, even though they all involve a background of (nonconsensual) institutional rules and expectations which sanction the entitlements and obligations at issue, it is easy to imagine *natural*, noninstitutional analogues for each case I mentioned

---

[37] Gaus and Lomasky deny that this obligation is consensual ("Are Property Rights Problematic?" p. 492), although they say only that they "doubt" that both parties have consented to the "system." But all that is necessary to render the case hopelessly disanalogous to the one which worries Waldron is that the obligated party has himself agreed to bear this particular obligation. And it seems plain that this is our normal understanding of the position of a department head, at least in any context in which we *would* take her to have an obligation to reward merit. We do not think that just *anyone* has an obligation to reward *any* kind of merit in any other person; one's exceptional performance in an academic department surely imposes no new obligations on, say, Madonna or Mother Theresa.

(that is, to describe moral rules which play the same sanctioning role in these cases).

Now it is true that in my cases the unilaterally imposed obligations are typically not very "onerous" — though they might be if, e.g., others were relying heavily on an inheritance (or a share of what "reverts to common") or on proceeds from inventions. But, of course, the parallel obligations to respect originally acquired property need not be onerous either — though they might be if, e.g., such acquisitions "make it morally difficult or morally impossible for others to secure their own survival."[38] Perhaps, then, we should understand Waldron's complaint as addressed only to *some* of the rights (purportedly) justified by *some* OA arguments, rather than as a general condemnation of all OA justifications of private property (as Waldron's own closing remarks in fact suggest).[39] If so, however, only the most extreme of the libertarian versions of OA justifications are threatened by this attack, and perhaps even they are threatened only with a call for revision or limitation, not a call for abandonment. Certainly the well-known classical OA justifications all either insisted on serious limits on rights of acquisition — so that genuinely onerous obligations could *not* be unilaterally imposed — or defended parallel, overriding rights for others to *take* from an appropriator's surplus the justly acquired goods which are needed by those others for their survival (see, e.g., Locke, I, 42).

I conclude from this that neither the final, general attacks considered in this section, nor the arguments from "remoteness" considered in the previous section, really tell against OA justifications of private property in a way that should lead us to put them away, as antiquated reminders of less philosophically sophisticated times. On the contrary, I have suggested that OA arguments, properly developed, promise substantial justificatory punch and direct contemporary relevance. I believe, further, that an OA justification of private property can in fact be advanced that is both plausible and satisfies contemporary standards of argumentative rigor; but I have done little here that should convince others to share my belief.[40] Rather, I hope primarily to have supplied some reasons to believe that OA arguments ought not to be hastily brushed aside in contemporary discussions of the possible justifications of private property.

Philosophy, University of Virginia

---

[38] Waldron, *The Right to Private Property*, p. 268. Schmidtz takes issue with this characterization of the acquisitions of our forebears in *The Limits of Government* (*supra* note 20), ch. 2.

[39] Waldron, *The Right to Private Property*, pp. 282–83. See Munzer, "Acquisition of Property Rights," pp. 667–68.

[40] I try to sketch the outlines of such an argument, following a reconstruction of broadly Lockean claims, in my *Lockean Theory of Rights*, esp. pp. 271–77, 292–94.

THE ADVANTAGES AND DIFFICULTIES OF
THE HUMEAN THEORY OF PROPERTY

By Jeremy Waldron

I. Locke, Rousseau, and Hume

In recent years there has been growing interest in the contrast between Humean theories of property, on the one hand, and Lockean and Rousseauian theories, on the other.[1] The contrast is a broad and abstract one, along the following lines.

Almost all theories of private property aim to secure the benefits that can accrue to society from market exchange. But those benefits can be obtained only if individuals and firms come to market already bearing alienable property rights in various commodities. There is an important question, therefore, about how the initial distribution of those property rights is to be determined and evaluated.

Rousseauian and Lockean theories are committed—though in different ways—to the proposition that the initial distribution of property rights must itself be morally defensible.

Rousseau's position is that the distribution of property ought to be subject to the general will of the whole society: society is entitled to establish a new distribution (or ratify an existing one) on the basis of broad principles of justice that reflect each person's status as an unconditional and equal partner in a contractarian social union.[2] John Rawls's conception of justice as fairness may be considered a modern version of this approach.[3]

Locke's position is that the initial distribution of property is determined in large part by morally legitimate acts of unilateral acquisition.[4] An individual who labors to wrest a resource from its natural condition invests

---

[1] See especially Brian Barry, *Theories of Justice*, vol. 1 of *A Treatise on Social Justice* (Berkeley: University of California Press, 1989).

[2] Jean-Jacques Rousseau, *The Social Contract*, ed. Maurice Cranston (Harmondsworth: Penguin Books, 1968), Bk. 1, chs. 6–9. This is Rousseau's normative position; for his account of the actual emergence of property rights, see Section VII below.

[3] John Rawls, *A Theory of Justice* (Oxford: Clarendon Press, 1971).

[4] John Locke, *Two Treatises of Government*, ed. Peter Laslett (Cambridge: Cambridge University Press, 1988), *Second Treatise*, ch. 5, sections 27ff. I say "in large part," because Locke acknowledges the possibility that some resources will become private property *after* civil society is set up, and intimates that, in these cases, the appropriate procedure is (what I have called) Rousseauian: see *ibid.*, sections 28, 38, 45, and 50. For an attempt, on the basis of these passages, to interpret Locke's theory *as a whole* in Rousseauian terms, see James Tully, *A Discourse on Property: John Locke and His Adversaries* (Cambridge: Cambridge University Press, 1980). For a refutation of Tully's interpretation, see Jeremy Waldron, *The Right to Private Property* (Oxford: Clarendon Press, 1988), pp. 232–41.

it with something of himself which, as Locke insists, "excludes the common right of other Men." Subject to one or two provisos,[5] the idea is that morally compelling rights of property may thus be established through individual enterprise without social ratification. Robert Nozick's sketch of a theory of historical entitlement may be considered a modern version of this approach.[6]

The position of David Hume, by contrast, is that it is a mistake to seek a moral justification for the initial premarket assignment of property rights. Whereas both Locke and Rousseau think it necessary to show that there is something natural or morally appropriate about each person's initial holding, Hume insists that "[t]he relation of fitness or suitableness ought never to enter into consideration, in distributing the properties of mankind."[7]

On the Humean model, we start from an assumption of conflict driven by limited altruism and moderate scarcity. People grab things and use them; they argue and fight over them. Over time, the holdings determined in this way are going to be largely arbitrary. Nevertheless, if any sort of stable pattern of de facto possession emerges, then something like a peace dividend may be available. It may be possible for everyone to gain, both in terms of the diminution of conflict and in terms of the prospects for market exchange, by an agreement not to fight anymore over possessions. I agree to respect what you have managed to hang on to, and you agree to respect what I have managed to hang on to: "By this means, every one knows what he may safely possess."[8] Such an agreement, if it lasts, may amount over time to a ratification of de facto holdings as de jure property.

The contrast, then, is based on Hume's agnosticism about distribution. We should not concern ourselves, he argues, with the distributive features of the possessory regime that emerges from the era of conflict. Our aim should be to ratify any distribution that seems salient—that is, any distribution support for which promises to move us away from squabbling about who should own what, and toward the benefits promised by an orderly marketplace.

If Rawls's theory is the modern embodiment of the Rousseauian approach, and Nozick's of the Lockean, then the exemplar of this Hum-

---

[5] The provisos most often mentioned are, first, that a unilateral acquisition of resources must leave "enough, and as good" for others (Locke, *Second Treatise*, section 27) and, second, that appropriated resources must not be allowed to spoil (*ibid.*, section 31). For doubts about the former proviso, see Jeremy Waldron, "Enough and as Good Left for Others," *Philosophical Quarterly*, vol. 29 (1979), pp. 319–28.

[6] Robert Nozick, *Anarchy, State, and Utopia* (New York: Basic Books, 1974), chs. 7–8.

[7] David Hume, *A Treatise of Human Nature*, ed. L. A. Selby-Bigge (Oxford: Clarendon Press, 1888), Bk. III, Part II, section iv, p. 514.

[8] *Ibid.*, Bk. III, Part II, section ii, p. 489.

ean position in the modern debate about property, justice, and markets appears to be James Buchanan.[9]

II. Advantages: Completing the Rational-Choice Paradigm

The advantages of the Humean position, assuming that it can be sustained, are considerable. In the first instance, enormous advantages accrue from this approach to what one might call the economists' paradigm in social theory.[10]

There cannot be a market unless there are property rights. To the extent that economics studies markets, the discipline presupposes a set of property entitlements. It is often assumed that economists have nothing to say about this initial distribution. It is a product of power, they will say, or a matter of moral philosophy, but, in all modesty, not a subject on which we as economists have anything distinctive to offer. This is not to deny its importance. The distributive features of a market equilibrium (who ends up with what) are profoundly affected by the initial distribution (who begins with what). If there are objections to the starting point, there will be objections to the finishing point, and nothing the economists say purports to address those objections. The point is not that a problematic set of initial endowments undermines the freedom or rationality of subsequent transactions (though that may also be true). It is simply a matter of legitimacy in, legitimacy out.[11]

However, although economists qua market theorists have nothing to say about initial holdings, there is no reason for the broader theory of rational choice to be silent on the issue. Hume's model provides a description which is congruent both with the market paradigm's assumptions about human behavior and with its moral minimalism (i.e., no more robust moral relations than Pareto-superiority and its derivatives).[12] The

[9] James M. Buchanan, *The Limits of Liberty: Between Anarchy and Leviathan* (Chicago: University of Chicago Press, 1975), esp. chs. 1–4.

[10] For a discussion of the relation between the economists' "market paradigm" and the broader "rational-choice paradigm," see Jules Coleman, *Risks and Wrongs* (Cambridge: Cambridge University Press, 1992).

[11] See David Gauthier, *Morals by Agreement* (Oxford: Clarendon Press, 1986), pp. 94–95:

> The operation of the market is to convert an initial situation specified in terms of individual factor endowments into a final outcome specified in terms of a distribution of goods or products among the same individuals. Since the market outcome is both in equilibrium and optimal, its operation is shown to be rational, and since it proceeds through the free activity of individuals, we claim that its rationality leaves no place for moral assessment. Given the initial situation of the market, its outcome cannot but be fully justified. But neither the operation of the market nor its outcome can show, or even tend to show, that its initial situation is also either rational or morally acceptable. . . . Market outcomes are fair if, but of course only if, they result from fair initial conditions.

[12] Throughout this essay I shall use "Pareto-superior," "Pareto-improvement," and "Pareto-optimal" in the following way: one situation S is Pareto-superior to another situa-

success of the model would therefore have the immense advantage of showing that a *complete* account of the institution and operation of a market economy can be given in rational-choice terms. Apart from Hume's story, economists have simply had to *assume* a set of initial entitlements; or else they have ambivalently bought into some version of the Lockean or Rousseauian approaches—purchases which have compromised the reductive purity of their paradigm. The Humean model promises an account of initial entitlements which uses the same terms (the terms of rational-choice theory) that are used in characterizing the market itself.[13]

It is not just a matter of methodological purity. The rational-choice basis of the Humean convention provides an attractive conception of a claim moral philosophers have been trying to sell ever since Socrates took on Thrasymachus: the claim that justice (here, *suum cuique tribuere*)[14] is necessarily to everyone's advantage:

> Instead of departing from our own interest, or from that of our nearest friends, by abstaining from the possessions of others, we cannot better consult both those interests, than by such a convention; because it is by that means we maintain society, which is so necessary to their well-being and subsistence, as well as to our own.[15]

On Hume's account, even those who have been making a living in a Hobbesian way, preying on others, and taking and consuming things that other people have found, grown, or made, may be better off observing rules of property, along the lines indicated by the convention, than they would be in a world in which everything was up for grabs. The Thrasymachus problem, after all, was that persons inclined to predation might ask proponents of justice for reasons why they should respect the holdings of others. The Humean account can offer such reasons, and ground them genuinely in the potential predator's own self-interest.

It is true that Rawls makes a similar claim in regard to his Rousseauian conception. He says that "everyone may expect to improve his situation if all comply with these principles, at least in comparison with what his prospects would be in the absence of any agreement."[16] But, as Brian Barry has shown, he makes no more than a half-hearted effort to argue

---

tion R if and only if at least one person is better off in S than he or she is in R and nobody is worse off in S than he or she is in R; a change is a Pareto-improvement if and only if it is a change from one situation R to another that is Pareto-superior to R; a situation R is Pareto-optimal if there is no situation Pareto-superior to R.

[13] This paragraph and the previous one are adapted from my review essay "Criticizing the Economic Analysis of Law," devoted to Jules Coleman's *Markets, Morals, and the Law* (Cambridge: Cambridge University Press, 1988); the review essay was published in *Yale Law Journal*, vol. 99 (1990), pp. 1441–71; see esp. p. 1461.

[14] "To each his own."

[15] Hume, *Treatise*, Bk. III, Part II, section ii, p. 489.

[16] Rawls, *A Theory of Justice*, p. 497.

for this, i.e., to show that there are none who might do better for themselves in a situation where no one observed Rawlsian principles than in a situation where everyone did.[17] Similarly, in response to an imagined complaint from a well-endowed person who has less on account of the difference principle, Rawls writes:

> [I]t is clear that the well-being of each depends on a scheme of social cooperation without which no one could have a satisfactory life. . . . The difference principle . . . seems to be a fair basis on which those better endowed, or more fortunate in their social circumstances, could expect others to collaborate with them when some workable arrangement is a necessary condition of the good of all.[18]

But again, this is just a gesture. It is not argued for; there is no basis in Rawls's model for arguing for it; and the logic of the "original position" is against it, inasmuch as that logic requires each party to bargain without any awareness of what he could hope to achieve for himself by trusting to his own force or cunning. The contrast could not be greater with Hume's theory, in which the spirit of the throwaway lines just quoted from Rawls informs every step of the argument.

Those are the general attractions of the Humean picture. In addition, it has a number of specific advantages over the other two models, which need to be discussed in detail. Before going on to review those, however, I want to warn the reader that some of the advantages just outlined are controversial. It is controversial whether a Humean peace dividend *can* be realized and a property-constituting convention arrived at among a population that includes predators.[19] I think it can, and I shall defend this position in Section VIII. More generally, it is controversial whether the ability of Hume's theory to answer the self-interested question "Why should I be just?" is not bought at too great a price. Many philosophers believe that by building this in as a definitional condition of justice, we distort and undermine its character as a critical value in society. I shall return to this at the end of the essay.

III. ADVANTAGES: AVOIDING MORAL CONTROVERSY

The theories we have been considering make different demands on moral consensus in the societies they are supposed to govern.

---

[17] Barry, *Theories of Justice*, pp. 71–74 and 241–54. Cf. Rawls, *A Theory of Justice*, pp. 134–35.

[18] Rawls, *A Theory of Justice*, p. 103. (The difference principle requires that social and economic inequalities be arranged so as to maximize the prospects of members of the least-advantaged group in society.)

[19] See Gauthier, *Morals by Agreement*, pp. 190–200; and Coleman, *Risks and Wrongs*, pp. 49–57.

Rousseau's model assumes acceptance in society of a strong set of moral principles for evaluating and reforming distributions. But in fact there is no such consensus: people disagree about distributive principles and about the content and relative importance of factors like need, desert, equality, and so on. Absent such consensus, Rousseau's approach appears to countenance the moralistic *imposition* of principles which are taken, on the basis of abstract contractarian reasoning, to be "the right ones to apply," whether people agree with them or not.

The Humean model makes no such unrealistic or dangerous assumptions. Its moral minimalism defies dissensus while removing the need for moralistic imposition. The idea is that, whatever one thinks about justice, everyone is made better off by their own lights through the peace dividend achieved in the move from conflict over possessions to a stable situation in which possession is ratified by convention as property.

In this regard, Hume's story also has advantages over the Lockean account. Locke's model, as much as Rousseau's, indicates that property rights are to be based on controversial moral principles—in this case, moral principles of acquisition and desert. The history of property theory indicates that there is no consensus on legitimate acquisition. Is it to be based on occupation or on labor? Is it to be subject to provisos (if so, which ones and how are they to be grounded)? Does acquisition require consent, or at least the notional imprimatur of hypothetical consent?[20] Is the Lockean approach based on desert? If so, how are controversies in the community about what counts as deserving activity to be resolved?[21] And so on. As much as the Rousseauian model, the Lockean approach either unrealistically presupposes the existence of a moral consensus on these matters, or it licenses the imposition by force of what are taken to be the correct principles of historic entitlement.

Nozick is evidently sensitive to this difficulty, and it is no doubt one reason for his notorious reluctance to specify content for the principles of acquisition and transfer that a full Lockean theory would comprise.[22] I suspect Nozick had it in mind to represent such principles as far as possible in Pareto terms and to minimize any more robust moral content, anticipating the integration of the Lockean model into the broader rational-choice paradigm (along the lines of our earlier discussion). This is obvious enough with the principle of justice-in-transfer, and it explains also the particular form of his Lockean Proviso on initial acquisition (no acquisition to make anyone worse off).[23] Even so, his approach remains quite distinct from the Humean model. For one thing, it is premised on

---

[20] See Waldron, *The Right to Private Property*, chs. 6–7.

[21] See Ronald Dworkin, "Liberalism," in his *A Matter of Principle* (Cambridge: Harvard University Press, 1985), pp. 198–200.

[22] See Nozick, *Anarchy, State, and Utopia*, pp. 150, 202–3, and 230.

[23] *Ibid.*, pp. 174–82.

very robust moral principles of self-ownership.[24] For another, it uses Pareto criteria as a basis for retrospective moral criticism and (where appropriate) rectification. If we can show that a move took place in the past that was not Pareto-superior, Nozick's approach requires us to condemn it and, if possible, to rectify the violation of liberty that it involved. This is entirely alien to the pragmatic spirit of the Humean approach.

IV. ADVANTAGES: AVOIDING PROBLEMS OF APPLICATION

The point just made indicates another enormous advantage of the Humean over the Lockean account. For even if the requisite moral principles are accepted in society, the Locke/Nozick approach still faces formidable difficulties about application which, in my view, simply remove it from the realm of the practicable.

The model purports to rest the legitimation of property on the integrity of chains of entitlement stretching back to the dawn of time. For Locke and Nozick, the justification of someone's controlling some piece of land now, depends on who he got it (bought it, inherited it, received it as a gift) from, and who that person got it from, and so on all the way back to the first human who took that land out of common use and into his exclusive possession. Break the chain anywhere, and who knows what justice now requires?[25]

In other words, the Lockean model fails to furnish the certainty and determinacy on which property systems depend. We can be as sure as we are of anything that, on any plausible Lockean principles, the history of property in the United States is largely a history of injustice, particularly in its early stages. Many alleged entitlements in modern society therefore have an illegitimate pedigree. Moreover, entitlements with an impeccable pedigree may be tainted by their coexistence with a discredited one (if rectifying injustice involves, as Nozick suggests, a subjunctive estimation of what would have happened if the injustice had not occurred).[26] Consequently, even one who accepts the moral force of Locke's principles now, has no idea which holdings they legitimate and which they call into question.

The Humean approach, by contrast, acknowledges that the early eras of human history are eras of conflict largely unregulated by principle and opaque to later moral enquiry. Unlike Locke and Nozick, Hume does not require us to delve into that history to ascertain who did what to whom, and what would have happened if they hadn't. Provided a settled pattern

---

[24] Though perhaps, in the end, Pareto principles, with their overtones of voluntarism, require such a grounding also. See Coleman, *Markets, Morals, and the Law* (*supra* note 13), pp. 122–29.

[25] See Jeremy Waldron, "Superseding Historic Injustice," *Ethics*, vol. 103 (1992), pp. 4–28.

[26] *Ibid.*, pp. 11–12. Cf. Nozick, *Anarchy, State, and Utopia*, p. 152.

of possession emerges, we simply draw an arbitrary line and say, "Property entitlements start from *here*."

V. Advantages: From Initial Specification to Markets

A third set of specific difficulties which Hume's model avoids has to do with a theory's articulation of its account of *initial* distribution into its account of the *subsequent* determination of holdings by market processes.

We have seen that the legitimacy of a market economy depends on the legitimation of the initial distribution of property rights. But market processes *transform* initial distributions. There is, then, a dilemma. We want a morally legitimate starting point. But if we insist too strongly on the moral credentials of the initial distribution, we may be unable to explain the morality of the quite *different* distributions that markets subsequently generate on that basis.

Thus, for example, the Rousseauian model seems to have the disturbing implication that if an initial premarket set of holdings is to be assessed on the basis of moral criteria of distribution (say, equality), then *any* set of holdings may be assessed on that basis. There is no justification for applying the Rousseauian criteria at t_1 which would not also be a justification for applying it at any subsequent time t_n.[27] And, as Nozick has pointed out, if the distribution at t_1 was transformed into that obtaining at t_n by market processes, the very criteria which approved the former distribution are likely to require substantial interference with the latter.[28]

The results of this constant application and reapplication of moral criteria, however, would be disastrous. The fear is that, in the end, redistribution would undermine market processes, either by continually reversing their effect or, worse still, by prohibiting market-based transformations of the initially approved distribution altogether.[29]

A similar difficulty arises for the Lockean model. Locke's own arguments focus almost all their philosophical energies on the issue of original acquisition. An individual who has worked to cultivate a piece of land has "mixed his *Labour* with, and joyned to it something that is his own." The

---

[27] For this argument (against what he calls "starting-gate theories"), see Ronald Dworkin, "What is Equality? Part 2: Equality of Resources," *Philosophy and Public Affairs*, vol. 10 (1981), pp. 308–11.

[28] Nozick, *Anarchy, State, and Utopia*, pp. 160–64.

[29] See also David Hume, *An Enquiry concerning the Principles of Morals*, Section III, Part II, in Hume, *Enquiries concerning Human Understanding and concerning the Principles of Morals*, ed. L. A. Selby-Bigge, 2d ed. (Oxford: Clarendon Press, 1902), p. 194:

> Render possessions ever so equal, men's different degrees of art, care, and industry will immediately break that equality. Or if you check these virtues, you reduce society to the most extreme indigence; and instead of preventing want and beggary in a few, render it unavoidable to the whole community.

land now *contains* his labor, so that if anyone else takes it, they will *eo ipso* be taking a part of the action and personality of that very individual.[30]

It is difficult to see how that same respect can be elicited in behalf of someone who has *purchased* the property from the original laborer.[31] Even if we establish that the initial appropriator (*P*) acquires by his labor an interest based on self-ownership that has a special claim to be respected, it does not follow that, when he transfers the land to someone else (*Q*), the latter acquires an interest with a similar degree of moral importance. The land does not contain *Q*'s labor, so a trespasser or government taker would not be violating *Q*'s personality in the way he would have violated *P*'s had he encroached on the property while it was still in *P*'s hands. *Q*'s right seems to be a watered-down version of *P*'s. Since the former is not based on self-ownership, it may well be less resistant, morally, to claims based on need or the social good than the latter.

This difficulty is *not* removed by showing simply that *P* is entitled to sell the property to *Q*. That must of course be shown, and Locke's own discussion of transfer is more or less entirely devoted to it.[32] But even if this argument goes through, it still does not show that *Q* has the same moral claim as *P* had.

As far as I can see, the only way out of this difficulty is the following. We accord property rights to *P* because we think it important for him to control a resource in which his labor is embedded. To recognize *P*'s control of the resource is to accede to his wishes about what should become of it. In transferring the resource to *Q*, *P* evidently intends that *Q* should acquire rights over it that are as powerful as his own. Thus, unless we recognize such rights in *Q*, we are going against *P*'s wishes and to that extent violating his entitlement to control what becomes of his labor. By respecting *Q*'s rights, then, we are still in a way respecting the labor and the personality of *P*.

---

[30] Locke, *Second Treatise*, section 27.

[31] This and the following paragraphs are adapted from Waldron, *The Right to Private Property*, pp. 259–62.

[32] Locke faces the following issue. People sell things because they have more resources than they themselves can personally use. But perhaps if one finds oneself with more resources than one can use, one should simply abandon the surplus goods and make them available for others to appropriate. That proposition must be refuted if exchange is to be possible in a Lockean world: *P* can be entitled to sell something to *Q* only if *P* is entitled to possess and exercise jurisdiction (e.g., powers of sale) over more goods than he can personally use. Locke attempts to establish this by arguing that the main moral objection to a person's possession of more goods than he can use is that surplus goods may rot or spoil in his possession without being used at all, by anyone. The force of that objection is avoided if *P* exchanges his surplus perishables for more durable items or for money from *Q*, which he can later exchange for other things he needs. (Seeing that the surplus perishables do not rot now becomes *Q*'s responsibility.) *P* is then in a position to "heap up as much of these durable things as he pleased; the *exceeding of the bounds of his* just *Property* not lying in the largeness of his Possession, but the perishing of any thing uselessly in it" (Locke, *Second Treatise*, section 46).

However, this argument casts enormous weight on our original recognition of P's entitlement. For that now includes being willing to support P's assignment of it to Q, and Q's assignment of it to yet another party, R, and R's assignment of it to S, and so on all the way down a chain of entitlements — and all on the basis of our respect for P's labor (because it is only P who has labor embedded in the resource). The problem is that Q, R, and S never acquire an interest along the way that is *intrinsically* worthy of respect in the way P's is. We respect S's use of the land because it was P's wish that the fate of the resource should be decided by the person to whom the person to whom the person to whom P transferred it, transferred it — and we want to respect P's wishes. As the syntax indicates, the argument becomes less and less manageable the further we are down the chain of entitlements. The price, then, of this solution is a considerable artificiality and an affront to intuition. Do we really want to say that the reason for respecting my control of a piece of property I own in England is because that is indirectly what is required by respect for some Celt who first invested it with his labor millennia ago?

Maybe an intermediate party acquires a moral stake of his own in these transactions by giving up one of his entitlements in order to purchase the property. Q may have mixed *his* labor with some resource which he now exchanges for a resource with which P's labor is mixed. Maybe in the process of exchange, P's labor and Q's labor change places, so that Q's labor is now embedded in the resource that he gets from P. But this is mere talk, and it's quite unclear what it amounts to. We may say that Q's labor is now *deemed* to be embedded in the object that P transferred to him (and vice versa); but the question is *why* we should deem this. If P gives Q an object to which P, having labored on it, has a very deep attachment, and Q in return gives P an object to which Q, having labored on it, has a very deep attachment, the result will be that *neither party ends up holding an object to which he has a very deep attachment*. No amount of loose talk about embedded labor zapping across in the exchange from one resource to the other alters the fact that the intimate connections between owners and objects are no longer what they were.

Enough of these epicycles. The point is this: What seems so difficult for a Lockean theory turns out to be laughably easy on the Humean model. For in this regard, Hume's theory has a shape that is almost exactly opposite to that of Locke's. In Hume's theory, almost *no* philosophical energy is put into the issue of original appropriation. Original appropriation is arbitrary: people just somehow get hold of things. What matters is the stability of possessions and the market exchanges that that makes possible. Any starting point will do, provided we get the process of transfer underway.

Hume's approach matches the solution very closely to the reason we are interested in having entitlements transferred in the first place. Precisely *because* the determination of initial holdings is so arbitrary, the initial distribution of property rights will "frequently prove contrary both to men's wants and desires; and persons and possessions must often be very ill adjusted."[33] Some peaceful way must be found to establish a better match between owner and object:

> To . . . allow every man to seize by violence what he judges to be fit for him, wou'd destroy society; and therefore the rules of justice seek some medium betwixt a rigid stability, and this changeable and uncertain adjustment. But there is no medium better than that obvious one, that possession and property shou'd always be stable, except when the proprietor consents to bestow them on some other person. This rule can have no ill consequence, in occasioning wars and dissentions; since the proprietor's consent, who alone is concern'd, is taken along in the alienation: And it may serve to many good purposes in adjusting property to persons.[34]

Thus, suppose P is arbitrarily accredited as the original owner of a piece of land, L — arbitrarily, because he was simply the one left holding L at the time property was set up.[35] P finds he has little use for L, and transfers it to Q. The result may be *slightly* less arbitrariness in the holding of L; Q has it now because P, to whom it was arbitrarily allocated, had less desire for it than he did. If Q subsequently transfers the resource to R, there may be still less arbitrariness in R's holding it, for now it has passed through two transactions designed to respond to the question of whose desire for L is greater. Appropriateness in holdings may thus be generated and enhanced through a series of transfers, rather than diminished as we saw in the Lockean model.

VI. Difficulties: The Possibility of a Bargaining Problem

Though the Humean model has these attractions, it also has its difficulties. In the remainder of this essay, I am going to focus on various worries that have been voiced — particularly those discussed by Jules Coleman and David Gauthier who, almost alone among modern writers on justice and markets, have given this model the critical attention it deserves.[36]

---

[33] Hume, *Treatise* (*supra* note 7), Bk. III, Part II, section iv, p. 514.

[34] *Ibid.*

[35] Buchanan suggests (*Limits of Liberty*, p. 30) that there may be some tendency to non-arbitrariness, even at this stage: "In the natural state, individuals will devote more effort to securing and protecting those final goods that stand relatively high in their own preference rankings." But, he goes on, there is no reason to believe that *relative* abilities to secure and defend goods will correspond closely with relative values placed on those goods by the respective participants.

[36] Though see also Richard Epstein, *Takings: Private Property and the Power of Eminent Domain* (Cambridge: Harvard University Press, 1985), chs. 1–2, for a discussion of similar topics.

The first objection that I want to discuss is set out by Coleman in his book *Markets, Morals, and the Law.* [37] Though Hume is not invoked by name, Coleman sets out (and criticizes) a hypothesis about the generation of premarket property rights that shares a number of features with the model I have outlined: [38]

> Suppose that individuals have holdings—possessions—but have no rights to these possessions that are themselves secure and enforceable. This is a premarket state of nature. In this premarket setting, individuals spend a share of their real resources in defending their holdings from attack and some of the rest of their resources in attacking others. [39]

A scheme in which such holdings were recognized and enforced as property by a convention among the holders might have advantages over this state of nature. The costs previously incurred in defending one's holdings would diminish, and the effectiveness of cooperatively provided defense might be greater than the defenses individuals were able to organize for themselves. There may be, then, as Coleman puts it, "an inefficiency in the premarket state of nature remediable by providing a property rights scheme that recognizes certain possessions as rightful and enforces claims in regard to them." [40]

However, inefficiencies like this are not overcome by magic. People have to reach an agreement, and the difficulty Coleman has with the Humean story focuses on the question of what the precise terms of cooperation are going to be. There is a bargaining problem involved in realizing the gains that accrue from cooperative protection. Though everyone in possession of a holding may stand to gain, how much each gains will, Coleman says, be a matter of negotiation. Moreover, since the initial holdings are certainly not given as equal, and since individuals are not equally capable of defending by themselves whatever holdings they have, their threat advantages are not the same. Some parties may hold out for a better deal, and this holding-out has costs for all. Coleman argues that we cannot simply assume from the fact that cooperative protection is more efficient in itself than individual protection, that it retains this edge of efficiency once the costs of bargaining are taken into account. [41]

The general point here is well-taken. Since a Pareto-improvement involves a potential surplus, since the improvement will not be made

---

[37] A lot of material in this section is adapted from Part IV of my review essay "Criticizing the Economic Analysis of Law" (*supra* note 13), pp. 1463–67.

[38] I shall draw attention to some differences toward the end of this section; as we shall see, the position that Coleman considers is somewhat more Hobbesian than Humean.

[39] Coleman, *Markets, Morals, and the Law* (*supra* note 13), p. 264.

[40] *Ibid.*

[41] *Ibid.*, p. 274.

unless the parties can reach a bargain concerning the division of the surplus, and since bargaining is itself not cost-free, we cannot infer that every Pareto-improvement that is in principle available will in fact be secured. In a perfectly competitive market, bargaining terms are set by prices determined independently of the transacting parties. But in the Humean case, where, *ex hypothesi*, market mechanisms are unavailable, the parties must bargain for the division of gains from trade or else they will not secure them.

Coleman's interest in this objection can be seen against the background of his general interest in the application of fairness standards in the rational-choice paradigm. The Humean story, as we know, is unconcerned with the fairness of the initial distribution; and in later sections, I will follow Coleman in asking whether agreements that embody such indifference can be sustained. It may be thought, however, that the present difficulty is not part of that wider problem, for although bargaining for the division of gains from cooperation involves *a* distributive issue, it does not involve *the main issue* of the distribution of wealth. The wealth that the parties bring to the bargaining table, and therefore the area on the Pareto-frontier[42] where their bargain may be struck, is determined independently of what the parties agree about in their bargaining.[43] Still, it seems likely that what the parties think about the division of the surplus will affect or be affected by what they think about distribution generally. Since the bargain to be struck is precisely an agreement to recognize holdings of wealth, disagreements about the division of the surplus are always liable to escalate into wider disagreements about the distribution of the holdings that are to be recognized.

One effect of the bargaining problem is that even though everyone gains, the bargain will leave some gaining less than they might: "[W]hatever agreement is reached, those who feel they are exploited will seek to destabilize the agreement, and there is ample opportunity for them to do so."[44] They will try constantly to force renegotiation to redistribute the cooperative surplus. Now, it is possible to interpret this as simply part of the *long-term* bargaining process that is involved in the emergence over time of a single Humean convention. After all, the rational-choice story is understood as a *model* of what happens, not a blow-by-blow account. All the same, whatever (finite) period we assign in our model to the negotiation of a Humean convention, there is no

---

[42] By "Pareto-frontier" I mean the ordered set of Pareto-optimal situations (represented, for example, as a curve on a diagram such as Figure 1 below).

[43] In the usual diagramming of utilities in a two-party case, the initial distribution determines a point such that all gains from bargaining must be northeast of that point; and the bargaining itself determines the slope of the northeasterly line from that point to the bargaining outcome. (The flatter the line, the more the bargaining favors the party whose utility is measured on the abscissa).

[44] Coleman, *Markets, Morals, and the Law*, p. 274.

guarantee that that convention will secure for all subsequent time the stability of the holdings that it recognizes. If the operation of the convention
changes the balance of power, that is likely to generate opportunistic challenges to its terms. I shall return to this in Section X.

The issue so far has been one of transaction costs: maybe the bargaining problem will exhaust the available Pareto-gains. As if that were not
bad enough, Coleman argues that the bargaining problem will be aggra-
vated by certain features of the property rights scheme. The institution
that is to provide cooperative protection will (necessarily) be a monopoly.[45] It may therefore have power that enables it to collect an amount
of revenue greater than that minimally needed to provide the necessary
protection, generating a surplus to be shared effectively as rent among
the providers. This aspect of monopoly taxation and rent-seeking may
seriously distort the payoffs associated with the original potential for
Pareto-improvement, and it will certainly further distort the bargaining
process.[46]

I am sure Coleman is right about this, but it is worth noting how the
argument depends on features of his version of the rational-choice story
which are a little different from the versions given by Hume and
Buchanan.

In the story Coleman considers, the potential for Pareto-improvement
consists in economies of scale and specialization so far as the protection
of holdings is concerned. What changes when the system of property
rights is set up, is that people no longer have to defend their holdings
themselves. Instead, they set up a specialist agency—something like a
Hobbesian sovereign. Coleman does not suggest that this institution
involves any mutual renunciation of predation. He seems to indicate that
the threat to holdings remains constant and that only the mode of defense
is altered.[47]

By contrast, the agreement in Hume's version of the story is nothing
but a convention of mutual restraint:

> I observe, that it will be for my interest to leave another in the pos-
> session of his goods, *provided* he will act in the same manner with
> regard to me. He is sensible of a like interest in the regulation of his
> conduct. When this common sense of interest is mutually express'd,
> and is known to both, it produces a suitable resolution and behav-
> iour; since the actions of each of us have a reference to those of the

---

[45] For discussion of the emergence of a monopoly protection agency and its transformation into a Weberian state, see Nozick, *Anarchy, State, and Utopia*, pp. 54–146.

[46] Coleman, *Markets, Morals, and the Law*, pp. 268–71.

[47] This is a little unclear. Coleman's technical account of the arithmetic of the Pareto-
improvement (*ibid.*, p. 264) suggests that the savings include the costs to oneself of attacking others' holdings.

other, and are perform'd upon the supposition, that something is to be perform'd on the other part.[48]

Property rights, according to Hume, do not arise out of the cooperative institution of enforcement mechanisms. They arise out of an agreement "concerning abstinence from the possessions of others."[49] The parties recognize that they gain more by not attacking one another's holdings, and by not having to defend their own against such attack, than they do from continuing to pursue the temptations and risks of predation. Moreover, the convention generates a sense of *obligation* in this regard, despite the fact that it does not involve setting up a coercive state. Obligations of justice are rooted primarily in the "internal aspect" of the practice that grows out of a shared understanding of the agreement, rather than in the external enforcement which characterizes Coleman's version of the model.[50]

All this makes a big difference to our picture of the bargaining problem. First, if the agreement is one of mutual restraint, it is not clear that there is any serious bargaining to be done before the gains to the parties can be realized. If each refrains from attacking the holdings of the others, then each gains (more or less automatically) an amount equal to the cost to himself of attacking others' holdings, plus the cost to himself of defending against others' attacks, plus the cost of the losses he would incur if his defenses failed (times, of course, the probability of their failing). And each party loses an amount equal to the amount by which he could augment his holding by attacking others' holdings (multiplied, this time, by the probability of *their* defenses failing). The Humean assumption is that the sum of these gains and losses is positive in the case of each person. My present point, however, is that such gains and losses accrue to the parties *as a direct consequence of mutual restraint*. Their accrual does not depend on bargaining. That X and Y agree to mutual restraint is all that is necessary for X to achieve this gain: his gain results directly from his not attacking Y and from his not being attacked by him.

Second, if the initial agreement securing the Pareto-improvement is simply mutual restraint, questions of monopoly pricing and rent-seeking do not arise (at least, not immediately). Since the agreement institutes only a shared normative order, the provision of the public good of mutual security does not require any specialized class or coalition of providers.

Third, if the agreement is construed in this Humean way, rather than along Hobbesian lines, then even if there is a modicum of bargaining to

---

[48] Hume, *Treatise*, Bk. III, Part II, section ii, p. 490 (emphasis in original).

[49] *Ibid.*

[50] *Ibid.*, pp. 491 and 495–501. For an account of the internal aspect of obligations that similarly does not rely on the existence of a coercive state mechanism, see H. L. A. Hart, *The Concept of Law* (Oxford: Clarendon Press, 1961), pp. 55–56, 82–88.

be done, the prospects (which we discussed earlier) of its escalating into the broader issue of the distribution of wealth are much diminished. By contrast, Hobbes's story envisages a level of premarket conflict among individuals that requires an enormously powerful sovereign to overawe them. A sovereign instituted on that scale will have such a capacity to redefine and redistribute holdings that the institution of property rights will be seen as nothing more than "the Act of that Power."[51] If any standards are brought to bear on such acts, they will presumably be (what I have called) Rousseauian in character, as the sovereign sets up property on a basis that seems right (to him). The intensity of the conflict preceding (and necessitating) the sovereign's institution makes it likely that patterns of de facto possession will be very precarious. It will be hard, therefore, for Hobbesian individuals to hang on to a sense — a sense that I think is essential to the *Humean* story — that the size and character of their post-institution holdings are determined on the basis of what they bring to the bargaining table (when they meet to institute social arrangements) rather than on the basis of what they transact there.

In brief, Hobbes's story has an independent power dimension that the Humean story lacks, and accordingly (as Coleman rightly observes) it gives rise to problems about the nature and exercise of such power that do not afflict the Humean model.

Coleman might say that if Hume's convention differs this much from the institution of a Hobbesian sovereign, the former is bound to be hopelessly fragile. Since it lacks an enforcement mechanism, since it is only a normative practice, individuals will always have a temptation to violate the rights that it recognizes. The immediate response is that the institutional solution only *seems* more powerful in Hobbes's story because the problem of conflict that elicits it is more intractable. In addition, however, there are some specific points to be made in defense of the Humean model.

(1) Though the model as I have presented it indicates a single act of agreement, Hume's version assumes more realistically that any agreement will crystallize out over a long period of time. It is not conceived as an instant promise, but as "a general sense of common interest":

> Nor is the rule concerning the stability of possession the less deriv'd from human conventions, that it arises gradually, and acquires force by a slow progression, and by our repeated experience of the inconveniences of transgressing it. On the contrary, this experience assures us still more, that the sense of interest has become common to all our fellows, and gives us a confidence of the future regularity

[51] Thomas Hobbes, *Leviathan*, ed. Richard Tuck (Cambridge: Cambridge University Press, 1991), ch. 18, p. 125.

of their conduct: And 'tis only on the expectation of this, that our moderation and abstinence are founded.[52]

Certainly there are going to be free-rider problems with a convention of this sort.[53] But Hume assumes in effect that the relevant collective-action problems are iterated, and that cooperative strategies may emerge as rational in the long-run even though violation is immediately tempting.[54]

(2) James Buchanan associates this dynamic aspect of the model with another. A Pareto-improvement is to be expected from a Humean convention only as the parties discover the limits of their respective predatory capacities. Since time immemorial, people will have been seizing, using, and fighting over resources:

> [A]s a result of the actual or potential conflict over the relative proportions of [resources] to be finally consumed, some "natural distribution" will come to be established. This cannot properly be classified as a structure of *rights*, since no formal agreement is made, although there might well exist mutual recognition of the appropriate bounds on individual action. Nonetheless, the natural distribution may represent a conceptual equilibrium, in which each person extends his own behavior in securing (defending) shares in [resources] to the limit where marginal benefits from further effort are equal to the marginal costs that such effort requires.[55]

Such a distribution might be equal or unequal, but the parties will already know that they cannot hope for a much better distribution by pitching their own strength yet again against that of others.

(3) I do not think either Hume or Buchanan is committed to the view that the conditions for a convention of this sort will always obtain, nor, when they do, that such a convention is always advantageous to everyone in a given territory. Certainly, neither of them provides grounds for supporting that view. As Coleman acknowledges in his later work, "cooperation that requires forgoing predation may not be a rational strategy for all agents."[56] The gains that one can continue to expect from predation may, in certain circumstances, exceed the benefits one could expect from mutual restraint, and it is quite wrong to suppose that all such calculations depend on the possibility of free-riding. If that is everyone's situation, no Humean cooperation is possible (and given the fact

---

[52] Hume, *Treatise*, p. 490.

[53] Coleman, *Markets, Morals, and the Law*, pp. 265–66.

[54] Hobbes makes similar assumptions in his argument against the "Foole," in *Leviathan*, ch. 15, pp. 101–3.

[55] Buchanan, *Limits of Liberty* (*supra* note 9), p. 24.

[56] Coleman, *Risks and Wrongs* (*supra* note 10), p. 57.

that Hobbesian sovereigns are difficult to institute, probably no Hobbesian cooperation either).[57] If it is the situation of a few, then Humean cooperation may be possible among the others, but it will also have to involve an element of self-defense against a rump of predators on whose allegiance the convention will have no claim whatsoever from either a moral or a rational-choice point of view.

(4) Hume acknowledges that there is eventually a role for a government to provide each person with an assurance that others will take a long-term view of the advantages of iterated cooperation and not succumb to "their violent propension to prefer contiguous to remote" advantages.[58] Men will agree to set up and obey a government that will enforce the terms of the original agreement, and thus "acquire a security against each others weakness and passion, as well as against their own."[59] Still, the institution of a coercive power is understood quite independently of the agreement on the bounds of property. Coleman's claims about the monopoly character of such a power remain valid, of course; but they are now at least theoretically distinguishable from whatever bargaining problem is involved in the agreement to recognize property.

VII. DIFFICULTIES: JUSTICE AND THE LIMITS OF PARETO-IMPROVEMENT

So far, I have looked at some technical difficulties with the Humean model. But the real objections that it faces are moral in character. For the rest of this essay, I shall examine the view that the Hume/Buchanan story fundamentally misrepresents the significance of *justice* in our thinking about the initial distribution of property rights.

Let us begin with the most radical critic of the Humean theory—Jean-Jacques Rousseau. The model I have called Rousseauian is that author's normative, even utopian proposal in *The Social Contract*. In his historical speculations, however, Rousseau tells the Humean story over again, only this time with a jaundiced irony regarding the convention to recognize property. Rousseau's historical story goes like this.

With the growth of metallurgy and agriculture, men found it necessary or desirable to guard patches of land on which they were working as their own, and to jealously keep others away from the benefits of their own labor. But differential talents led over time to the gradual unfolding of inequality and with it the will to domineer over others, a division between rich and poor, and something akin to a Hobbesian war of all

---

[57] Actually, determining whether the two possibilities stand or fall together would require detailed analysis that I cannot undertake here. For the conditions favoring Hobbesian cooperation, see the discussion in Jean Hampton, *Hobbes and the Social Contract Tradition* (Cambridge: Cambridge University Press, 1986), ch. 5.

[58] Hume, *Treatise*, Bk. III, Part II, section vii, p. 537.

[59] *Ibid.*, p. 538.

against all. In time, people reflected on the horrors of this situation —
particularly the rich, who saw their possessions endangered and who
were acutely aware that, since their own wealth was founded on force,
they would have little ground for complaint if others forcibly took it from
them:

> Destitute of valid reasons to justify and sufficient strength to defend
> himself, able to crush individuals with ease, but easily crushed him-
> self by a troop of bandits, . . . and incapable, on account of mutual
> jealousy, of joining with his equals against numerous enemies united
> by the common hope of plunder, the rich man, thus urged by neces-
> sity, conceived at length the profoundest plan that ever entered the
> mind of man.[60]

The plan was to propose a Humean convention to the poor:

> "Let us join," said he, "to guard the weak from oppression, to
> restrain the ambitious, and to secure to every man the possession of
> what belongs to him: let us institute rules of justice and peace, to
> which all without exception might be obliged to conform; rules that
> may in some measure make amends for the caprices of fortune by
> subjecting equally the powerful and the weak to the observance of
> reciprocal obligations."[61]

The common people bought the idea, and as Rousseau writes, "ran headlong to their chains." The state of war ceased and possession became ratified as property. But far from being a pact of mutual advantage, the
initial convention was actually a fraud:

> Such was, or may well have been, the origin of society and law,
> which bound new fetters on the poor, and gave new powers to the
> rich; which irretrievably destroyed natural liberty, eternally fixed the
> law of property and inequality, converted clever usurpation into
> unalterable right, and, for the advantage of a few ambitious indi-
> viduals, subjected all mankind to perpetual labour, slavery, and
> wretchedness.[62]

Is Rousseau's indictment a fair one? Is the Humean convention simply
an artifice to subdue the poor and consolidate the gains of the powerful?
    Certainly, it is hard to avoid that appearance if we focus on it as a his-
torical possibility rather than as a theoretical model. To begin with, we

---

[60] Jean-Jacques Rousseau, *A Discourse on the Origin of Inequality*, Part II, in *The Social Contract and Discourses*, ed. G. D. H. Cole (London: J. M. Dent & Sons, 1973), p. 88.
    [61] *Ibid.*, p. 89.
    [62] *Ibid.*

know that the possessions ratified by the convention may involve the most radical inequality. There is nothing necessarily creditable about the procedures by which holdings are acquired, nothing particularly attractive about the personal features (strength, cunning, ruthlessness, and luck) on which the outcome is likely to be patterned, nothing, in short, that is likely to contribute to the moral legitimacy of holdings considered on their own. Now, the basic idea of the model is that fairness is irrelevant at this stage: all that matters is that the distribution of de facto holdings have the stability characteristic of Buchanan's "natural equilibrium":

> [T]here are . . . considerable differences among separate persons in a precontract setting. To the extent that such differences exist, post-contract inequality in property and in human rights must be predicted. . . . There is nothing to suggest that men must enter the initial negotiating process as equals. Men enter as they are in some natural state, and this may embody significant differences.[63]

It is all a matter of grabbing and fighting and defending what one can while one tries to get as much as possible from others; and it settles down into something that can be turned into a system of property only when everyone has tested his strength and cunning against others' and worked out who in the long run is likely to be able to hang on to what. As a result of this, some individuals, families, or groups who are weaker, less well-placed or strong-willed or fortunate than the rest, will have next to nothing to hold on to when the convention is established. Hungry, cold, terrified, and despairing, they will doubtless face a proposal to ratify and legitimize their dispossession with considerable alarm. As rules of property develop, even the worst off will be taught and expected to obey them. But doing so may be a costly and demanding—perhaps mortally demanding—form of self-restraint. The rights which conventional ratification places beyond his reach may cover just the resources that the poor person needs to survive. What, then, can be said to him in their defense? Why should he abide by the rules of this convention?

It may be responded, "Well, at least the poor are in possession of themselves and their bodies; they can look to the convention as a basis for ratifying their self-ownership." But even that may be assuming too much. The reference to human rights in the passage from Buchanan just cited indicates that some may reach the natural equilibrium possessed of the bodies or persons of others. Since there is nothing to be said morally about the basis of de facto possession, there is nothing to rule out slavery or cannibalism as features of the holdings that are ratified by the convention.

Even in this extremity, the convention may be defended as amounting to a Pareto-improvement. Everyone benefits—or, at least, nobody loses.

---

[63] Buchanan, *Limits of Liberty*, pp. 25–26.

Those in possession of great wealth benefit because they save the cost of defending their holdings. Those whose holdings are negligible are at the very least freed from the worry that they will lose what little they have, and they benefit too from the overall stability and certainty introduced into the system of holdings and from the prospects of market transaction which that stability makes possible. And while those who have nothing or less than nothing may not actually benefit, they are no worse off than they would have been anyway, convention or no convention, and thus they too should applaud the Pareto-superiority of the move. That is the Humean defense.

But this line of argument greatly exaggerates the justificatory significance of a Pareto-improvement.[64] If Pareto-superiority justifies anything, it justifies only the move that confers the benefits and justifies it only to those who receive them. As we have seen, there are likely to be significant moral concerns about the pre-convention distribution of holdings, on the Humean model. The fact (if it is a fact) that some benefit and no one loses at the time of the convention does not allay those concerns: the most it does is mitigate a bad situation. Even if everyone agrees to the improvement, they can do so without undermining their insistence that both the pre-improvement and the post-improvement distributions remain unfair.

Also, one must be very careful in inferring anything about obligation from the possibility of a Pareto-improvement. What happens in a Pareto-improvement is that some benefit and others do not (though no one loses). Now it may make some sense (*perhaps*) to say that the beneficiaries have an obligation not to upset the move. But it makes no sense whatever to say that those who are left just as they were have such an obligation. Their moral position vis-à-vis the Pareto-improvement is one of sheer indifference, and it is absurd to say that they may be called upon in the name of efficiency and the general welfare to support it.

Even for those who do benefit, it matters greatly exactly *what* the Pareto-improvement is taken to be. In the abstract, the sheer reduction of conflict may benefit most people. But that does not show that *any scheme which reduces conflict* is a Pareto-improvement. A given scheme may have side effects and incidental consequences, and these must be counted too before any Pareto conclusion is reached. In Hume's story, we are imagining something which is not merely the reduction of conflict, but the reduction of conflict by the institution of a scheme of *property rights*. To reduce conflict, the parties concur in recognizing one another's holdings not only as relatively invulnerable (as they are, once a natural equilibrium is established), but as *rightful*, as *just*, as *their due*, and so on. Hume has well described how "artificial virtues" such as honesty and fair-

---

[64] See note 12 above for definitions of "Pareto-superior," "Pareto-improvement," and "Pareto-optimal."

ness grow up around the recognized holdings, giving them extra legitimacy and a secure foothold in conscience and consciousness. To take
something from these holdings now is not only dangerous, but perceived
as dishonest and shameful. To challenge their legitimacy is to be accused
of envy and injustice. These are not trivial matters: they have their effect
(exactly the effect they are designed to have) in insulating existing holdings from redistributive challenge. One result of that is to diminish the
risk of subsequent disorder. But another result is to make the economic
situation of the rich more secure—and *a fortiori* (in a condition of moderate scarcity), to make the economic prospects of the poor less hopeful
than they were immediately before the convention.

Thus, although the poorest parties to the convention gain the benefits
of a reduction in violent conflict, they may suffer a significant decline in
their long-term prospects. Since resources are scarce, and since the poor
have precious little with which to enjoy the benefits of market exchange,
their prospects remain inversely proportional to the resilience of the holdings of those who have more than they do. Since the latter holdings are
made immeasurably more robust by legitimation and by the emergence
of the artificial virtues of honesty and respect for property, the former are
made poorer to that extent. So Rousseau was right: the price the poor pay
for order and peace is to be confronted with a more secure set of holdings
and a greatly reduced chance of ever being able to challenge them.

It is difficult to know how to characterize all this in the language of
Pareto-superiority. Strictly speaking, if the convention to ratify possession
has long-term consequences which work to the detriment of the poorest
members of society, then the move is not a Pareto-improvement. If the
reduction of conflict has the effect of entrenching them in their poverty,
they may be worse off, not better off, as a result of the move. In theory,
then, the Humean model—predicated as it is on the assumption that no
one loses as a result of the convention—will be inapplicable to this change
if the situation is as I have just described it. The trouble is that the respect
in which the poor are made worse off according to Rousseau's critique—
a lesser long-term prospect of their being able to reverse their dispossession—is difficult to quantify and thus difficult to compare with the
immediate and tangible benefits to all of a reduction in conflict. Various
economic models for comparing the two might be imagined—models that
characterize prospects for change in terms of expected utilities. But there
is an ideological, not just an analytical issue, about whether a diminution
in such prospects is actually commensurable with the costs and benefits
that the Pareto analysis tends to focus on.[65] These issues cannot be
resolved here.[66] They indicate, however, the depth and subtlety of the

---

[65] For an excellent discussion, see Steven Lukes, *Power: A Radical View* (London: Macmillan, 1974).
[66] I shall say a little more about the difficulties of applying the Humean model to the real
world in Section X below.

Rousseauian critique: his critique does not so much challenge the Humean calculations as call into question the assumptions about quantifiability and commensurability that underlie them.

VIII. A POSSIBLE SOLUTION: THE DANGERS OF BARGAINING WITH PREDATORS

How might a Humean respond to the point that the convention to recognize possession is likely to ratify extreme inequality? What is the Humean response to the charge that this is an inadequate basis for developing a theory of justice?

In his most recent examination of the model, Jules Coleman toys with a possible solution. It is not intended to rebut the difficulty, and it is not clear that Coleman actually wants to go to bat for it;[67] but it is worth considering all the same as a way of incorporating fairness considerations into the overall structure of the rational-choice paradigm.

The response that Coleman outlines questions the assumption I have been making so far, that issues of distributive fairness can be separated from issues concerning the stability of the Humean convention. He relies on the intuitive idea that an egregiously unfair distribution will be unstable for exactly that reason. A peace dividend is not possible on the basis of injustice: "No justice, no peace." People will not put up with it, and they will not trust the good faith of those whose predatory activities have led to the acquisition of grossly disproportionate holdings.

The detail of the argument turns on the Humean premise that I highlighted in Section VI—that the convention to recognize property must already be, in essence, self-enforcing before there can be any question of the institution of a Hobbesian enforcement mechanism. Thus, Coleman directs our attention to the possibility that stability requirements might be satisfied only with regard to distributions that are fair:

> A bargain that is not enforceable cannot be rational. . . . Rational parties will not enter bargains that are unstable . . . because doing so promises only to make them worse off than they currently are. If third-party enforcement mechanisms exist, they relieve much of the pressure of finding an enforceable agreement. In a state of nature no third-party mechanisms exist, and so in order to be rational a bargain must be self-enforcing. In order to be stable or self-enforcing, agreements in a state of nature *must be fair*. In that case, rational bargaining will yield fair agreements or no agreements.[68]

In a moment, I shall ask *why* Coleman thinks that an agreement can be self-enforcing only if it is fair. Before proceeding, however, it is worth

---

[67] See Coleman, *Risks and Wrongs*, pp. 57–59.
[68] *Ibid.*, p. 54.

posing a couple of abstract questions. Is "fairness," as it is used in this argument, supposed to connote some objective distributive standard arrived at independently of the process of forming a convention? Is it, for example, supposed to connote the sort of standards that are deployed in either the Rousseauian or the Lockean approach to the emergence of property rights? In particular, can "fairness" as an objective standard be used to critically evaluate the participants' own views about what is fair and what is not?

One natural interpretation of Coleman's suggestion is that a Humean convention will be stable only if the participants *think* it is fair. But if fairness is an objective characteristic, they may be mistaken in their assessment. In any case, the participants are certainly likely to disagree among themselves about what counts as a fair distribution. Though we are not assuming a Hobbesian sovereign, we should not neglect Hobbes's insight that, since people naturally disagree about right and wrong, instability is as likely as stability to be the result of the participants' making fairness an issue.

Alternatively, the suggestion might be that the stability of an agreement is itself a criterion of its fairness (whatever the parties *think* about it). Coleman inclines to this interpretation, saying that "[t]he compliance and fairness problems are resolved simultaneously; they are, in effect, the same problem."[69] But this implies that if a stable convention does emerge on the basis of a distribution that we would judge — apart from its viability — as grossly unfair, then that appearance of unfairness is to be regarded as misleading: the stability of the arrangement refutes it. Now this is certainly the upshot of the Hume/Buchanan view, but for that very reason it may not be regarded as an answer to the underlying criticism we are considering. For the assumption of the model is precisely that the stability of the convention is everything and that the virtue of fairness is simply an artifact of that stability. The objection, on the other hand, is that fairness seems — to us, at least — to be more than that, and to operate as a distinct and independent moral standard.

Let us assume, then, that in Coleman's theorem — "In order to be stable or self-enforcing, agreements in a state of nature *must be fair*"[70] — "fairness" is to have some Lockean or Rousseauian content independent of stability, and independent of any participant's views about it. The question remains: What reason is there to accept such a theorem?

Coleman himself attributes the theorem to David Gauthier, but the argument of the latter in chapter 7 of *Morals by Agreement*, directed against Buchanan's version of the Humean model, is somewhat different.

Gauthier's argument turns on a connection between injustice and coercion: an unjust distribution, he seems to suggest, is a distribution sus-

[69] *Ibid.*
[70] *Ibid.*; emphasis in original.

tained by force (though he fails to make it clear whether this is supposed to be true by definition, or simply a matter of common experience). Gauthier insists that "[t]he initial bargaining position must be non-coercive."[71] If the natural equilibrium involves any element that is sustained by coercion, he argues, then that element must be expected to evaporate in a post-agreement world. After all, the post-agreement situation is Pareto-superior to pre-agreement conflict precisely because everyone saves the energy that they previously put into the use, and the defense of themselves against, violence. Gauthier reckons that they cannot *both* realize these savings *and* maintain a distribution of rights that has its origins in coercion.

We can illustrate this with an example (mine, not Gauthier's), scrutinizing the suggestion noted earlier that a Humean convention may involve the ratification of slavery. Suppose P is captured and enslaved by Q in pre-convention times and forced to work for him. Sometimes P refuses to work; sometimes he tries to run away altogether. Every time he tries to run away, Q brings him back and beats him. But sometimes (let us say particularly nighttimes) when Q tries to get P to work, P refuses and Q cannot make him budge no matter how hard he beats him. Thus, a natural equilibrium emerges: P never succeeds in escaping, but he can never be made to work nights. Let us call this situation X. If X persists for any period of time, P and Q are likely to come to the realization that they are wasting an awful lot of energy attacking and resisting one another. P can save a lot of running and Q a lot of chasing and beating, if they settle that P is to remain on Q's farm as his slave. And Q can save a lot of beating by simply recognizing that P will never work nights: P becomes "entitled" to his evenings off. The new arrangement (call it situation Y) is Pareto-superior, since the parties save the costs of exercising and resisting coercive force. But Gauthier believes Y is unstable. He will ask, "Why should we expect P to remain Q's slave at all, even with his nights off, now that Q's coercion has been removed (in pursuit of a peace dividend)? Surely P will now just wander off, a free man." Call the situation that results from his doing so, Z.

My inclination is to say that Q will chase P as before, seize him, and bring him back, so that we return to situation X. Gauthier's reply is: "Why should Q do that? The reintroduction of coercion will be costly to both parties and thus irrational for Q. Hence, we must suppose that a stable agreement ends at Z, even if the parties actually begin in X. The eventual outcome is as if there had never been a predatory capture of P by Q."[72]

But Gauthier's reasoning here is flawed. Unless it depends on something uninterestingly contingent, like Q being caught off-guard by P's

[71] Gauthier, *Morals by Agreement* (*supra* note 11), p. 200.
[72] This reply is adapted from *ibid.*, pp. 196–97.

escape in a post-agreement world, it presupposes that the utilities of P and Q at X, Y, and Z are as shown in Figure 1. On this account, Q must necessarily lose by moving from Z to X.[73] But if Z were to the northeast of X, as it is in Figure 1, then the coercive outcome X would *always* have been irrational for Q, and, *ex hypothesi*, that is not the case. Gauthier is right to note that the reintroduction of coercion is *costly* for Q, but wrong to infer that it is therefore not worthwhile. If Q's coercive retention of P was rational in the pre-agreement situation, then the utilities at X, Y, and Z must be as shown in Figure 2. Thus, if P moves the situation from Y to Z by wandering off, a move back from Z to X must be worth the costs for Q.

What Gauthier has forgotten, in other words, is that the Humean convention remains stable only so long as it ratifies roughly the distribution of holdings secured by a coercive equilibrium. To the extent it disrupts such equilibrium, the parties have an incentive to renege on their agreement to renounce force, and to do whatever they can to restore the equilibrium they began with. To suppose that they are somehow incapable of doing so—i.e., that their disarmament in the move from X to Y is irrevocable, so that it is impossible to reintroduce force—is to make exactly the sort of Hobbesian assumptions on whose absence this whole strategy of argument depends. And even if such assumptions could be made, no party would agree to such a one-sided convention: Q would never agree to a convention that allowed P to disrupt the equilibrium by wandering off while prohibiting Q from using force to restore it.

Enough about Gauthier.[74] Let us return to Coleman's argument about

---

[73] This is exactly the shape of Gauthier's Figure 9 in *ibid.*, p. 228, where X = Gauthier's I_n, Y = B_n, and Z = B_c.

[74] See also the critique of Gauthier's argument in Jody S. Kraus and Jules L. Coleman, "Morality and the Theory of Rational Choice," *Ethics*, vol. 97 (1987), esp. pp. 725-31.

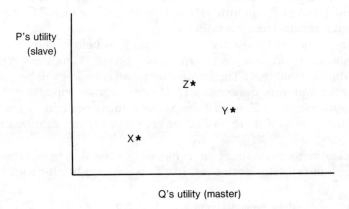

P's utility (slave)

Z★

Y★

X★

Q's utility (master)

FIGURE 1.

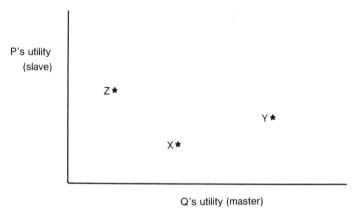

FIGURE 2.

predation and cooperation. His case turns on the claim that people will not cooperate with those who have proved themselves predators.

There is a trivial sense in which this is true. As we saw in subsection (3) of Section VI, there may be some who are predators in the sense that they are better off not being parties to a Humean convention, no matter what anyone else does. Let us call such a person a predator[1]. Of course it is folly to try and cooperate with such an individual. A predator[1] is, in Locke's terms, "a *Lyon* or a *Tyger*, one of those wild Savage Beasts, with whom Men can have no Society nor Security."[75] But this shows nothing about the wisdom of entering into an agreement with predators who evidently *do* stand to gain from a Humean peace dividend.

A putative participant in a Humean convention may be defined as a predator in any one of three other senses. A predator[2] is a person who has grabbed things forcibly from others in the pre-agreement situation. A predator[3] is a person who comes to the Humean bargaining table with more than his fair share[76] even though this is not a result of his being a predator[2]. In other words, a predator[3] is a predator purely in terms of his holding and consuming goods that, if things were fair, would be held and consumed by others. A predator[4] is a person who, though he would be benefited by a Humean convention, is disposed to free-ride upon it.[77]

There is no doubt that the presence of a predator[4] is disruptive and destabilizing. In the absence of Hobbesian enforcement, the parties have every incentive to find out who such persons are and to make their free-

---

[75] Locke, *Second Treatise*, section 11.

[76] Thus, people who disagree about what counts as a fair share will of course disagree about whether to describe a given individual as a predator in this third sense. See also the discussion in the last paragraph of this section (in the text accompanying note 88 below).

[77] These four senses of "predator" are mine, not Coleman's.

riding not worth their while by eliminating them, or threatening to eliminate them, as far as possible from cooperative schemes. The predator$_4$
is the "Foole" of *Leviathan*, chapter 15, and Hobbes's response to him
remains appropriate. Coleman is therefore right to insist that "[r]ational
agents will constrain themselves from cooperating with others who take
advantage of them" in this sense, and he is right too to infer, along
Hobbesian lines, that individuals who stand to gain from the stability of
a Humean convention have reason not to pursue a predatory$_4$ strategy.[78]

But Coleman uses this to argue for a much more doubtful claim. From
what we have just said, he infers that rationality "precludes bargaining
from threat advantages secured in a war of all against all."[79] This can be
interpreted in two ways, depending on how we understand "threat
advantages." That phrase may mean (a) advantages secured by threatening to behave as a predator$_4$; or it may mean (b) whatever advantages
one can reasonably expect to secure in the absence of an agreement. The
latter is the usual game-theoretic understanding, but an equivocation
from sense (b) to sense (a) has often been used to attack the Humean
model. There is insufficient space to go into that here.[80] Let us simply
concede that Coleman's claim is right in sense (a) of threat advantage: if
it is irrational to cooperate with a predator$_4$, and if predators$_4$ can be
identified, then it is irrational to be a predator$_4$; and if it is irrational to be
a predator$_4$, in most cases it will be irrational to threaten to be a preda-
tor$_4$. Still, absent equivocation, this shows nothing about the acceptabil-
ity of Coleman's claim if "threat advantage" is read in sense (b).

In the end, Coleman's argument seems to be that there is some sort of
natural connection between being a predator$_4$ and being a predator in
one of the other senses.

Clearly this is not the case with predator$_3$. A perfectly decent person
may be a predator$_3$ by accident. Born in an exceptionally fertile spot, he
may not even realize that he has vastly more resources than his fellow
bargainers until he comes to the bargaining table. Coleman surely cannot
be suggesting that it is impossible to cooperate reliably with such a person. A predator$_3$ may be evidently ready to stick with any mutually
advantageous bargain struck between him and his poorer neighbors: the
mere fact that he *has* more resources need affect neither his cooperative
disposition nor their perception of it.

Coleman may respond that the other parties will complain at the bargaining table about the disproportionate size of the predator$_3$'s holding
and that if he refuses to even things out immediately, he becomes *ipso
facto* a predator in a more dangerous sense. But why should this be? The
person may deny or resist the charge that he has more than a fair share.

[78] Coleman, *Risks and Wrongs*, p. 52.
[79] *Ibid.*
[80] There is an excellent discussion in Barry, *Theories of Justice* (*supra* note 1), pp. 68–76.

His doing so may be evidence only of the position that Hobbes, Hume, and Buchanan have all recognized—that there is likely to be no consensus about fairness in advance of an agreement. Certainly his dissent is not evidence of his unreliability as a potential cooperator. The others may accuse him of unreliability in trying to foist on them an agreement which is unstable because it is unfair (by their lights)—trying in effect to trick them into fruitless compliance. But then they would be begging the very question we are discussing: viz., are unfair agreements *ipso facto* unstable?

If Coleman's argument is to be sustained, the claim must be specifically that a predator$_2$ cannot reliably be cooperated with. The claim must be that a person who has made a practice of grabbing things from others in the pre-agreement situation cannot be expected to restrain himself from grabbing things from people in the post-agreement situation. Notice that, even if this were true, it would take us only part of the way to establishing the instability of unfair agreements. For not all unfair distributions of initial holdings result from predation$_2$; not all unfairness results from people showing a bad character in the sense Coleman needs. Disproportionate initial holdings can be the result of differential luck, initial placement, and so on (as we saw with predator$_3$).

In any case, there are good reasons for doubting Coleman's correlation between predator$_4$ and predator$_2$. Behaviorally, the dispositions are quite different. Predator$_4$ reneges on his agreements and tries to take advantage of others' cooperation: he is, as I said, like Hobbes's "Foole." Predator$_2$, by contrast, seizes things in situations where there is no framework for cooperation and thus neither a Hobbesian nor a Humean basis for reproaching him. If such a person professes a readiness to cooperate with others in securing a peace dividend that will depend on mutual restraint, there is no reason to doubt him. His posture is exactly that stipulated by Hobbes as the first law of nature: "That every man, ought to endeavour Peace, as farre as he has hope of obtaining it; and when he cannot obtain it, that he may seek, and use, all helps, and advantages of Warre."[81] Perhaps Coleman wants to quarrel with Hobbes's view that it is possible both to pursue a predatory$_2$ war and to hold oneself ready "*in foro interno*" to cooperate with others in the event that cooperation becomes both safe and rational.[82] But if he does, he must see that it takes more than the simple equivocation implicit in "One cannot cooperate with a predator."

There may also be some equivocation on the concept of "free-rider" here. A predator$_4$ is a free-rider in the strict game-theoretic sense, while a predator$_2$ is a free-rider in the more informal sense of one who takes advantage of others' efforts, by seizing things that they have grown or

---

[81] Hobbes, *Leviathan*, ch. 14, p. 92.
[82] *Ibid.*, ch. 15, p. 110.

made. But the verbal similarity between these two meanings of "free-riding" does not establish any substantial correlation.

Before abandoning this line of argument, I want to pursue two final gambits. It is possible to imagine a society consisting largely of Lockean farmers who produce holdings for themselves on the basis of independent, noncooperative but nonpredatory$_2$ activity, but comprising also one or two predators$_2$ who seek occasionally to wrest from the farmers the products of their labor. If the disparity in size between the two groups is big enough, the farmers may find it worth their while to enter into a Humean convention among themselves ratifying their Lockean holdings as mutually recognized property rights. Relative to that convention, the rump of predators$_2$ will have the status of predators$_1$; and certainly, it will be foolish for the farmers to attempt to cooperate with them on the basis of this convention. However, to the extent that the predators$_2$ constitute a danger or even a nuisance, the members of both groups may find that they will do better for themselves by setting up a second convention to supersede the first—a second convention which will ratify whatever holdings the predators$_2$ have managed to secure along with the holdings of the farmers, modified accordingly to reflect the limits of the defensive capabilities of all parties.[83] Coleman's position seems to be that if it was dangerous to cooperate with the predators$_2$ in the first convention, it must continue to be dangerous to cooperate with them in the second. But again, there is no reason adduced to show that this is the case.

Gauthier argues that by entering into the second convention the Lockean farmers evince a disposition that if advertised in advance may encourage predation$_2$: "Someone disposed to comply with agreements that left untouched the fruits of predation would simply invite others to engage in predatory and coercive activities as a prelude to bargaining."[84] But this is unlikely to be of any importance. Either predation$_2$ is independently rational in the pre-convention situation or it is not: if it is, then even the honest Lockean farmers have to come to terms with its fruits if they want to secure a peace dividend; if it is not, it is unlikely that knowledge of the farmers' disposition to enter negotiations with predators when that is mutually beneficial will tilt the balance of costs and benefits for a potential predator$_2$ in any but the most marginal cases. Certainly such cases have no hope of affording a general argument for the theorem that unfair agreements are unstable.

A final line of argument that Coleman considers (together with fellow author Jody Kraus) eschews the idea of predation altogether, and addresses directly the possibility that people do best by cultivating a disposition (labeled "narrow compliance") to cooperate only in schemes and conventions that are fair.[85] There is insufficient space here to fully out-

---

[83] See Buchanan, *Limits of Liberty*, pp. 60–64.

[84] Gauthier, *Morals by Agreement*, p. 195.

[85] Kraus and Coleman, "Morality and the Theory of Rational Choice," pp. 732 ff.

line Kraus and Coleman's analysis of this possibility. They demonstrate that narrow compliance is likely to be a rational strategy only for a disadvantaged person,[86] and even then only if that person is assured that a sufficient number of others have also cultivated the disposition. The latter condition is unlikely to be fulfilled, "for it will never be rational for any one individual to become narrowly compliant in the first place."[87]

In any case, this possibility—along with any argument that invokes the concept of fairness at this stage[88]—is subject to an immediate difficulty in the context of the Humean model. Whatever the assurance and collective-action problems involved in narrow compliance, they are compounded fatally by the fact that people disagree about fairness, so that the bargains with which narrow compliance disposes me to comply may be different from those with which narrow compliance disposes you to comply. That disagreement is no incidental matter; on the contrary, it is a central assumption of the model and it accounts for much of the conflict in the state of nature. One can wish it away, theoretically, if one likes; but then one will have wished away the problems that gave the Humean model its interest for us in the first place.[89]

IX. Difficulties: The Independent Importance of Justice

So much for a possible solution. The general difficulty we are confronting is this. The Humean model is supposed to explain not only the emergence of a stable set of holdings, but also the emergence of property *rights*, and with a sense of rights a sense also of *fairness* and *justice*. But it is not at all clear that it can do that. No doubt some sense of an immutable *balance of power* might emerge from Humean negotiation, similar to the sense that characterizes international diplomacy. But why should we expect heavily moralized standards like justice and fairness—standards that connote the idea of the rightfulness of the proportion of one person's holding to another's—to emerge from the essentially amoral process that Hume and Buchanan describe? The Humean model purports to give an account of rights, justice, and fairness; but it turns out that these notions are accorded no independent critical force and are presented as simple derivatives of a *modus vivendi* based amorally on an equilibrium of force.

A defender of the model may respond by saying it was overambitious of Hume to describe his theory as an account of the origins of *justice*. Its aim is to characterize the emergence of an initial set of property rights in

---

[86] An advantaged person (i.e., one with more than his fair share), of course, stands to benefit from complying with at least some unfair arrangements, viz., those that entrench his advantaged position.

[87] Kraus and Coleman, "Morality and the Theory of Rational Choice," p. 745.

[88] This applies, for example, to any argument turning on the notion of predation$_3$. See note 76 above.

[89] I have benefited from many conversations with Jules Coleman on these issues.

rational-choice terms, and that (as we saw in Section II) is a sufficient achievement in terms of paradigm-unification, whether or not it succeeds in the further task of characterizing our sense of justice. Who knows where our sense of distributive justice comes from? It largely doesn't matter, for as Hume points out,

> [t]hat there be a separation or distinction of possessions, and that this separation be steady and constant; this is absolutely required by the interests of society. . . . What possessions are assigned to particular persons; this is, generally speaking, pretty indifferent; and is often determined by very frivolous views and considerations.[90]

It is difficult, however, to sustain this breezy indifference to justice, even *within* the terms of the model. For although the Humean wants to say that we should forget about establishing positive standards of distributive justice, he also wants to insist, negatively, that it is wrong or irrational to use such standards, if we have them, to call into question the distribution that the convention sustains. He may not be able to show positively that the ratified holdings are fair; but he wants it very much to be the case that the holdings are *immune* from further assessment in terms of fairness. That may not be an immunity to which his model entitles him.

Hume's own strategy is to insist that issues of justice—important as they are—are logically posterior to settlement on property rights. If justice is a matter of "To each his own," then no question of it can be raised until some system of "mine" and "thine" is agreed upon.[91] However, this purely logical point fails to show that standards of justice, once established, may not subsequently be turned against the initial settlement. An example will illustrate this point.

Suppose a Humean convention has been set up, so that people recognize and respect one another's holdings. What happens if new resources are discovered or come into existence? Are we then to go through the same process all over again—fighting and grabbing until a pattern of retention emerges? Hume answers with an adamant "No":

> [T]ho' the rule of the assignment of property to the present possessor be natural, and by that means useful, yet its utility extends not beyond the first formation of society; nor would anything be more pernicious, than the constant observance of it; by which restitution

[90] Hume, *Enquiry*, Appendix III, p. 309n.
[91] Hume, *Treatise*, Bk. III, Part II, section ii, pp. 490–91:

> After this convention, concerning abstinence from the possessions of others, is enter'd into, and everyone has acquir'd a stability in his possessions, there immediately arise the ideas of justice and injustice; as also those of *property*, *right*, and *obligation*. The latter are altogether unintelligible without first understanding the former.

wou'd be excluded and every injustice would be authoriz'd and rewarded. We must, therefore, seek for some other circumstance, that may give rise to property after society is once establish'd. . . .[92]

He argues for first occupancy as a post-convention principle of acquisition (on several grounds, including the disutility of leaving any issue of property rights unsettled while a new resource passes through several hands). [93] But if this principle gets established in the popular consciousness as *the* appropriate standard to use to judge post-convention acquisitions, it is not unimaginable that people may be tempted in time to apply it also to what they know about the origin of *pre*-convention holdings. And what they will find is an incongruity, since, if anything, the principle on which pre-convention holdings were recognized was a principle of *last* occupancy, not *first* occupancy, relative to the moment of the convention. No matter who first held or occupied or made or cultivated some resource, no matter how many times it was subsequently lost or seized or grabbed, the person who got the benefit of the rights established through the convention was the person left holding it at that moment. People are likely, therefore, to criticize that process, much as we find critics bringing quasi-Lockean standards to bear on issues of aboriginal rights. Now if those governed by the convention deploy their new standards of justice in this way, Hume can hardly argue that they are making a logical mistake. Even though they could not have had such standards to apply to any acquisition unless pre-convention holdings had been ratified, still, once the deployment of such standards has gotten underway, there is nothing contradictory about turning them on the pre-convention holdings themselves and calling the whole basis of subsequent transactions into question.

Thus, showing (as Hume does) that recognition of existing holdings is a precondition for the deployment of any principle of justice is not, in itself, a way of showing that the recognized holdings and the market outcomes that flow from them cannot be scrutinized by such a principle.

Buchanan, by contrast, attempts to resist justice-based critiques of the initial distribution on substantive rather than logical grounds. According to Buchanan, the Humean convention will not secure the benefits at which participants aim—peace and secure market transactions—unless its effect is to preclude any post-convention questioning of the holdings that it ratifies. Indeed, the way Buchanan sees it, the person who questions the initial distribution on grounds of justice is a kind of free-rider, for his questioning assumes that we can persist with some settled distribution

[92] *Ibid.*, Bk. III, Part II, section iii, p. 505.

[93] "[T]his affords us an easy reason, why we annex the idea of property to the first possession, or to occupation. Men are unwilling to leave property in suspence, even for the shortest time, or open the least door to violence and disorder" (*ibid.*).

of property, only not *this* one.[94] The convention must therefore be established as a matter of constitutional law, and insulated from day-to-day
majoritarian decision making in the society that enjoys its benefits.[95]

But this argument of Buchanan's fails on two fronts. First, it underestimates the robustness of modern economies. Although it is clear that
markets would be impossible if every property right were at every
moment subject to redistributive consideration, our experience has not
been that markets become impossible whenever any property rights are
scrutinized in that way. Clearly, benefits like stability, security, and the
possibility of exchange can accrue from a Humean convention even if the
convention does not put the pattern of holdings utterly beyond question.
Most modern economies work reasonably well despite the absence of
anything equivalent to Fifth Amendment protection for property
rights;[96] and even in America, economic interaction seems to flourish in
spite of continuing debates about social justice, economic inequality,
appropriate levels of progressive taxation, and so on. Property systems
are much more resilient and flexible than the apprehensions of their conservative defenders might lead us to believe.[97] They can survive regulation, abrogation, even income tax, without any of the dire predictions of
chaos, collapse of expectations, and a return to Hobbesian conflict coming true.

On the other side, Buchanan's approach simply underestimates the
moral urgency associated with the sentiment of justice. People have been
heard to say, "*Fiat iustitia, ruat caelum*,"[98] and though that may be hyper-
bole, it is a reasonable indication that we are in the presence of a value
that may not be rebutted simply by showing that its invocation would
make it difficult for James Buchanan to buy fruit from a watermelon
stand.[99] Presented by its proponents as "the first virtue of social institutions,"[100] justice is likely to trump any apprehension that questions
raised in its name may defeat the economic purposes that motivated the
original Humean agreement.

[94] Buchanan, *Limits of Liberty*, pp. 26–27.

[95] *Ibid.*, pp. 82–90. Actually, since (as we shall see) Buchanan does not countenance an
entirely static post-convention world, any subsequent reallocation of holdings can take place
only on the basis of unanimous agreement.

[96] The Fifth Amendment to the United States Constitution provides, among other
things, that no person shall "be deprived of life, liberty, or property, without due process
of law; nor shall private property be taken for public use, without just compensation."

[97] See Hume's discussion of whether property and rights admit of degrees, in *Treatise*,
Bk. III, Part II, section vi, pp. 530–31. See also the attempt to drive a wedge between Hume
and Buchanan in Barry, *Theories of Justice*, pp. 173–75.

[98] "Let justice be done though the heavens fall."

[99] The tale of this transaction is the starting point of the discussion in Buchanan, *Limits
of Liberty*, p. 17.

[100] Rawls, *A Theory of Justice* (*supra* note 3), p. 3.

X. DIFFICULTIES: FROM MODEL TO REALITY

In Section IV, I criticized the Locke/Nozick model for its impracticability. How can we *now* ascertain which holdings are legitimate in Lockean terms and which are not? I suggested there that Hume's theory does not encounter such difficulties, for it does not require of the holdings it legitimizes the impeccable pedigree that the Lockean model does. Still, there are some difficulties with the real-world application of the Humean model, and they connect in an interesting way with the problems we have been considering.

The fact is that no one in our society is aware of having been a party to a Humean convention. There appear to be property rights, sure, and they have some constitutional protection. But most of us simply find that they exist, that they have been foisted on us, and that they appear to be strongly defended. Many of us participate opportunistically in the institution as homeowners and investors, but few of us think we are precluded thereby from criticizing it, or arguing in favor of state regulation, or even urging large-scale egalitarian redistribution. Private property, like most controversial social institutions, seems to come packaged with its opposition, and that opposition occasionally, as I have said, surfaces in laws and policies that, at least at the margin, modify property rights or reallocate them from one person to another.

How is this reality to be reconciled with the Humean model? To answer this question, we have to work from both ends. The model needs to be made a little more sophisticated, and the reality has to be represented in terms of the framework that the model provides.

First, the model. In Section VI, I emphasized the dynamic character of Hume's theory. The theory assumes the gradual emergence over time of a stable equilibrium of possession, and the convention itself is conceived more on the model of the gradual emergence of a language or a currency than as a decisive social contract.[101] In Section VIII, I suggested also that the model might accommodate the possibility of one convention's superseding another, as the parties expanded the number of persons with whom they wanted to live on peaceful terms.

In general, if the situation in a society is evolving as ours is, with continuing disputes about holdings, there are two ways we can model it. (i) We can say that the society continues in a conflictual state of nature, until *all* outstanding conflicts, physical and ideological, settle down into a pattern of stable equilibrium; and *then* a convention is conceived which ratifies that equilibrium. (ii) Alternatively, we can postulate successive conventions, responding to changes in circumstances as well as alterations in the balance of power subsequent to the initial ratification of

---

[101] See Hume, *Treatise*, Bk. III, Part II, section ii, p. 490; Hume, *Enquiry*, Appendix III, pp. 306-7.

(possibly unequal) holdings. Of these approaches, (i) is more attractive from a theoretical point of view, since it draws a clear line between a phase of conflict and a settlement of property rights. But (ii) offers a more realistic account, since it accommodates the possibility, with which *we* are well acquainted, that holdings will be perceived (albeit ambivalently) as *property*, indeed as property *rights*, while disputes about their legitimacy continue.

In Buchanan's version, model (ii) is used to characterize the possibility of continuing conflict and to dovetail with his requirement that alterations in property rights be made matters of constitutional unanimity. He acknowledges that, once a Humean convention has been set up, the new arrangements may alter the balance of power among the property holders:

> Suppose that A and B, in anarchistic natural equilibrium, secure final stocks of consumables measured at ten units and two units respectively. These stocks are net of the effort expended in defense and in predation. A disarmament contract is negotiated, and the post-constitutional imputation becomes fifteen units for A, seven units for B, with each person having secured the equivalent of an additional five units. This settlement continues to be in existence for some time, but let us assume that, after X periods, the relative strengths of the two parties is thought to change. Although the natural distribution, in anarchy, is no longer observable, let us suppose that A now thinks that the two parties would fare equally in genuine anarchy, that the distribution would, in fact, be closer to 6:6 than to the original 10:2. In such a situation, A may well recognize the extreme vulnerability of the 15:7 imputation in the status quo, its vulnerability to violation by B. In order to secure for himself some greater assurance that predictable order will continue, A may willingly accept a proffered change in nominal rights, a move to a new distribution, say that of 13:9.[102]

Buchanan insists that this readjustment still has the character of unanimity. "Society," acting for example in a majoritarian way, does not reallocate holdings: reallocation takes place only as each of the affected property-holders "comes to predict that [his] claim will be eroded or undermined unless the structure is modified."[103] All the same, Buchanan is no longer in a position to condemn unilateral or fractional or majoritarian attacks on the status quo in this situation, for it is precisely the recognition of the possibility and rationality of such attacks that is going to

---

[102] Buchanan, *Limits of Liberty*, p. 79.
[103] *Ibid.*, pp. 78–79.

motivate the property-holder to acquiesce willingly in the renegotiation of his holding.

Turning now from the (modified) model to the reality, we find ourselves in fact facing a situation that has (a) some of the features of a post-convention settlement (e.g., we talk of property, not just possession; and relative stability in holdings is already yielding the benefits of market transactions), and (b) some of the features of pre-convention conflict (e.g., there is a continuing political and ideological battle over who should own what).

Now we could just let things go on in this way. However, to the extent that (b) is the result of human decision – people choose to protest current distributions, to propose majoritarian changes, etc. – it is in some sense *up to us* how far the status quo will resemble the post-convention settlement envisaged in the model. Buchanan's suggestion, as I understand it, is addressed normatively to these choices: we should evaluate the status quo "as if it were legitimate contractually." [104] Since the status quo is what exists, and since, on Humean grounds, any settlement about property is better than none, we should stop calling the existing distribution into question and we should behave toward it as though we had already ratified it along Humean lines.

This suggestion cannot be impugned on the ground that it makes the Humean convention merely notional, a retrospective artifact of our present choice not to disrupt the status quo. For as Hume himself emphasized, nothing hinges on the character of the convention as a voluntaristic promissory act: all it is, is "a general sense of common interest," [105] and that is exactly what Buchanan recommends.

But it is important to see that Buchanan's recommendation can carry no weight against a person who figures that his agitation against the existing distribution might be *successful*. A notional convention presupposes a notional version of Buchanan's natural equilibrium. And if there are protestors with a fair chance of carrying the day against the existing distribution, either on the basis of their own efforts or on the basis of whatever political mechanisms happen to exist, then there can be no question but that the requisite equilibrium of force in society does not exist.

XI. Justice, Self-Interest, and Dissensus

In Section X, I followed Buchanan in failing to distinguish between opposition (to an existing distribution) based on self-interest, and opposition (to an existing distribution) born out of a sense of justice. In *The Limits of Liberty*, Buchanan is noncommittal about this: he says he is simply

---

[104] *Ibid.*, p. 85.
[105] Hume, *Treatise*, Bk. III, Part II, section ii, p. 490.

trying to see how far one can get with a rational-choice analysis without invoking external moralistic norms.[106]

In a later book, his position is more aggressive. He suggests that "justice"-talk is nothing but a dressed-up way of saying "I like it," and that its introduction "spells the end of rational discourse." Such sentiments, he says, are best analyzed in rational-choice terms like any other expressions of self-interest.[107] This reductionism has been roundly criticized by Brian Barry:

> It is rather strange that "rational discourse," for Buchanan, entails jettisoning everything that might normally be thought of as constituting rational discourse (such as arguments about the justice or injustice of alternative arrangements). . . .[108]

And others have suggested that there are limits to our ability to represent sentiments of justice as personal preferences without distortion.[109]

Even so, Buchanan has a point. Sentiments of justice may not be exactly like personal interests; but conflicts among incompatible sentiments of justice are at least as intractable as conflicts of interest, probably much more so. Nothing that I have said in the last four sections about the inability of the Humean theory to properly characterize distributive justice detracts from my argument earlier, in Section III, that theories which make justice central face enormous difficulties about moral dissensus. People disagree about the standards appealed to in Lockean and Rousseauian theories: the standards of occupancy, labor, and fair trading; or the standards of equality, need, and desert. For all that these principles are put forward under the banner *"Fiat iustitia, ruat caelum,"* there is no agreement whatever among their respective proponents about the exact nature of the value for whose sake we should allow the economic heavens to fall.

At its best, the Humean model is put forward as a response to that difficulty. Like all good theories of politics, it recognizes that not man, but men, inhabit the earth[110] — not moral philosophy, but dozens of quarreling philosophers. There is no question of our being in a position to determine the distribution of property on the basis of justice. A single tyrant might predicate property rights on some single standard of justice, but *we*, in our plurality, cannot do that, for no one such standard can be sin-

---

[106] Buchanan, *Limits of Liberty*, p. 80.

[107] James Buchanan, *Freedom in Constitutional Contract* (College Station: Texas A&M Press, 1977), pp. 82–83.

[108] Barry, *Theories of Justice*, pp. 174–75.

[109] Amartya Sen, "Rational Fools: A Critique of the Behavioral Foundations of Economic Theory," *Philosophy and Public Affairs*, vol. 6 (1977), pp. 317–44.

[110] See Hannah Arendt, *The Human Condition* (Chicago: University of Chicago Press, 1958), p. 243.

gled out as *ours*. Of course, we can vote on the matter or fight over it, but — to be realistic — what will prevail as a result will be "the views of the majority" or "the views of the victors" and not "the best theory of justice" as such. The point is that if we are prepared to accept *that* sort of arbitrariness, why not accept the arbitrariness implicit in the Humean model, which at least has the additional benefit of predicating itself upon stability and involves the lowest transaction costs in moving from the status quo?

That is the best case I can present for the Humean model (though I am not sure it is ultimately convincing). It has the advantage over Locke and Rousseau of taking moral pluralism seriously, and it has the advantage over Hume's own theory, and Buchanan's too, in its open acknowledgment that any settlement of property will be accompanied by undercurrents of justice-based resistance. It rests its case, in the end, on the intractability of the disagreements that persist among the partisans of justice, rather than on the peremptory dismissal of their partisanship as "frivolous" or "indifferent" [111] or as merely "empty arguments about personal values." [112]

Jurisprudence and Social Policy, University of California, Berkeley

---

[111] Hume, *Enquiry*, Appendix III, p. 309n.
[112] Buchanan, *Freedom in Constitutional Contract*, p. 83.

CORRECTIVE JUSTICE AND PROPERTY RIGHTS

By Jules L. Coleman

Suppose the prevailing distribution of property rights is unjust as determined by the relevant conception of distributive justice. You have far more than you should have under that theory and I have far less. Then I defraud you and in doing so reallocate resources so that our holdings *ex post* more closely approximate what distributive justice requires. Do I have a duty to return the property to you?

There are many good reasons for requiring me to return to you what I have taken. One is that while you may have no right in justice to all that you own, it does not follow that I do, or that I have a right to take it. Thus, requiring me to return the property to you is a way of recognizing that I had no right to take it from you in the first place.

If I have no right to take your property, then justice might require that I give up my unjust enrichment. It hardly follows, however, that I should turn over my gains to you, since, *ex hypothesi*, you have no "right" to them either.[1] Perhaps I should be made to deposit my ill-gotten gains in a public coffer created for the purpose of general redistribution. One thing we might be tempted to say about a practice of compensation, then, is that it cannot be a requirement of justice if the underlying property rights that are sustained by it do not themselves conform to the requirements of distributive justice. Compensation is a matter of justice only if the underlying property rights scheme that is sustained by such a practice is itself required by justice.[2]

If compensation is demanded by justice only if the underlying property rights are themselves required by distributive justice, it will be difficult to understand important legal practices, especially tort law, as expressing or implementing demands of justice. That is because the prevailing distribution of property rights is probably not the one required by the best conception of distributive justice. Perhaps our tort practice is best understood on, broadly speaking, consequentialist grounds. How is that?

Even if doing so has the effect of sustaining an unjust distribution, making compensation or repair can be justified in order to discourage individuals from making matters worse by taking redistribution into their

---

[1] To clarify: You have no right to them in the best theory of distributive justice. The purpose of this essay is to determine the conditions under which you would have a certain kind of "right" to the property: a right that is sustainable by corrective justice, even if it is not one that follows from the best theory of distributive justice.

[2] See Section II for an argument against this claim.

own hands. To be sure, sometimes agents are in the best position to real-locate resources privately. This occurs in the typical voluntary exchange, sanctioned by the law of contract, in which individuals have adequate information about, among other things, their preferences. On the other hand, individuals may not be in the best position to *force* transfers in the name of distributive justice, since most individuals lack the information necessary to produce "justice-enhancing" forced reallocations, and many are poorly motivated to try. Worse, efforts to force private redistribution are likely to be met with private resistance, with its attendant injury, loss of additional property, and loss of life. Therefore, someone who takes from another has to make repair even if the taking in a particular case makes matters better (from the point of view of distributive justice), sim-ply because individuals cannot be counted on to make matters better in the aggregate or over the long term. Requiring compensation discourages private redistribution.

Interestingly, requiring compensation does not discourage private redistribution altogether. Suppose that the "taker" values the property more than does the property right holder. Then, the taker will be better off even after he compensates the property right holder than he was before the taking. Because he gains by the taking, the "injurer" will not be discouraged from engaging in private redistribution by a practice requiring him to compensate for his taking. A practice requiring compen-sation for harms to property rights will not fully discourage forced, pri-vate redistribution.

Moreover, it is not obvious that coercive private redistribution should be stifled completely. In the typical voluntary exchange, adequately informed individuals reallocate resources between or among themselves. This private reallocation is normally justified because it is voluntary and the participants are sufficiently knowledgeable about their preferences to insure that the transaction is mutually advantageous. Voluntary ex-changes among informed, rational agents are generally welfare enhanc-ing. One way of looking at an exchange is to view the parties to it as "taking" but compensating *ex ante*, where the terms of compensation are set by agreement. Both contract and forced, but compensated, transfers involve the same elements: "taking" and "compensation."

From the welfare-maximizing perspective, the difference between con-tract and forced, but compensated, exchange, is that in the latter case, compensation occurs *ex post* and its terms are set by a third party (typi-cally a court), whereas in the former case, compensation is established *ex ante* by mutual agreement. As long as the compensation is adequate, both kinds of transfers produce net gains.

By requiring compensation for takings, each potential taker (or "forced transferrer") is put in the position of determining whether he will bene-fit sufficiently by harming another to make it worth his while to do so. In order for someone rationally to decide, he will need sufficient information about his benefit schedule and the damage schedule of his victim. When he has the relevant information, he may find it rational to force a "mutually advantageous transfer."[3]

If individuals have the kind of information about their private interests and preferences that justifies allowing them to reallocate resources voluntarily (via exchange), then a practice of requiring takers to compensate property right holders will encourage individuals to gather information regarding benefit and damage schedules. It will also allow those with adequate information about their preferences and the damage schedules of property right holders to force transfers that, because they are welfare enhancing, are justified on certain kinds of consequentialist grounds. What the practice of compensation does is discourage wealth- or welfare-reducing transfers: precisely those forced transfers that are, from this perspective, undesirable.

From the welfare-maximizing perspective, the choice between exchange and forced transfer depends on the difference between transaction and compensation costs, not on the relative voluntariness of the transaction. Typically, but not always, voluntary exchanges are less costly than forced ones, and are preferable on those grounds.[4] There is a natural connection between our practices of voluntary exchange and forced, but fully compensated, transfers. Under differing empirical circumstances, both practices allow resources to move to more highly valued uses. If this is correct, then the best way of looking at our prevailing practice of requiring individuals to compensate the victims of their takings is that doing so allows the value of those resources to rise when circumstances do not permit voluntary exchange, or when the costs of voluntary transfer exceed the costs of *ex post* compensation.

It would be a mistake to deny the power of consequentialist arguments for our current legal and moral practices. On the other hand, we should not abandon the possibility of understanding our current practices as reflecting or implementing certain demands of justice. The plausibility of this line of argument depends on the claim that individuals can have a moral duty to support institutions that are not themselves fully just. And that is precisely the argument I want to make. Repairing certain losses can

---

[3] It is a little misleading to refer to forced transfers as "mutually advantageous," even when full compensation is paid. That is because the victim does not ordinarily gain from the transfer, even when he is fully compensated. Instead, he is made indifferent between his *ex ante* and *ex post* positions. This problem can be easily fixed in either of two ways: To insure that forced exchanges are in fact mutually advantageous, compensation should exceed what it would take to render a victim indifferent between his *ex ante* and *ex post* positions by epsilon (or one dollar, say); or instead of referring to forced, but fully compensated, transfers as mutually advantageous, we might simply refer to them as welfare-enhancing transfers in which no one is made worse off.

[4] A voluntary exchange that involves many bargainers all capable of behaving strategically can be more socially costly than a forced transfer in which compensation is not subject to negotiating and is instead set by a third party.

be a requirement of justice even when the net effect of doing so is to sustain a less than fully just allocation of property rights.

Not every distribution of property rights, however, can be sustained by a practice of corrective justice. Thus, the burden of this essay is to set out the conditions under which a property rights scheme can be sustained by corrective justice. This will require quite a few preliminary distinctions and substantial groundwork. Indeed, the bulk of the argument sets out the relevant conception of corrective justice. I reach the problem of specifying the relationship between corrective justice and property rights only in the last section, and then only in a preliminary fashion.

I. CORRECTIVE JUSTICE

What are the conditions that a scheme of property rights must satisfy in order for it to be sustained by a practice of corrective justice? Answering this question, even in a preliminary fashion, requires a conception of corrective justice; I will draw on the conception of corrective justice I have defended in my recent book *Risks and Wrongs*.[5] According to corrective justice, individuals have a duty to repair the wrongful losses for which they are responsible. Thus, any conception of corrective justice requires conceptions of *loss*, *wrongfulness*, and *responsibility*.

A. Loss

A *loss* is a diminution in an individual's welfare or well-being as judged relative to an appropriate baseline.[6] So conceived, a loss is the kind of thing that can give rise to reasons for acting. The fact that you have suffered a diminution in welfare—that you have been rendered worse off than you otherwise would have been (as determined by the relevant baseline)—is the sort of fact about you that could provide me with a reason for acting, for doing something with respect to alleviating your current state. Sometimes, losses give everyone reasons for acting. Thus, in a community of a certain type, the fact that all your family possessions have been destroyed by a flood, or by some other natural disaster that you could have neither guarded against nor otherwise anticipated, may give everyone else in the community a reason for contributing to a general fund that will help you get back on your feet.

On other occasions, the losses you suffer may give some individual a reason for acting, a reason that no one else has to come to your aid or to

---

[5] Jules L. Coleman, *Risks and Wrongs* (New York: Cambridge University Press, 1992), esp. chs. 16–20.

[6] It does not matter for my immediate purposes which formulation—welfare or well-being—we use, nor does the general account presuppose any particular conception of what is to count as the appropriate baseline.

alleviate your condition. If I have caused your loss, then I may have a reason to do something about alleviating your condition that no one else has.

Different principles and practices connect individuals with the losses that others have suffered. In order for a particular person to be connected with another's loss via the principle of corrective justice, the loss itself must be *wrongful* and the individual in question must be *responsible* for it. Other practices can give rise to agent-specific reasons for acting in which neither the wrongfulness nor the responsibility condition may be satisfied. Thus, if I unintentionally knock you down as the result of an unanticipated, involuntary muscular twitch, then I may have a duty to lift you up, to apologize, or, if necessary, to assist in finding emergency help, and so on. I may have these agent-specific reasons for acting even though your loss is not wrongful in any obvious way, and even though it is at least arguable that I am not morally responsible for it.

The duty imposed by corrective justice — namely, to render compensation — requires not just a loss, but a wrongful one, and not just causation, but responsibility. This means that we need an account of what makes a loss wrongful as well as an account of what it means to be responsible for a wrongful loss.

B. Wrongfulness

A loss is *wrongful* in the sense required by corrective justice if it results either from *wrongdoing* or *a wrong*. Wrongdoing is conduct that falls below the relevant norm or standard of behavior. If individuals ought to exercise reasonable care, then failure to do so constitutes a kind of wrongdoing in this sense. Individuals can fail to exercise reasonable care without harming anyone, without invading anyone's rights. In contrast, someone wrongs another whenever he invades that person's rights. Thus, wrongdoing is a failure to comply with a relevant norm; a wrong is an action contrary to another's right. Conduct that is wrongful because it involves either wrongdoing or a wrong can give rise to wrongful losses, losses for which those responsible can incur a duty to repair in justice.[7]

---

[7] Since wrongs are invasions of rights, we have to understand what it is to have a right in order to understand what it is to commit a wrong. In understanding rights, the important distinction is between their *content* and their *structure*. The structure is the analysis of rights, an account of what is analytically true of rights — what it means, in other words, to have a right. Some (like Joel Feinberg) hold that rights are *valid claims*; others (like Joseph Raz) argue that rights are *normative grounds of duties*; still others (like Ronald Dworkin) claim that rights are *trumps in political arguments*.

Suppose that Feinberg is correct; what is true of rights analytically (that is, as part of their structure) is that they are valid claims. It is one thing to note that rights are claims; it is another to reveal the particular claims individuals have. That will depend on the *content* of the specific rights individuals have and the substance of the particular claims associated with each individual right or with rights of certain types. The kinds of valid claims that comprise rights will range over various domains. Thus, if someone has a property right of a certain kind, that will entail that he has valid claims regarding, among other things, the terms of

Wrongs are invasions of rights. Whether a particular act constitutes a wrong depends on the content of the relevant right. If I take something of yours over which you have the power to exclude and alienate, then I wrong you. On the other hand, if I take something of yours over which you have a power only to demand compensation, then (provided I compensate you) I have not wronged you.

If I act contrary to your right, then I wrong you *whether or not I am justified in doing what I did*. I may dock my boat at your slip to protect my family from an impending storm even if I have no right to do so without your permission. Suppose you refuse me permission. Then it is possible that I could be justified in my action even though it is invasive of your rights. There are many examples of this sort, including the famous torts case of *Vincent v. Lake Erie*.[8] This suggests a distinction between two ways of invading rights: *violating* and *infringing* them. Infringements are justifiable or permissible invasions of rights; violations are wrongful invasions of rights. Violations are not only wrongs; they are wrongdoings as well. That is, they fall below the relevant standard of acceptable behavior, and that is just another way of saying that they are unjustifiable departures from the background norms. Infringements are wrongs; but they are not wrongdoings. An infringement involves conduct that is permissible, sometimes justifiable, and, perhaps, even laudatory on balance.

We also distinguish between rights and interests. Rights are special ways of protecting legitimate interests. Not all interests rise to the level of rights. Both rights and interests can be set back or harmed. The harm-

---

its transfer. The terms of transfer specify the conditions that must be satisfied in order for transfers of resources to comply with the constraints imposed by rights. The terms of transfer constitute what I call the *transaction domain*.

Whereas the structure of rights is given by a philosophical account of what it is to have a right, the content of rights is given by a *normative* theory of rights that specifies, among other things, the terms of legitimate transfer. If I have a right to a resource of some sort, say, a painting, part of what that means, *its structure*, is that I have certain claims with respect to the painting. This tells me nothing yet about the specific claims or powers I have with respect to the painting. I might have the power to exclude others from viewing the painting other than on terms agreeable to me; or I might only have the power to charge people a fee for viewing it. I might have the power to set that fee, or I might have to accept a fee set by an agency of some sort. I might have the power to sell the painting and to exclude others from taking it without my consent. Or I might have the power to sell the painting, but not to exclude others from taking it, provided they compensate me. I might have the power to determine the level at which compensation is to be set, or I might have to accept compensation determined by an art agency. And so on. All of these possibilities are compatible with the claim that I have a right to the painting. They differ with respect to the content of that right, the powers the right confers on me, and the constraints it imposes on others.

The content of rights depends on the underlying normative theory of rights. Suppose that the point of having rights is to promote welfare understood in, broadly speaking, utilitarian terms. Rights are valuable to the extent they are welfare maximizing. The norms governing transfer of rights will then reflect the goal of welfare maximization. Thus, the constraints imposed by rights, the powers and claims conferred by them, will be sensitive to empirical conditions and their possible impact on utility.

[8] 109 Minn. 456, 124 N.W. 221 (1910).

ing of a legitimate interest can create a wrongful loss only if it is the result of another's wrongdoing; the harming of a right can occasion a wrongful loss whether or not the conduct of another is wrongful or at fault. Wrongful losses can result either from wrongs, that is, invasions of rights, or wrongful harming of legitimate interests. The latter kind of wrongful loss depends on the injurer having done something wrong or unjustifiable, the former does not: indeed, it is compatible with the agent's conduct being morally desirable on balance.

There is a normatively significant feature of the difference between interests that are rights and those that are not. If you set back an interest of mine that is not a right, I have been harmed; I may well suffer a loss, but not necessarily a wrongful one. In order for my loss to be wrongful, you would have had to set back my interest unjustifiably, impermissibly, or wrongfully. Only then would the loss I might suffer as a consequence be wrongful.

If, in contrast, you were to harm an interest of mine that is a right — in other words, if you were to wrong me — then whatever losses resulted would be wrongful in the sense required by corrective justice. More importantly, it would be no defense against your duty to make repair to point out that you were justified in what you did. So if I had a right to a successful career, pointing out that my work is full of mistakes would be honorable, but would nevertheless constitute a wrong to me. In the case of interests that are rights, it is not part of my claim to repair that you acted impermissibly, whereas in the ordinary case in which I have a legitimate interest, but no right, that is precisely what I need to show. By the same token, you can free yourself of the duty to make repair by showing that you acted permissibly or justifiably in the case of a harm to a legitimate interest, but your efforts will be to no avail if my interest is a right.

C. Responsibility

The concepts of wrongdoing and wrong implicated in corrective justice are not those of *moral* wrongdoing and *moral* wrong. Consider the latter first. A person can wrong another by acting in morally justifiable ways, by permissibly invading the rights of others. The conception of a wrong, therefore, does not suggest that the agent has acted in a morally reprehensible fashion. If the point of offering an *excuse* is to show that one's conduct is not morally blameworthy or reprehensible, then such an excuse is irrelevant to determining whether conduct is a wrong — at least from the point of view of corrective justice. If it is irrelevant to determining whether conduct is a wrong, it is irrelevant to determining whether a loss is, in that sense, wrongful. The same is true of conduct that is wrongdoing. Recall that conduct is wrongdoing if it falls below the relevant standard of conduct. It is one question whether conduct falls below the relevant norms; it is another whether the actor is to blame for this failure, whether the fault in his conduct marks a moral fault in him. The point of corrective justice is not to penalize or punish the agent for his conduct, but to recognize the *victim's loss* as wrongful and worthy of repair. The question is whether the victim's loss is morally significant; it is not whether the injurer's conduct is morally culpable. The primary role of wrong and wrongdoing bears on assessing the kind of loss the victim has suffered, not the kind of character the injurer has exemplified.

Culpability is not a condition of corrective justice; responsibility is, however. Corrective justice imposes a *duty* of repair on those *responsible* for the wrongful losses of others. And does not the notion of responsibility presuppose that the agent has no excuse for his conduct, for his wronging or wrongdoing?

Once again, we need to draw a distinction—this time between two different kinds of excuses: those that, if sound, defeat ascriptions of *blame*, and those that, if sound, defeat ascriptions of *agency*. Excuses of the first sort are typically offered to show that the agent's action does not exemplify a defect in his character or motivation. Excuses of the second sort are designed to show lack of volition. So if I hit you, but only because I was pushed by someone else, then although it was me who hit you, my doing so was the result of no action of mine. The consequences of my *actions*, in contrast, are my responsibility even when they do not evidence a defect in my character or motivation. I am, in the normatively interesting sense, responsible for them even if I am not to blame for them. Thus, excuses that defeat agency are relevant to corrective justice, even when those that defeat culpability or blame are not. Corrective justice *connects* agents with losses by the criterion of responsibility. Excuses that defeat agency sever the relationship between loss and agent. Other excuses that admit agency, while denying culpability, are therefore irrelevant.

The next question is whether agency is all that is required to connect an actor with a wrongful loss—whether agency is enough in the sense of sufficient under corrective justice to make another's loss the agent's responsibility. It is not. To see this, consider a rather straightforward counterexample to the claim that it is.

Suppose the actions of both Mike and Ike are causally necessary for the loss that Pike suffers, but that only Ike is at fault: only Ike, in other words, has failed to exercise due care. In that case, Pike has suffered a loss owing to the wrongdoing of another (Ike). His loss, therefore, is wrongful. That loss is connected by the principle of agency with the conduct of both Mike and Ike, in the sense that it would not have occurred but for the conduct of both. There is wrongful loss and there is agency (in both Mike's and Ike's actions). Were causal agency sufficient to connect actors with others' wrongful losses under corrective justice, Mike, as well as Ike, would then be connected to Pike's loss in a way that would impose a duty to repair on both of them. And this seems wrong. Mike's conduct contributed to Pike's injury, but he did nothing wrong. It is not

Mike's conduct that makes Pike's loss a wrongful one. It is Ike's. This suggests that more than agency or causal power is required by corrective justice as a link between injurers and wrongful losses.

Someone can be *responsible* for a loss in the sense required by corrective justice only if the loss is *his fault*. So what we need is an account of the truth conditions (or assertability conditions) of sentences of the form: Such-and-such harm is so-and-so's fault. My tentative suggestion is the following.

A loss L is some individual S's fault if and only if:
(1) S is at fault (that is, his conduct falls below the appropriate norm).
(2) That aspect of S's conduct that is at fault is causally connected in the appropriate way to L.
(3) L falls within the scope of the reasonably foreseeable risks in virtue of which S's conduct is at fault.
(4) S does not have an agency-defeating excuse for his conduct.

This analysis is surely controversial, but let me briefly say something about important aspects of it. First, in the Mike-Ike-Pike example, the possibility of holding Mike liable in justice to Pike is eliminated by (1): Mike is not at fault. Therefore, Pike's loss cannot be his fault; and if it cannot be his fault, he cannot have a duty to repair it. Clauses (2) and (3) are designed to rule out perverse cases of the following sort. I go out driving and in the course of doing so my car hits yours. Now suppose that my driving is at fault because my rear brake-lights were broken. If my driving is otherwise flawless or reasonable, then your loss is connected to my driving, but it is not connected to that aspect of my driving that is negligent.[9] Moreover, there might be cases in which your loss is connected to that aspect of my driving that is negligent, but in which it is not the sort of loss that falls within the scope of the risks that lead us to think of the conduct as negligent or at fault in the first place. This analysis attempts to remove those cases from the realm of responsibility.

This analysis of responsibility for loss cannot apply in all cases involving wrongful loss. The reason is that in some cases — those involving infringements — there is no fault in the doing. Clause (1) is never satisfied. Instead, we need to focus only on whether the loss results from a rights-infringement and on whether the loss falls within the scope of the risks protected by the right. In other words, the questions we need to ask are: "Did the injurer's conduct invade the victim's right, that is, was it action contrary to the demands or constraints imposed by the right?"; and "Was the loss the victim suffered within the scope of the interests protected by that right?"

[9] If, however, your car rear-ended mine (due to my faulty brake-lights), then my negligence would have been responsible for *that*.

D. *Local justice*

We have accounts of both wrongful losses and the principle of responsibility. We do not yet have a complete conception of corrective justice, however. The reason is that corrective justice, unlike other principles of justice, is said to constitute a form of "local justice" — justice between the parties. We need to give some content to this aspect of corrective justice.

Suppose I make you a promise to meet you for lunch tomorrow, and suppose promises give rise to rights and duties of a certain sort. Then if I fail to show up, other things being equal, I have wronged you. I have not only done something wrong, in the sense of violating the norms governing promising, I have wronged you. If the wrong was simply breaking a promise, it would be problematic, some might say, that you should have a claim against me. No particular person can have a claim against me just because I have done something wrong. Some might say, then, that the reason you have a claim against me — whether to insist that I apologize or otherwise make amends — is that I have *wronged you*. And that is the essence of local, as opposed to global, justice; that is the essence of justice between us: I owe you something — I have a duty to you — because I wronged you.

This suggests that in order for a duty (or a right) in corrective justice to arise, there must be some sort of first-order right that already governs (normatively) the relationship between the parties, a right whose invasion provides the grounds for a claim in corrective justice to repair. Corrective justice is justice between the parties because it builds on, or is layered on, rights that already govern the relationship between the parties.

This conception of local justice is too narrow, however. It explains why certain private rights-violations give rise to duties in corrective justice, but it does not explain the connection between *wrongdoing* — in which no rights are involved — and corrective justice. The problem, then, is to square this fact about wrongdoing with the prevalent view of corrective justice as "local." In what sense can violations of "general" norms create local duties of repair?

My suggestion is that the *locality* of local justice does not have to do only with the *parties*; rather it has to do with the baseline or background norms governing wrongdoing within a particular community, and with "local understandings" of more general norms.

Norms that are general may depend on local practices and understandings for their content. In our culture, there is a general practice of restricting one's behavior so that it is not unreasonably risky to others. But the content of the norm varies; it is partially given by norms and conventions that arise within "local" communities of risk-takers. The actual standard of care imposes different substantive requirements depending on the community's conventions and local practices. So, to use an obvious example, reasonable risk-taking on a football field is different from reasonable risk-taking in a schoolyard during recess; and reasonable risk-taking during recess differs from reasonable risk-taking in the classroom.

American legal practice also recognizes this distinction by its reliance both on customary practice as a criterion of reasonable risk-taking and on the role of criminal statutes in setting *per se* negligence standards. The idea in the first case is that manufacturers in a particular industry, for example, are in the best position to determine what is reasonable practice among themselves. In the second case, the legislature is presumed to speak as the representative of the community as a whole over a relevant domain.[10]

It should be clear from these remarks that the notion of a "local" community is not a geographic one. It should also be clear that the notion of community is not identical with affective or intentional communities. It refers to groups of individuals whose interests bring them together in relevant ways—ways that make it important for each of them that all of them abide by certain reliable and enforceable practices. Such communities are defined by the norms that govern interaction among their members. They may be smaller or larger, more or less tightly knit, and so on. The sorts of norms whose violation can give rise to claims to repair in corrective justice are local in this sense. They are typically conventions and norms that arise within communities. It is in this sense that corrective justice is local justice, or justice between the parties.

If I fail to do what *distributive* justice requires of me, and if you, therefore, have less than you ought to have under the principle of distributive justice, and I have more than my share, then *distributive* justice says I have too much and you too little. It is distributive justice that says a correction is in order, not corrective justice as an independent moral ideal. By the same token, if I act inefficiently and impose inefficient costs on you, then it is efficiency that says a correction is in order, not corrective justice as an independent ideal. Not every justified correction is itself required by corrective justice. Corrective justice, in other words, grounds a subset of justified corrections. Put another way, all corrections are forms of *redistribution*. The case for redistribution can be grounded in distributive justice, efficiency, benevolence, utility, or corrective justice. (There may be other justifications as well.)

The norms enforced or sustained by corrective justice are local norms and conventions of the sort mentioned above. It is likely that these norms

[10] The relationship between community standards, custom, and criminal statutes, on the one hand, and negligence (or unreasonable risk-taking), on the other, is unsettled and quite controversial. Should custom, for example, *constitute* the standard of reasonable care? Or instead, should it establish the prima facie standard of reasonable care? Does it establish a rebuttable presumption of care? Or strong evidence of it? Or simply evidence? Or does it have no special claim at all? My point is that the content of even general norms can have an important "local" dimension in the sense that the duties the general norm imposes on individuals differ depending on the norm's content, and its content often depends on local understandings and practices.

will be efficient since their stability depends in part on the extent to which they are mutually beneficial, that is, wealth maximizing.[11] It is also true that they will be sufficiently fair or equitable to be stable within the community. Since the primary means of enforcement of informal norms within a community are also informal, reliance is typically placed on internalization and reciprocal private sanction. Thus, it would not be surprising to find that the norms governing, for example, reasonable risk-taking, within most liberal, nonoppressive communities are both relatively efficient and fair. But it is neither their efficiency nor their fairness that gives rise to the duty in corrective justice to repair losses resulting from their violation.

The problem is that corrective justice imposes *moral* reasons for acting. If neither the efficiency nor the fairness of the norms is necessary in order to sustain duties in corrective justice, what is? Put another way: What conditions must be satisfied in order for norms to be sustained by the imposition of duties in corrective justice? In order to be sustained by corrective justice, the norms must be local, that is, part of the background or baseline norms governing behavior within communities. But it hardly follows that "local norms" or conventions will necessarily give rise to moral reasons for sustaining or protecting them. What else must be true of them in order that a practice of corrective justice should apply to them? To answer this question, let us focus primarily on the local or conventional norms governing property rights or holdings.

II. Property Rights and Corrective Justice

One thing someone might hold is that corrective justice does not reach the underlying property rights or holdings. It applies only to the norms or practices governing the *transfer* of holdings. Suppose that the underlying property rights are both unfair and inefficient. Even so, we will need norms to specify the conditions of their transfer. These background or baseline norms are the ones sustained by a practice of corrective justice, not the norms that specify the property holdings themselves. This is just another way of saying that corrective justice is a dimension of *transactional* justice. The rights, wrongs, norms, and losses that are its concern are those governing transfer, not those governing the justice of the underlying claims. So it is simply a mistake to phrase the problem of corrective justice as we have: that is, as the question of what conditions must be satisfied in order that a scheme of property rights be sustainable by a practice of corrective justice.

Corrective justice only indirectly affects property rights schemes. It sustains transactional schemes or norms. We should have asked a different

---

[11] See Robert C. Ellickson, *Order without Law* (Cambridge: Harvard University Press, 1989).

question: namely, "What must be true of a scheme of transactional norms in order that they be sustainable by a practice of corrective justice?"

However plausible this line of argument may be, I reject it for at least two different reasons: one conceptual, the other normative. To the conceptual concern first: I reject the distinction between underlying rights and transactional "rights." On the account of rights given above, rules governing their transfer are part of the content of rights; transactional rights are part of the underlying rights, not distinct from them. Second, and more importantly, the normative concern: Corrective justice imposes *moral reasons for acting*. If it happens that applying corrective justice has the effect of sustaining a distribution of resources that is simply unjust, then how can an individual have a duty in morality to do so? To this question, it may be no answer to say that one does not have a moral duty to sustain an unjust system of property rights, but that one does have a duty to sustain a just system of transfer, even if sustaining the just system of transfer has the effect of sustaining an unjust system of property rights. Indeed, one might wonder whether a system of transfer could be just if sustaining it under normal circumstances had the effect of entrenching an unjust system of property rights.

I do not want to suggest that no arguments on behalf of some such position can be constructed. My point is the more modest one that in order to determine the conditions of being under a moral duty to make repair, we must determine what conditions, if any, would justify the practice of making repair in such cases. Thus, we cannot simply dissociate the duty to make repair from the status of the underlying entitlements and treat the latter as if it had no bearing on the grounds or content of the former.

Here is a schematic answer to the question of what conditions must be satisfied in order for a scheme of property rights to be sustainable by a practice of corrective justice: The rights sustained by corrective justice must be ones that justify their enforcement against infringements and invasions by the actions of others, *even if they would not be enforceable against the actions of a state seeking to implement the correct allocation of property rights under the best available theory of distributive justice*. This schematic answer is not without content, however. It implies, among other things, that the state has an authority—to redistribute for the purposes of implementing a just distribution of property holdings—that private individuals do not have. Suppose there exists a set of holdings that satisfies this condition. Then it would follow that even if an individual could further distributive justice by not paying compensation for a loss he wrongfully caused another (either by keeping his gain or by redistributing it in some other way), he would have no authority to do so; indeed, he would have a duty to repair in justice, whereas the state would be justified in not paying compensation. Of course, part of the reason the state would be free of the burden of compensation is that, unlike the private individual, it can implement the demands of distributive justice *systematically*, over the community as a whole. And part of what that means, at least implicitly, is that the state would be authorized to infringe a property right to implement distributive justice without owing compensation, provided it did so in a reasonably systematic fashion. And that is part of the reason why the state, in the United States at least, would have a duty of compensation under the "takings clause" of the Fifth Amendment to the Constitution even if the property it takes is not one that would be held by the "victim" under the best theory of distributive justice, and even if the point of the taking is redistribution according to that theory. The typical "taking" is not part of systematic redistribution aimed at implementing the correct distribution of resources.

The fact that the liberal state has an authority that private individuals do not have, and that it is one that depends in part on the state's ability to implement redistribution systematically, might help us to fill out the content of the principle stated above. Whatever their ultimate justice (or efficiency), schemes of holdings, and the norms regulating them, help to create stable expectations on which individuals can rely in coordinating their behavior with one another. Coordination allows individuals to create a framework of norms and institutions within which individuals formulate and execute projects and plans and pursue goals. Norms and institutions are essential, in other words, to personal autonomy and to individual and collective well-being. A scheme of property rights, of holdings secured by enforceable powers of exclusion and alienation, provides a good example. There is a wide range of possible principles according to which property rights might be allocated. Some of these are likely to be more just than others. A range of these, however, will serve reasonably well in providing the framework within which individuals can formulate meaningful projects and plans, and make the necessary investments to execute them.

The very idea of tying together autonomy in the formulation and pursuit of individual projects and goals with the framework of property rights suggests some constraints on the kinds of property rights schemes that are justifiable. They must provide individuals with an adequate range of opportunities and with the capacities to successfully pursue them (other things being equal). The scheme of norms cannot, moreover, be incompatible with the concept of autonomy; and part of what that means is that the scheme of holdings cannot be oppressive, or enforceable only through oppressive means. Beyond that, practical considerations, especially those of stability, will constrain the set of enforceable (by moral duties in corrective justice) property rights schemes.

In short, the basic idea I am reaching for is this: The set of property rights enforceable by duties in corrective justice need not itself conform with any abstract ideal or demand of distributive justice. The norms, and the rights they create, however, must be central to individual autonomy and well-being. The roles norms play in this regard are complex and connected. First, they create a framework within which individuals formulate and pursue their projects and plans. Second, they provide part of the wherewithal necessary to formulate and pursue those plans. Thus, any distribution sustainable by corrective justice must be stable and facilitate coordination, and it must provide the ingredients required by the liberal conception of autonomy. Any set of underlying property holdings that satisfies these substantive constraints is, I suggest, enforceable by duties of corrective justice.

Two final remarks: The first seeks to connect these substantive constraints with the notion of locality implicated in the principle of corrective justice. The norms that evolve among individuals within various communities allow coordination. Coordination provides individuals with a framework of reliable and stable expectations that, I have argued elsewhere, is necessary if investments in one's private projects are to be rational.[12]

The second seeks to connect these remarks about property rights with our initial concern about the relationship between corrective and distributive justice. At the outset, I said that I would defend the position that corrective justice could sometimes impose a moral duty to make repair even if doing so had the effect of sustaining a less than just distribution of resources. What I have argued is that distributions of resources that are less than ideal can be sustained by corrective justice. One way of interpreting my argument is that it is based on a distinction between "first" and "second" best conceptions of distributive justice. Corrective justice does not apply only to cases of first-best distributions of resources, nor will it apply to all second-best distributions. It will apply to some second-best sets of holdings, those in which certain threshold requirements are met. Those threshold requirements are themselves to be determined, at least in part, by the relevant first-best or ideal theory. If one has a theory of distributive justice of the sort I do — a theory that emphasizes human well-being and autonomy — then a practice of corrective justice can sustain a scheme of property rights provided that scheme sufficiently allows for individual autonomy, the possibility of human development, and the like. Instead of saying that corrective justice can sustain a property rights scheme that is not just, we might say that a practice of corrective justice can sustain second-best distributions of holdings or property rights that meet or satisfy threshold requirements of allowing for adequate autonomy and the possibility of achieving significant levels of well-being.

Jurisprudence and Philosophy, Yale Law School

---

[12] Coleman, *Risks and Wrongs*, esp. ch. 21.

PROVING OWNERSHIP*

By Gary Lawson

Philosophers and lawyers are apt to view property law from different perspectives. At the risk of gross overgeneralization, philosophers who discuss property rights tend to focus on the abstract principles that underlie ownership claims, while lawyers are more likely to focus on the practical problems of adjudicating concrete disputes within the constraints of a functioning legal system. Lawyers, for example, are likely to be more sensitive than philosophers to the real-world problems of *proof* that often accompany legal claims of ownership. For a lawyer, the key question is not whether any given theory of property rights is true in some metaphysical sense, but whether, *given* the theory of property rights employed by a particular legal system, a litigant within that system can *prove* an ownership claim to the satisfaction of an officially constituted tribunal.

Of course, this difference in perspective is largely one of emphasis. Philosophers with any interest in the real-world implications of their theories must be concerned to some degree with the concrete problems of proving ownership claims, and lawyers must pay some attention to the abstract principles that justify (or fail to justify) property rights.[1] But the difference in emphasis is important. The fate of a lawyer's client depends, not on what *is*, but on what can be *proved* under stylized conditions. Thus, while philosophers can choose to be truth-seekers if that is their inclination, lawyers qua lawyers must typically concern themselves with legal justification.[2]

Philosophers and lawyers considering the problem of proving propositions about ownership can gain by carefully reflecting on the lawyer's distinctive methods of justification. While much ink has been spilled by

---

* I am grateful to Ronald J. Allen and Patricia B. Granger for their characteristically insightful comments.

[1] Of course, the lawyer will be less concerned with the objective justice or injustice of those principles than with whether he can formulate rhetorically appealing arguments about justice that can maximize the client's wealth position. Or at least, if the lawyer intends to pursue abstract justice rather than maximization of the client's wealth, he ought to tell the (ex-)client before collecting his fee.

[2] *Legal* justification is simply justification within the confines of a given legal system. The principles that will justify a proposition for purposes of legal adjudication can be very different from the principles that will justify a metaphysical truth claim. For example, legal systems can and do, for policy reasons, employ evidentiary rules of admissibility that purport to forbid decision makers to consider much evidence that is metaphysically relevant. See Richard A. Posner, *The Problems of Jurisprudence* (Cambridge: Harvard University Press, 1990), pp. 205–6. Accordingly, legal justification is always relative to a specific legal system.

philosophers over the the centuries about the circumstances, if any, under which people can legitimately claim ownership rights over tangible or intangible entities, there has been surprisingly little discussion about the critical problem of selecting the appropriate *standards of proof* for evaluating propositions about ownership.[3] Standards of proof, however, are essential to analysis of propositions about property rights in at least three ways. First, one must know how to determine whether a particular theory of ownership—that is, a theory that specifies the actions and/or conditions necessary to establish an ownership claim—is known to be true *with enough certainty to warrant adoption by the legal system as a basis for generating legal rules*. Is it sufficient to produce legal obligations that a particular theory of ownership is merely better than its competitors, or must a theory meet some higher threshold of proof, such as a preponderance-of-the-evidence or a beyond-a-reasonable-doubt standard, before the law should act upon it? Second, given a theory of ownership that serves as the foundation for the selection of legal rules, one must know how certain the law must be that any proposed rule is in fact properly derivable from the governing theory before the rule will be given effect as law. Third, given a set of legal rules for evaluating ownership claims, one must know how certain the law must be that those prescribed conditions for ownership have been satisfied in a specific case before the putative owner will be afforded legal protection. Thus, standards of proof are critical to the selection of a theory of property rights, to the derivation of legal rules from that theory, and to the application of legal rules to concrete disputes.

Despite the central importance of standards of proof at all stages of inquiry, philosophers have been remarkably silent about the role of standards of proof in analysis of property rights. Even lawyers, who are trained to be sensitive to the importance of standards of proof, typically discuss standards of proof only in the context of the application of legal rules to concrete disputes, not to the selection of a theory of ownership or the derivation of legal rules from that theory. This narrow focus reflects our legal system's general tendency to pay close attention to standards of proof with respect to *factual* but not *legal* propositions. Once the legal system has chosen its abstract criteria for ownership, the question of whether those criteria are satisfied in a specific case is conventionally labeled by lawyers a question of *fact* ("If first physical occupancy establishes legal ownership, was *A* in fact the first physical occupant, and hence the legal owner, of *X*?"). Lawyers universally acknowledge that the law must specify a standard of proof for all relevant factual propositions in litigation.[4] Lawyers, however, have not been so quick to recognize that the justification of conventionally labeled propositions of *law* ("first physical

---

[3] At least, I am unfamiliar with any such discussions. I would welcome correction.

[4] In the American legal system, that standard can range from proof by a preponderance of the evidence (the ordinary rule in civil cases) to proof beyond a reasonable doubt (the rule in criminal cases for questions relevant to guilt).

occupancy establishes legal ownership") equally requires the selection of
an appropriate standard of proof. The legal criteria of ownership themselves, no less than the application of those criteria to specific cases, must
be justified in accordance with formal epistemological principles that
include the choice of a standard of proof as an essential element.

This essay explores some of the positive and normative problems posed
for property rights theorists by the inescapable need to employ standards
of proof in any act of justification. In Section I, I describe in general terms
the formal structure of justification, in the law and elsewhere.[5] In Section II, I show how that formal structure applies to the justification of
theories of property rights and to the derivation of legal rules from those
theories. In Section III, I examine the claim that the law should select the
best available theory of property rights and the *best available* legal rules that
can be derived from the chosen property rights theory. I demonstrate that
this "best-available-alternative" standard of proof, which tacitly drives the
American legal system and much scholarly discourse, is not inevitable:
the law can, and sometimes does, judge legal propositions in accordance
with more demanding standards of proof. Finally, in Section IV, I
describe the consequences of adopting for legal propositions about ownership a standard of proof that is more demanding than a best-available-
alternative standard. I then try to identify the normative considerations
that seem to be driving the law's sometimes peculiar treatment of standards of proof.

I do not purport to tell philosophers or lawyers which particular stan-
dard(s) of proof they should employ in any given circumstance, but I do
assert that any discussion of property rights must employ *some* standard
of proof. My goal is thus to bring some of the many problems pertaining
to standards of proof to the forefront of studies of property rights, where
they can receive the attention that they have so long deserved.

I. The Nature of Justification

Every lawyer knows the formal requirements for proving, or justifying,
a factual proposition in a legal proceeding.[6] First, you must present to
the trier of fact evidence that satisfies the law's stylized *principles of admissibility*, which in the American system are typically set forth as articulated
rules of evidence. Second, you must persuade the trier of fact to give the

---

[5] This discussion draws heavily on a prior essay in which I discuss in more detail the formal structure of justification and its significance for legal analysis. See Gary Lawson, "Proving the Law," *Northwestern University Law Review*, vol. 86, no. 4 (Summer 1992), pp. 859–904.

[6] Of course, the practical requirements may be very different from the law's formal
requirements. In some legal contexts, the best, or even only, way to "prove" a factual proposition may be to get the trier of fact either to ignore the evidence or to consider evidence
that the law deems formally inadmissible. My concern here is exclusively with the formal
structure of legal justification.

admissible evidence the appropriate degree of weight or significance. The law, by and large, does not prescribe a detailed set of rules for assigning significance to evidence, but it is obvious that some significance-assigning process must take place before the decision maker can reach a conclusion. The lawyer thus must invoke and apply *principles of significance*. Finally, the lawyer must convince the trier of fact that the evidence, taken as a whole, supports the relevant factual proposition[7] with whatever degree of certainty is legally necessary to enable that proposition to support a judgment for the lawyer's client. The requisite degree of certainty will be different in different contexts. In a routine civil case, the relevant facts must be established by a preponderance of the evidence by the party bearing the burden of proving them.[8] In a criminal case, facts relevant to guilt must be proved by the prosecution beyond a reasonable doubt. In other contexts, the law requires proof in accordance with some intermediate standard, such as a clear-and-convincing-evidence standard. Legal proof of the relevant proposition, in sum, must satisfy the applicable *standard of proof*.

The choice of a standard of proof can obviously affect the justifiability of propositions. Assume that principles of admissibility and significance are given: we know what counts as evidence for or against the truth of a proposition and how much weight that evidence deserves. Evidence for a relevant factual proposition that may (in accordance with those admissibility and significance principles) be sufficient to meet a preponderance-of-the-evidence standard, and hence to warrant liability in a civil case, may be insufficient to prove the same fact beyond a reasonable doubt, and hence insufficient to warrant a finding of guilt in a criminal case. Thus, principles of admissibility, principles of significance, and standards of proof are all essential to the legal justification of propositions.[9]

A moment's reflection will show that the law's structure of justification reflects something very fundamental about the nature of knowledge. *Any* act of epistemological justification involving *any* proposition in *any* intel-

---

[7] There is substantial debate within the legal community about how to define the factual propositions that need to be proved in adjudication. The conventional theory identifies a set of distinct propositional elements that, in conjunction, establish the plaintiff's case. Some scholars have suggested, however, that this conjunction-of-elements approach generates logical absurdities and cannot explain actual legal practice. See generally Ronald J. Allen, "The Nature of Juridical Proof," *Cardozo Law Review*, vol. 13, no. 2 (November 1991), pp. 373–422. These scholars suggest that the factual "propositions" that are actually passed upon at trial are comprehensive, integrated stories about events. For my purposes, it does not matter how one defines the relevant factual propositions that must be justified, as the formal structure of justification will be the same in any instance.

[8] The *burden* of proof is distinct from the *standard* of proof. The burden of proof identifies the party who must, as a normative matter, provide the relevant legal authorities with reasons to act or not act. The standard of proof, together with principles of admissibility and significance, defines the extent of that burden. The American legal system typically assigns the burden of proof to the party seeking legal action; a criminal defendant, for example, goes free unless proven guilty. Different legal systems could adopt different default positions.

[9] See Lawson, "Proving the Law" (*supra* note 5), pp. 867–71.

lectual discipline must employ the same formal structure that the law employs for the proof of facts. I can make no hard demonstration of this claim, but I have yet to find a counterexample.[10] Imagine any proposition, then try to imagine whether it is possible adequately to justify the proposition without answering each of the following three questions: "what did you count, or not count, as evidence of truth or falsity; how heavily did you count it; and how much evidence, and of what quality, did you require before making your claim?"[11] It seems intuitively clear that this tripartite structure embodies universalizable principles of justification.

II. Justification and Meta-Justification

If the structure of justification described above is indeed universalizable, it of course applies to both legal and factual propositions concerning property ownership or theories of property ownership. Neither philosophers nor lawyers, however, have adequately recognized that the selection of a standard of proof is therefore an indispensable, and indeed an inescapable, part of any attempt to justify propositional claims about property rights.

Philosophers have hotly debated the conditions under which claims of ownership can justifiably be made. They have argued about the kinds of events or actions that can constitute (or lead to) ownership claims and the degree of significance that should be given to these different events or actions. In my terminology, they have debated the appropriate *principles of admissibility and significance* for justifying claims of ownership. Competing theories of ownership present competing sets of such principles. How does one decide which, if any, of those competing sets of principles are worthy of adoption for any given purpose?

Plainly, if one is to choose among competing theories of property rights, one must have some meta-theory that prescribes how that choice should be made. One needs to know, in other words, how to recognize a correct theory of property rights when one comes across it.[12] In order for a meta-theory to perform this function of justifying the selection of a

---

[10] For an illustration of how standards of proof necessarily inform general philosophical discussions of epistemology, see *ibid.*, pp. 871–74 (examining the assumptions about standards of proof implicit in the Cartesian argument for skepticism and some of the responses thereto).

[11] *Ibid.*, p. 871.

[12] A wag might suggest at this point that we also need a meta-meta-theory that tells us how to evaluate meta-theories, and so on in an infinite regress. As with all epistemological regresses, the inquiry into foundations must end with criteria that are presupposed by any attempt to question, deny, or justify them (and which are therefore true beyond a rational doubt). In other words, we must ultimately ground all inquiry into property rights in axioms. See Lawrence C. Becker, *Property Rights: Philosophic Foundations* (London: Routledge & Kegan Paul, 1977), pp. 45–46.

theory or set of theories, the act of justification must conform to the formal epistemological requirements for justification. Thus, just as a theory of property rights must, at a minimum, specify what counts as evidence toward establishing a claim of ownership and how much significance that evidence should be given, any meta-theory that tells you how to choose among competing theories must also specify what counts as evidence, and how much it counts, for or against any particular theory. But admissibility and significance principles alone are not enough for an act of justification.[13] To say that a theory is correct — that it is justified in light of some meta-theory — is necessarily to say that the affirmation of that theory has met a *standard of proof* that warrants a conclusion of correctness. Therefore, the governing meta-theory for choosing among theories of property rights must specify the appropriate standard of proof for that choice: it must specify when enough evidence, as admitted and evaluated in accordance with the meta-theory's admissibility and significance principles, has been amassed so that a particular theory can be deemed correct.

The selection of a standard of proof profoundly affects the kinds of claims that can properly be made about various property rights theories. There are numerous competing theories of property rights that set forth different principles for determining ownership. It may well be that, given the admissibility and significance principles of the correct meta-theory, no single theory of property rights is correct *beyond a reasonable doubt*. If the beyond-a-reasonable-doubt standard is the appropriate standard of proof for evaluating theories of property rights, then in such a case no theory can be justified, and hence no theory can be proclaimed correct. It may even be the case that no single theory can claim to be supported by a preponderance of the evidence, and hence that no theory can claim to be correct even by that less-demanding standard. One can also readily imagine a circumstance in which one theory is supported by a preponderance of the evidence but not by evidence that is persuasive beyond a reasonable doubt. Thus, if the relevant principles of admissibility and significance for judging theories are stipulated, the choice of a standard of proof obviously determines whether the theory in question can be said to be "correct" or justified. This graphically illustrates that the choice of a standard of proof is implicit in any notion of "correctness" or justification. With-

[13] In nonlegal settings, inquiries into admissibility and significance tend to merge. The law often deems evidence inadmissible for reasons having nothing to do with metaphysical truth. For the philosopher, however, the only criterion of admissibility is relevance. If evidence has relevance, that means that it is epistemologically entitled to some significance in the decision maker's cognitive process. Nonetheless, one might have reason even in nonlegal settings to distinguish *whether* something counts as evidence for a proposition from *how much* it counts as evidence. A deontologist, for example, might want to say that consequentialist considerations are simply *inadmissible* in the proof of moral propositions, even if that is functionally identical to saying that such considerations are admissible but entitled to no significance.

out specification of a standard of proof, it is not possible even in principle to conclude a dialogue about property rights, as one will never know when to say "enough."

What is true of meta-theories with respect to standards of proof is obviously true of theories of property rights as well. Given the admissibility and significance principles of a specific theory of property rights, one cannot tell whether any asserted legal rule is justified by the theory unless one knows the standard of proof that such propositions must satisfy. To speak of justification without reference to a standard of proof is to speak nonsense.

III. Is the Best Alternative Good Enough?

An obvious answer to the standard-of-proof problem suggests itself, and indeed has been tacit in many discussions of property rights. While it is possible that no theory of property rights can satisfy either a beyond-a-reasonable-doubt or a preponderance-of-the-evidence standard, surely we can at least say, given a set of admissibility and significance principles for judging theories,[14] that some theories are *better* than others. Except in the most bizarre circumstances in which the evidence for two theories is precisely balanced, we should even be able to say that some one theory is the *best* among the available alternatives. And, one might argue, once we can say that a theory is best, surely there is no reason not to deem it correct. After all, the argument continues, we must choose *some* theory, and while it may be unfortunate that the best available theory does not meet a threshold of certainty as high as (for example) a preponderance-of-the-evidence standard, the only alternative is to choose a *worse* theory, which cannot be the right course of action. In other words, it takes a theory to beat a theory.[15]

While this argument is tempting, it does not withstand close analysis. It is simply not true that we *must* choose some theory of ownership. There is always the option of throwing up one's hands and saying "none of the above." Suppose, for example, that given a meta-theory for judging theories of property rights, there are ten plausible competing theories from which we may choose. Assume further that it is possible to assign numerical probabilities to each theory's chances of actually satisfying the

[14] Obviously, we cannot know whether any theory of property rights can meet any specific standard of proof unless we know the admissibility and significance principles that ought to be employed to judge theories. My goal in this essay, however, is solely to explore the standard-of-proof problem and to show that it exists *independently* of the particular admissibility and significance rules that one selects.

[15] See, e.g., Tibor R. Machan, *Individuals and Their Rights* (La Salle, IL: Open Court, 1989), p. xxxi: "The evaluation of a substantive theory must . . . be comparative. . . ." But see Becker, *Property Rights* (*supra* note 12), p. 33: "[T]he absence of a valid alternative proves nothing about the validity of the case at hand."

meta-theory's admissibility and significance principles.[16] Obviously, a theory can be the best available alternative under these circumstances while having barely a ten percent chance of satisfying the governing substantive criteria for a correct theory. It is hardly irrational to refuse to give assent to such a theory, even if all other theories are even more unlikely to satisfy the governing criteria. Pneumonia might be better than malaria, but one would not rush to embrace either alternative.

But, it might be countered, even if philosophers and scholars have the option of saying "none of the above" in such circumstances, the law does not. The law must resolve disputes, and it must select legal rules for resolving those disputes. Accordingly, it must select some theory for generating those legal rules. If a theory is not chosen directly, the argument continues, it will necessarily be chosen indirectly, so one might as well go with the best option available.

This argument, however, also has its problems, as can be seen by reexamining the law's approach to the proof of facts. Suppose that the plaintiff and defendant in a civil trespass action are arguing about whether the defendant (or instrumentalities for which the defendant bears responsibility) crossed onto the plaintiff's land. They agree completely about the governing legal rules; the defendant concedes that if the plaintiff can prove by a preponderance of the evidence that the defendant performed the alleged actions, the plaintiff can recover. Each side presents its evidence, makes its arguments about the evidence's significance, and awaits the jury's verdict.

In order for the jury to find for the plaintiff, it *necessarily* must conclude that a certain fact about the defendant's conduct is true with the requisite certainty specified by the law's governing standard of proof, which in this case is a preponderance-of-the-evidence standard. But in order to find for the defendant, the jury *need not* conclude, in accordance with the applicable standard of proof, that the defendant *did not* commit the acts in question. If they do reach such a conclusion, the defendant of course wins, but the defendant can win even in the absence of such a conclusion. Because the plaintiff bears the burden of proof, the defendant wins whenever the jury *reaches no conclusion at all* about the relevant facts. It is open to the jury to say, "Neither party has persuaded us by a preponderance of the evidence that its version of the facts warrants assent. Therefore, we choose to conclude nothing about what happened, and the plaintiff, who is affirmatively seeking the law's aid, loses the case." Hence, the law functions perfectly well by requiring factual propositions to satisfy a fixed threshold of proof, even though that standard can generate a choice among the proffered propositions of "none of the above."

---

[16] In reality, no such numerical measure is available, and any comparative assessment of theories must be ordinal. But an example cast wholly in ordinal terms would be much more difficult to construct and grasp. For a discussion of how standards of proof can be expressed in ordinal terms, see Lawson, "Proving the Law" (*supra* note 5), pp. 869–70.

There is no reason why the law could not also function with similarly demanding standards of proof for the selection of legal rules and for the selection of theories to generate legal rules. Consider the process of selecting legal rules, on the assumption that we know the admissibility and significance principles that ought to guide that process. It is clear from observation of the American legal system (though judges and scholars seldom discuss the issue) that, as a general matter, propositions of law are accepted by courts when they are the best available candidates to serve as the governing rules. But that is hardly an inevitable standard, and the legal system sometimes deviates from it. Propositions of *foreign* law, for example, must be proved by a preponderance of the evidence, and failure adequately to prove the applicable foreign law can result in dismissal of one's lawsuit.[17] Similarly, some jurisdictions require the government in criminal cases to prove relevant legal propositions beyond a reasonable doubt, just as it must prove relevant factual propositions by that lofty standard.[18] In principle, propositions about property, or any other legal subject, could also be evaluated in accordance with the same kinds of proof standards used in these other cases.

So why does the law, and in particular the law of property, not generally require legal propositions to be proved in accordance with the same standards of proof as factual propositions? The answer is not altogether clear, but it may lie in the consequences of large-scale application of such proof standards to legal questions. My final task is to explore those consequences and the normative questions they raise.

IV. Lawlessness versus Coercion

Consider a variation on the facts of the famous case of *Pierson v. Post*.[19] Pierson is hunting a fox, and the chase takes him onto wasteland of unknown ownership. Pierson succeeds in tiring out the fox, but before he can close for the kill, the fox is independently spotted by Post, Peters, and Petrov. All three shoot at the fox, one of them hits it, and the fox drops dead. Post is the first to reach and physically possess the fox's carcass. All four parties wind up in court to contest ownership of the fox. Pierson claims ownership by virtue of the chase, Post claims ownership by virtue of first physical possession, and Post, Peters, and Petrov all individually claim ownership by virtue of having fired the killing shot. Assume that there are no relevant regulations asserting a supreme governmental property right in wild animals. Who owns the fox?

---

[17] See *ibid.*, pp. 898–99.

[18] See Robert Batey, "Techniques of Strict Construction: The Supreme Court and the Gun Control Act of 1968," *American Journal of Criminal Law*, vol. 13, no. 2 (Winter 1986), pp. 133–35. I am profoundly indebted to Professor Batey for bringing these jurisdictions to my attention. It should be noted that Professor Batey saw before I did that the justification of legal propositions, at least in criminal cases, requires specification of a standard of proof.

[19] *Pierson v. Post*, 3 Cai. R. 175 (N.Y. Sup. Ct. 1805).

Clearly, under existing American law, none of these parties can claim by a preponderance of the evidence (or any higher standard) to be the rightful owner of the fox. *The owner of the land* is, with a very high degree of certainty, the rightful owner, because ownership of the land usually confers an exclusive right to reduce wild animals on that land to possession and ownership.[20] One option for the law is therefore to adopt a preponderance-of-the-evidence standard, throw all four parties out of court, and wait for the true owner to assert his or her rights. The effect of such a ruling would be to leave the status quo in place, at least for the moment. In our example, that means that the law would not interfere at this point with Post's physical possession.

Suppose that after such a ruling, Peters seizes the fox from Post and acquires physical possession. Post now runs to court asking for the return of his fox. "Ah," says Peters, "but it *isn't* your fox. It may not be mine either, but it certainly isn't yours. If the law would not entertain our earlier claims because none of us could prove a right to ownership by the appropriate preponderance-of-the-evidence standard of proof, there is no reason why the law should entertain your claim now." And indeed, the logic of the argument is the same. If the plaintiff cannot make out a case for recovery in accordance with the governing standard of proof, the law should not act. The law acts only when prompted to do so by legally justified claims, and the demands of legal justification have not, by hypothesis, been met in this case.

The effect of legal inaction is to leave physical possession where it lies. In such circumstances, successful self-help will always be rewarded. Of course, if the self-help efforts are tortious, perhaps because they result in a trespass or battery, the tortious self-helper will be liable for any damage caused by those torts, but presumably possession of the appropriated item will stay with the tortious self-helper until a plaintiff comes along who can prove ownership in accordance with the necessary standard of proof. A consequence of an absolute proof standard[21] for ownership may thus be to increase the number of instances in which the law affords no means for allocating ownership, leaving the parties essentially in a state of nature. Where the law cannot be proved, it effectively does not exist.[22]

The law has responded to this potential for gaps in legal coverage by

[20] See *Restatement of Property* (Philadelphia: American Law Institute, 1944), section 450, comment g, p. 2906.

[21] An "absolute" standard of proof is simply a standard which relies on criteria other than a relative ranking of the alternative propositions facing the decision maker. Functionally, a standard is absolute if it is possible in principle for all of the available alternatives to fail to meet it.

[22] This point is strongly made—and urged as a criticism of the use of absolute proof standards for legal propositions—by Larry Alexander in an essay responding to my earlier, more general treatment of standards of proof in the law. See Larry Alexander, "Proving the Law: Not Proven," *Northwestern University Law Review*, vol. 86, no. 4 (Summer 1992), pp. 907–11.

adopting a "best-available-alternative" standard for proving legal propositions about property ownership. Although some people describe ownership as a claim against the entire world,[23] the American law of property is prepared to accept considerably more modest claims as adequate grounds for forcible legal intervention. In a lawsuit between A and B, it is generally not necessary for A to show that he has an ownership claim against the entire world in order to prevail against B. It is enough to show that his claim is *better* than B's. If some third party, C, has a claim superior to A's, C can prevail in a separate lawsuit or as an intervenor, but B cannot normally invoke C's claim as a defense.[24] In other words, the law will determine the *relative rights* of the parties by passing judgment only on those alternatives directly available to it in the lawsuit at hand.[25] Thus, A must only prove, using whatever admissibility and significance rules the law prescribes, that "A owns X" is a better alternative than any other legal conclusion (e.g., "B owns X") presented to the court.[26] Hence, if Pierson can show that tiring out the fox, even if it does not establish a universally valid claim to ownership, establishes a *better* claim to ownership than does shooting the tired-out fox or seizing its carcass, the law will intervene on behalf of Pierson. Similarly, if seizure of the carcass establishes the best claim, Post wins. If shooting the fox establishes the best claim, Pierson is out and Post, Peters, and Petrov must resolve among themselves the *factual* question of whose bullet struck the killing blow. That is, once we have determined that whoever shot the fox has the best claim to ownership among the available claimants, we still must determine whether anyone can prove himself to be that person with the requisite certainty.

If we reach a stage where that latter determination must be made, however, the best-available-alternative standard ceases to govern. The law applies that relative standard to the selection of legal rules — that is, to the

[23] See Richard A. Epstein, "Property and Necessity," *Harvard Journal of Law and Public Policy*, vol. 13, no. 1 (Winter 1990), p. 3.

[24] For a comprehensive discussion of this general rule of the relativity of title, and the exceptions thereto, see Charles Donahue, Jr., Thomas E. Kauper, and Peter W. Martin, *Cases and Materials on Property: An Introduction to the Concept and the Institution*, 2nd ed. (St. Paul, MN: West Publishing Co., 1983), pp. 56–108.

[25] One can argue at length about when a legal alternative is "available" to a court in a particular case. Suppose, in our example, that the owner of the land, who we know with the requisite degree of certainty is the true owner of the fox, is not a formal party to the lawsuit but is known to the parties and the court. That is, we not only know *that* there is a true owner whose claim is superior to the parties' claims, but we know the *identity* of that true owner. Is such knowledge alone sufficient to defeat the claims of all of the actual parties? Some courts would say yes. See, e.g., *Barwick v. Barwick*, 33 N.C. 80, 81–83 (1850); Annotation, "Mere Possession in Plaintiff as Basis of Action for Wrongfully Taking or Damaging Personal Property," *American Law Reports Annotated*, vol. 150 (1944), pp. 186–89.

[26] One could argue that in these circumstances it is a mistake to discuss the issue in terms of *ownership*, as the law would merely protect *possession* as an independent interest. That is no doubt true, but it does not alter the analysis. The law still must determine which acts and events constitute possession, and that determination is subject to the same standard-of-proof considerations as are determinations regarding ownership in any larger sense.

determination of what actions or events generate legally recognizable claims of ownership. But once those legal rules are selected, the *factual* question of whether the conditions they prescribe have been satisfied by a particular litigant is governed by the preponderance-of-the-evidence standard that generally governs civil cases. If the evidence consists only of the fact that three guns fired and the fox died, it is doubtful whether any one of the hunters could show, by a preponderance of the evidence, that his bullet made the kill. (Of course, sophisticated ballistics evidence could perhaps resolve the question even beyond a reasonable doubt, but let us assume that no such evidence is presented.) Accordingly, the law could not conclude with the requisite certainty that any litigant satisfies the criteria demanded by the best available legal rule for determining ownership. One could either end the inquiry at that point and leave the fox with Post (as the law does when parties fail to carry their factual burden of proof after the law has been determined), or one could then move to the next best alternative legal rule, on the ground that the first proposed legal rule is not really "available."[27]

The law's schizophrenia concerning standards of proof, whereby it chooses legal rules on a best-available-alternative basis but resolves factual, or law-applying, questions on an absolute, preponderance-of-the-evidence (or higher) standard, is difficult to explain, partly because legal writers have expressly said so little about the problem. Nonetheless, it is possible to identify the competing considerations that no doubt drive the selection of these different standards. In favor of a best-available-alternative approach, one can invoke the dangers of lawlessness noted above. When the law does not provide some orderly means for choosing among competing claimants, self-help emerges as an attractive option, and the law has reasons for wanting to discourage self-help efforts by providing a reliable dispute-resolving mechanism. An absolute proof standard leaves open the possibility of situations literally ungoverned by law whenever no proposed rule can satisfy the relevant standard of proof.

On the other hand, in defense of the law's absolute standards for proof of facts, one can raise the moral concerns previously noted about engaging in forcible intervention without good reasons. When the law operates, it does so coercively. A valid judgment is an authorization for official agents of the legal order to use violence, if necessary, to enforce its terms. That is not a step that the law takes, or ought to take, lightly. One needs to have very good reasons for waving guns in people's faces, and concluding that some legal ruling is the best available alternative simply may not amount to sufficient reason. Indeed, it is not even obvious that a preponderance-of-the-evidence standard is strict enough to warrant such dramatic action as legal coercion. The law does not regard a preponder-

---

[27] Or conceivably the law could allow Post, Peters, and Petrov to pool their claims and split the proceeds. It is clear, after all, that *as a group* their joint claim is superior to Pierson's.

ance of the evidence on factual questions as adequate grounds for action in criminal cases, and it is not self-evident that a different standard ought to govern civil cases.

There are thus credible normative reasons to support both a best-available-alternative standard and an absolute proof standard of some sort. It is therefore not surprising that the law tries to have it both ways. But is adopting a lesser, or relative, standard of proof for legal (or law-determining) questions while maintaining an absolute standard of proof for factual (or law-applying) questions the only, or a satisfactory, way to reconcile these competing tensions? Recall that the justification of propositions about ownership requires three elements: principles of admissibility, principles of significance, and a standard of proof. When applied to property rights, the first two elements, which tell you what to look for and how much to count it, constitute what we ordinarily think of as a substantive theory of property rights. The law is worried that these principles, in conjunction with an absolute proof standard, might lead to numerous situations in which legal rules provide no resolution to disputes and thus lead to undesirable self-help efforts. But proof problems always result from the *interplay* between the substantive theory and the standard of proof. Thus, the law can accommodate those concerns about lawless situations either by adopting a lesser standard of proof *or by selecting admissibility and significance principles that generate clear outcomes even with a higher standard of proof*. The ability to generate clear outcomes, in other words, may be a *substantive* virtue in a system of legal rules for determining property rights. A meta-theory for selecting theories of property rights thus could specify that an ability to resolve, under an absolute standard of proof, all or most disputes that are likely to arise in the legal system is an important criterion in the theory-selection process. Hence, one can increase the dispute-resolving capacity of a legal system either by holding admissibility and significance rules constant and lowering the standard of proof or by holding the standard of proof constant and changing the admissibility and significance rules. There is no obvious normative reason to prefer one option to the other.

It may seem, however, as though changing the substantive theory to increase the system's dispute-resolving capacity is letting the tail wag the dog. Surely, one might argue, the legal system should conform to a correct theory of property rights rather than vice versa. The problems of administering a legal system just do not seem like the sorts of considerations that ought to be significant, or perhaps even admissible, in deriving a theory of property rights. But a *full* theory of property rights, if by that we mean a method for justifying propositions about ownership, must include a standard of proof. If administrative considerations are not legitimate considerations in selecting a legal system's admissibility and significance principles, it is hard to see how they could be legitimate considerations in selecting a legal system's standard of proof. Accordingly, one must either hold that both the substantive theory and the standard of proof should be selected on normative grounds that are independent of the practical needs of the legal system, or acknowledge that the practical needs of the legal system can, in principle, affect both the substantive theory and the standard of proof.

In sum, one can respond to consequentialist concerns about the ability of a system of property rights to resolve disputes in at least five ways. First, one can deny that such concerns have any relevance in selecting or administering a system of property rights, in which case one needs some independent normative justification for selecting the admissibility and significance principles and the standard of proof to be employed at any level of the inquiry. Second, one can accept those consequentialist concerns as relevant but deem lawlessness an advantage.[28] Third, one can treat concerns about lawlessness as legitimate, deny that they ought to affect the admissibility and significance principles for selecting legal rules, and maintain that the standard of proof ought to be chosen to accommodate these concerns. Fourth, one can hold the standard of proof constant and make the admissibility and significance principles for selecting legal rules bear the brunt of the load in enhancing the law's dispute-resolving capacity. Or fifth, one can let these consequentialist concerns affect one's choice both of admissibility and significance principles and of a standard of proof.

I have no firm view on which of these approaches is best (even if being "best" is indeed the appropriate standard of correctness in this context). But the law's present choice to treat admissibility and significance principles as constants while varying the standard of proof for propositions of law requires a justification that has not yet been provided. To the extent that scholars similarly bifurcate the treatment of admissibility and significance principles on the one hand and standards of proof on the other, they too owe an explanation for this practice. If standards of proof are somehow qualitatively different from admissibility and significance principles, the reasons for that difference are not to be found in the nature of justification.

Law, Northwestern University

---

[28] This position, however, requires not merely an aversion to state action but an aversion to organized legal action of any kind. Even an anarchist who believes that law should be privately administered has an interest in the law's dispute-resolving capacity.

ABORIGINAL PROPERTY AND WESTERN THEORY: RECOVERING A MIDDLE GROUND*

By James Tully

I. Introduction

During the last forty years, the Aboriginal peoples of the Americas, of the British Commonwealth, and of other countries colonized by Europeans over the last five hundred years have demanded that their forms of property and government be recognized in international law and in the constitutional law of their countries. This broad movement of 250 million Aboriginal people has involved court cases, parliamentary politics, constitutional amendments, the United Nations, the International Court of Justice, the development of an international law of Aboriginal peoples, and countless nonviolent and violent actions in defense of Aboriginal systems of property and cultures. The Aboriginal peoples of New Zealand, Canada, and the United States have been at the forefront of the movement, and it is in these countries that the greatest legal recognition has been achieved.[1]

I have come to the conclusion that many of the representative Western theories of property do not provide an impartial conceptual framework in which these demands for justice with respect to property can be adjudicated. Even the recent attempts to stretch some Western liberal theories to accommodate a plurality of systems of property do not give fair recognition to Aboriginal property.[2] However, it does not follow that there is no impartial conceptual framework available. I will argue that the constitutional common law of the British Commonwealth, Canada, and the United States does provide a form of recognition and negotiation of Aboriginal and European-American systems of property that meets the criteria of justice shared by both Aboriginal peoples and non-Aboriginal North Americans.[3] This form of conceptualization of property developed

* I would like to thank Ellen Frankel Paul and the other contributors to this volume for their exceptionally helpful comments.

[1] See Julian Burger, *First Peoples: A Future for the Indigenous World* (New York: Anchor Books, 1990), for an overview; see *ibid.*, p. 15 for the figure of 250 million, not including Africa. See also Augie Fleras and Jean Leonard Elliott, *The Nations Within: Aboriginal-State Relations in Canada, the United States, and New Zealand* (Toronto: Oxford University Press, 1992).

[2] See, for example, Will Kymlicka, *Liberalism, Community, and Culture* (Oxford: Clarendon Press, 1991).

[3] Although I believe my argument could be extended to other countries, this essay is restricted to Canada and the United States.

in practice during the early modern period and was given authoritative expression in the documents accompanying the Royal Proclamation of October 7, 1763, and in the Supreme Court decisions of Chief Justice John Marshall in the early nineteenth century. In the Royal Proclamation and the decisions of John Marshall, the ways in which Aboriginal and Western property in North America had been conceptualized in major European and European-American political theories were replaced by a fairer common-law alternative.

During the same period, the Aboriginal peoples, or "First Nations" as they are called in Canada, developed a form of mutual recognition and negotiation of French and British property in North America which is commensurable with the common-law tradition. The cross-cultural "middle ground" composed of early modern Aboriginal and common-law conceptions of the constitutional relations between their two systems of property, and their authoritative traditions of interpretation, is now being rediscovered and reconstructed by a young generation of Aboriginal and non-Aboriginal legal scholars, and is being employed to justify the property rights of the Aboriginal peoples of North America.[4] I do not mean to suggest that this Aboriginal and common-law system (as I will call it)[5] for the establishment and adjudication of property relations has been faithfully followed in practice by governments and courts since 1763. Quite the contrary. It has been criticized, denied, ignored, and violated many times.[6] Nonetheless, it provides a normative framework for property rights that meets both Aboriginal and non-Aboriginal criteria of justice.

The reason why many Western theories of property do not provide an impartial framework is that they share a set of assumptions which misrecognize the political organizations and property systems of the Aborig-

[4] See Joseph William Singer, "Sovereignty and Property," *Northwestern University Law Review*, vol. 86, no. 1 (1991), pp. 1–56; Charles Wilkinson, "Native Sovereignty in the United States: Developments during the Modern Era," in *Aboriginal Self-Determination*, ed. Frank Cassidy (Halifax: Institute for Research on Public Policy, 1991), pp. 219–32; Brian Slattery, "Understanding Aboriginal Rights," *Canadian Bar Review*, vol. 66, no. 1 (1987), pp. 727–83; and Brian Slattery, "Aboriginal Sovereignty and Imperial Claims," in Cassidy, ed., *Aboriginal Self-Determination*, pp. 197–219.

[5] "Aboriginal and common-law system" refers to both the Aboriginal and common-law modes of argument, authoritative traditions, and concepts, *and* the institutions of property and practices of cross-cultural negotiation these modes of argument are associated with. The *locus classicus* for this approach is Ludwig Wittgenstein, *Philosophical Investigations* [1953], trans. G. E. M. Anscombe (Oxford: Basil Blackwell, 1988), sections 240–42. See James Tully, "Wittgenstein and Political Philosophy: Understanding Practices of Critical Reflection," *Political Theory*, vol. 17, no. 2 (May 1989), pp. 172–204; and compare Philip Bobbitt, *Constitutional Interpretation* (Oxford: Basil Blackwell, 1991), pp. 141–77, and Dennis Patterson, "Conscience and the Constitution," *Columbia Law Review*, vol. 93, no. 1 (January 1993), pp. 270–307.

[6] For judicial and government deviation from the Aboriginal and common-law system, see Milnar Ball, "Constitution, Court, Indian Tribes," *American Bar Foundation Research Journal* (now *Law and Social Inquiry*), vol. 1 (1987), pp. 1–139; Robert N. Clinton, "The Proclamation of 1763: Colonial Prelude to Two Centuries of Federal-State Conflict over the Management of Indian Affairs," *Boston University Law Review*, vol. 69 (1989), pp. 329–85; and the works cited in note 4 above.

inal peoples. From the seventeenth century to the present, Western theories of property conventionally begin from one of the following three premises that purport to represent the initial conditions for thinking about property: (1) equal individuals in a state of nature, behind a veil of ignorance, or in a quasi-ideal-speech situation, prior to the establishment of a legal system of property, and aiming to establish one society; (2) individuals within a set of shared and authoritative traditions and institutions derived from European history; or (3) a community bound together by a set of shared and authoritative traditions and institutions. The suggestion of this essay is that a theory of property which begins from any of these three conventional and well-known premises of liberal, critical, and communitarian theory cannot be justly applied to reflect on property in Canada and the United States, because the premises misrecognize and occlude the initial conditions of property in North America. The initial conditions are that when Europeans arrived and began to establish systems of property, the Aboriginal peoples were already there, organized into First Nations with their own systems of property and authoritative traditions, many of which are over ten thousand years old. As Chief Justice Marshall classically stated in *Worcester v. the State of Georgia* (1832):

> America, separated from Europe by a wide ocean, was inhabited by a distinct people, divided into separate nations, independent of each other and the rest of the world, having institutions of their own, and governing themselves by their own laws. It is difficult to comprehend the proposition, that the inhabitants of either quarter of the globe could have rightful original claims of dominion over the habitants of the other, or over the lands they occupied; or that the discovery of either by the other should give the discoverer rights in the country discovered, which annulled the pre-existing rights of its ancient possessors.[7]

This would be of interest only to historians of political theory if the Aboriginal peoples had been subsequently and justly conquered or assimilated, and their original systems of property and government superseded; for then one, perhaps any one, of the three conventional premises would represent their (changed) status accurately. But this has not occurred. Neither the Aboriginal people themselves nor international law acknowledge the conquest, assimilation, or supersession of the First Nations.[8]

---

[7] *Worcester v. the State of Georgia*, 6 Peter 515 (U.S.S.C. 1832), p. 542, reprinted in John Marshall, *The Writings of Chief Justice Marshall on the Federal Constitution* (Littleton, CO: Fred B. Rothman & Co., 1987), pp. 426–27.

[8] For international law, see Maureen Davies, "Aspects of Aboriginal Rights in International Law," in *Aboriginal Peoples and the Law*, ed. Bradford Morse (Ottawa: University of Carleton Press, 1991), pp. 16–47, esp. pp. 37–40. Although there is agreement that the

Consequently, the initial conditions for theorizing and reflecting on property rights in America are of a (European) people who arrive on a continent of roughly five hundred established Aboriginal nations and systems of property and who do not wish to become citizens of the existing Aboriginal nations, but wish to establish their own nations and systems of property in accordance with their European institutions and traditions. The question of justice with respect to property is thus a question of political and cultural pluralism: How can non-Aboriginal systems of property be justly established under such conditions? This is the fundamental problem of property in North America properly stated – a problem for which, I will argue, there is a solution: the Aboriginal and common-law system. To imagine or presuppose that the conditions are a state of nature, a veil of ignorance, or an ideal-speech situation of pre-political and undifferentiated individuals, in which no system of property exists, or a set of authoritative European traditions and institutions, or an already existing community, is to beg the problem – it is to dispossess the Aboriginal peoples of their property rights, forms of government, and authoritative traditions without so much as an argument. The imposition of any one of these three premises constitutes the injustice.

The historical reason why the Western theories of property constructed on these three premises misrepresent the initial condition of property in North America is *not* that the theorists were uninterested in European settlement in America or unaware of the Aboriginal peoples of America and their systems of property. Just the opposite. One of the leading problems of political theory from Hugo Grotius and Thomas Hobbes to Adam Smith and Immanuel Kant was to justify the establishment of European systems of property in North America in the face of the presence of "Indian Nations." Almost all the classic theorists advanced a solution to this problem of justifying what was seen as the one of the most important and pivotal events of modern history. They constructed and used these three premises to justify European settlement on the one hand, and to justify the dispossession of the Aboriginal peoples of their property on the other. Substantial sections of the early modern theories are given over to trying to show that the three premises do fairly represent the initial conditions in North America – sections which are standardly overlooked today because the three premises are taken for granted. Hence, to understand how they misrecognize the initial conditions, and why Chief Justice Marshall repudiated them, it is necessary to survey the errors in the arguments and assumptions the classical theorists used to establish the premises.

Aboriginal peoples are not conquered, there is less agreement on what their status is. The United Nations' forthcoming declaration on the rights of indigenous peoples may clarify this. See *Discrimination against Indigenous Peoples: First Revised Text of the Draft Universal Declaration on the Rights of Indigenous Peoples*, U.N. Doc. E/CN.4/Sub.2/1989/33 (1989).

Accordingly, the remainder of this essay consists of three sections. Section II is a critical survey of the shared assumptions of representative theories of property used to justify the establishment of European property in North America. Section III is a recovery and reconstruction of the overlapping common-law and Aboriginal conceptions of their two systems of property and of the reasons for believing this normative framework meets both Western and Aboriginal criteria of justice. It provides a system for establishing and adjudicating property relations, by consent, in a genuinely bicultural and bilegal situation. Section IV seeks to show what effect this argument should have on property *theory* in North America today. Western theories of property are not invalid just because their premises misrecognize, in a biased manner, the initial conditions of property relations in North America. Rather, once their bias has been corrected, they have a legitimate role to play in the critical reflection on property in North America today, but only within the broader framework of the Aboriginal and common-law system.

One further introductory point is necessary to situate this essay in its appropriate context. There are two opposed views in the literature on Aboriginal property in North America. Some argue that the property systems of Canada and the United States are unjust, because they rest on the theft of Aboriginal property and the usurpation of Aboriginal governments.[9] The only remedy would be to overthrow the present systems of property. Others argue that the Canadian and U.S. systems are just, in virtue of the legal positivist principle of effective occupation and use over the last three centuries.[10] No remedy would be required. This essay can be said to present a third view somewhere between these two.[11] I agree with the proponents of the first view that many grave injustices have been and continue to be committed, and that the principle of effective occupation and use applies in the first instance to the Aboriginal peoples, rather than to the land claims of the Canadian and U.S. governments. It does not follow, however, that justice demands the overthrow of the present systems of property in the two countries. For the Aboriginal and common-law system is a normative framework that is just by both Aboriginal and non-Aboriginal standards. It has been consented to and

<hr/>

[9] See, for example, Ward Churchill, *The Struggle for the Land: Indigenous Resistance to Genocide, Ecocide, and Expropriation in Contemporary North America* (Toronto: Between the Lines, 1991); and John Howard Clinebell and Jim Thomson, "Sovereignty and Self-Determination: The Rights of Native Americans under International Law," *Buffalo Law Review*, vol. 27, no. 1 (1987), pp. 669–714.

[10] See, for example, L. C. Green, "Claims to Territory in Colonial America," in *The Law of Nations and the New World*, ed. L. C. Green and Olive P. Dickason (Edmonton: University of Alberta Press, 1989), pp. 1–131.

[11] For two different middle positions, see Russell Barsh and James Youngblood Henderson, *The Road: Indian Tribes and Political Liberty* (Berkeley: University of California Press, 1980); and Brian Slattery, "First Nations and the Constitution: A Matter of Trust," *Canadian Bar Review*, vol. 71, no. 1 (1992).

is immanent to some extent in the practice of the present systems of property, specifically in the treaty system. It thereby provides the already shared framework for the negotiated redress of claims to property in North America. (It is sufficient to note in passing that the claims of injustice advanced by the first view appeal to standards that are part of the Aboriginal and common-law system.) To say this is not to endorse the status quo, as the proponents of the second view conclude, but to reform it in accordance with its best standards.

II. WESTERN THEORIES OF PROPERTY

In this section, I seek to show how Western theories tend to misrepresent the initial conditions of appropriation in America; I do this by critically analyzing assumptions of some exemplary and influential theories. This critical survey provides the clarification necessary to appreciate the superiority of the Aboriginal and common-law system, which I reconstruct in the next section, and to see the appropriate place for Western property theory, suitably corrected, within the conceptual framework established by the Aboriginal and common-law system in the final section.[12] I start with John Locke because he gathered together many of the arguments of the early seventeenth century and because his theory set the terms for many of the later theories that were used to justify the establishment of European property in America. Also, it was Locke's theory that Chief Justice Marshall repudiated, in *Johnson and Graham's Lessee v. M'Intosh* (1823), before he put forward his alternative.[13]

A. Locke's theory

In the *Second Treatise* of the *Two Treatises of Government* (1690), Locke set out four sets of arguments, contrasts, and assumptions that were widely accepted and taken for granted by later theorists, providing the unexamined conventions of many Western theories of property. The four sets of arguments conjoin to misrecognize two conditions of Aboriginal peoples at the time of European arrival and settlement: their systems of property and their political organizations. I do not mean to suggest that all four sets of arguments have found their way into theories of property that start from any of the three premises set out in the introduction. The Lock-

[12] The argument of Sections II and III is constructed on the basis of detailed historical scholarship in two previous essays: James Tully, "Rediscovering America: The *Two Treatises* and Aboriginal Rights," in Tully, *An Approach to Political Philosophy: Locke in Contexts* (Cambridge: Cambridge University Press, 1993), pp. 137–78, and "Placing the *Two Treatises*," in *Political Discourse in Early Modern Britain*, ed. Nicholas Phillipson and Quentin Skinner (Cambridge: Cambridge University Press, 1993), pp. 253–82.

[13] *Johnson and Graham's Lessee v. M'Intosh*, 8 Wheaton 543 (U.S.S.C. 1823), pp. 567–71, reprinted in Marshall, *Writings of Chief Justice Marshall*, pp. 257–61.

ean arguments are most closely associated with theories constructed on the first premise. I do, however, wish to suggest that assumptions of some of the four sets of arguments have found their way into theories of property which start from the other two premises, and these assumptions function there to misrecognize Aboriginal property and political organization.

The first set involves the belief that Aboriginal peoples are in a pre-political "state of nature." The state of nature represents the "pattern" of a "first age" in a process of historical development all societies go through: "[I]n the beginning all the World was *America*." European societies represent the most advanced or "civilized" age in this process.[14] In the first age there is no established system of property or government and economic activity consists of subsistence hunting and gathering. In contrast, the European civilized age is characterized by established legal systems of property, political societies, and commercial or market-oriented agriculture and industry.[15] This first set of contrasts makes up the background assumption of the "stages view" of historical development which tends to be taken for granted in political (and economic) theory to this day.[16]

Second, the Aboriginal peoples of America, possessing neither government nor property in their hunting and gathering territories, have property rights only in the products of their labor: the fruit and nuts they gather, the fish they catch, the deer they hunt, and the corn they pick.[17] Unlike citizens in political societies, anyone in a state of nature is free to appropriate land without the consent of others, as long as the land is uncultivated and "there is enough, and as good left in common for others."[18] Illustrating his theory throughout with examples drawn from America, Locke draws the immensely influential conclusion that Europeans are free to settle and acquire property rights to vacant land in America by agricultural cultivation without the consent of the Aboriginal people:

> [L]et him [a European] plant in some in-land, vacant places of *America*, we shall find that the *Possessions* he could make himself upon the *measures* we have given, would not be very large, nor, even to this day, prejudice the rest of Mankind, or give them reason to complain, or think themselves injured by this Man's Incroachment. . . .[19]

[14] John Locke, *Two Treatises of Government*, ed. Peter Laslett (Cambridge: Cambridge University Press, 1970), *Second Treatise* (II), sections 14, 30, 49, 108, 109; the quote in the text is from section 49.

[15] *Ibid.*, II, 30, 38, 45, 50, 87, 107, 108.

[16] See Ronald Meek, *Social Science and the Ignoble Savage* (Cambridge: Cambridge University Press, 1976); and Tully, "Placing the *Two Treatises*," pp. 262–66.

[17] Locke, *Two Treatises*, II, 28, 30, 34, 36, 37, 41–43, 48–49.

[18] *Ibid.*, II, 27.

[19] *Ibid.*, II, 36.

It might appear from the phrase "vacant places" that Locke means that Europeans may cultivate and settle without consent only in those parts of North America that are not the hunting and gathering territories of the Aboriginal peoples. But the text will not bear this interpretation. Locke stipulates that he means by "vacant" land any land that is "uncultivated" or "unimproved" by labor: that is, land that is used for hunting and gathering is vacant.[20] The reason why the American Indians have no property in their hunting and gathering territories is that the title to property in land is "labor," and labor is defined in terms of European agriculture and industry: cultivating, subduing, tilling, and improving.[21] Consequently, the hunters and gatherers have no rights in the land and thus no reason to complain. Moreover, if the Aboriginal peoples attempt to subject the Europeans to their laws and customs or to defend the territories that they have mistakenly believed to be their property for thousands of years, then it is they who violate natural law and may be punished or "destroyed" like "savage beasts" by the European settlers.[22]

At the beginning of chapter 5 of the *Second Treatise*, Locke explains that the justification of appropriation without consent is the problem he sets out to solve, and he repeats twice that he has solved it.[23] The reason why the argument was so contentious is that it bypasses one of the basic principles of Western law, the principle of consent, or *quod omnes tangit ab omnibus tractari et approbari debet* ("what touches all must be agreed to by all"). This principle constrained most earlier theorists of European settlement to insist on deeds or treaties as a sign of consent and a condition of legitimate property acquisition. This second set of arguments came to be called the "agricultural" or "cultivation" justification for settlement, and it was widely used in the eighteenth and nineteenth centuries until Chief Justice Marshall repudiated it.

Whereas the second set of arguments justifies appropriation by alleging that the Aboriginal peoples have no rights in the land, the third set of arguments justifies appropriation by claiming that the Aboriginal peoples are better off as a result of the establishment of the commercial system of private property in land. Locke claims that a system of European commerce based on the motive to acquire more than one needs, satisfied by surplus production for profit on the market, is economically superior to the American Indian system of hunting and gathering based on fixed needs and subsistence production. It is superior in three crucial respects: it uses the land more productively; it produces a greater quantity of conveniences; and it produces far greater opportunities to work and labor by expanding the division of labor.[24] The standard of comparison of the two

[20] *Ibid.*, II, 42, 45.
[21] *Ibid.*, II, 32.
[22] *Ibid.*, I, 130–31; II, 10, 11, 16.
[23] *Ibid.*, II, 25, 39, 51.
[24] *Ibid.*, II, 37, 40–43, 48–49.

systems is which produces the "greater quantity of conveniencies" (an early formulation of the gross domestic product), including not only finished products but also the opportunities to labor.[25] Commercial agriculture, Locke suggests, uses one-tenth the amount of land that hunting and gathering does to produce the same quantity of conveniences. Then he revises the ratio to one one-hundredth the amount of land. In the following sections commercial societies are said to create one hundred, and then one thousand, times as many "conveniencies of life" as hunting and gathering from the same amount of land, and Locke famously concludes that a day-laborer in England is one hundred times better off than an Indian King with his huge yet unimproved territory in America.[26]

The Aboriginal peoples are better off as a result of conversion to the commercial system, for they too share in its greater abundance of commodities and jobs. As we have seen, Locke sets out the problem of original appropriation without consent with the proviso that any legitimate appropriation must leave enough and as good in common for others. Although agricultural appropriation does not leave enough and as good *land*, it unquestionably leaves more than enough and as good of the objects of comparison: namely, opportunities to labor and products of labor. Appropriation by means of cultivation and industry is non-zero-sum in this (much celebrated) sense.[27] It is difficult to overestimate the influence of this argument in justifications of original acquisition and in normative comparisons of competing property systems. Even theorists who believe that Aboriginal peoples have rights in their territories, contrary to Locke, often argue that they are nevertheless more than *compensated* for their loss of land by the material bountifulness and greater productivity of the commercial system. Locke's standard of comparison of "greater conveniences" in its many reformulations is taken for granted as an impartial standard, whereas it measures all systems in terms of the goods of the commercial system without weighing these against the goods of, for example, a steady-state, hunting and gathering system.[28]

The fourth set of arguments establishes a broad and influential picture of the historical development of systems of property and government. It explains why Aboriginal peoples have no recognizable systems of property and government and why Europeans do. A fixed and recognizable system of property in land is defined as an institutionalized legal system of property, and a political society is defined as an institutionalized sys-

[25] *Ibid.*, II, 34, 37.

[26] *Ibid.*, II, 40, 41, 42.

[27] *Ibid.*, II, 37, 43. For this interpretation of Locke's solution to the "enough and as good" or "sufficiency" proviso, see Stephen Buckle, *Natural Law and the Theory of Property* (Oxford: Clarendon Press, 1990), pp. 150–53; Barbara Arneil, *All the World Was America: John Locke and English Colonization* (London: University of London Ph.D., 1993); and Gopal Sreenivasan, *The Limits of Lockean Rights in Property* (Oxford: Oxford University Press, 1994).

[28] For a critical survey of the recent literature and a defense of this argument, see Tully, "Property, Self-Government, and Consent" (forthcoming).

tem of law, with legislature and executive.[29] By defining systems of property and government in terms of the institutions of early modern European state-formation, it is easy for Locke to show that Aboriginal societies lack both. He concedes that American Indians govern themselves by means of popular councils and chiefs, and that they are usually called nations and kingdoms by Europeans. However, in chapter 8 of the *Second Treatise*, a chapter on the history of state and property formation, he points out that the authority of the chief rests on the unanimous, non-delegated and ongoing consent of the council of the people, not on delegated and institutionalized majority rule through a legislature, and the right to declare war remains vested in the people, not delegated to the executive.[30] Hence, Aboriginal societies are not recognized as "political societies" or states by these defining criteria, but are considered to be in the state of nature. It follows that Europeans can deal with the Aboriginal peoples not on a nation-to-nation basis but as individuals under natural law.[31]

Aboriginal peoples lack the institutions of government and property according to Locke because they have no need of them at their level of economic development. They have "few Trespasses, and few Offenders," "few controversies" over property, and therefore "no need of many laws to decide them."[32] They can thus decide controversies on an *ad hoc* basis as in the state of nature. In turn, the explanation for this underdevelopment, which explains their whole system, is that they have limited and fixed desires for property, and thus produce for the sake of subsistence rather than for surplus. That is, they lack the desire to enlarge their possessions which comes into effect with the introduction of money and markets and leads to disputes over property, and so to the need for institutionalized political and property systems to settle the disputes.[33] Europeans, in contrast, live in commercial societies. Once money and trade develop, they spur the growth of population and the applied arts. An elastic desire for more than one needs comes into effect, uprooting forever the pre-monetary economy of limited desires and needs. People seek to enlarge their possessions in order to sell the surplus on the market for a profit.[34] As a result of the dynamic productivity of market-oriented labor, land becomes scarce, property disputes increase, and people set up political societies with institutionalized legal and political systems to regulate and protect property.[35]

---

[29] Locke, *Two Treatises*, II, 30, 38, 87.

[30] *Ibid.*, II, 107–8, and the quotation in the editorial footnote to II, 107.

[31] *Ibid.*, II, 9, 108.

[32] *Ibid.*, II, 107.

[33] *Ibid.*, II, 108.

[34] *Ibid.*, II, 37, 48–49.

[35] *Ibid.*, II, 50. See Tully, "Rediscovering America," pp. 164–66, for a defense of this interpretation.

B. Aboriginal governments

Let me draw a rough sketch of Aboriginal forms of government and property that Europeans encountered in eastern North America, in order to show how Locke's four sets of arguments misrecognize them. After observing and studying the Indian nations of the northeast in the early seventeenth century, Roger Williams famously concluded, in opposition to Locke's later view, that "the wildest Indians in America agree on some forms of Government . . . [and] their civill and earthly governments be as lawfull and true as any Governments in the World."[36] The typical form of Aboriginal government was a nation governed by a council or longhouse of chiefs (*sachems*) drawn from the clans. Each nation had a clearly demarcated and defended territory, a decision-making body, a consensus-based decision-making procedure, and a system of customary laws and kinship relations. The nations, in turn, often associated in international relations of confederation of various kinds and engaged in the international activities of trade, diplomacy, war, and peace. There were no standing armies, bureaucracies, police forces, prisons, or written laws. They did not have the definitive institutions of European states, yet they governed themselves and their complex systems of property.[37] Aboriginal societies were not only called "nations" by Europeans, and often treated as such, as we shall see; they were seen by many Europeans besides Chief Justice Marshall to meet the four criteria of nationhood or statehood in international law: a permanent population, a form of government, the recognized occupation of a territory over time, and the ability to enter into relations with other governments.[38]

Locke was knowledgeable about American Indian societies from his interest in the colony of Carolina, his seat on the Board of Trade, which

[36] Roger Williams, "The Bloody Tenant . . . ," in *The Complete Writings of Roger Williams* (New York: Russell & Russell, 1963), vol. 3, p. 250. See Ruth Barnes Moynihan, "The Patent and the Indians: The Problem of Jurisdiction in Seventeenth-Century New England," *American Indian Culture and Research*, vol. 2, no. 1 (1977), pp. 8–18.

[37] See Francis Jennings, *The Ambiguous Iroquois Empire: The Covenant Chain Confederation of Indian Tribes with English Colonies from Its Beginnings to the Lancaster Treaty of 1744* (New York: W. W. Norton and Co., 1984); and Daniel Richter and James Merrell, eds., *Beyond the Covenant Chain: The Iroquois and Their Neighbours in Indian North America* (Syracuse: Syracuse University Press, 1987).

[38] For these four criteria for statehood and sovereignty in international law, see Davies, "Aspects of Aboriginal Rights" (*supra* note 8), pp. 24–28. For the argument that Aboriginal nations meet the criteria, see Grand Council of the Crees (of Quebec), *Status and Rights of the James Bay Crees in the Context of Quebec's Secession from Canada*, submission to United Nations Commission on Human Rights, 48th session (January 27–March 6, 1992). For the widespread recognition of their nationhood in the early modern period, see Richter and Merrell, *Beyond the Covenant Chain*; Richard White, *The Middle Ground: Indians, Empires, and Republics in the Great Lakes Region, 1650–1815* (Cambridge: Cambridge University Press, 1991), pp. 305–17; and Six Nations, *The Redman's Appeal for Justice: The Position of the Six Nations That They Constitute an Independent State* (Brantford, Ontario: The Six Nations, 1924). For doubts, see generally S. James Anaya, "The Capacity of International Law to Advance Ethnic or Nationality Rights Claims," *Iowa Law Review*, vol. 75 (1990), pp. 837–82; and L. C. Green, "Claims to Territory in Colonial America" (*supra* note 10).

administered the colonial system, and his collection of anthropological literature on travel and exploration in the Americas.[39] In his interpretation of Aboriginal government, he highlights three features of their organization to the neglect of the customary system of government that underlies them. He interprets the war-chief from a European perspective, as a kind of proto-European sovereign, and stipulates that because he does not possess the right to declare war and peace he does not, by definition, possess the degree of sovereignty necessary to statehood. But the war-chief was not, and is not today, a proto-sovereign. He was a temporary military commander subordinate to political authority. Second, the chiefs and the council often appointed *ad hoc* arbitrators of justice. These *ad hoc* procedures may be a source of Locke's concept of individual and non-delegated self-government in the state of nature, but he overlooks the appointment procedure and the unwritten yet orally transmitted culture of customary law and sanctions that governs it. Third, Locke emphasizes the lack of crime, property disputes, and litigation in Aboriginal societies, and he explains these by reference to their limited desires and material possessions. Yet he disregards the national, clan, and family systems of sanctions that help prevent and resolve disputes.

With respect to Aboriginal property, the territory as a whole belongs to the nation (or, more accurately, the nation belongs to the territory) and jurisdiction over it is held in trust by the chiefs. The identity of a nation as a distinct people is inseparable from their relation to and use of the land, animals, ecosystems, and spirits that co-inhabit their territory. Clans and families have a bundle of rights and responsibilities, usually matrilineal, of use and usufruct over the land and waterways for various purposes. That is, property rights and duties inhere in the clans and families and apply to forms of activity and to the geographical territories or ecosystems in which the activities take place, not to the products of the activities, as in Locke's account. The activities include hunting, trapping, gathering berries, seasonal agriculture, clam-bed cultivation, fishing, and so on. The distribution and trade of the products is governed by custom and kinship traditions. These systems of property are transmitted from generation to generation, not by myths of a state of nature or veil of ignorance but by the stories families and clans are responsible for learning and telling at public feasts. When the coastal nations made property agreements with the settlers, as Roger Williams explained, they were granting them rights and responsibilities of co-use of the land, not alienable rights to the land itself.[40] Finally, families and individual members own their goods, yet there is a relatively casual attitude toward possessions and an overriding custom of sharing and gift-giving (typical of subsistence econ-

[39] See Tully, "Rediscovering America" (*supra* note 12), pp. 140–41.

[40] John Cotton, "John Cotton's Reply to Roger Williams," in *The Complete Writings of Roger Williams*, vol. 2, pp. 46–47. See Moynihan, "The Patent and the Indians."

omies). From an Aboriginal perspective, the European settlers were appropriating land that was not in the state of nature, but in their nations, and was not unowned, but was under their ownership and jurisdiction.[41]

In his depiction of Aboriginal property, Locke highlights one specific, European form of property-generating activity, industrious labor, and in this light, so to speak, fails to recognize the Aboriginal system of national territories, the bundle of property rights and responsibilities in activities and their locales, and the customs governing distribution. Of course, if he had recognized these forms of property, settlement in America without consent would have been unjust by his own criteria, for the land would have been owned, rather than unowned and common as the original-appropriation argument requires.

C. Later Western theorists

The four sets of argument presented by Locke were widely used throughout the eighteenth and nineteenth centuries to simultaneously dispossess Aboriginal peoples of their nationhood and property, and justify European settlement and expansion in America. In 1725, for example, John Bulkley of Connecticut published "An Inquiry into the Right of the Aboriginal Natives to the Land in America" in order to refute the claim advanced by the Mohegan nation that they constituted a sovereign nation with jurisdiction over their territory in Connecticut.[42] His argument was based entirely on the passages of Locke's *Two Treatises* that I have summarized above. In *The Law of Nations or the Principles of Natural Law* (1758), one of the most widely cited legal texts in America, Emeric de Vattel echoed Locke in using the agricultural argument to justify French and British settlement:

> The cultivation of the soil . . . is . . . an obligation imposed upon man by nature. Every Nation is therefore bound by the law of nature to cultivate that land which has fallen to its share. There are others who, in order to avoid labour, seek to live upon their flocks and the fruits of the chase. Now that the human race has multiplied so greatly, it could not subsist if every people wished to live after that fashion. Those who still pursue this idle mode of life occupy more land than they would have need of under a system of honest labour, and they may not complain if other more industrious nations, too

[41] This synopsis of Aboriginal property systems is based on numerous anthropological studies. Two of the best are Anthony F. Wallace, "Political Organization and Land Tenure among Northeastern Indians, 1600–1830," *Southwestern Journal of Anthropology*, vol. 13 (1957), pp. 301–21; and William A. Starna, "Aboriginal Title and Traditional Iroquois Land Use," in *Iroquois Land Claims*, ed. Christopher Vecsey and William A. Starna (Syracuse: Syracuse University Press, 1988), pp. 31–49.

[42] John Bulkley, "An Inquiry into the Right of the Aboriginal Natives to the Land in America," in Roger Wolcott, *Poetical Meditations* (New London, 1726), pp. i–lvi.

confined at home, should come and occupy part of their lands. . . .
[W]hen the Nations of Europe . . . come upon lands which the savages have no special need of and are making no present and continuous use of, they may lawfully take possession of them and establish
colonies in them.[43]

Ronald Meek and other scholars have traced how Locke's four sets of
arguments became conventional features of the four-stages theories of
property in the Scottish and French Enlightenments, even when the theorists disagreed with Locke in other respects.[44] Once the broad picture
that Locke's arguments set in place was accepted to different degrees, the
inevitability of European settlement and dispossession was assured.
When theorists of what John Pocock calls the "competing traditions" of
rights, virtues, and commerce debated the nature of modernity in terms
of the relative merits of Locke's rights-bearing and industrious agricultur-
ist, James Harrington's virtuous republican, and Adam Smith's polished
and civilized commercialist, they gave the implantation of European civilization in America the impression of historical inevitability; for all three
conceptions of modernity were defined in contrast to, and in supersession of, the Aboriginal peoples they displaced in practice—the propertyless and economically wasteful hunter-gatherers, the vicious savages, and
the rude and primitive Indians, respectively.[45]

Features of Locke's four sets of arguments did not come to be accepted
only in the background conventions of the great liberal and republican
theories of property. Similar modes of argument are woven into the
theory of Immanuel Kant, who is often seen as founding an independent
tradition of liberal political theory. In "Idea for a Universal History with
a Cosmopolitan Intent" (1784) and "Perpetual Peace" (1795), Kant argues
that humanity can achieve full moral progress and freedom only after
commerce and republican constitutions are spread around the world.[46]
Although there are important differences between Kant's concept of a
republican constitution and Locke's concept of a political society, they
both share the characteristically European features that are said to mark

[43] Emeric de Vattel, *Le droit des gens, ou principes de la loi naturelle* [1758]; reprinted as
The Law of Nations or the Principles of Natural Law, trans. Charles G. Fenwick (Washington:
Carnegie Institute, 1902), pp. 207–10.

[44] See note 16 above.

[45] I defend this claim in "Placing the *Two Treatises*" (*supra* note 12), pp. 279–80. For the
authors cited, see John Pocock, *Virtue, Commerce, and History* (Cambridge: Cambridge Uni-
versity Press, 1985); James Harrington, *The Political Writings of James Harrington*, ed. J. G. A.
Pocock (Cambridge: Cambridge University Press, 1977); and Adam Smith, *Lectures on
Jurisprudence*, ed. Ronald Meek, D. D. Raphael, and L. G. Stein (Indianapolis: Liberty
Press, 1982).

[46] Immanuel Kant, "Idea for a Universal History with a Cosmopolitan Intent" and "Perpetual Peace: A Philosophical Sketch," in *Perpetual Peace and Other Essays*, trans. Ted Humphrey (Indianapolis: Hackett Publishing Company, 1983), pp. 29–40 and pp. 107–44; see
esp. pp. 33, 111, 114.

them as different from and superior to Aboriginal forms of government: institutionalized legal and constitutional rule of law and representative government.[47] Once these civilizing institutions are established, progress toward moral freedom occurs by means of the mechanism of "unsocial sociability": that is, markets and constitutional government constrain self-interested individuals ("a people comprised of devils") to cooperate with others in order to satisfy their desires for more than they need for bare subsistence.[48]

In contrast, the systems of property and government of Aboriginal peoples are misrecognized and dismissed, and European institutions are set in their place and justified as the baseline for moral and political theory and practice. The uncivilized hunting and gathering peoples of America, Kant argues, lack secure property because they have not made the transition to the life of agriculture. They have, in their pre-political state of nature, what he calls the "lawless freedom of hunting, fishing, and herding," which, of "all forms of life, . . . is without doubt most contrary to a civilized constitution."[49] Agriculture, commerce, and republican constitutions are spread to non-Europeans by means of war, and then commerce.[50] Although Kant condemns the excesses of the European wars of imperial expansion, especially outright conquest,[51] and prefers expansion by means of trade, economic sanctions, and diplomacy, he commends the overall effect of spreading the economic and political institutions of moral progress, going so far as to say that it is "our duty to work towards bringing about this goal."[52] The justification European nations possess, again quite similar to Locke, is the third definitive article for perpetual peace that Kant proposes for international law.[53] This is "the right of hospitality," which gives Europeans the right to engage in commerce with native inhabitants, and to defend their traders if the native inhabitants deny the right. "In this way," Kant concludes, "distant parts of the world can establish with one another peaceful relations that will eventually become matters of public law, and the human race can gradually be brought closer and closer to a cosmopolitan constitution."[54]

In contemporary political theory the premises and modes of argument laid down by theorists such as Locke and Kant continue to be taken for

---

[47] Ibid., pp. 112–15.

[48] Ibid., pp. 31–32, 124. For the philosophical background to the concept of "unsocial sociability," see Istvan Hont, "The Language of Sociability and Commerce: Samuel Pufendorf and the Theoretical Foundations of the 'Four Stages Theory'," in The Languages of Political Theory in Early-Modern Europe, ed. Anthony Pagden (Cambridge: Cambridge University Press, 1987), pp. 253–76.

[49] Kant, "Perpetual Peace," pp. 111, 122 and note.

[50] Ibid., p. 123.

[51] Ibid., p. 119.

[52] Ibid., p. 125.

[53] Ibid., pp. 118–19.

[54] Ibid., p. 118.

granted as the initial conditions for theorizing about property in North America. Whereas Locke and Kant at least presented arguments to jus-tify the elimination of Aboriginal claims to aboriginal property and gov-ernment, contemporary theorists tend to take the conclusion of their arguments for granted as the original starting point of a theory, without even raising the question of Aboriginal property. Original-acquisition theories overlook Aboriginal acquisition. This is obvious, of course, in theories which start from what I call the first premise, some variation of a Lockean state of nature and individual self-ownership, such as Robert Nozick's theory in *Anarchy, State, and Utopia*.[55] But it is no less true in theories which start from a more Kantian premise, such as John Rawls's *A Theory of Justice*, as Vernon Van Dyke has pointed out.[56]

In the last decade Rawls has suggested that his theory can be seen in a slightly different way, as a theory written within the framework of an authoritative moral and political tradition and history (what I have called the second premise). The tradition which sets the horizons of the theory consists entirely of a set of institutions and forms of thought that derive from post-Reformation Europe (toleration, rule of law, representative gov-ernment, markets, and individual rights), and the role of the philosopher is to articulate "the basic intuitive ideas that are embedded in the politi-cal institutions of a constitutional democratic regime and the public tra-ditions of their interpretation."[57] This move thus effectively posits Kant's threshold institutions, and their traditions of interpretation, as the author-itative framework for theorizing about property, thereby effacing the pre-existence of independent Aboriginal government, property, and traditions, and assimilating Aboriginal peoples into this European-derived frame-work. Theorists working within this framework who notice Aboriginal property claims, such as Will Kymlicka, take up these claims *within* the Kant-Rawls framework, failing to recognize that the Aboriginal claim is to a system of property and tradition that is independent of, and prior to, the one Rawls posits.[58] Nor do recent communitarian theories of prop-erty and justice fare any better. They generally agree with Rawls that political theory must take a set of entirely European traditions and insti-tutions as the authoritative framework, disagreeing with Rawls only over

[55] Robert Nozick, *Anarchy, State, and Utopia* (New York: Basic Books, 1974). See David Lyons, "The New Indian Claims and Original Rights to Land," in *Reading Nozick: Essays on Anarchy, State, and Utopia*, ed. Jeffrey Paul (Totowa, NJ: Rowman and Littlefield, 1981), pp. 355–79.

[56] John Rawls, *A Theory of Justice* (Cambridge, MA: Harvard University Press, 1971); see Vernon Van Dyke, "Justice as Fairness — For Groups," *American Political Science Review*, vol. 69 (1975), pp. 607–14.

[57] John Rawls, "Justice as Fairness: Political not Metaphysical," *Philosophy and Public Affairs*, vol. 14 (1985), p. 225. This premise is incorporated in John Rawls, *Political Liberal-ism* (New York: Columbia University Press, 1993).

[58] See Kymlicka, *Liberalism, Community, and Culture*; and Allen Buchanan, *Secession: The Morality of Political Divorce from Fort Sumter to Lithuania and Quebec* (Boulder: Westview Press, 1991).

which European traditions are authoritative and over their interpretation, as for example in the work of Alasdair MacIntyre and Michael Walzer.[59] Aboriginal claims are either ignored or, at best, misrecognized as claims for some sort of minority status within the European-derived normative framework of an overarching national community, to the same effect. Many theorists of "difference," finally, continue to work within some of the four sets of assumptions associated with the three main Western premises, for they misrecognize Aboriginal property claims as demands for the recognition of difference within, again, some overarching framework of non-Aboriginal institutions and modes of argument, not as an independent system of property and authoritative traditions.[60]

III. The Common-Law System

Let us now turn to the Europeans and colonists who did recognize, to some extent, the property and government of the Aboriginal peoples. Most of the colonists were aware that the Aboriginal peoples possessed political organizations and forms of property. A second form of property acquisition, in competition with the Lockean agriculturalist argument for appropriation without consent, arose on this basis. Colonists (even some who paid lip service to the agriculturalist argument) often negotiated a treaty or deed of cession, on the presumption that the Aboriginal people had some sort of prior claim and that consent was thus required. One of the most bitter struggles over property in New England in the mid-seventeenth century was between Roger Williams and his Plymouth followers, who negotiated treaties with the local First Nations for the use of their land, and Governor Winthrop and his Boston followers, who claimed, in a proto-Lockean way, that settlement and cultivation were sufficient to establish property.[61]

The classic statement of the "treaty" theory of property acquisition was written by Samuel Wharton in his famous text *Plain Facts: Being an Examination into the Rights of the Indian Nations of America to Their Respective Territories* (1781) to justify the acquisition of, and speculation in, the rich lands of the Ohio Valley in the latter half of the eighteenth century. Wharton dismisses the argument that the land of the Aboriginal peoples can be appropriated without consent. He argues that the Enlightenment ideals of rights and equality must be applied to the Aboriginal peoples. Consequently, they have "an absolute exclusive right to the countries

---

[59] Alasdair MacIntyre, *Whose Justice? Which Rationality?* (Notre Dame: University of Notre Dame Press, 1988); Michael Walzer, *Spheres of Justice: A Defense of Pluralism and Equality* (New York: Basic Books, 1983).

[60] For example, see the otherwise impressive work by Iris Marion Young, *Justice and the Politics of Difference* (Princeton: Princeton University Press, 1990).

[61] Francis Jennings, *The Invasion of America: Indians, Colonialism, and the Cant of Conquest* (New York: W. W. Norton and Co., 1975), pp. 128–46.

they possess" in virtue of their occupation and use of them and of their (ironically) Lockean right to the means of preservation.[62] It follows from this absolute and therefore alienable property right, according to Wharton, that the Aboriginal peoples may sell parcels of their land to individual colonists or, as in his own case, to land speculation companies. The land then falls under colonial law.[63]

A third, widely employed claim to property was a land grant from a colonial assembly. The assumption was that a colonial assembly had sovereignty over its territory and thus possessed the right to allocate property to its citizens. This justification was often based on the compact theory of colonial independence, derived from the *Two Treatises* — as, for example, in the writings of James Otis and Thomas Jefferson.[64] The question it raises is how the colonial assembly acquired independence from the Crown and sovereignty over the lands of the Aboriginal peoples. The answer to the question about sovereignty was: either through a Lockean settlement and cultivation argument, an argument that the land had been ceded to the assembly by treaties, or an argument that it had been acquired through conquest.

The British Crown dismissed all three of these theories of property acquisition and slowly developed a common-law way of conceptualizing the status and relations of the different systems of property of the Aboriginal peoples and the European newcomers that was fair to both. The Crown formalized this in the Royal Proclamation of 1763 by recognizing the Aboriginal First Nations as a mirror image of itself: as equal in status to European nations and to be dealt with on a nation-to-nation basis.[65] It followed from this form of recognition that the Crown (or other European crowns) was the only agent with the authority to negotiate with the Aboriginal peoples, considered as nations, and to secure non-Aboriginal title to property in North America. If an individual were to negotiate property acquisition from a First Nation by agreement (although this was discouraged by the Crown), then he would hold it under the Aboriginal law of that nation. The motivation for formalizing this form of recogni-

[62] Samuel Wharton, *Plain Facts: Being an Examination into the Rights of the Indian Nations of America to Their Respective Territories, and a Vindication of the Grant of the Six United Nations* (Philadelphia, 1781), p. 7.

[63] For the context, see Robert A. Williams, *The American Indians in Western Legal Thought: The Discourse of Conquest* (Oxford: Oxford University Press, 1990), pp. 257–300.

[64] James Otis, *Rights of the British Colonies Asserted and Proved* (Boston, 1764); Thomas Jefferson, *A Summary View of the Rights of British America* [1775], ed. T. P. Abernethy (New York: Columbia University Press, 1943). See Tully, "Placing the *Two Treatises*" (*supra* note 12), pp. 266–75.

[65] For this way of articulating the form of mutual recognition expressed in the Royal Proclamation, see John Pocock, "A Discourse of Sovereignty: Observations on the Work in Progress," in *Political Discourse in Early Modern Britain*, pp. 417–21. The Royal Proclamation is reprinted in *Documents of the Canadian Constitution, 1759–1915*, ed. W. P. M. Kennedy (Toronto: Oxford University Press, 1918), pp. 18–21.

tion in the Royal Proclamation is obvious.[66] The Aboriginal nations of the Ohio Valley and the Old Northwest (up to the Great Lakes) resisted the invasion of their territories and property rights by settlers and land speculators, bearing agriculturalist arguments and dubious deeds, and this defensive war threatened to disrupt British-Native trade and military relations. The recognition of the Aboriginal peoples as nations concentrated the control of all property relations in the Crown's Privy Council and gave it the authority to remove the interloping settlers from the Ohio Valley. This move was a major cause of the War of Independence, because it blocked the expansion of the colonies, especially Virginia and New York, and land speculators into the Aboriginal nations of the Ohio Valley. Consequently, one of the great ironies of American legal history is that Chief Justice Marshall, a Virginian, decided that the way to solve the post-revolutionary conflict over title to land in the west, and to strengthen the Union, was to transfer the old, hated doctrine of Crown recognition of Aboriginal sovereignty to the new federal government.[67]

The common-law recognition of two different but juridically equal systems of property in America, enunciated in 1763, is based on the practice of the Privy Council and the North American agents of Indian Affairs over the previous century. As early as 1665, a Royal Commission repudiated the "agriculturalist" argument that land in North America was "vacant waste" and concluded that it belonged to the Aboriginal people: "[N]o doubt the country is [the Indians'] till they give it or sell it, though it be not improoued [sic]." In the 1690s, the colony of Connecticut claimed jurisdiction over Mohegan lands on a combination of Lockean and treaty grounds (as argued by John Bulkley; see Section II above). The Mohegan nation claimed sovereignty under the law of nations and appealed to the Privy Council that it would negotiate only with the Crown. This was one of the most famous cases in colonial history, lasting over eighty years and employing some of New York's brightest lawyers on the Mohegan side. The Privy Council found in favor of the sovereignty of the Mohegan nation in 1705 and, when Connecticut appealed, again in 1743.[68]

---

[66] For the context, see Brian Slattery, *The Land Rights of Indigenous Canadian People as Affected by the Crown's Acquisition of Their Territory* (Saskatoon: University of Saskatchewan Press, 1979); and Jack Stagg, *Anglo-American Relations in North America to 1763 and an Analysis of the Royal Proclamation of 7 October 1763* (Ottawa: Department of Indian and Northern Affairs, 1981).

[67] Dorothy V. Jones, *License for Empire: Colonialism by Treaty in Early America* (Chicago: University of Chicago Press, 1982).

[68] The quotation is from N. B. Shurtleff, ed., *Records of the Governor and Company of the Massachusetts Bay in New England* (Boston: W. White, 1853–54), p. 213, cited in Clinton, "The Proclamation of 1763" (*supra* note 6), p. 334. The Mohegan case is in J. H. Smith, *Appeals to the Privy Council from the American Plantations* (New York: Oxford University Press, 1950), pp. 417–22. See Clinton, "The Proclamation of 1763," pp. 335–36; and Bruce Clark, *Native Liberty, Crown Sovereignty: The Existing Aboriginal Right of Self-Government in Canada* (Toronto: McGill-Queens University Press, 1990).

The Royal Proclamation and Chief Justice Marshall's interpretation of it provide the classic enunciation of the Aboriginal and common-law system. We are now in a position to appreciate its superior recognition of the initial conditions of property in America. First, as Chief Justice Marshall later explained, when the Crown discovered and occupied territory in America, it gained a right to continue to occupy this territory, on the internationally recognized title of use and occupation, but only with respect to the exclusion of all other *European* nations. The title of long use and occupation did not, however, confer on the Crown any right with respect to the Aboriginal peoples, since, from their perspective, they held the superior title of long use and occupation. Discovery and occupation confers sovereignty only if the land is "vacant" (*terra nullius*), and, contrary to Locke, this was not the case in North America.[69]

Therefore, the second and crucial step in establishing the Crown in America was to establish a juridical relationship with the Aboriginal peoples. This could be done by conquest or consent. Although Chief Justice Marshall entertained the fiction of conquest in an earlier case (*Johnson and Graham's Lessee v. M'Intosh* [1823]), he repudiated it in the later and authoritative *Worcester v. the State of Georgia* (1832). Conquest was never the doctrine of the Crown.[70] It should be noted that even if the wars against the Aboriginal peoples were considered wars of conquest, the systems of property and government of the Aboriginal peoples would have continued intact by the international convention of "conquest and continuity." When one civilized nation conquers another, the property and government of the conquered nation continue, under the *imperium* of the conqueror, unless and until the conqueror expressly discontinues them. If the conqueror recognizes them, then the option of discontinuity is extinguished. Chief Justice Marshall refers to this convention; the Crown applied it to Canada in the Quebec Act (1774), after the "conquest" of 1760, and to Grenada in *Campbell v. Hall* (1774), and Locke himself applies this liberal convention to the Norman Conquest of Anglo-Saxon England.[71]

Hence, the principle governing relations between the Crown and Aboriginal nations is the oldest principle of Western law: the principle of consent (*quod omnes tangit*, or "what touches all must be agreed to by all"), which Locke sought to get around by his theory that appropriation could

[69] *Johnson and Graham's Lessee v. M'Intosh*, pp. 573–74, in Marshall, *Writings of Chief Justice Marshall* (*supra* note 7), pp. 263–64; and *Worcester v. the State of Georgia*, pp. 543–47, in ibid., pp. 427–33. Compare Brian Slattery, *Ancestral Lands, Alien Laws: Judicial Perspectives on Aboriginal Title* (Saskatoon: University of Saskatchewan Press, 1983), p. 26, and see quotation accompanying note 7 above.

[70] *Johnson*, pp. 588–89, in Marshall, *Writings of Chief Justice Marshall*, pp. 274–75; and *Worcester*, pp. 544–45, in ibid., pp. 428–29.

[71] *Johnson*, p. 589, in ibid., p. 275; *Worcester*, p. 547, in ibid., p. 431; *Campbell v. Hall*, 1 Cowp. 204 (1774); *The Quebec Act*, 14 George III, c.88 (1774); Locke, *Two Treatises*, II, 182–85, 192–96.

proceed without consent because it did not affect the rights of the Aboriginal peoples. The Royal Proclamation sets out three conditions for consensual negotiations between the Crown and Aboriginal nations in which their coordinate "sovereignty" is recognized and continued through the negotiations of treaty relations between them: (1) the negotiations are between the Crown and the chiefs of an Aboriginal nation, thereby recognizing nation-to-nation status; (2) the negotiations must take place in a public place, recognizing and employing both Aboriginal and Crown forms of negotiation and reaching agreements; and (3) the negotiations cannot be initiated by pressure from the Crown. Although the subject of the negotiations can involve anything of concern to the parties, they typically concern land cessions to the Crown, or agreements on the co-use and management of resources, in exchange for protection and other benefits to the Aboriginal peoples. The land in America not ceded to the Crown in this manner is "reserved" to the Aboriginal peoples and remains under their governments and property systems.[72]

The three conditions of the Royal Proclamation provide the normative framework for over five hundred treaties that the Aboriginal peoples have negotiated with the Crown and, after 1867, the federal government of Canada. The Proclamation is constitutionalized in section 25 of the Canadian Charter of Rights and Freedoms, and all treaties are constitutionally protected.[73] The treaties have given rise to a network of trust-like relations of interdependent property and government between the First Nations and the federal government in Canada which constitutes a system of "treaty federalism": that is, the Aboriginal peoples and the federal government are recognized as forming a federation of nations bound together by treaties. In the U.S., Chief Justice Marshall's interpretation, rather than the Royal Proclamation itself, provides the normative framework. The crucial feature is that the Aboriginal nations' juristic status as nations and their systems of government and property remain intact through the negotiated relations of treaty federalism, even when, as is quite common, they conditionally entrust some powers of self-government and rights of property to the federal government over the lands reserved to themselves or placed under joint resource and environmental management.[74]

This normative framework has been violated, either by ignoring or denying it, on more occasions in the past than it has been honored in Canada and the U.S. However, in the last twenty years the courts of both

[72] "The Royal Proclamation," in Kennedy, ed., Documents (supra note 65), pp. 20–21. Compare Clinton, "The Proclamation of 1763," pp. 354–60; and Darlene Johnston, The Taking of Indian Lands in Canada: Consent or Coercion? (Saskatoon: University of Saskatchewan Native Law Centre, 1989).

[73] See Bruce Wildsmith, Aboriginal Peoples and Section 25 of the Canadian Charter of Rights and Freedoms (Saskatoon: University of Saskatchewan Native Law Centre, 1988).

[74] Compare the similar arguments of Barsh and Henderson, The Road, for the U.S., and Slattery, "First Nations and the Constitution," for Canada (supra note 11).

countries, and constitutional amendments in Canada, have tended to some uneven extent to approximate several features of it.[75] My argument is not that this framework *determines* the legal and constitutional practice of the two countries; nor is my argument that the Royal Proclamation and Chief Justice Marshall give perfect expression to it. The framework can be theoretically reconstructed and defended independently of either formulation, since its norms of recognition of equality, political and cultural continuity, and consent are shared by Western and Aboriginal traditions, even though, as we have seen, they have not been adhered to in Western theory with respect to Aboriginal peoples. It is, however, part of my argument that the Royal Proclamation and the interpretation of Chief Justice Marshall constitute two (partial) expressions of this framework, and that at least some of the relations between Aboriginal peoples and the governments of Canada and the U.S. over the last two hundred years are based on the norms of the framework as formulated in the Royal Proclamation and by Chief Justice Marshall. If this is true, then the Aboriginal and common-law system, with its institutions and traditions of interpretation, has priority with respect to the institutions and traditions which the proponents of the three premises, especially the second, appeal to as authoritative. Of course, many of the institutions and traditions these proponents appeal to are included in the Aboriginal and common-law system, albeit in a modified form (as we shall see in Section IV). This practice-based part of the argument is thus important (but not indispensable), because it challenges the presumption of all three premises that Aboriginal forms of property and traditions do not form any of the *actually* recognized authoritative institutions and traditions of property in America—that is, that the argument I am advancing is not grounded in the legal and constitutional traditions of North America. Therefore, I want to defend my reading of the Royal Proclamation and Chief Justice Marshall's interpretation of it against the claim that neither one comes near to recognizing the coexistence and equality of Aboriginal forms of property and government.

Lawyers, judges, and commentators often read the Royal Proclamation and the Marshall cases to the effect that they assert sovereignty over the Aboriginal peoples and their land and subject them to the Crown or the federal government.[76] This interpretation is surprising, because the Crown made no attempt to govern the Aboriginal peoples at the time, and the documents surrounding the Proclamation and treaties repeatedly, though

---

[75] See notes 4, 6, and 11 above for recent court cases and constitutional developments. For a comprehensive analysis of a recent Canadian lower court denial of the normative framework (based on the four sets of Eurocentric assumptions summarized in Section II) which has been successfully appealed, see Frank Cassidy, ed., *Aboriginal Title in British Columbia: Delgamuukw v. The Queen* (Montreal: Institute for Research on Public Policy, 1992).

[76] See, for example, L. C. Green, "Claims to Territory in Colonial America," pp. 99–105, 110–11, 116–23; see also the examples in note 6 above.

not without exception, acknowledge the sovereignty and independence of the Aboriginal nations.[77] Here is the relevant passage:

> It is just and reasonable and essential to our Interest, and the Security of our Colonies, that the several Nations or Tribes of Indians with whom We are connected, and who live under our Protection, should not be molested or disturbed in the Possession of such parts of Our Dominions and Territories as, not having been ceded to or purchased by Us, are reserved to them, as their Hunting grounds.[78]

In *Worcester v. the State of Georgia* (1832), Chief Justice Marshall provides an answer to the attempt to read this passage as the assertion of Crown sovereignty over the Aboriginal peoples. *Worcester* also provides a step-by-step clarification and correction of Marshall's earlier views in *Johnson and Graham's Lessee v. M'Intosh* (1823), thereby providing a response to later commentators who take this earlier decision as authoritative.[79] First, the phrase "Our Dominions and Territories" does not imply sovereignty with respect to the Aboriginal peoples, but, as we saw above, a claim to exclude other European powers, to treaty with the Aboriginal nations for land cessions, and to assert sovereignty over the ceded land.

Second, the Proclamation does not discontinue the sovereignty of the Aboriginal nations to "live under" the protection of the Crown. Chief Justice Marshall lays this down in no uncertain terms, ironically invoking Emeric de Vattel's concept of "guardianship" to represent the continuity of Aboriginal sovereignty in relation to the federal government:

> [T]he settled doctrine of the law of nations is, that a weaker power does not surrender its independence, its right to self-government, by associating with a stronger, and taking its protection. A weak state, in order to provide for its safety, may place itself under the protection of one more powerful, without stripping itself of the right of self-government, and ceasing to be a state. Examples of this kind are not wanting in Europe. "Tributary and feudatory states," says Vattel, "do not thereby cease to be sovereign and independent states, so long as sovereign and independent authority are left in the administration of the state."[80]

---

[77] See Johnston, *The Taking of Indian Lands in Canada* (*supra* note 72); and *Worcester*, p. 547, in Marshall, *Writings of Chief Justice Marshall*, p. 431.

[78] "The Royal Proclamation," in Kennedy, ed., *Documents*, p. 20.

[79] There is considerable evidence that Marshall was dissatisfied with his judgment in *Johnson* and welcomed the opportunity to correct it. See Joseph C. Burke, "The Cherokee Cases: A Study in Law, Politics, and Morality," *Stanford Law Review*, vol. 21 (1968), pp. 500–31.

[80] *Worcester*, p. 560 in Marshall, *Writings of Chief Justice Marshall*, p. 446.

It was only in the late nineteenth century, when government policy in the United States and Canada came under the spell of doctrines of racial superiority, that "under the protection" was misinterpreted as a "guardian-child" relation and the independence and consent of the Aboriginal nations was systematically violated.[81]

Chief Justice Marshall goes on to show that the status of the First Nations as "sovereign nations" and "states" was never discontinued, but in fact was recognized and affirmed by the many treaties with the Crown and later with Congress. These treaties are not mere contracts but are like "international" treaties between crowned heads of state in Europe. The "several Indian nations" are "distinct political communities, having territorial boundaries, within which their authority is exclusive," and their "right to all the lands within those boundaries . . . is not only acknowledged, but guaranteed [sic] by the United States." Furthermore, the phrase "hunting grounds" does not in any sense restrict the Aboriginal peoples to that activity.[82]

Chief Justice Marshall concludes that the Aboriginal nations are to be conceived as, and to continue as, "domestic dependent nations." That is, they are independent, self-governing nations with internal sovereignty. Their protection by the United States government "diminishes" their sovereignty only in the following respects. They cannot engage in military alliances with foreign governments; their trade is regulated by Congress; and Congress may build roads through their nations and use their waterways for navigation. Any other relations of federalism must be worked out by fair treaty negotiations.[83]

Although this "diminished" sovereignty is acceptable to almost all the First Nations of the United States (with the exception of the Haudenosaunee confederacy, which claims undiminished sovereignty), the Canadian Royal Commission on Aboriginal Peoples has rejected this definition of "domestic dependent nations" as a diminution of their legitimate status. In advancing this reply, the First Nations of Canada do not signal a desire to form independent sovereign states, but rather to ensure that their equality and coexistence with the Canadian government is recognized and affirmed through all the negotiated relations of dependency.[84]

IV. THE ABORIGINAL SYSTEM

As we have seen, the Royal Proclamation form of recognition of Aboriginal and non-Aboriginal relations was formulated in the context of decades

[81] J. R. Miller, *Skyscrapers Hide the Heavens: A History of Indian-White Relations in Canada* (Toronto: University of Toronto Press, 1989), pp. 83–210.

[82] *Worcester*, pp. 544, 548, 551, 553–54, 559–61, in Marshall, *Writings of Chief Justice Marshall*, pp. 428, 433, 436, 438–39, 445–47.

[83] *Worcester*, p. 555, in *ibid.*, p. 440; and *The Cherokee Nation v. the State of Georgia*, 5 Peter (1829), pp. 14–20, in *ibid.*, pp. 412–18.

[84] Royal Commission on Aboriginal Peoples, *The Right of Aboriginal Self-Government and the Constitution: A Commentary* (Ottawa, February 13, 1992), p. 15.

of negotiations with the First Nations of northeastern North America. It is not surprising, therefore, that it is fairly close to, and overlaps with, the form of recognition that the Aboriginal peoples themselves developed to establish and negotiate property relations with the non-Aboriginal newcomers. Let us now turn to the Aboriginal side of the Aboriginal and common-law system. When the Europeans arrived, the Aboriginal peoples of the northeast were organized into nations and federations, and they had a system of international customary law developed over centuries of use. This is codified in an exemplary way in the oldest living constitution in North America, *Kaianereko:wa* or the Great Law of Peace of the Haudenosaunee (Six Nations or Iroquois) confederacy, established in the mid-fifteenth century.[85] The First Nations sought to understand and negotiate with the Dutch, French, and British in light of their centuries' old practices of federal and international negotiations, just as the Europeans conceptualized negotiations within their traditions as we have seen, developing from 1645 to 1815 a complex multinational system that spanned half the continent.[86] At the heart of their practice of international relations is a normative framework called the Two Row Wampum Treaty, or *Kahswentha*, of the Haudenosaunee, which has been adopted by many First Nations across North America. This representation of negotiated relations is symbolized in the belts made of wampum beads exchanged at treaty negotiations from the first French-Iroquois treaty in 1645 to the negotiations at Oka Quebec in the summer of 1990. A background of white wampum beads symbolizes the purity of the agreement; two rows of purple beads symbolize the Aboriginal and non-Aboriginal nations involved; and the three beads separating the two rows symbolize peace, friendship, and respect. The two central and parallel rows of purple beads

> symbolize two paths or two vessels, travelling down the same rivers together. One, a birch bark canoe, will be for the Indian people, their laws, their customs and their ways. The other, a ship, will be for the white people and their laws, their customs and their ways. We shall each travel the river together, side by side, but in our own boat. Neither of us will try to steer the other's vessel.[87]

First, the Aboriginal peoples and the European Americans, the two vessels, are reciprocally recognized as equal and coexisting nations, each

[85] A. C. Parker, ed., *The Constitution of the Five Nations, or The Iroquois Book of the Great Law* (Albany: State University of New York, 1916; Iroqrafts Reprints, 1984).

[86] For the history of early treaty relations, see Francis Jennings et al., eds., *The History and Culture of Iroquois Diplomacy* (Syracuse: Syracuse University Press, 1985); and White, *The Middle Ground* (*supra* note 38).

[87] The quotation is from the Haudenosaunee confederacy's presentation to the Canadian House of Commons Committee on Indian Self-Government (1983), reprinted with commentary in Michael Mitchell, "An Unbroken Assertion of Sovereignty," in *Drumbeat: Anger and Renewal in Indian Country*, ed. Boyce Richardson (Toronto: Summerhill Press — The Assembly of First Nations, 1989), pp. 109–10.

with its own customs and laws of government and property, just as in the Royal Proclamation. This is the principle (of recognition) of *Kahswentha* or equality. The second feature is that, as the two peoples become bound together by relations of trust by means of treaties, the Aboriginal traditions, governments, and property systems continue through their negotiated relations of interdependency and guardianship over time. It is symbolized by the parallel rows of beads, the vessels carrying on "side by side," and by neither people trying to steer the other. This feature, similar to the international principle of continuity expressed in the Royal Proclamation and in Chief Justice Marshall's judgment in *Worcester*, is one of the oldest conventions of Aboriginal international relations. The Great Law of Peace, for example, states that, "whenever a foreign nation is either conquered or has by its own will accepted the Great Peace [i.e., joined the Haudenosaunee confederacy], their own system of internal government may continue."[88]

The third feature of the Aboriginal normative framework is the treaty negotiations themselves. The Aboriginal negotiators negotiate in accordance with their complex traditions of consensus government and diplomacy. The negotiations can involve the delegation (but never the alienation) of some of their powers of self-government, cession of land, agreements on the co-use of land and co-management of resources, establishment of reserves, redress of injustices in past treaties, and so on. The form of political association with Canada and the U.S. is thus properly called "treaty federalism," since the Aboriginal nations have the ability to voluntarily delegate some powers to the Canadian and U.S. governments for specific purposes, thereby placing themselves in a guardian relationship, while retaining their status as independent nations. This Aboriginal form of federalism is also commensurable with the liberal traditions of federalism and continuity that underlie the Royal Proclamation. As long as the first two features are firmly established, as the initial and continuing conditions for negotiations over property, the negotiations cannot extinguish the status of Aboriginal societies as nations with independent systems of property and traditions of thought, any more than the negotiations can extinguish the equal status of the U.S. and Canada. As a result, the Aboriginal peoples cannot be brought under the sovereignty of non-Aboriginal laws, institutions, and traditions of interpretation without their consent. Rather, they bring themselves by their consent, expressed in their own ways, into the federation constituted by the Aboriginal and common-law system of laws, institutions, and traditions of interpretation.[89]

---

[88] Parker, ed., *The Constitution of the Five Nations*, section 84, p. 53.

[89] For Aboriginal accounts of treaty negotiations, see Richardson, ed., *Drumbeat: Anger and Renewal*. For liberal traditions of federalism commensurable with the Royal Proclamation and Two Row, see James Tully, "Diversity's Gambit Declined," in *Canada's Constitutional Predicament*, ed. Curtis Cook (Montreal: McGill-Queens University Press, 1994).

The Two Row Wampum Treaty has provided the Aboriginal people with a way of conceptualizing the foundation and negotiation of Aboriginal and Western systems of property in America for over three hundred years. Although Two Row is grounded in Aboriginal world-views and serves to protect Aboriginal systems of property, the features of it that serve to establish a framework for recognizing, establishing, and negotiating relations of property overlap with the three similar features of the common-law framework, based on Western traditions and designed to protect Western systems of property in America.

V. Conclusion

In conclusion, there exists in Aboriginal and common-law traditions and practices a cross-cultural form of recognition of and negotiation between two different systems of property in North America. This Aboriginal and common-law system is the normative basis of the constitutional history of Aboriginal-U.S. and Aboriginal-Canadian property relations. It is also a very flexible bicultural and bilegal system, capable of providing the framework for overlapping systems of property as diverse as the James Bay and Northern Quebec Agreement of 1975–81, the Sechelt Self-Government Agreement of 1987 in British Columbia, the new Inuit province of Nunavut of 1992 in Northern Canada, and the negotiated redress of hundreds of treaty and reserve violations, from the Haudenosaunee claims in New York to the Sioux claims in the Black Hills of South Dakota.[90] In addition, the negotiations, court cases, appeals, renegotiations, and armed resistances over the centuries in accordance with and in violation of the system have given rise to hundreds of inter-subjective conventions (such as Marshall's concept of guardianship and Canada's concept of a fiduciary trust between the Crown and First Nations) which provide the common grounds for each successive property negotiation.

It is therefore the suggestion of this essay that a theory of property applicable to North America will be just only if it begins from the Aboriginal and common-law conceptual framework as its premise, for this is the just representation of the initial conditions of property at the foundation of Canada and the United States. Unfortunately, as we have seen, many current theorists of property either ignore the foundations of property in North America, by uncritically assuming that European-American institutions and traditions are exclusively authoritative and applying one or more of the three premises mentioned in the introduction, or they mistake Aboriginal property for a problem of recognizing some kind of cultural or

[90] For these examples, see Ken Coates, ed., *Aboriginal Land Claims in Canada: A Regional Perspective* (Toronto: Copp Clark Pitman Ltd., 1992); Vecsey and Starna, eds., *Iroquois Land Claims* (*supra* note 41); and Edward Lazarus, *Black Hills, White Justice: The Sioux Nation versus the United States, 1775 to the Present* (New York: Harper Collins, 1991).

minority difference within the sovereignty of a liberal or communitarian framework. In either case the sovereignty of non-Aboriginal institutions and traditions of thought is taken for granted and the Aboriginal peoples are subjected to it without their consent, thereby unwittingly perpetuating a form of conceptual imperialism in legal and political philosophy. The legitimacy of these modes of argument and institutions of property rests on the prior recognition of the coordinate legitimacy of the Aboriginal traditions and institutions of property and the network of treaty relations between the two peoples.

Hence, the modes of argument of Western theories of property should be used in North America only *within* the Aboriginal and common-law framework. They are authoritative for an issue of property in North America that is concerned exclusively with the legitimate non-Aboriginal systems of property. Reciprocally, Aboriginal traditions are authoritative for any issue of property concerned exclusively with the Aboriginal systems of property. (Of course any interlocutor is free to introduce arguments from the other traditions as best he can.) For any issue of property on the now large middle ground where the Aboriginal and non-Aboriginal systems of property overlap in a multiplicity of ways, Aboriginal and non-Aboriginal modes of argument are always on equal footing. In this unique cross-cultural speech-situation, the negotiators are bound together by three shared norms (and by all previous, justified agreements) of the system: that the equality of their respective traditions and institutions is recognized and continued, that the negotiations and argumentation respect the forms of negotiation of both cultures, and that the treaty relations of property they reach by negotiation will be based on consent, not on force or deceit. The Aboriginal and common-law system comprising these three shared norms is the philosophical foundation and, to the extent that the existing property systems are just, practical foundation of property in North America.

Philosophy, McGill University

PROPERTY RIGHTS, INNOVATION, AND CONSTITUTIONAL STRUCTURE

By Jonathan R. Macey

I. Introduction

The Industrial Revolution caused an expansion of our ideas of property to include other forms of wealth, such as innovations and productive techniques. And the modern age has caused a further expansion of our ideas of property to include inchoate items, particularly information. The Framers of the U.S. Constitution presumed that government not only took an expansive view of the nature of property rights, they also believed that such rights should be protected. To James Madison and the other Framers, property was a "broad and majestic term" that "embraces everything which may have a value to which man may attach a right."[1]

Because of this earlier broad conception, the American legal system has had little trouble adjusting to the changing nature of property rights. While there has been an explosion in recent years in litigation dealing with rights in information, this is to be expected in a world economy in which information is playing an increasingly prominent role.

Consistent with the view that property is an expansive concept, the Supreme Court has held that inside information about corporate takeovers is property, and the Securities and Exchange Commission (SEC) rules against insider trading must therefore be construed to protect property rights in information.[2] Similarly, the Court has held that medical researchers may decide whether and to whom to release their raw data;[3] television manufacturers have property rights in information about their products, including a limited right to confidentiality with respect to accident reports;[4] and the property interest reflected by shares of stock in a corporation includes the potential to control that corporation.[5]

Unfortunately, despite the broad conception of property rights embraced by James Madison and the Framers, the legislative assault on property rights in America that began in the 1930s is proceeding at an

---

[1] James Madison, "Essay on Property," in *The Writings of James Madison*, ed. Gaillard Hunt (New York: G. P. Putnam's Sons, 1906), vol. 6, pp. 101, 103.

[2] Jonathan R. Macey, "From Fairness to Contract: The New Direction of the Rules against Insider Trading," *Hofstra Law Review*, vol. 13, no. 1 (Fall 1984), pp. 9–52.

[3] *Forsham v. Harris*, 445 U.S. 169 (1980).

[4] *Consumer Product Safety Commission v. GTE Sylvania, Inc.*, 447 U.S. 102 (1980).

[5] *Manges v. Camp*, 474 F.2d 97 (5th Cir. 1973).

ever-quickening pace.[6] Cultural and constitutional protections for property owners that existed for decades have eroded. These incursions on property rights come in an incredible variety of forms, from advertising regulations to zoning restrictions.

The purpose of this essay is to examine the causes of the remarkable diminution in the quality of property rights protections under American law. In a nutshell, the argument is that politicians and interest groups have ingeniously avoided the protections for property rights contained in the U.S. Constitution. The forces of innovation and technological change in the organizational structure of Congress have conspired to diminish substantially the protection afforded to property rights by the Constitution. In particular, the Constitution attempted to protect property rights by erecting structural impediments, in the form of the separation of powers and divided government, to passing statutes that eroded property rights. While the basic structure of the Constitution has not changed, the efficacy of the structural protections for property rights established in the Constitution has diminished.

This essay begins, in Section II, with a description of the nature and purpose of property rights, and their current treatment in the American legal system. The purpose of this section is to distinguish between the two primary mechanisms for obtaining wealth—wealth transfers and wealth creation—and to sketch out the normative implications of this distinction. In addition, Section II will describe the various forms that property rights can take, and will explain how the framework developed in this essay is consistent with the Framers' original conception of the nature and function of property rights.

Section III will describe the Framers' belief that property rights could be protected under the Constitution, and will set out the strategies employed by the Framers to achieve such protection in some detail. It will also discuss the failure of the Constitution to fulfill the Framers' expec-

---

[6] Until the 1930s, Congress and the judiciary in the United States were very respectful of property rights. Prior to the 1930s, "a *laissez faire* ideology based on classical economics was the dominant ideology of the educated classes in society" (Richard A. Posner, *Economic Analysis of Law*, 3d ed. [Boston: Little, Brown and Co., 1986], p. 21). This ideology was reflected in judicial opinions which strongly protected property rights, e.g., *Lochner v. New York*, 198 U.S. 45 (1905) (declaring unconstitutional a New York statute limiting the number of hours a baker could work, on the grounds that it impaired the freedom of employers and employees to contract). During the 1930s, the Roosevelt administration launched an intensive legislative assault on property rights and contractual freedom, and the Supreme Court ultimately cooperated in this assault by dramatically curtailing its interpretation of the Constitution with respect to property rights and contractual freedom. For example, in *West Coast Hotel Co. v. Parrish*, 300 U.S. 379 (1937), the Court upheld the constitutionality of a Washington statute imposing a minimum wage for women. The Court in this case declined to afford any weight to the economic liberty of the parties being regulated. Wholesale judicial approval of every aspect of New Deal legislation followed shortly thereafter. See, e.g., *United States v. Darby*, 312 U.S. 100 (1941) (upholding the Fair Labor Standards Act); *NLRB v. Jones & Laughlin Steel Co.*, 301 U.S. 1 (1937) (upholding the National Labor Relations Act); *Wickard v. Filburn*, 317 U.S. 111 (1942) (upholding the Agricultural Adjustment Act).

tations concerning such protection. Finally, Section IV will examine the changes that have undermined the Framers' efforts to provide protection for property rights.

II. Property Rights and Constitutional Law

While questions concerning the nature, function, purposes, and legitimacy of property have long been topics of debate among philosophers, these issues are fairly well-settled among economists. Something which has the inherent capacity to be held and controlled as an economic asset is property. In turn, an economic asset is anything that can be used in a market transaction. In other words, something which has real or potential value in voluntary exchange is property. The economic function of voluntary exchange is well established. Exchange is the mechanism through which individuals and firms create wealth. The notion that exchange benefits its individual participants is axiomatic. If a party to an exchange did not benefit from the transaction, he would not participate.

A. Morals and property rights

Voluntary exchange transactions benefit not only the individual parties who participate in such transactions but also society at large, as entrepreneurs are "coaxed by competitive forces to provide what others want on improved terms, a serendipitous benefit to the public that was in no way a part of the entrepreneur's intentions."[7] In other words, property is anything that has value in exchange. The creation and free exchange of property are critical to human flourishing because it is only through this pattern of creating property and entering into voluntary exchange transactions that human beings can improve their economic well-being in the long run. While voluntary exchange through consensual market transactions constitutes the only way that human beings can benefit themselves both individually and as a group, there is another way that individuals can derive benefit, at least personally, and over the short term. The alternative to wealth creation through private exchange is to seek wealth transfers either through outright theft, or lawfully, in the legislative arena, by seeking legal rules that transfer wealth from one group to another. The process of seeking wealth through legislative exchange rather than through market exchange is known as "rent-seeking."

Unlike market transactions that increase individual and aggregate wealth, both theft and lawful legislative wealth transfers impose signifi-

---

[7] This point is most often attributed to Adam Smith. The phrasing here is Richard McKenzie's. See Richard B. McKenzie, "Introduction," in *Constitutional Economics*, ed. Richard B. McKenzie (Lexington, MA: Lexington, 1984), p. 4.

cant costs on society. Foremost among these costs are those that innocent third parties must incur to block legislation that threatens to transfer wealth to rent-seeking groups. In addition, deadweight losses will occur to the extent that rent-seeking groups (also known as interest groups) must expend resources to obtain these transfers. An interest group will find it worthwhile to spend up to $99.99 to obtain a $100.00 wealth transfer. This $99.99 is a deadweight social loss, because it represents a sum that could have been spent to create wealth. Similarly, the groups who must pay for this wealth transfer will be willing to pay up to $99.99 to block a wealth transfer of $100.00.[8] Consequently, the process of seeking wealth transfers through government becomes a negative-sum game: the various affected parties will spend more than the total amount of the transfer in efforts to block or to obtain the transfer. Indeed, rent-seeking would be a negative-sum game even if the parties did not spend more than the total amount of the transfer in efforts to block it. *Any* expenditures to obtain transfers represent waste, because the money used to obtain such transfers would otherwise be put to productive use.

Rent-seeking regulation is manifested in a variety of subtle forms in advanced economies.[9] In particular, firms will attempt to gain a competitive edge by obtaining legislation that creates unnecessary regulation, imposing greater costs on some firms than on others. Import tariffs are an example of this form of regulation. Gasoline taxes are another. Where such regulations exist, more deadweight losses result as parties must expend resources simply to comply with the requirements of the regulation. From a property rights perspective, a related element of rent-seeking is that the resulting regulations cause economic resources to be diverted from their highest and best uses to less valuable—but unregulated—uses.

Moreover, the power of the government to effectuate wealth transfers imposes costs even on markets that appear to be operating free of governmental intervention. Even in such unregulated markets, economic actors must expend resources to keep their markets clear of governmental regulation. This phenomenon is known as "rent extraction." It is distinguishable from rent creation, the more widely understood phenomenon where government creates a protected niche for a particular industry subgroup by enacting regulations that favor that group at the expense of consumers or rival producers.[10]

---

[8] Jonathan R. Macey, "Transaction Costs and the Normative Elements of the Public Choice Model: An Application to Constitutional Theory," *Virginia Law Review*, vol. 74, no. 2 (March 1988), p. 478.

[9] For a full discussion of why rent-seeking legislation often does not attempt to impose direct cash transfers among groups, but instead takes a variety of more subtle forms, see Jonathan R. Macey, "Promoting Public-Regarding Legislation through Statutory Interpretation: An Interest Group Model," *Columbia Law Review*, vol. 86, no. 2 (March 1986), pp. 223–68.

[10] Fred S. McChesney, "Rent Extraction and Rent Creation in the Economic Theory of Regulation," *Journal of Legal Studies*, vol. 16, no. 1 (January 1987), p. 103.

In other words, while private market exchange transactions benefit both the parties to such transactions and society as a whole, rent-seeking in the public sector harms everyone in society, save the individuals or groups that directly benefit from such transactions. The pervasiveness of this detriment is due to the fact that people must expend vast resources to obtain rent-seeking legislation, to comply with it, to avoid having to comply with it, to adjust to it, and to prevent it from being enacted in the first place.

The basic question of what constitutes property thus yields a straightforward and uncontroversial response. By contrast, the question of what constitutes the legitimate means of acquiring property is far more controversial. The above discussion has demonstrated that there is a critical normative distinction between the acquisition of resources through consensual market transactions on the one hand, and the acquisition of resources through governmental intervention on the other.

When resources are acquired through consensual market transactions, there are no losers, only winners among the parties to such transactions. In my view, such transactions cannot be challenged on moral grounds. Indeed, without such transactions, human growth and flourishing simply would not be possible. By contrast, when resources are acquired through governmental fiat, there generally will be more losers than winners. As noted above, this surprising result is a straightforward implication of public-choice analysis. The fact that resources must be spent not only to obtain transfers from the government but also to resist such transfers produces this result.

B. Allocation and creation of property rights

While the basic contours of what constitutes property are well established, at least in principle, the question of how such rights initially are created and allocated has been the subject of far more vigorous debate, even among economists. For example, a number of economists take the view that property rights are defined as the *permissible* use of resources, goods, and services, either privately or collectively.[11] The critical assumption in this formulation, of course, is that both property and rights in property are regarded simply as social constructs that exist because of the state's acquiescence in their creation.

Within economic and legal circles, the most prominent adherent to this perspective is Judge Richard Posner, who takes the view that individuals lack natural rights to anything, including the right to contract. Under Posner's approach to property rights, all rights are socially constructed,

[11] Richard B. McKenzie, *Economics* (Boston: Houghton Mifflin Co., 1986), ch. 4, p. 76.

and result from power relationships, which are, in turn, tolerated by the state. According to this conception of rights, economic rights in general, and property rights in particular, are "luxuries enabled by social organizations(s)" such as the state.[12] By contrast, a natural-law perspective on rights emphasizes the permanent nature of the concept of reason, and posits that man is governed by universal rules of reason that transcend the actions of any particular sovereign.[13] Natural law sets the parameters for civil law and cabins its outer reach. Because justice is prior to every aspect of civil law, state power that intrudes on people's individual rights is illegitimate and may be ignored or rebelled against.

Rejecting the concept of natural rights and natural liberty, Posner asserts that the state "has a right to take away the difference between my income and that of the average resident of Bangladesh."[14] There are two critical flaws in Posner's analysis. First, the analysis confuses the concept of "right" with the concept of "power." Merely because the government or some other social organization has the raw power to take away my wealth or my ability to earn wealth, does not mean that it has the right to do so. Nor does it mean that I lack either the right to the wealth that is in my possession, or the right to earn additional wealth. Thus, a state's mere exercise of its power to deprive citizens of their property rights does not mean that these rights do not exist. The idea of natural rights refers to those rights that human beings possess by virtue of their status as human beings.[15]

The second flaw in Posner's analysis is far more serious, because it concerns the process by which property rights come into being. Posner notes that one of the primary benefits of social interaction is to enhance the value of an individual's property. From this, Posner concluded that an individual's rights cannot be natural if they are a product of social interaction rather than of his skills and efforts alone.[16] But the fact that the skills and efforts of a social group combine to enhance the value of an individual's natural endowment does not diminish the fact that initial endowment *belongs* to the individual. Clearly, Chris Webber's ability to prosper from his basketball talents would be diminished if there were no professional basketball league. But this does not mean that Mr. Webber's basketball talents are not naturally his. (Mr. Webber, who attended the

---

[12] Richard A. Posner, "Hegel and Employment at Will: A Comment," *Cardozo Law Review*, vol. 10, nos. 5–6 (March/April 1989), Part II, pp. 1625–36.

[13] By the term "natural law" I refer to the norms and rules that must exist in order for man to exercise his natural rights without interference either from the state or from other men.

[14] Posner, "Hegel and Employment at Will: A Comment," p. 1627.

[15] The foremost exponents of these views of natural rights include John Locke, *Two Treatises of Government*, ed. T. Cook (New York: Hafner Publishing Company, 1947), *Second Treatise*, ch. 2; and Charles Louis de Secondat, Baron de Montesquieu, *The Spirit of the Laws*, trans. T. Nugent (New York: Hafner Publishing Company, 1949), ch. 12.

[16] Posner, "Hegel and Employment at Will: A Comment," p. 1626.

University of Michigan for a time, but did not graduate, recently signed a fifteen-year, $74.5 million contract with the Golden State Warriors.)

Similarly, but even more fundamentally, Posner assumes that because our ability to prosper is a result of civil society, we owe our livelihood, and hence our property, to that civil society. But, as noted above, if one takes the position that certain rights are natural, or at least pre-political, then civil society must be viewed simply as a social construct whose purpose is to enhance our well-being and capacity for human flourishing by defining and protecting the property rights that exist in nature. Thus, it simply does not follow that those who benefit from the existence of a properly functioning civil society do not have natural rights merely because they happen to receive the benefits associated with living in such a society.

The fact is that human beings have the ability to identify and acquire property, and to benefit themselves and others by engaging in mutually beneficial exchanges of that property for other valuable property. As long as human beings recognize that phenomenon, they will have a substantial incentive to *construct* civil societies that facilitate the identification and acquisition of property and the consummation of mutually beneficial exchanges. Thus, just as the ability to bargain and exchange property makes property valuable, the ability to construct a civil society that protects property rights makes bargaining and exchange valuable.

In one sense the distinction I seek to establish between the concept of power and the concept of right is trivial, and in another sense it is significant. The distinction is trivial in the sense that once the state has exercised its power to deprive an individual of his right to do something such as acquire property or engage in mutually consensual contractual arrangements, the issue of whether that individual has been deprived of a natural right, or whether that natural right never existed in the first place, is wholly academic. I would argue that, in such an instance, the state has deprived the individual of his ability to do something, but he retains his natural right to do the thing.

Thus, there is a difference between natural rights and inalienable rights. There probably are no inalienable rights, because the state, which enjoys a virtual monopoly on force, can successfully deprive people of their ability to make practical use of their rights. The fact that the state possesses such power does not mean, however, that there are no natural rights. Following Posner, those who reject the idea of natural rights might argue that an individual loses his right to engage in a particular activity the moment the state passes a law forbidding that act;[17] I would

---

[17] One might argue that Posner is at least implicitly acknowledging the rights perspective because individuals cannot lose a right that they never had to begin with. Posner's response would seem to be that the state's rights trump those of individual citizens, although it is not obvious why this is the case. See Posner, "Hegel and Employment at Will: A Comment," p. 1627. Alternatively, Posner might respond that the individual had the right at first

argue that the state simply has exercised its *power* to prevent the individual from exercising his (natural) rights. From a consequentialist perspective, of course, this distinction is meaningless, because the tangible effects
on a person affected by the law are the same in either case: he will be
required to comply with the dictates of the state.

However, from a jurisprudential perspective, the distinction between
those who take the Posnerian view that natural law does not exist, and
those, like myself, who think it does exist, is quite significant. Those who
believe that natural law does not exist, obviously believe that such law
can have no effect on the contours of civil law. By contrast, a natural-
rights orientation is of practical value, because it places the moral burden
of persuasion on the state whenever it wishes to deprive a person of some
right. This orientation, it seems to me, is far superior to an orientation
that believes that the existence of rights is determined by pragmatic concerns, such that, e.g., if someone can organize a political coalition that is
successful in obtaining passage of a statute requiring Chris Webber's salary to be turned over to that person, then he has the "right" to that salary. A dramatic example of the potentially immense practical significance
of the philosophical distinction I am making between "rights" and
"power" is found in the remarkable transformation in American jurisprudence that occurred between 1937 and 1947 (the "post-*Lochner*" era).[18]
During this time the Supreme Court largely abandoned its long-held commitment to the protection of property rights.[19] In particular, the Court
abandoned its protection of the right of the individual to enhance the

---

because the government gave it to him. But this would be factually inaccurate, because the
government has not enacted laws covering every activity that individuals can engage in.

[18] The term "*Lochner* era" derives from the Supreme Court's landmark 1905 decision in
Lochner v. New York, 198 U.S. 45 (1905), which concerned the constitutionality of a New York
law limiting the number of hours a baker could work to sixty hours per week or ten hours
per day. This New York statute was held unconstitutional in the U.S. Supreme Court on
the grounds that it violated the constitutional right to contract of the employers and employees covered by the statute. Richard Epstein has found that the labor practices being regulated
by the New York law did not exploit workers. Rather, the proposed legislation placed small,
family-owned bakeries at a competitive disadvantage with respect to large, unionized bakeries. Richard A. Epstein, "Toward a Revitalization of the Contract Clause," *University of Chicago Law Review*, vol. 51, no. 2 (Spring 1980), pp. 732–34. For a more complete discussion
of the evolution of the treatment of economic liberties under the Constitution, see Bernard
H. Siegan, *Economic Liberties and the Constitution* (Chicago: University of Chicago Press, 1980).

[19] The *Lochner* decision in 1905 began an era in the Court's history, lasting until 1937, in
which approximately two hundred economic regulations were struck down on the grounds
that they violated citizens' rights to substantive due process. During the *Lochner* era, the
Court protected private property rights from governmental interference and adopted a
laissez-faire attitude toward economics and wealth distribution. Regulations of the terms
and conditions of employment were routinely struck down by the Court. For example, in
Adkins v. Children's Hospital, 261 U.S. 525 (1923), the Court struck down minimum-wage laws
for women on the grounds that these regulations merely promoted wealth redistribution for
women, and did not promote a legitimate health objective. Similarly, in *Coppage v. Kansas*,
236 U.S. 1 (1919), the Court held that a state statute outlawing so-called "yellow dog" labor

value of his property rights by engaging in mutually consensual exchange transactions free of governmental interference. As Cass Sunstein has pointed out, the crucial transformation that occurred during this period was not a change in the institutional role of the judiciary in overseeing the political process, but rather a change in the Court's conception of the meaning of rights.[20]

The fact that the judiciary has not completely abdicated power to Congress or to the state legislatures since 1937 is amply demonstrated by the Court's consistent willingness to overturn legislative enactments in areas that do not involve property rights.[21] Nor has the Court abandoned its belief that mutually consensual market transactions are beneficial both to the participants in such transactions and to society as a whole. Indeed, the justices remain committed, at least in principle, to the ideals of free enterprise and private property.[22]

Rather, the crucial jurisprudential event in the 1930s was the Supreme Court's rejection of the idea expressed in the Declaration of Independence that certain "fundamental" rights are natural and pre-political and there-

---

contracts, which required employees to sign a waiver of their right to join a union as a condition of employment, was invalid because it infringed upon the employers' and employees' freedom of contract.

The *Lochner* era began to crumble in 1934 with the Court's decision in *Nebbia v. New York*, 291 U.S. 502, upholding a regulatory scheme for fixing milk prices. The Court rejected the *Lochner*-era idea that governmental price regulation could only be extended to business in extremely rare circumstances, and allowed states to enact economic regulations that could be construed by legislators as promoting public welfare. The *Lochner* era was dealt its most crushing blow in 1937, when the Court overruled *Adkins v. Children's Hospital*, 261 U.S. 525 (1923), and upheld a minimum-wage law for women in *West Coast Hotel Co. v. Parrish*, 300 U.S. 379 (1937). The decline of the *Lochner* era was due, in great part, to the Court's belief that New Deal programs were necessary for the nation's economic survival during the Great Depression. A shift in the membership of the Court contributed to *Lochner*'s demise. New Deal reformers criticized the justices on the Court that decided *Lochner* for trying to protect the interests of capitalists at the expense of the general public's interest. The New Dealers succeeded overwhelmingly in shifting the Court away from its philosophical orientation in favor of property rights. Since 1937, no economic regulations have been struck down on substantive due process grounds.

[20] Cass R. Sunstein, "Beyond the Republican Revival," *Yale Law Journal*, vol. 97, no. 8 (July 1988), pp. 1539–80.

[21] Perhaps the most famous example of the Court's willingness to overturn legislative enactments that infringe on real or perceived noneconomic rights is *Roe v. Wade*, 410 U.S. 113 (1973), which established a constitutional right to abortion on the grounds that women enjoy a fundamental right to privacy. Similarly, in *Texas v. Johnson*, 491 U.S. 397 (1989), the Court upheld the right of citizens to burn the American flag by overturning a Texas statute making it a crime to desecrate or otherwise mistreat the flag. The opinion was based on the constitutional right to freedom of speech. And, in *Florida Star v. B.J.F.*, 491 U.S. 524 (1989), the Court held that free-speech rights allowed newspapers to publish the names of rape victims despite a Florida statute banning the practice. In *Pierce v. Society of Sisters*, 268 U.S. 510 (1925), the Court struck down a statute requiring that children attend only public schools, thereby upholding the rights of parents to send their children to private schools, so long as such schools meet basic educational standards.

[22] John E. Nowak, Ronald D. Rotunda, and J. Nelson Young, *Constitutional Law* (St. Paul: West Publishing Co., 1978), pp. 77–78.

fore exist outside the realm of politics.[23] In place of this natural-rights conception of law that existed until 1937, the Court has embraced a conception of rights as a purely political manifestation of "a well-functioning deliberative process."[24] It was this important change that permitted the Court to abandon its commitment to economic liberty and to abdicate its role to check and balance the excesses of Congress and the state legislatures.

C. Implications for constitutional planning

In the above discussion I have argued that property consists of assets that have value in exchange. Property rights are rights to command resources, either directly or through exchange transactions. While consensual market transactions are mutually beneficial, coerced governmental wealth transfers benefit only one party to the transaction and reduce aggregate wealth in the ways described above.

The problem, of course, is that the very collective (governmental) force used to define and protect property rights can also be used to effectuate governmental wealth transfers. The primary problem facing people who are involved in constitutional ordering is how to create a governmental structure that is sufficiently powerful to protect citizens' property rights, and to provide for public goods such as national defense, without creating a governmental structure that encourages rent-seeking.

This problem is particularly acute because powerful factions and interest groups will be willing to pay governmental actors (in the form of either outright bribes, promised political support, or other currency) for legislation that is of particular benefit to them, while free-rider and collective-action problems will cause individuals and groups to be reluctant to pay for the public goods that the government is supposed to provide, e.g., defense, interstate highways, protection of navigable waterways.

---

[23] The shift in the Court's reasoning reflected a greater trust in legislative judgments about social issues. The Court disclosed a willingness to defer to the legislature about what sorts of measures would promote public welfare. The change began in *Nebbia v. New York*, 291 U.S. 502 (1934), when the Court stated that "a state is free to adopt whatever economic policy may reasonably be deemed to promote public welfare" (*ibid.*, 537). Gradually, the Court rejected the idea that substantive due process was a viable legal theory. The result has been a deference to legislative authority that has manifested itself in cases such as *Home Building & Loan Association v. Blaisdell*, 290 U.S. 398 (1934) (upholding a statute granting local courts the power to relieve a mortgagor from foreclosure sales despite his violation of the terms of the mortgage, so long as he has paid a reasonable portion of the fair rental value of the property); *P. F. Peterson Baking Co. v. Bryan*, 290 U.S. 570 (1934) (upholding a Nebraska statute regulating the weight of every loaf of bread made for sale in Nebraska on grounds of protecting bakers from unfair competition); and *Norman v. Baltimore & Ohio R.R. Co.*, 294 U.S. 240 (1955) (permitting the government to interfere with private contracts by invalidating agreements specifying that payments for services must be in gold).

[24] Sunstein, "Beyond the Republican Revival," pp. 1539–80.

Mancur Olson has provided the best summary of the normative implications of the interest-group model of political behavior.[25] The very existence of a collectivity capable of effectuating wealth transfers provides
strong incentives for special-interest coalitions and organizations to
emerge in the first place. These organizations "reduce efficiency and
aggregate income in the societies in which they operate and make political life more divisive."[26] In addition, these coalitions "slow down a society's capacity to adopt new technologies and to reallocate resources in
response to changing conditions, and thereby reduce the rate of economic
growth."[27] Finally, special-interest groups increase "the complexity of
regulation, the role of government, and the complexity of understandings,"[28] thereby retarding the social evolution of a society and raising
the costs of all forms of economic activity.

It is for all of these reasons that, like theft, efforts to obtain resources
through governmental wealth transfers are both amoral and ultimately
self-destructive as they cause individuals to obtain property through coercion, rather than through consent. By parity of reasoning, the opposite
applies to efforts to obtain resources through market transactions, because these sorts of transactions increase efficiency and aggregate income,
improve the ability of a society to respond to new technologies, and
improve the quality of understandings by establishing a pattern of dealings that can be mimicked by others.

These insights have led to depressing conclusions. Olson has argued
that, in advanced, organized societies, the apparently irrepressible efforts
of special-interest groups to organize into effective political coalitions in
order to effectuate wealth transfers to themselves from less powerful
groups, imply that democratic economic systems will ultimately crumble,
as governments slowly but systematically remove private parties' incentives to create wealth.[29] While Olson's analysis may ultimately prove correct, there are at least two gaps in his analysis, one theoretical and one
empirical, that provide a basis for hope. The empirical gap in Olson's
analysis is that, by predicting the decline of all advanced, industrial societies, he fails to account for the sustained postwar economic success of
Japan and Germany, or for the long-term success of such diverse countries as Switzerland, Hong Kong, South Korea, and Singapore.

The theoretical gap in Olson's analysis is that so long as the members
of a community recognize that the establishment of a civil society will

[25] Mancur Olson, *The Rise and Decline of Nations* (New Haven: Yale University Press, 1982), p. 74.
[26] *Ibid.*
[27] *Ibid.*
[28] *Ibid.*
[29] *Ibid.*, p. 77.

bring with it the problems of rent-seeking, all members of society have an incentive *ex ante* (that is, at the time the constitutional rules of the civil society are formulated) to devise rules that protect private property rights and discourage rent-seeking. To put the matter a bit more formally, rational members of society will recognize that once the civil society has formed, each member will face a collective-action problem in the form of a Prisoner's Dilemma that prevents society as a whole from reaching collective outcomes that further the aggregate welfare of the group.

The term "Prisoner's Dilemma" describes the situation that arises when two prisoners have been apprehended and accused of committing a crime. Each prisoner, when separated from the other, will find that it is in his individual interest to confess, even though both prisoners would be better off if they could coordinate their activities and forge an enforceable agreement to remain silent. For example, a Prisoner's Dilemma arises where each prisoner is told that he will receive a jail term of five years if both confess. Each prisoner is also told that if one of them confesses, and the other does not, the confessing prisoner will receive a lighter sentence of one year, while the uncooperative prisoner will receive a more severe sentence of ten years. Finally, the prisoners are told that if both remain silent, they can only be convicted of a lesser charge (say possession of a dangerous weapon, instead of attempted robbery), and hence will receive only two years each.

Under these circumstances, the best outcome for each prisoner would be obtained by confessing and having the other party remain silent. On the other hand, the worst outcome for each prisoner would be to remain silent while the other prisoner confesses. Thus, in the absence of an ability to coordinate their actions, the two parties will both confess in order to avoid the worst possible outcome and to have a chance at the best possible outcome.

In the context of constitutional design, future citizens recognize that after the moment of constitutional formation, they will be in a Prisoner's Dilemma. The best outcome for each individual will be obtained if that citizen, and the groups to which that individual belongs, have their own property rights protected from confiscation but simultaneously are able freely to pursue wealth transfers from government. The worst outcome for each citizen, of course, will be obtained if that citizen, and the groups to which that individual belongs, have little or no protection for their own property rights and are prevented from pursuing wealth transfers from government.

The critical point here, of course, is that so long as citizens realize that this state of the world will exist at some later date, each citizen has a strong interest in agreeing *ex ante* (i.e., at the time of constitutional creation) to protect property rights and to constrain rent-seeking. By forging such an agreement, everybody can be made better off, provided of course that the agreement can be enforced. This is a straightforward implication of the fact that rent-seeking is a negative-sum game.[30]

Indeed, even if certain groups and individuals expect to be net winners from the wealth-transfer game, such groups and individuals either can be excluded from the new collectivity or else can be induced to join the constitutional scheme through side payments that are given in exchange for a commitment to support a constitutional regime that restricts coercive, inefficient wealth transfers.[31] Thus, the interest-group dynamic during times of constitutional creation may be completely different from the dynamic during times of ordinary politics, when wealth transfers can be expected to dominate the political landscape.

III. The Framers' Design

Interestingly, the Framers of the United States Constitution were fully aware of the nature of the dilemma they faced. In fact, one of the basic justifications offered by the Framers for their new Constitution centered around its usefulness in controlling interest groups.[32] The Framers' perspectives and assumptions about constitutional law find their most complete expression in "Federalist No. 10," in which James Madison expressly embraced the notion that what would separate the American

---

[30] This analysis presumes that *ex ante* none of the parties think that they will be net winners in the rent-seeking process. This presumption will be robust in any society in which there are a large number of different factions, groups, and interests. In such a society, individuals will be members of losing factions more often than they will be members of winning factions, because the rent-seeking process is characterized by wealth transfers through the political system from large, disparate groups to small, discrete interest groups. Individuals may receive net benefits when they happen to be allied with small, discrete groups. But these same individuals will find themselves on the giving end of wealth transfers far more often than they find themselves on the receiving end, because they will not be members of most of the small, discrete groups that participate in the rent-seeking process.

[31] Individuals who expect to be net winners in the political process can be bought off easily because of the threat of exclusion from the new civil society. By demanding a side payment in the first place, those individuals who expect to be net winners reveal themselves as being a net drag on the productivity of the future society. This disclosure will reduce dramatically the willingness of other potential members to include them in the first place.

[32] See James Madison, "Federalist No. 10," in *The Federalist Papers*, ed. Clinton Rossiter (New York: Mentor, 1961), p. 77 ("[a]mong the numerous advantages promised by a well-constructed Union, none deserves to be more accurately developed than its tendency to break and control the violence of faction"); Alexander Hamilton, "Federalist No. 22," in *ibid.* (applauding political stalemate and governmental inaction); Madison, "Federalist No. 37," in *ibid.*, p. 231 (describing the Framers' "deep conviction of the necessity of sacrificing private opinions and partial interests to the public good"); Madison, "Federalist No. 51," in *ibid.*, p. 322 (explaining the Framers' "policy of supplying, by opposite and rival interests, the defect of better motives," in order to ensure stalemate rather than action at the behest of private interests); see also Cass R. Sunstein, "Interest Groups and American Public Law," *Stanford Law Review*, vol. 38, no. 1 (November 1985), p. 29: "[T]he problem of faction has been a central concern of constitutional law and theory since the time of the American Revolution."

Constitution from its predecessors in world history would be a more realistic conception of human nature. In particular, the Framers understood
that the post-constitutional world would be motivated by self-interest
rather than by virtue.[33] And the Framers recognized that in post-
constitutional politics, citizens' self-interest would manifest itself in the
form of factions or special-interest groups whose goal would be to effectuate wealth transfers to themselves from the population as a whole. The
distinctive feature of the American Constitution, then, was that it was the
first constitution in world history expressly designed to confront the problems of faction and interest-group opportunism.

   Thus, the Framers attempted to guide transactions away from the political sphere and toward the marketplace, because they recognized that the
same invisible hand that leads to wealth creation in private market transactions, leads to economic inefficiency and social instability in the political sphere.[34] In designing a Constitution that would protect private
property rights and retard rent-seeking, the Framers had three possible
strategies at their disposal: language-based strategies, incentive-based
strategies, and structurally based strategies. The Constitution reflects the
use of each of these, at least to some extent, although for the reasons
specified below, structurally based strategies dominated the Framers'
efforts.

A. Language-based strategies

   The Constitution is replete with manifestations of the Framers' efforts
to protect private property interests and retard rent-seeking through the
use of language. Most notable among the explicit protections is the Fifth
Amendment prohibition against the taking of private property "for public use, without just compensation."[35] In addition, the Constitution protects property rights by prohibiting the government from requiring that
soldiers be housed in private residences without the consent of the
owner,[36] and by acknowledging the "right of the people to be secure in
their persons, houses, papers, and effects against unreasonable searches
and seizures."[37] More importantly, the Ninth Amendment seems to presume the existence of a set of natural rights retained by the people against
the state. It provides that "[t]he enumeration in the Constitution, of certain rights, shall not be construed to deny or disparage others retained by
the people."[38] Furthermore, the Tenth Amendment stipulates that

---

[33] Jonathan R. Macey, "Competing Economic Views of the Constitution," *George Washington Law Review*, vol. 56, no. 1 (November 1987), p. 56.

[34] See Olson, *Rise and Decline of Nations*, pp. 36–74.

[35] U.S. Constitution, Amendment V.

[36] U.S. Constitution, Amendment III.

[37] U.S. Constitution, Amendment IV.

[38] U.S. Constitution, Amendment IX.

"powers not delegated to the United States by the Constitution, nor prohibited by it to the States, are reserved to the States respectively, or to the people."[39]

The problem with these language-based protections of property rights is that they are not self-enforcing. They depend on the willingness of public servants to interpret the language in ways that are often contrary to the immediate interests not only of those public servants, but also of powerful, self-interested political coalitions. Moreover, the Darwinian forces of electoral processes in democratic governments are likely to weed out politicians who attempt to remain faithful to constitutional language that is designed to protect property rights. This is because rival politicians who promise to ignore such language will be more popular with the economic and political interests that must be served to win popular elections.

Thus, language-based systems for controlling interest-group wealth transfers and protecting property rights, while inexpensive to construct, are not likely to prove effective.

B. Incentive-based strategies

One way that constitutional architects can protect property rights and reduce the incidence of rent-seeking is by creating a constitution that provides appropriate economic incentives for government officials. The theory is simple: just as corporations in the private sector compensate managers for productivity through bonuses and other incentive-based mechanisms, so too could governmental actors be compensated for protecting property rights, and resisting rent-seekers. The U.S. Constitution does this, albeit to a limited extent. One way that the Constitution provides incentives for governmental actors to protect property rights is by establishing a federal system that creates competition among the providers of legal rules, thereby causing politicians to suffer the costs associated with citizen exit if they enact suboptimal legal rules.

Put another way, as long as there are viable substitutes for the existing political regime, a state will find it difficult to extract wealth from its constituents if there are other states to which its constituents may move at low cost. The American Constitution created a system in which individual states would be forced to compete for citizens.[40] The free flow of people across borders was assured, and the Constitution provides that "[t]he Citizens of each State shall be entitled to all Privileges and Immunities of Citizens in the several States."[41] While this aspect of the constitutional

---

[39] U.S. Constitution, Amendment X.

[40] The states' independence from the federal government permits them "to provide real, if today very limited, competitive alternatives for consumers of governmental services" (Richard Posner, "The Constitution as an Economic Document," *George Washington Law Review*, vol. 56, no. 1 [November 1987], pp. 4–38).

[41] U.S. Constitution, Article IV, Section 2, Clause 1.

design has worked rather well, the Framers did not envision the inexorable transfer of power from the states to the federal government that has largely undermined the efficacy of the incentive system created by the existence of jurisdictional competition among rival sovereigns.[42]

Unfortunately, the lack of a pricing mechanism for the value of governmental services places significant constraints on the efficacy of incentive systems other than jurisdictional competition that might serve as mechanisms for protecting property rights. It is easy for investors to judge the claims of performance made by rival firms, because share price performances of such firms can be readily compared. By contrast, it is extremely difficult for citizens to judge the claims of rival politicians or rival political parties in the absence of a pricing system.

Thus, in theory, compensation levels for executives should generally be linked to share price performance, because share prices reflect both the current observable performance of the firm and expectations about the firm's future performance (discounted to reflect present value).[43] Thus, those with an interest in a particular firm can monitor its performance and its expected future performance simultaneously by observing share prices. No analogous measure of a politician's performance exists, however. This lack of any appropriate benchmark for measuring and monitoring political performance is a primary justification for adopting a political regime that replaces governmental decision making with the private ordering of the marketplace. It also explains why incentive-based systems for rewarding politicians and bureaucrats are so difficult to devise.

For example, elected officials could be compensated based on some measure such as the growth in gross domestic product (GDP); however, unlike share prices, GDP measures only current output. Such a scheme would give politicians incentives to favor short-term growth over long-term considerations. Schemes to link politicians' compensation to employment levels have similar problems. Politicians would be inclined to engage in debt-finance government spending in order to keep employment levels high.

Thus, apart from providing for competition among governmental jurisdictions by permitting firms and individuals to move freely from one jurisdictional authority to another, the standard incentive mechanisms used in corporate governance cannot be replicated easily in the political

---

[42] However, the anti-Federalists did anticipate this transfer of power to the federal government. See "Agrippa," in *The Complete Anti-Federalist*, ed. H. Storing (Chicago: University of Chicago Press, 1981), p. 99.

[43] There has been a great deal of controversy in recent months over the salaries of top corporate officers, in part because executive compensation appears to have been increasing without a corresponding increase in corporate profits. It appears that compensation for top management is not as closely linked to performance as one might expect. See Michael C. Jensen and Kevin J. Murphy, "Performance Pay and Top Management Incentives," *Journal of Political Economy*, vol. 98, no. 2 (Winter 1990), pp. 225–64.

sphere. Unlike the corporate sphere with its public market for shares, nothing in the political realm provides citizens with a low-cost mechanism for observing and evaluating the performance of politicians and bureaucrats. Thus, the incentive-based strategies for assuring agents' performance in the private sector do not hold the same promise for success in the public sector.

C. Structurally based strategies

In light of the weaknesses inherent in both language-based and incentive-based strategies, it is not surprising that the Framers of the U.S. Constitution looked to structurally based strategies as their preferred mechanism for controlling politicians in the post-constitutional world. Indeed, a careful examination of the Constitution from a structural perspective reveals a remarkable level of sophistication in the sorts of structurally based strategies employed to combat the assault on property rights caused by rent-seeking.

At their core, structurally based strategies are designed to protect property rights and reduce rent-seeking by raising the costs to special-interest groups of passing legislation generally. The structural features in the Constitution that protect property rights by reducing the efficacy of interest-group activity are: (a) the provision for a bicameral legislature in which the House and the Senate are of different sizes and represent different constituencies; (b) the provision for an executive veto; (c) the provision for an independent judiciary.

1. Bicameral legislature. With regard to the bicameral legislature, Robert McCormick and Robert Tollison have demonstrated empirically that for a fixed number of total legislators, interest groups fare better in the market for legislation where the legislators are distributed equally between the houses of a bicameral legislature.[44] By contrast, where the members of each house represent different constituencies, and where the two houses must concur to pass a law, it is more difficult and more costly for interest groups to ensure the passage of legislation that furthers their interests. This is because the cost of making collective decisions goes up in a nonlinear fashion—these costs increase at a faster rate than the growth in the size of the legislature.[45] As a result, if the total size of the legislature is held constant, increasing the size of one house (with a concomitant decrease in the size of the other) raises the cost to an interest group of obtaining agreement in that house by an amount greater than the group's savings in the other house.

[44] Robert E. McCormick and Robert D. Tollison, *Politicians, Legislation, and the Economy: An Inquiry into the Interest Group Theory of Government* (Boston: Martinus Nijhoff, 1981), pp. 45–57.

[45] Mancur Olson, *The Logic of Collective Action: Public Goods and the Theory of Groups* (Cambridge, MA: Harvard University Press, 1971), pp. 53–65.

Thus, for example, the cost to an interest group of obtaining a wealth transfer in a bicameral legislature of 200 representatives will increase if the legislature moves from a structure in which there are 100 representatives in each house, to a structure in which there are 160 representatives in one house and 40 in another. This is because the dynamics of collective action dictate that the increase in costs to interest groups of effectuating wealth transfers in the body of 160 will increase by more than the decrease in the cost of purchasing influence in the body of 40.

Consistent with this analysis, Article I of the Constitution, which sets forth the composition of the Senate and the House of Representatives, clearly envisions a bicameral legislature in which the houses are of radically different sizes. Article I, Section 2, Clause 3 provides that membership in the House of Representatives shall not exceed one for every thirty thousand people, while Article I, Section 3, Clause 1 provides that the Senate shall be composed of two Senators from each state.

Similarly, the provision in Article I, Section 2, allowing for the growth of the House of Representatives as the population grows,[46] is another structural feature designed to protect property rights by controlling the efficacy of interest groups. This is because rent-seeking is expected to increase as the population grows larger, but to become more difficult and costly as the legislature grows.

2. *Executive veto.* The executive veto raises costs to interest groups in much the same way as the bicameral legislature. The veto permits the executive branch to act as a third house of the legislature, thus furthering the cost to interest groups of obtaining favorable legislation.

3. *Independent judiciary.* The provision for an independent judiciary also protects property rights by raising the costs to interest groups of destroying such rights. While it is clear that the independent judiciary fails to fully live up to its intended role as a vehicle for protecting property rights,[47] it is also clear that the judiciary continues to play an important, if needlessly self-constrained, role in this area.

---

[46] U.S. Constitution, Article I, Section 2, Clause 3.

[47] The most complete expression by the Framers of the role of the independent judiciary in protecting against rent-seeking is contained in "Federalist No. 78":

> But it is not with a view to infractions of the Constitution only that the independence of the judges may be an essential safeguard against the effects of occasional ill humors in the society. . . . [T]he firmness of the judicial magistracy is of vast importance in mitigating the severity and confining the operation of such [unjust and partial] laws. It not only serves to moderate the immediate mischiefs of those which may have been passed but it operates as a check upon the legislative body in passing them; who, perceiving that obstacles to the success of an iniquitous intention are to be expected from the scruples of the courts, are in a manner compelled, by the very motives of the injustice they meditate, to qualify their attempts. (Alexander Hamilton, "Federalist No. 78," in Rossiter, ed., *The Federalist Papers* [*supra* note 32], p. 470)

The Framers intended the judiciary branch to be a distinctly separate, independent mechanism for securing "a steady, upright and impartial administration of the laws" (*ibid.*, p. 471) and for strictly upholding the rights guaranteed by the Constitution. While the judicial

Prior to the New Deal era, the independent judiciary in general and the Supreme Court in particular were strong believers in market systems, and embraced a laissez-faire ideology based on classical economics. These views caused them to be more ardent protectors of property rights than modern judges, who are more likely to believe in the virtues of the regulatory state.[48] The protections that the Court traditionally afforded to economic liberties of all kinds, particularly property rights, stemmed from two sources. First, the Court respected the Founders' judgment that the very fate of the republic hinged on their ability to construct a government that would provide adequate protections for property rights. The Framers recognized that the greatest challenge facing them was to control the threat to property rights posed by the rent-seeking activities of interest groups (known to the Framers as "factions"):

> The latent causes of faction are thus sown in the nature of man; and we see them everywhere brought into different degrees of activity. . . . *[T]he most common and durable source of factions has been the various and unequal distribution of property.* Those who hold and those who are without property have ever formed distinct interests in society. Those who are creditors, and those who are debtors, fall under a like discrimination. A landed interest, a manufacturing interest, a mercantile interest, a moneyed interest, with many lesser interests, grow up of necessity in civilized nations, and divide them into different classes, actuated by different sentiments and views. *The regulation of these various and interfering interests forms the principal task of modern legislation. . . .*[49]

Indeed, the Framers rejected the idea of government through pure democracy because democratic structures were thought to provide inad-

---

branch was intended to serve as a check on legislative excess, it was also designed to be the weakest of the three branches, having only the power of judgment and neither the independent power to enforce its decrees nor the ability to influence or control the financial affairs of the nation. To effectuate this, the Framers believed it was necessary for all federal judges to hold their positions, pending good behavior, for life terms. Life tenure ostensibly would remove the political pressures exerted over other government officers and would allow for the long, detailed study of precedent that was necessary, the Framers believed, to just administration of the laws.

The power of judicial review was not expressly granted by the Constitution. The Supreme Court's role as the final arbiter of the Constitution was a product of judicial construction, in *Marbury v. Madison*, 1 Cranch 131 (U.S. 1803), where Chief Justice Marshall reasoned that a denial of judicial review of the constitutionality of legislative enactments would force the courts to ignore the Constitution in violation of their oath of office, which requires them to support the Constitution.

[48] As an example of the pre–New Deal attitude toward property rights, see the decision handed down in *Lochner v. New York*, 198 U.S. 45 (1905) (described in note 18 above).

[49] James Madison, "Federalist No. 10," in Rossiter, ed., *The Federalist Papers* (*supra* note 32), p. 79; italics added.

equate protections against special-interest groups' efforts to undermine property rights:

> [D]emocracies have ever been spectacles of turbulence and contention; have ever been found incompatible with personal security or the rights of property; and have in general been as short in their lives as they have been violent in their deaths.[50]

From the founding of the American republic until the New Deal era, the Supreme Court and the lower federal courts respected the Framers' view that protecting property rights was in the long-term interest of the nation.

A second, independent reason why the Supreme Court protected property rights prior to the New Deal stemmed from the justices' "independent reading of the Constitution and the historic freedom of action in American life. . . ."[51] In particular, the commerce clause and the takings clause were thought to compel the invalidation of laws that unreasonably infringed on property rights or free enterprise.[52]

But gradually, beginning in the mid-1930s, the Supreme Court abandoned its commitment to providing constitutional protections from governmental interference with property rights. Cultural, political, and ideological pressures combined over time to cause the judiciary to virtually eliminate the explicit constitutional protections traditionally provided for property rights.[53]

[50] *Ibid.*, p. 81.

[51] Nowak, Rotunda, and Young, *Constitutional Law* (*supra* note 22), pp. 77–78.

[52] Under Article I, Section 8, of the Constitution, Congress is given explicit authority "[t]o regulate Commerce with foreign Nations, and among the several States and with the Indian Tribes." In addition to being a positive grant of authority to Congress, this provision has been construed as limiting the power of state legislatures, by depriving them of the power to enact statutes that interfere with interstate commerce. In *Gibbons v. Ogden*, 9 Wheat 1 (1824), the Court held that only Congress and not state legislatures could regulate commerce affecting more than one state. States can only regulate commercial activity that does not affect interstate commerce.

The Fifth Amendment to the Constitution provides that "[n]o person shall be . . . deprived of life, liberty, or property, without due process of law; nor shall private property be taken for public use, without just compensation." Under current Fifth Amendment jurisprudence, the states and the federal government have the right to take private property so long as the private owner is justly compensated for such use. If property is merely subjected to regulatory restrictions, however, no compensation is required. To avoid having a regulatory act classified as a compensable taking, the government must prove that the regulation substantially promotes legitimate governmental interests and does not deny the owner of the property any economically viable use of his land, see *Agins v. City of Tiburon*, 447 U.S. 255 (1980). In theory, a taking is never justifiable except for a "public use." However, the Court has interpreted the public-use requirement so broadly that now any interference with ownership that is "rationally related to a conceivable public purpose" satisfies the public-use requirement; see *Hawaii Housing Authority v. Midkiff*, 467 U.S. 229 (1984).

[53] In general, the diminution in protections for property rights came when the Court abandoned its belief in the virtues of private property and free markets. In particular, in hun-

Despite the fact that the judiciary routinely ignores property rights when it reviews legislative enactments for constitutional infirmity, the independent judiciary still provides important, albeit subtle, protection for property rights. In particular, whenever an interest group obtains passage of a statute that threatens property rights through governmental regulation, there is a danger that the statute will have to be interpreted by a court. When judges interpret statutes they are likely to ignore the nature of any bargains that interest groups have struck with legislatures, because these judges were not party to such deals and do not stand to benefit from them. Moreover, the judges who interpret statutes will generally be unable to enforce interest groups' bargains with Congress even if they want to, because Congress generally disguises its statutory wealth transfers to interest groups by claiming that such statutes have been enacted to benefit the public.

Special-interest legislation is often drafted with a public-regarding gloss because the gloss raises the cost to the electorate and to rival interest groups of discovering the true effects of the legislation. In other words, public values are engrafted onto statutes in order to "justify the exercise of governmental power."[54] Typically, legislation that impinges on property rights is justified on the grounds that such legislation is a valid exercise of the government's "police power." The police power refers to the power to enact and enforce laws that promote the public health, welfare, and safety. The police power has been cogently described as "a hugely expansible excuse for a host of governmental interventions . . . [which] has been stretched to justify such governmental tampering with the mar-

dreds of constitutional cases involving the takings clause, the commerce clause, and due-process rights, the Court has balanced the articulated interests of the state against the property interests involved in the case, and has exalted the state interests over the property interests. For example, in *Penn Central Transportation Co. v. New York*, 438 U.S. 104 (1978), the Supreme Court held that New York law could prohibit Penn Central from building a multistory office building above Grand Central Station. The Court held that the severe restrictions on property rights that came as a result of the designation of Grand Central Station as a historic landmark did not constitute a taking.

It is simply impossible for a litigant to succeed in persuading a court that a legislative act violates substantive due process norms. And it is extremely difficult for a litigant to succeed in establishing that a regulatory action constitutes an unconstitutional taking. To prevail, a plaintiff must either show a permanent physical occupation of his land, or a complete destruction of the value of the land as a consequence of the government's action, or that the government has reneged on a commitment it has made, thereby frustrating distinct investment-backed expectations on the part of the plaintiff; see *Lucas v. South Carolina Coastal Council*, 112 S.Ct. 2886 (1992). Thus, unless one can show that the government's action has harmed some particular discrete and insular minority that has been singled out for special protection by the Court, legal protests against government-imposed wealth transfers generally are in vain. For an extended discussion of the reasons why the Court abandoned its protections for property rights, see Jonathan R. Macey, "Some Causes and Consequences of the Bifurcated Treatment of Economic Rights and 'Other' Rights under the United States Constitution," *Social Philosophy & Policy*, vol. 9, no. 1 (Winter 1992), pp. 141–70.

[54] Sunstein, "Beyond the Republican Revival" (*supra* note 20), p. 1577.

ket as minimum wage and maximum hours laws, workmen's compensation acts, zoning, and usury laws."[55]

Thus, like the executive veto and the bicameral legislature, the independent judiciary is a structural device that raises the costs to interest groups of effectuating legislative wealth transfers that undermine property rights. And the failure of the judiciary to afford economic liberty constitutional protection, while deplorable, should not be viewed as evidence of the complete failure of the Framers' efforts to protect property rights through the creation of an independent judiciary. In this context, it is worth noting that the Framers appear to have realized that statutory interpretation, rather than the power to review legislative acts for constitutional infirmity, provided the best defense for the establishment of an independent judiciary.[56]

In a nutshell, traditional methods of statutory interpretation by an independent judiciary comprise an additional way in which property rights are protected by the structural elements of the Constitution. By lowering the probability that special-interest legislation will be interpreted in the way the interest-group sponsors envisioned, the judiciary lowers both the value of such legislation to interest groups, and the willingness of such groups to pay for the legislation. This, in turn, lowers the quantity of special-interest legislation.[57]

IV. CHANGES UNDERMINING STRUCTURAL PROTECTIONS OF PROPERTY RIGHTS

The purpose of the preceding discussion was to demonstrate that of all the strategies employed within the U.S. Constitution to protect property rights, only the structurally based strategies have proven successful over time. Unfortunately, while structurally based strategies have been more successful than the alternatives, such strategies have at best provided incomplete protections for such rights. The purpose of this section of the essay is to explain why structurally based strategies have met with only partial success.

A. The internal organization of Congress

The succinct answer to this question is that both interest groups and Congress have used innovative techniques to undermine the structural protections afforded to property rights under the Constitution. In other words, while the Constitution creates a number of structural obstacles to

---

[55] Ellen Frankel Paul, "Moral Constraints and Eminent Domain," review of Richard Epstein, *Takings: Private Property and the Power of Eminent Domain, George Washington Law Review*, vol. 55, no. 1 (November 1986), pp. 174–75.

[56] See, e.g., Hamilton, "Federalist No. 78" (*supra* note 47), p. 470.

[57] Macey, "Promoting Public-Regarding Legislation" (*supra* note 9), pp. 251–56.

interest-group wealth transfers, such groups, with the cooperation of Congress, have developed innovative strategies for avoiding these obstacles.

A critical structural feature of the Constitution that protects property rights is the provision for a bicameral legislature in which various members of Congress, as well as the president, serve different constituencies. The fact that the two houses of Congress and the president must all cooperate, at least to some extent, in order to pass legislation, raises the cost of interest-group wealth transfers by increasing the level of consensus required before legislation can be enacted. Put another way, the bicameral legislature and the presence of a presidential veto create the functional equivalent of a supermajority voting rule, which raises decision costs and makes favorable treatment less likely for special-interest groups.[58]

Similarly, as noted above, one of the more subtle structural protections for property rights contained in the Constitution was the creation of a bicameral legislature in which one house was significantly larger than the other. The virtue of this feature was that it would be particularly difficult to reach consensus in the larger house, because the costs of reaching decisions increase at an increasing rate.

Unfortunately, two technological innovations within Congress itself, the invention of logrolling and the modern committee system, have effectively undermined the structural protections described above. Logrolling is the legislative practice of giving support to another politician on one issue in exchange for receiving support on another. This provides a mechanism by which Congress can reduce the costs of generating legislation that transfers wealth to favored interest-group clients.

The committee system also significantly reduces the cost to interest groups of obtaining collective action by Congress in support of rent-seeking legislation. The ability of committees within Congress to logroll with other committees enables small numbers of legislators to make credible commitments to interest groups that they will not renege on previous promises. Suppose, for example, that there are two groups of legislators. One group is seeking passage of a discrete piece of legislation such as the building of a dam. The other is seeking to have an administrative agency established to benefit its favored constituency.[59] The structurally induced problem facing the interest groups seeking to obtain these statutes is clear. The first group, after building its dam, might pass a new bill revoking the law establishing the administrative agency. This possibility makes it less likely that either law will be enacted, since the two

[58] James M. Buchanan and Gordon Tullock, *The Calculus of Consent: Logical Foundations of Constitutional Democracy* (Ann Arbor: University of Michigan Press, 1965), pp. 233–48.

[59] This example is drawn from Barry R. Weingast and William Marshall, "The Industrial Organization of Congress," *Journal of Political Economy*, vol. 96, no. 1 (February 1988), pp. 132–63.

groups of lawmakers may be unable to bind themselves to a mutual exchange of political support. A nonbinding agreement will be worthless to the legislators.

This so-called nonsimultaneity of performance problem is solved by the introduction of the committee system into Congress. After the dam is built, the politicians who got the credit for building it will be unable to enact legislation to dismantle the legislative agency even if a majority prefers that the regulatory agency be dismantled. This is because, by hypothesis, the legislators who want the administrative agency to be established are the legislators on the committee responsible for reporting out the legislation concerning the agency. As committee members, they are in charge of determining whether any legislation banning the administrative agency ever makes it to the floor for a vote. If proponents of the agency think they will lose the vote, they will not let the matter reach the floor.

The committee system is a remarkably successful device for reducing the efficacy of the structurally based strategies employed by the Framers for protecting property rights. Congressional committees are not representative of the entire Congress. Rather, each committee is disproportionately populated by Congressmen with particularly close ties to the interest groups whose activities fall under the committee's jurisdiction. Thus, politicians with ties to labor tend to serve on the Education and Labor committee, those with ties to urban groups serve on the Banking and Currency committee, while those with ties to agriculture serve on the Agricultural committee.[60] In this way, the costs to interest groups of collective action are reduced, because such groups need only to persuade the members of the relevant committees that legislation they favor should be passed or that legislation they oppose should be blocked. Thus, while the Framers intended that interest groups should have to obtain approval of a supermajority of legislators to achieve passage of a law, the congressional innovations known as the modern committee system and the logrolling process permit such groups to obtain favorable legislation by obtaining approval of only a small fraction of congressmen.

The logrolling process is facilitated by the ability of Congress to package many unrelated laws together in omnibus bills. This innovation makes logrolling easier by solving the contracting problems that exist among legislators. Legislators with favored projects in the omnibus bill can make credible promises to support legislation favored by other legislators in exchange for the support provided on their projects, because all of these projects will be approved simultaneously. Legislators cannot disapprove other projects without disapproving their own.

The practice of bundling large numbers of unrelated measures into omnibus bills also undermines the efficacy of the presidential veto,

---

[60] Barry R. Weingast, "The Political Institutions of Representative Government: Legislatures," *Journal of Institutional and Theoretical Economics*, vol. 145, no. 4 (December 1989), pp. 693–703.

because Congress can bundle measures that it finds important together with measures that the president finds important. In this way Congress is able to hold hostage new laws that are important to the president by making a credible threat that if the president vetoes the bill, he will have sacrificed passage of legislative measures that he believes to be important.

The Constitution determined the basic structure of government, but the Framers permitted Congress to design its own internal rules of governance. Thus, while the Framers recognized that the future of American politics after the ratification of the Constitution would "not be one long glorious reenactment of the American Revolution,"[61] they failed to contemplate ways in which Congress would be able to reduce the efficacy of the structural protections provided for property rights by the Constitution. The basic problem is that Congress has transformed itself, since the founding of the Republic, from a loose collection of unaffiliated individuals from all parts of the country, into a highly efficient, well-organized *organization* dedicated to effectuating wealth transfers to favored groups in order to insure the reelection of its incumbent members. Put succinctly, the Framers envisioned that Congress would act as a market for new legislation, but it has turned out that Congress has organized itself as a firm and not as a market.[62]

For example, during the period immediately following the ratification of the Constitution, new laws were not formulated and approved by committees and subcommittees before coming to the full Congress. Rather, bills were considered and approved in principle by the Committee of the Whole before they were sent to a congressional committee to be put into legislative syntax.[63] As a consequence, anyone who wanted to propose a statute had to persuade a majority of the entire legislature that the statute was worth pursuing, because deliberation by the entire body preceded markup by the specialists.[64]

By switching the system so that bills are first discussed at the committee level, the current system facilitates logrolling, because committee members can easily take part in political trading among themselves. This insures that bills coming out of committees have broad-based bipartisan support, if only because of the nature of the compromises reached at the committee level. The current system also facilitates interest-group wealth transfers by making it cheaper for interest groups affected by a particular piece of legislation to identify *ex ante* the relevant legislators to target regarding that legislation. By targeting their lobbying efforts toward the

---

[61] Bruce Ackerman, "The Storrs Lectures: Discovering the Constitution," *Yale Law Journal*, vol. 93, no. 6 (May 1984), p. 1015.

[62] See Weingast and Marshall, "The Industrial Organization of Congress," pp. 132–43.

[63] William T. Mayton, "The Possibilities of Collective Choice: Arrow's Theorem, Article I, and the Delegation of Legislative Power to Administrative Agencies," *Duke Law Journal*, vol. 1986, no. 3 (December 1986), pp. 948–56.

[64] For a complete discussion of the operation of the committee system, see Weingast and Marshall, "The Industrial Organization of Congress."

members of the relevant committee, these interest groups can economize greatly on lobbying costs.

Thus, the rules governing internal organization turned out to play an unexpectedly important role in the legislative outcomes generated by the political process. And, consistent with what one would expect, the rules that Congress has designed to govern its own internal workings have been designed to further the rational self-interest of the legislators themselves. In particular, these rules have been designed to reduce to the fullest extent possible the problems facing interest groups and politicians who wish to undermine property rights by passing interest-group-oriented legislation. These legislators benefit by passing large numbers of laws that provide highly concentrated benefits to discrete groups, and pay for those benefits by taking property from diffuse, poorly organized individuals. These deprivations of property come in the form of taxes, regulatory burdens, licensing restrictions, and the innumerable other manifestations of the modern regulatory state.

B. The rise of the modern administrative state

Interestingly, the modern administrative state emerged during the mid-1930s at precisely the same time that the Supreme Court began to refuse to afford constitutional protections for property rights. The rise of the administrative state is yet another manifestation of Congress's ability to evade the Constitution's structurally based mechanisms for protecting property rights.

The Constitution was designed to protect property rights by raising the costs to interest groups of passing laws. By creating a system of divided government, and requiring some level of approval from all three branches in order to secure passage of a new law, the Framers hoped that each branch of government would check the rent-seeking proclivities of the others.

Administrative agencies typically combine, in a single bureaucracy, legislative functions with judicial and executive functions. The rise of these agencies is probably the greatest departure from the system of government envisioned by the Framers. This is particularly true in light of the fact that when Congress organizes such agencies, it grants them open-ended delegations of administrative power, permitting interest groups to bypass the deliberative processes of the tripartite system of government, and thereby facilitating the ability of interest groups to destroy property rights by capturing the administrative agencies ostensibly created to regulate them.

While interest groups do capture administrative agencies, such captures are unusual. Agencies are generally created amid controversy and conflict among competing interest groups, when legislators are uncertain about the costs and benefits of pursuing alternative courses of action. In such circumstances, the optimal political decision for legislators is to create an administrative agency. An agency creates a regulatory auction at which interest groups can bid for wealth transfers, while Congress avoids accountability for the consequences.

The implications of this phenomenon for property rights are clear:

> Legislators delegate authority to [administrative agencies] in order to reduce various costs of legislating, which allows them to legislate more *private* goods. Stated differently, delegation [of regulatory authority to administrative agencies] reduces the legislator's marginal cost of private-goods production, which *ceteris paribus*, yields more legislation and more public-sector private-goods production.[65]

The very existence of administrative agencies is a glaring contradiction of the carefully crafted structurally based strategy for protecting property rights contained in Article I of the Constitution, which requires envisioning the separate involvement of the House, the Senate, the president, and the federal courts in order to obtain a legislative enactment. These institutions represent different constituencies and have different preferences. This diversity of interests, combined with the requirement that all must acquiesce if a bill is to become law, raises the costs to interest groups and politicians of depriving citizens of their property rights.

Thus, the broad delegations of power to administrative agencies that are a hallmark of the modern legislative system are an additional cause of the diminution in property rights protections caused by the erosion of structurally based mechanisms for protecting property rights. Such broad delegations undermine the lawmaking process contemplated by Article I and make it easier for politicians and interest groups to use the political process to effectuate wealth transfers.

V. CONCLUSION

Property rights are worth protecting for both moral and economic reasons. In order to protect property rights, a legal system must encourage the voluntary transactions that occur in the private sector. Such transactions yield the economic benefit of providing all parties involved in them with a net welfare gain. Such transactions have a broader significance because they provide net gains to the society generally as entrepreneurs are forced by competitive pressures to provide high-quality goods and services at low prices.

By contrast, the social-welfare implications of transactions that occur because of legislative fiat are indeterminate. Some may provide net

[65] P. Aranson, E. Gellhorn, and G. Robinson, "A Theory of Legislative Delegation," *Cornell Law Review*, vol. 68, no. 1 (Fall 1982), pp. 1–60.

improvements in social welfare, many clearly do not. Often these transactions reflect the triumph of raw political power over the disorganized
public at large. Moreover, these transactions are both morally and economically suspect because they reduce aggregate social wealth, because
they make some people better off while making many others worse off,
and because they require people to waste their private time and resources
in combating such transfers. Moreover, rent-seeking reduces the incentives of people to save and invest. This is because the riskiness of investments necessarily increases as property rights become uncertain, as
people can never be sure that the potential gains associated with their
investments will not be subject to new regulatory restrictions, new taxes,
or both.

All of this was well understood by the Framers. Yet history has shown
that the Framers failed to achieve their central goal of providing enduring protections for property rights against the post-constitutional on-
slaught of factions. The reason for this is that Congress has developed
ingenious institutional responses, particularly the committee system and
the modern administrative agency, to overcome the structural protections
for property rights contained in the Constitution.

Law, Cornell Law School

PROPERTY, RIGHTS, AND FREEDOM*

By Gerald F. Gaus

I. Monistic Classical Liberalism

William Penn summarized the *Magna Carta* thus: "First, It asserts *Englishmen* to be free; that's Liberty. Secondly, they that have free-holds, that's Property."[1] Since at least the seventeenth century, liberals have not only understood liberty and property to be fundamental, but to be somehow intimately related or interwoven. Here, however, consensus ends; liberals present an array of competing accounts of the relation between liberty and property. Many, for instance, defend an essentially instrumental view, typically seeing private property as justified because it is necessary to maintain or protect other, more basic, liberty rights. Important to our constitutional tradition has been the idea that "[t]he right to property is the guardian of every other right, and to deprive a people of this, is in fact to deprive them of their liberty."[2] Along similar lines, it has been argued that only an economic system based on private property disperses power and resources, ensuring that private people in civil society have the resources to oppose the state and give effect to basic liberties.[3] Alternatively, it is sometimes claimed that only those with property develop the independent characters that are necessary to preserve a regime of liberty.[4] But not only have liberals insisted that property is a means of preserving liberty, they have often conceived of it as an embodiment of liberty, or as a type of liberty, or indeed as identical

*This essay was written during my tenure as a Visiting Scholar at the Social Philosophy and Policy Center, Bowling Green State University. I would like to thank the Center for its generous support. My thanks also go to David Conway, Bob Ewin, Julian Lamont, Loren Lomasky, Fred Miller, Chris Morris, Ellen Paul, Jeffrey Paul, and Kory Swanson—and to the other contributors to this volume—for their comments and criticisms.

[1] Quoted in Michael Kammen, *Spheres of Liberty: Changing Perceptions of Liberty in American Culture* (Madison: University of Wisconsin Press, 1986), p. 25. Compare Alexander Hamilton, "Federalist No. 85," in *The Federalist Papers*, ed. Clinton Rossiter (New York: Mentor, 1961).

[2] Albert Lee of Virginia, quoted in James W. Ely, Jr., *The Guardian of Every Other Right: A Constitutional History of Property Rights* (New York: Oxford University Press, 1992), p. 26.

[3] As F. A. Hayek writes: "There can be no freedom of the press if the instruments of printing are under government control, no freedom of assembly if the needed rooms are so controlled, no freedom of movement if the means of transport are a government monopoly." See Hayek, "Liberalism," in his *New Studies in Philosophy, Politics, Economics, and the History of Ideas* (London: Routledge and Kegan Paul, 1978), p. 149.

[4] See Alan Ryan, *Property* (Milton Keynes: Open University Press, 1987).

209

to liberty.[5] This latter view is popular among contemporary libertarians or classical liberals.[6] Jan Narveson, for instance, bluntly asserts that "Liberty is Property," while John Gray insists that "[t]he connection between property and the basic liberties is constitutive and not just instrumental."[7]

My subject in this essay is the latter, more intimate, constitutive view of the relation between liberty and property. For not only does it advance an interesting claim about liberty and property, but it points to a particularly elegant theory of liberalism. If liberalism's fundamental commitments are to liberty and property, and if it turns out that these are essentially the same thing (or that one is an instance of the other), then it seems possible that liberalism as a political theory rests on a single value or political principle.[8] In this sense classical liberalism would be a *monistic political theory*. Now no doubt those raised on Isaiah Berlin's "Two Concepts of Liberty" will find this characterization surprising, not to say disturbing. Berlin, of course, charges that monism is the root of anti-liberal ideologies while liberal tolerance derives from appreciating the ultimate plurality of values.[9] As Berlin's analysis of T. H. Green and positive

[5] John W. Chapman advocates an intermediate position, according to which "[i]n a genuinely liberal society, freedom and property stand in a relation, not of opposition, but of mutual justification and support." See Chapman, "Justice, Freedom, and Property," in *NOMOS XXII: Property*, ed. J. Roland Pennock and John W. Chapman (New York: New York University Press, 1980), p. 317.

[6] Henceforth, I shall not distinguish these. I suspect that, ultimately, this is an error: classical liberals tended to be rather more flexible on questions of government intervention in the economy and assistance to the working class than is typical of contemporary libertarians. For instance, Loren Lomasky's very modest welfarism is enough for Tibor Machan to conclude that "Lomasky gives too much to advocates of the welfare state by conceding that some measure of state welfare is appropriate. In my view this undermines the integrity of free constitutional law and government." See Machan, *Individuals and Their Rights* (La Salle: Open Court, 1989), p. xv. Cf. Loren E. Lomasky, *Persons, Rights, and the Moral Community* (New York: Oxford University Press, 1987), pp. 125–29. For the views of classical liberals on these matters, see my "Public and Private Interests in Liberal Political Economy, Old and New," in *Public and Private in Social Life*, ed. S. I. Benn and G. F. Gaus (New York: St. Martin's Press, 1983), pp. 184–95. See also Norman P. Barry, *On Classical Liberalism and Libertarianism* (New York: St. Martin's Press, 1987).

[7] Jan Narveson, *The Libertarian Idea* (Philadelphia: Temple University Press, 1988), p. 66; John Gray, *Liberalism* (Milton Keynes: Open University Press, 1986), p. 62. The description in the text applies to Gray's 1986 position, and not necessarily to his current views. For Gray's itinerary through liberalism to conservatism, see his *Liberalisms* (London: Routledge, 1989), especially the postscript. See also Loren E. Lomasky, "Liberal Obituary?" *Ethics*, vol. 102 (October 1991), pp. 140–54.

[8] In most cases, it is important to distinguish value-based arguments from principled arguments; the appropriate response to values is usually to promote and protect them, while principles demand respect. But nothing turns on this point here. See S. I. Benn, *A Theory of Freedom* (Cambridge: Cambridge University Press, 1988), ch. 1. For a related discussion, see David McNaughton and Piers Rawling, "Honoring and Promoting Values," *Ethics*, vol. 102 (July 1992), pp. 835–43.

[9] Isaiah Berlin, "Two Concepts of Liberty," in his *Four Essays on Liberty* (Oxford: Oxford University Press, 1969), p. 167:

> One belief, more than any other, is responsible for the slaughter of individuals on the altars of the great historical ideals — justice or progress or the happiness of future gen-

liberty shows, however, political liberals have not been immune to monistic ambitions.[10] I suggest here that not only Green's "new liberalism," but classical liberalism too has often manifested the monistic impulse to harmonize, claiming that basic liberal values are, if properly understood, really one. However, it needs to be stressed that my concern is not with values or principles *simpliciter*, but with *political* values or principles. Even if classical liberalism is monistic with respect to its foundational political principle, the justification of liberty and private property could still derive from the ultimate pluralism of nonpolitical values.

It is useful at the outset to distinguish three forms of political monism. My concern in this essay is with what might be called *identity monism*, according to which two or more values or principles that are prima facie distinct really are ultimately analyzable into each other. I shall thus concern myself with claims that liberty can be analyzed as a type of property, or property as a type of liberty. This is to be contrasted to *harmony monism*, which insists that two values, though distinct and independent, can never conflict with each other in the sense that in order to promote one, a person must act contrary to the other. Berlin's critique of monism is directed at both varieties — he aims to show that values are plural (hence identity monism is erroneous) and that they can conflict (hence harmony monism is to be rejected). However, I restrict myself here to showing that property rights and liberty are distinct, and thus that classical liberalism cannot rest on identity monism. The next task would be to consider whether it could still embrace a harmony monism of liberty and property.[11] Lastly, both of these can be contrasted to what can be called *reductive monism*, according to which apparently distinct values can be understood as instances of some third, master value, such as happiness or utility. Arguments upholding the "incommensurability of values" are often cases against a reductive monistic claim that, for instance, all values can be reduced to some single value and so placed on a single met-

---

erations, or the sacred mission or emancipation of a nation or race or class, or even liberty itself, which demands the sacrifice of individuals for the freedom of society. This is the belief that somewhere, in the past or the future, in divine revelation or in the mind of an individual thinker, in the pronouncements of history or science, or in the simple heart of the uncorrupted good man, there is a final solution. This ancient faith rests on the conviction that all positive values in which men have believed must, in the end, be compatible, and perhaps even entail one another.

[10] Remember, Berlin acknowledges that "Green was a genuine liberal" (*ibid.*, p. 133n). I examine Green's liberalism in my *The Modern Liberal Theory of Man* (New York: St. Martin's Press, 1983). For a specific analysis of the relation between Green's idealism and his liberalism, see my "T. H. Green, Bernard Bosanquet, and the Philosophy of Coherence," in *The Routledge History of Philosophy*, vol. 7, *The Nineteenth Century*, ed. C. L. Ten (London: Routledge, 1994).

[11] I have argued elsewhere that property rights, like all rights, restrict liberty. See Gerald F. Gaus and Loren E. Lomasky, "Are Property Rights Problematic?" *The Monist*, vol. 73 (October 1990), pp. 484–503.

ric.[12] Insofar as classical liberalism is based on utilitarianism, it is clearly monistic in this sense. Again, this is not my concern here: I restrict myself to the idea that classical liberalism's view of liberty and property is an instance of identity monism.

Sections II and III examine two versions of the identity monistic claim: (i) that all rights, including liberty rights, are property rights, and (ii) that property rights are themselves liberty rights or directly follow from liberty rights. I shall argue that neither view is plausible given classical-liberal views of ownership and liberty. I conclude in Section IV by briefly examining the relation between rights and freedom and by very briefly commenting upon the prospects for a pluralistic, rather than a monistic, libertarianism.

II. THE "ALL RIGHTS ARE PROPERTY RIGHTS" THESIS

A. Personal rights and ownership: The intuitive view

Narveson claims that each person owns his own body, and this apparently in a straightforward sense that he possesses toward it the standard rights of ownership. Furthermore, it seems that these straightforward rights of ownership account not only for rights to bodily integrity but for rights to liberty too. You own your eyes and that is why they cannot be removed, and because you own your arm, it is up to you to decide whether to lift it or not. To be free to do something is just to be free to use what is yours—your property; so all your freedom rights concern your property. Indeed, Narveson claims, "[it] is plausible to construe *all* rights as property rights." [13]

Pretty clearly, analyzing all rights in terms of property rights requires having a clear grasp of the latter. If, however, we embrace the widely accepted thesis that property is best understood as a (shifting) bundle of rights, it becomes hard to determine just what the "All Rights Are Property Rights" thesis entails. Certainly we cannot understand the thesis as necessarily supposing what A. M. Honoré describes as "full" or "liberal" ownership.[14] It is, of course, a commonplace that many perfectly straightforward examples of property rights do not include all eleven of Honoré's elements.[15] More interesting, perhaps, is that insisting that all rights (e.g., rights to one's body) are instances of full liberal ownership imme-

[12] See my *Value and Justification: The Foundations of Liberal Theory* (Cambridge: Cambridge University Press, 1990), pp. 175ff.

[13] Narveson, *The Libertarian Idea*, p. 66.

[14] See A. M. Honoré, "Ownership," in *Oxford Essays in Jurisprudence*, ed. A. G. Guest (Oxford: Clarendon Press, 1961), pp. 107–47. See also James O. Grunebaum, *Private Ownership* (London: Routledge and Kegan Paul, 1987), ch. 1; and Lawrence C. Becker, *Property Rights* (London: Routledge and Kegan Paul, 1977), pp. 18–19.

[15] For instance, a person can be said to own a building, even though it is a historic landmark and he does not have the right to destroy it.

diately leads to counterintuitive and implausible claims. If one owns one's body in Honoré's sense, then it is subject to "liability of execution" — it can be taken away if one does not repay one's debts.[16] Although some hard-headed proponents of the "All Rights Are Property Rights" thesis may be prepared to embrace even this, we would do well to concentrate on a somewhat more moderate, and plausible, interpretation. Judith Jarvis Thomson, for example, maintains that

> ownership really is no more than a cluster of claims, privileges, and powers; and if the cluster of rights that a person X has in respect of his or her body is sufficiently like the clusters of rights people have in respect of their houses, typewriters, and shoes, then there is no objection in theory to saying that X does own his or her own body. . . .[17]

No doubt, but just how much alike is sufficient? In the context of an analysis of liberal theory, it would be useful to possess some idea of a core cluster of rights, powers, etc., that are at least necessary for liberal ownership. Possessing such an idea, we could say that a cluster of rights that does not contain rights $R_1 \ldots R_n$ falls short of the minimum liberal understanding of what it means to own something. This, then, would provide a negative test of the claim that a right to P is sufficiently like a property right to be called one. I stress that this yields only a negative test; if a cluster does not contain $R_1 \ldots R_n$, it is not sufficiently like liberal property — this, of course, does not mean that it *is* sufficiently like liberal property if it *does* contain $R_1 \ldots R_n$.[18]

It seems reasonable to suppose that for Alf to have unimpaired liberal ownership rights over some thing P, he must have at least the following rights: [19]

(1) *Right of Use:* Alf has a right to use P, i.e.,
   (a) It is not wrong for Alf to use P, and
   (b) It is wrong for others to interfere with Alf's using P.

---

[16] I owe this point to Jeremy Waldron.

[17] Judith Jarvis Thomson, *The Realm of Rights* (Cambridge: Harvard University Press, 1990), p. 225.

[18] I suspect that Wittgensteinian-inclined philosophers will resist the idea that liberal property rights — or for that matter anything else — have an essential core. To turn Wittgenstein on his head: Do not suppose that, of course, property rights don't have a core — look and see. Cf. Ludwig Wittgenstein, *Philosophical Investigations*, 3d ed., ed. G. E. M. Anscombe (New York: Macmillan, 1953), section 66.

[19] Here I am following Frank Snare, "The Concept of Property," *American Philosophical Quarterly*, vol. 9 (April 1972), pp. 200–206. I have significantly altered the fourth condition. Snare provides two additional conditions; again, I am concerned here with necessity, not sufficiency.

(2) *Right of Exclusion:* Others may use *P* if and only if Alf consents, i.e.,

    (a) If Alf consents, it is prima facie not wrong for others to use *P*; and

    (b) If Alf doesn't consent, it is prima facie wrong to use *P*.[20]

(3) *Right of Transfer:* Alf may permanently transfer the rights in rules (1) and (2) to specific persons by consent.

(4) *Right to Compensation:* If Betty damages or uses *P* without Alf's consent, then Alf typically has a right to compensation from Betty.[21]

If Alf does not have at least these rights, then his ownership of *P* is, at best, attenuated. Thus, entail (the restricting of inheritance to the owner's lineal descendants) was a restraint on liberal ownership just because it drastically restricted the right of transfer.[22] If we are going to be owners of our bodies in a way consistent with the aspirations of libertarians, then at least these four conditions must be satisfied.

When the matter is put thus, it becomes clear that maintaining we possess liberal ownership rights over our own bodies is not an explication of our current intuitions but is instead highly revisionary, since rights of transfer are not typically associated with body rights. To be sure, we do have transfer rights over some parts of our body, such as the rights to sell blood and semen, but many bodily rights violate rules (2)(a) and (3).[23] Consent—rule (2)(a)—is not usually taken as rendering killing prima facie not wrong. And it is even more counterintuitive to claim a right to transfer one's right not to be murdered or beaten. My point right now is not that such transfer would be conceptually incoherent (see below, Section IIC), but rather that such transfers are not part of law or of most people's normal understanding of rights to bodily integrity. Now I think this is of some importance, for libertarians often suggest that our intuition that,

---

[20] I shall not comment much on Snare's prima facie clauses. The second is intended to take account of Locke's remark that we would be justified in pulling down a man's house in order to keep a fire from spreading; see Snare, "The Concept of Property," p. 203. Adam Smith too argues that we can justifiably violate natural liberty by imposing "an obligation of building party walls, in order to prevent the communication of fire"; similar reasoning leads Smith to support infringing natural liberty by regulating the banking trade. See Adam Smith, *The Wealth of Nations*, ed. Edwin Cannan (Chicago: University of Chicago Press, 1976), vol. 1, pp. 344–45. For a view of property rights that points to a stronger interpretation of rules (2)(b) and (4), see Guido Calabresi and A. Douglas Melamed, "Property Rights, Liability Rules, and Inalienability: One View of the Cathedral," *Harvard Law Review*, vol. 85 (April 1972), pp. 1089–1128.

[21] This last condition raises complex problems of compensatory justice. I consider these problems in more depth in my essay "Does Compensation Restore Equality?" in *NOMOS XXXIII: Compensatory Justice*, ed. John W. Chapman (New York: New York University Press, 1991), ch. 2.

[22] See S. I. Benn and R. S. Peters, *Social Principles and the Democratic State* (London: Allen and Unwin, 1959), p. 156.

[23] See Stephen R. Munzer, *A Theory of Property* (Cambridge: Cambridge University Press, 1990), ch. 3. See also Munzer's contribution to the present volume.

say, it is wrong to carve up a person also shows that it is wrong to tax him; both, we are told, are unjustified expropriations of his property.[24] However, the former intuition is grounded on the supposition that rights to personal integrity are different from property rights, and crucial to this difference are the different conditions placed on their transferability.[25] Given that alienability or transferability seems a crucial divide between property and most body rights,[26] our intuitions would appear strongly to suggest that taxing a person's property is not at all similar to taking his eyes or kidneys for use by others.

Now it might be thought that all this rests on a confusion between (i) Alf alienating his property right to P, and (ii) Alf relinquishing his right to hold property. Joel Feinberg, for example, is careful to distinguish alienating a right from forfeiting, annulling, waiving, and relinquishing it. Important for our purposes is the distinction between relinquishing the right to property and alienating property.[27] Liberal ownership requires that one be able to alienate one's property in the sense that one can transfer one's right to any P to others. But this is entirely consistent with the right to property being inalienable in the sense that a person cannot relinquish his right to hold property. For instance, it has been argued that a piece of property cannot itself be a property owner;[28] hence, it is conceptually impossible for a slave to be a property owner. If so, then if property is an inalienable right in this second sense, it follows that one cannot sell oneself into slavery, as that would extinguish one's right to own property. Now, given this distinction, it may be thought that no asymmetry obtains between property rights and, say, personal rights. To be sure, rights to bodily integrity cannot be relinquished, but neither (it might be argued) can the right to hold property.[29] To insist that property rights are inherently alienable, the objection runs, is to say that one can alienate any or all pieces of property, not that one can relinquish the right to hold property. In a similar sort of way, even if one cannot relinquish the right not to be beaten, one can waive it on particular occasions, as when one agrees to participate in a boxing match. (To be sure, this raises some problems regarding the right to life — can it be waived without being

[24] Cf. Narveson's claims in *The Libertarian Idea*, p. 66; Robert Nozick, *Anarchy, State, and Utopia* (New York: Basic Books, 1974), pp. 72, 228–30; and Machan, *Individuals and Their Rights*, p. 122.

[25] "Hegel regards alienability as a mark of something really being property — which is why lives and liberty cannot be property." Alan Ryan, *Property and Political Theory* (Oxford: Basil Blackwell, 1984), p. 129.

[26] See Randy Barnett, "Contract Remedies and Inalienable Rights," in *Philosophy and Law*, ed. Jules Coleman and Ellen Frankel Paul (Oxford: Basil Blackwell, 1987), pp. 194–95.

[27] See Joel Feinberg, "Voluntary Euthanasia," in his *Rights, Justice, and the Bounds of Liberty* (Princeton: Princeton University Press, 1980), p. 243.

[28] Grunebaum, *Private Ownership* (*supra* note 14), p. 9.

[29] Of course, some insist that all these rights can be relinquished. See Thomson, *The Realm of Rights*, pp. 283–84.

relinquished? — but Feinberg shows that analogous proposals are possible even here.)

Note that this reply does not establish a real symmetry between personal and property rights. In the case of the former, the argument points to the distinction between, on the one hand, a temporary or at least revocable decision not to exercise one's right and, on the other, a once-and-for-all alienation of the right. But surely, when one sells a piece of property, one is not making a temporary or revocable decision to refrain from exercising one's property right: one transfers it to another. But more importantly, even if the argument succeeded in demonstrating this symmetry between property and personal rights, so far from assisting the "All Rights Are Property Rights" thesis, it helps undermine it. For that thesis claims that all one's rights are property rights, and it remains undisputed that if one has a liberal property right to P, one can sell it. What the reply really shows is that our right to hold property, like other personal rights, is not itself a property right, and thus the "All Rights Are Property Rights" thesis does not even apply to our right to hold property.

Though appeal to intuitions is by no means decisive, it is worth noting the loss to basic rights theory of forgoing appeal to intuitions about rights. To an extraordinary extent, rights theory has relied on declarations of rights; such declarations provide little in the way of justificatory argument but are nevertheless forceful in proclaiming widely agreed-upon rights. Moreover, it remains both fascinating and important that the dominant libertarian account — Robert Nozick's *Anarchy, State, and Utopia* — has very little to say about the foundations of the rights on which it builds. This has usually been taken as a deep criticism of Nozick's enterprise, and has spurred some of his followers to provide various (conflicting) foundations.[30] Yet it is unclear whether these foundationalists have enhanced the appeal of the libertarian position. I say this not as a criticism of their efforts, but to suggest that the intuitive appeal of basic rights is more powerful than any demonstration of their foundations, no matter how skilled. To the extent that this is so, libertarians who quickly abandon currently held conceptions of rights for a highly revisionary one may inadvertently undermine the attractiveness of their position.

B. Waivability and transferability

Although it has more dangers than may strike one at first, let us explore a more revisionist approach to personal rights. Some revision

[30] The critical essay here was Thomas Nagel's "Libertarianism without Foundations," in *Reading Nozick*, ed. Jeffrey Paul (Totowa, NJ: Rowman and Littlefield, 1981), pp. 191–206. Tibor Machan explicitly says that his recent book is a response to Nagel's criticism (Machan, *Individuals and Their Rights*, p. xiii); Loren Lomasky begins his book by stating that "[r]ights without foundations are treacherous entities" (Lomasky, *Persons, Rights, and the Moral Community*, p. vii). See also the similar remark of Samuel C. Wheeler III in his "Natural Property Rights as Body Rights," *Noûs*, vol. 14 (May 1980), p. 172. For Nozick, see note 24 above.

may well be possible without undermining the intuitive force of rights claims. Moreover, there is widespread support — not just among libertarians but among many liberal rights theorists — for the (revisionary) claim that all, or nearly all, personal rights are (or ought to be) waivable. Joel Feinberg, for instance, argues that fundamental to "rights-ownership" is that one is typically at liberty either to exercise or to waive a right as one sees fit; and though Feinberg acknowledges that some rights are "mandatory" (i.e., their exercise is not discretionary), he clearly thinks them somewhat deviant.[31] Thus, it may be argued that our current understanding of some personal rights as mandatory or not waivable does not conform to our general concept of rights, and so should be abandoned.

However, as rule (3) makes clear, waivability is not sufficient for liberal property rights; a property owner is not simply able to waive his property right over P — in which case P would become unowned — but is able to transfer it to someone else.[32] The question, then, is whether the libertarian can build transferability into all rights. Having already insisted on universal waivability, the libertarian might be attracted to Hobbes's proposal, which depicts transferring a right as a benefit-directed waiving of it:

> Right is laid aside, either by simply renouncing it; or by transferring it to another. By *simply* RENOUNCING; when he cares not to whom the benefit thereof redoundeth. By TRANSFERRING; when he intendeth the benefit thereof to some certain person, or persons. And when a man hath in either manner abandoned, or granted away his right; then he is said to be OBLIGED or BOUND, not to hinder those, to whom such right is granted, or abandoned, from the benefit of it; and that he *ought*, and it is his DUTY, not to make void that voluntary act of his own: and that such hindrance is INJUSTICE, and INJURY, as being SINE JURE; the right being before renounced or transferred.[33]

It is not pellucid just what Hobbes means by intending a benefit, but two interpretations are worth exploring: (i) that Alf indiscriminately renounces or waives his right, with the intention that Betty benefits, and (ii) that Alf selectively renounces his right only in relation to Betty.

Suppose that at present Alf has rights of exclusive use of his 1975 Ford Pinto. According to rule (1), it is permissible for Alf to use the Pinto, and it is wrong for anyone to interfere with his use; and according to rule (2),

---

[31] Joel Feinberg, "A Postscript to The Nature and Value of Rights," in his *Rights, Justice, and the Bounds of Liberty*, pp. 156–58. Because Feinberg sees mandatory rights as the deviant case, he asks: "Why then are they called rights at all?" Though he answers the question, the important point for our purposes is that he asks it. See also L. W. Sumner, *The Moral Foundation of Rights* (Oxford: Clarendon Press, 1987), pp. 98ff.

[32] See Thomson, *The Realm of Rights*, pp. 283–84.

[33] Thomas Hobbes, *Leviathan*, ed. Michael Oakeshott (Oxford: Blackwell, 1946), p. 86. For a discussion, see Gregory S. Kavka, *Hobbesian Moral and Political Theory* (Princeton: Princeton University Press, 1986), pp. 302–3.

if Alf consents, it is prima facie permissible (not wrong) for others to use his Pinto, but if Alf does not consent it is prima facie wrong. The most literal reading of Hobbes's text would suggest that Alf renounces all these rights *in relation to everyone*, with the intention that Betty benefits. Pretty obviously, though, his mere intention would not be enough: if he has renounced all his rights of exclusive use, then Charlie is no longer prima facie wrong to drive the Pinto away, even if Alf never intended him to benefit. We cannot be this literal.

A more plausible interpretation is suggested by Hobbes's remark that "[t]he mutual transferring of right, is that which men call CONTRACT."[34] Perhaps Hobbes has in mind a person who selectively renounces his right. Say, for example, Alf (i) totally renounces his right of use, (ii) renounces his right to exclude Betty, and (iii) renounces his right to give permission to use the Pinto, except to Betty, to whom he gives permission in perpetuity. After this, Alf no longer has the right to use the Pinto or let others use it, he has no right to exclude Betty, and it is prima facie permissible for her to use it. Does Betty now own the Pinto? Clearly not. She has not yet obtained the right to allow others to use it; she can use it, and they cannot, but she does not have the rights of rule (2). Simply by renouncing his own rights, no matter how selectively, Alf cannot transfer rights to Betty.[35] Transfer cannot be analyzed into selected waivability.

It might seem that the following would work.[36] Alf might exercise his right of use by allowing Betty *or her designees* to use the Pinto, and at the same time waive any future rights to use it himself. Betty in turn may allow Charlie and his designees to use it, and waive her future rights to use it herself. But suppose that Doris ignores Charlie's claim to exclusive use and drives the Pinto away. Whose right has been violated — Alf's or Charlie's? This case recalls the dispute between those upholding beneficiary theories of rights and critics such as H. L. A. Hart. In its unqualified form, the beneficiary theory of rights maintains that one has a right if one is the beneficiary of another's duty; in the qualified form endorsed by David Lyons, it asserts that one has a right if one is in some way the direct or intended beneficiary of a duty.[37] In opposition, Hart insisted that third-party beneficiaries do not possess rights: if *A* promised *B* to take care of *C* while *B* is on vacation, Hart argued, it is *B* who holds the

[34] Hobbes, *Leviathan*, p. 87.

[35] For Hobbes, of course, everyone already has a liberty to do everything, so this problem, though relevant to his account of contracts in general, does not cause difficulties for his account of empowering the sovereign. For an extensive analysis, see Jean Hampton, *Hobbes and the Social Contract Tradition* (Cambridge: Cambridge University Press, 1986).

[36] I owe this suggestion to David Friedman.

[37] See David Lyons, "Rights, Claimants, and Beneficiaries," *American Philosophical Quarterly*, vol. 6 (July 1969), pp. 181ff.

right against *A*, even though *C* is the beneficiary.[38] And that seems to be essentially the same as our case, where Alf is the property owner and Charlie benefits from Alf's right. If we follow Hart—and I think there is much to be said for his position—although Charlie is certainly harmed by Doris's violation of the property right, it is not clear that he has been wronged. Alf seems to have suffered the wrong. But we do not have to side with Hart here. Even if we grant that Charlie has *a* right because he is the direct beneficiary of Doris' duty, it must be the case that Alf still has a right against Doris. It is permissible for Charlie to use the Pinto and prima facie wrong for Doris to interfere only because Alf still has some rights over it, though he has so arranged things that Charlie and not he benefits from his rights.[39] Consequently, even if we allow that, as a beneficiary, Charlie too has rights, it remains the case that Alf continues to possess rights against Doris. Transfer, then, has not been completed.

An analogy may help make the point clearer. Suppose that Wade Stadium, home of the Duluth Dukes, installs a new entry gate; it scans the handprints of people, and is programmed to admit season-ticket holders. For every positive scan, one person is admitted. Alf has a season ticket; he is, of course, free not to use it. Moreover, he can let Betty in by putting his hand on the scanner, allowing her to go through. But no combination of using his right and waiving it can transfer to Betty the ability to pass through on her own, or to admit others by putting her hand on the scanner. Alf can let her in the game, and he can stay out, but that does not make Betty a season-ticket holder; he has not *transferred* his right, though he can allow Betty to benefit from it (and in so doing Betty may have gained some rights—for the security guard to eject her from the stadium may well violate a right of hers).

The upshot is that even if we grant the libertarian waivability of all rights, he has not shown that all rights can be transferred. This, I think, is important. It is tempting to suppose that only a paternalist could wish to interfere with treating all personal rights as property rights. As Nozick famously argues, Locke's insistence that one does not have a right to kill oneself has a paternalistic ring to it; Nozick's own "nonpaternalistic position holds that someone may choose (or permit) another to do to himself *anything*, unless he has acquired an obligation to some third party not to

---

[38] H. L. A. Hart, "Are There any Natural Rights?" in *Theories of Rights*, ed. Jeremy Waldron (Oxford: Oxford University Press, 1984), pp. 81–82. For critical discussions of third-party beneficiary cases, see Lyons, "Rights, Claimants, and Beneficiaries"; and Joel Feinberg, "Duties, Rights, and Claims," in his *Rights, Justice, and the Bounds of Liberty*, pp. 131–32.

[39] The stronger interpretation of the beneficiary view is that being the beneficiary of another's duty is a necessary as well as a sufficient condition for having a right. If so, it might be argued that since Alf no longer receives any benefit, he can no longer be said to have any rights to the Pinto. I have argued elsewhere that one can indeed have a right to φ even if φ-ing sets back one's interests; see my "Does Compensation Restore Equality?" (*supra* note 21). See also note 107 below.

do or allow it."[40] However, this can lead only to full waivability; the transfer of property rights involves the transfer of powers (see Section IIIB), and thus a general anti-paternalistic position cannot justify transferability.

C. Liberty rights as immunities

To be sure, as Stephen Munzer notes, all this does not itself show that body rights are in no way property rights; they could be limited property rights, akin to the rights of an owner of a historical landmark or an entailed property.[41] Even without transferability, one still has the right of exclusive use, which many have seen as central to property.[42] Yet such a level of ownership falls short of minimum liberal aspirations, and thus constitutes a restriction of liberal ownership. If the "All Rights Are Property Rights" thesis claims that all rights are *liberal* property rights, our very limited property rights in our own body provide scant support for it. Rights to freedom provide even less. A basic right such as freedom of religion does not seem to involve any of the crucial rights of ownership at all. The First Amendment to the U.S. Constitution assures citizens an immunity: it bars Congress from enacting laws establishing a religion, thus providing citizens with an immunity from legislation. According to Wesley Hohfeld, this immunity held by citizens corresponds to a disability on the part of Congress to pass such laws; that is, the crux of the right to freedom of religion as specified by the First Amendment is an inability or lack of authority on the part of Congress to pass laws establishing a religion.[43] Now it is not even clear what it could mean to waive this right: if Congress lacks the authority to establish a religion, it is hard to see how any decision by an individual citizen can alter this. But it is even more puzzling to see in what sense this right can be transferred: it is the lack of Congressional authority that is the heart of the right, and it is utterly mysterious how individual citizens can transfer their immunity to others. Moreover, insofar as free-speech rights are comprised of immunities, the

---

[40] Nozick, *Anarchy, State, and Utopia*, p. 58. Of course, given Locke's views about our relation to God, the argument is not paternalistic. Note that Nozick never actually says Locke's view is paternalistic.

[41] Munzer, *A Theory of Property* (*supra* note 23), pp. 43ff.

[42] For characterizations of property that focus on this, see E. F. Carritt, *Ethical and Political Thinking* (Oxford: Clarendon Press, 1947), p. 166; and J. R. Lucas, *The Principles of Politics* (Oxford: Clarendon Press, 1966), p. 183.

[43] For Wesley Hohfeld's classic analysis, see his "Some Fundamental Legal Conceptions as Applied in Judicial Reasoning," *Yale Law Review*, vol. 23 (1913), pp. 16–59. For an excellent explication and development of Hohfeld's analysis, see R. E. Robinson, S. C. Coval, and J. C. Smith, "The Logic of Rights," *University of Toronto Law Review*, vol. 33 (1983), pp. 267–78.

same applies to them.[44] If libertarians are to insist that all genuine rights are liberal property rights, they must maintain that rights to ϕ that are essentially immunities due to the lack of authority to regulate ϕ-ing are not really rights. This would indeed be highly revisionary. Thomson, I think, is manifestly correct that some of the rights most important to us are essentially immunities.[45] This is not to deny that property rights might be relevant to a right such as freedom of religion; a government that did not officially and explicitly establish a religion but prohibited all sects but one from using any building for religious purposes would run afoul of freedom of religion.[46] Nevertheless, it remains true that the establishment clause is plausibly understood as asserting a right of citizens but most implausibly understood as establishing any liberal ownership rights.

D. The "Property Rights Derive from Self-Ownership" thesis

Thus far, I have been supposing that, according to the "All Rights Are Property Rights" thesis, standard liberal property rights are the basic sort of right, and all rights—including rights to bodily integrity—are simply specific types of property rights. But perhaps the tie between bodily rights and property rights is rather different. It has long been argued that a person's right to his own body—a form of self-ownership—is the basic right, and rights to external property are derived from this fundamental self-ownership. As Stephen Buckle shows in his study of natural-law theories of property (in which he includes Locke's theory), natural-law theorists insisted on an intimate connection between a person's rights and what

[44] See Frederick Schauer, *Free Speech: A Philosophical Enquiry* (Cambridge: Cambridge University Press, 1982), ch. 8. H. L. A. Hart acknowledges immunity rights, but insists that "[a]n individual's immunity from legal change at the hands of the law is spoken and thought of as a right only when the change in question is adverse, that is, would deprive him of the rights of other kinds (liberty-rights, powers, rights correlative to obligations) or benefits secured to him by law." See Hart, "Legal Rights," in his *Essays on Bentham: Studies in Jurisprudence and Political Theory* (Oxford: Clarendon Press, 1982), pp. 190–92. Though the first clause may well be correct—that only an immunity against an adverse change is a candidate for a right—it is dubious that this adversity must be measured against a baseline of preexisting legal rights or legally secured advantages.

[45] See Thomson, *The Realm of Rights*, p. 59, chs. 11, 14.

[46] Cf. James Buchanan's remark that "it should be obvious . . . that there is really no categorical distinction to be made between the set of rights normally referred to as 'human' and those that are referred to as 'property.' Does A's right to speak, sometimes labelled a 'human right' encompass the authority to enter a house that B owns, a 'property right,' and shout obscenities?" I am not sure precisely what Buchanan means by "categorical," but clearly, property rights and speech rights can clash, and more importantly, speech rights sometimes require use rights, e.g., a free press. But none of this shows that they are not different categories of rights. See James Buchanan, *The Limits of Liberty* (Chicago: University of Chicago Press, 1975), p. 10.

"belongs" to that person. This idea of what belongs to a person, or *suum*, concerns a set of "essential possessions": life, limbs, and liberty. Thus understood, says Buckle, the *suum* is "what naturally belongs to a person because none of these things can be taken away without injustice."[47] Now, crucially, natural-law theorists held that *suum* could be extended. As Buckle says concerning Locke, "[t]he property in one's own person thus has a dynamic quality, in that it needs to grow to survive—it requires the acquisition of certain things. The *suum* must be extended—'mixed' with things—in order to be maintained."[48] Thus, by extending *suum* into the external world, external private property in goods is generated.[49]

Now on the face of it, this may seem to be no more than a play on words; if we adopt an extremely wide sense of "property" such that whatever belongs to a person is his property, then it is simple enough to show that "rights" and "ownership" are coextensive; if you have a right to it, it is yours, and so you "own" it. Hence the complaint that Locke's use of "property" is so broad as to "gobble up under this term anything that a person has or that can be said to be 'his', including his life and his liberty."[50] However, the claim that external private property is justified by extending *suum* makes Lockean theory more interesting, for it insists that ownership of external goods is an extension of one's essential attributes, thus providing an argument upholding the monistic view of liberty and property rights. Monistic unity is achieved not by a play on the words "belongs" and "rights," but via the justificatory mechanism of extending *suum* to generate external private property.

Although the extension claim makes the theory interesting, it also poses the chief barrier against its serving as the foundation of a libertarian monism, as it is doubtful that the extended *suum* will look much like liberal ownership. As Buckle points out, Locke insists that our property in our persons is inalienable: it is no part of the idea of *suum* that one can alienate it. Now if property is an extension of *suum*, required so that our essential attributes can thrive, it may well be that significant parts of the external *suum* will be inalienable as well:

[47] Stephen Buckle, *Natural Law and the Theory of Property* (Oxford: Clarendon Press, 1991), p. 29. Because *suum* includes one's body, Locke's theory does commit him to holding that we own our body parts, such as limbs. Thus, though Locke talks of owning our own persons, it is not really a mistake to interpret him as claiming that we own our bodies (*ibid.*, pp. 169–70). Cf. Jeremy Waldron, *The Right to Private Property* (Oxford: Clarendon Press, 1988), pp. 177ff., 361n.

[48] Buckle, *Natural Law and the Theory of Property*, p. 171. Buckle argues for the applicability of the concept of *suum* to Locke's theory on pp. 168–74. See also A. John Simmons, *The Lockean Theory of Rights* (Princeton: Princeton University Press, 1992), pp. 226–27.

[49] Note here a basic similarity to the Hegelian account of property, pointing to a less stark division between the Lockean and Hegelian accounts than some would suggest.

[50] A. I. Melden, *Rights and Persons* (Oxford: Blackwell, 1977), p. 178. See below, Section IV.

[I]f slavery is excluded because of the property all men have in their own persons, it can only be because this basic form of property cannot be alienated (voluntarily or otherwise). Further, if our appropriation of what is *necessary* for our subsistence (that is, leaving aside the questions of surpluses, and also of traded goods) depends on our duty to preserve ourselves, then neither will these appropriations be alienable. So Locke accepts that at least some forms of property — including the fundamental form from which more extensive properties are derived — are not alienable. This is sufficient to set his concept of property apart from the modern conceptions of property that preoccupy the philosophers in question.[51]

Put simply, it would seem that we have no right to alienate something that is necessary to maintain us, and thus no right, say, to play the ponies when we need to pay our rent or buy food.

Interestingly, Samuel C. Wheeler III essentially repeats the natural-law argument in defending libertarian property rights.[52] According to Wheeler, because we have a right to exist as agents, we have a "right to move and use our own bodies as we please," and others have an obligation not to interfere with these rights of exclusive use.[53] Our right to exist as agents thus justifies our rights to exclusive use of our bodies. And, again in just the way a natural-law theorist would have argued, Wheeler maintains that we can extend these basic body rights into the external world, thus generating external property.[54] Wheeler too, however, has difficulty showing that transferability is justified by this argument. "Transfer rights," he argues,

are derived from our right to *use* our bodies. So, suppose you need a kidney and I need an arm. You have an arm you can get along without and I have a spare kidney. If we both have a right to use our bodies as we see fit, it seems that we can trade one part for another, using an arm to get a kidney and vice versa.[55]

---

[51] Buckle, *Natural Law and the Theory of Property*, p. 180, note omitted.

[52] In their analysis of Wheeler's argument, Douglas B. Rasmussen and Douglas J. Den Uyl stress the distinction between the extension of self-ownership and the extension of property rights in one's body. Though it is not without importance, I have suggested in note 47 that this distinction may not be fundamental to the natural-law account. See Rasmussen and Den Uyl, *Liberty and Nature: An Aristotelian Defense of Liberal Order* (La Salle: Open Court, 1991), pp. 124–27.

[53] Wheeler, "Natural Property Rights as Body Rights" (*supra* note 30), p. 187.

[54] David Braybrooke dismisses this view, apparently assuming that it is a libertarian invention. See Braybrooke, "Our Natural Bodies, Our Social Rights: Comments on Wheeler," *Noûs*, vol. 14 (May 1980), pp. 195–202.

[55] Wheeler, "Natural Property Rights as Body Rights," pp. 185–86.

Thus, he concludes that if you can use your body as you want, you can give away parts or transfer them to others. But we have seen that this is not so: rights of exclusive use plus waivability do not yield transferability of *rights* (of course, you can physically transfer the *thing*, in the sense that possession of the kidney has been transferred from you to the other fellow).[56] When you renounce ownership of a body part, rights of exclusive use — rules (1) and (2) from Section IIA — are not transferred.

I suspect that the only plausible argument that the extension of *suum* leads to unrestricted rights to transfer external property is based on the supposition that our basic rights to life, liberty, and bodily integrity are not only waivable, but themselves freely transferable. But this is pretty deeply counterintuitive; it is not part of our normal understanding of these rights, nor is it even part of a moderately revisionist one. Moreover, as I have stressed, restricting transferability need not be paternalistic; indeed, as we shall see in the next section, it is not even properly understood as restricting negative freedom at all. So a commitment to universal transferability cannot, as we shall see, be deduced from a commitment to negative liberty. However, it seems that the libertarian monist employing a Lockean argument must insist that all our basic rights are transferable. Unless he does, he is confronted by Buckle's question: How can the extension of nonalienable rights of use generate freely transferable external ones?

E. A dilemma

The arguments of this section point to a dilemma for the classical-liberal monist who seeks to demonstrate that all rights are liberal property rights. As we saw in Sections IIA through IIC, if he starts out with standard liberal rights of ownership, he cannot show that all rights (e.g., personal rights) meet even the minimum requirements of liberal ownership. On the other hand, if (following Locke) the classical-liberal monist begins with our standard personal and liberty rights and takes these as the model of what is properly one's own, then it becomes most dubious whether the external property rights so justified amount to liberal ownership. To be sure, the libertarian monist can "escape" this dilemma simply by insisting that everything and anything deserving the title "right" can be transferred to another, but such a move severely weakens the intu-

---

[56] Wheeler suggests that if another can incorporate your body part into his body, then it would become his property. But then you are not really transferring the right. You relinquish it, the body part becomes unowned, and the first person to integrate it into his body becomes the new owner. See *ibid.*, p. 186. The problem here is much the same as that confronted by the Hobbesian analysis of transfer in terms of indiscriminate waiving. See Section IIB above.

itive force of the rights being claimed. Moreover, as we are about to see, this move cannot be grounded on a commitment to negative freedom.

III. The "Property Rights Are Liberty Rights" Thesis

A. Is property itself a liberty?

The claim that all rights are property rights is ambitious. And it is more than is necessary for monistic libertarianism. A more modest, but sufficient, claim is that property rights are a sort of liberty or directly follow from liberty (we have already seen that liberty rights are not a subset of property rights). This is, moreover, a common claim. Property rights, we are told, derive from liberty, are necessary for liberty,[57] or are themselves a type of liberty.[58] To evaluate the claim that property rights are a type of liberty right or inherently a part of liberty, it is necessary to specify in some general way what a liberty right is. The problem, as we shall see in Section IV, is that in a way all rights are conducive to a free life; hence, there is some tendency to collapse the idea of a liberty right and rights in general. Whether or not that is enlightening will occupy us presently; for now, I wish to focus on a specific right to liberty — one that concerns protecting liberty in a way that, say, a right to a social-security check does not. Given that my interest is in the possibility of a classical-liberal monist theory, the point of departure must be some notion of a right to negative liberty or noninterference.[59]

On the face of it, there is much to be said for the idea that property rights protect negative liberty. A property owner is free (at least within rather broad boundaries) to use his property without interference. Certainly liberty is an element of property rights. But if the "Property Rights Are Liberty Rights" thesis is to succeed, that is not enough: not only must property include liberty, but it must not go beyond it. If there is more to property than liberty, then a justification of liberty will not suffice to justify liberal ownership. The problem, once again, is the right of transfer. In the last section, I argued that transfer rights are essential to liberal ownership, but are not a part of many standard freedoms and personal rights. I now make a further claim: transfer rights cannot be explicated primarily in terms of freedom.

---

[57] Anthony Fressola, "Liberty and Property," *American Philosophical Quarterly*, vol. 18 (October 1981), p. 316.

[58] Sumner, *The Moral Foundation of Rights* (*supra* note 31), p. 77; Lomasky, *Persons, Rights, and the Moral Community* (*supra* note 6), p. 132; Lucas, *Principles of Politics* (*supra* note 42), p. 184.

[59] I assume, then, that negative liberty is a fundamental classical-liberal value. For an interesting argument disputing this, arguing instead for positive liberty as the foundation of libertarianism, see Horacio Spector, *Autonomy and Rights: The Moral Foundations of Liberalism* (Oxford: Clarendon Press, 1992).

B. *Transfer as a power*

The right of Alf to transfer his property to Betty implies a power on Alf's part to modify Charlie's moral status without Charlie's consent.[60] Say, for example, that Alf and Charlie are neighbors; they like each other a good deal, and have no difficulty respecting each other's property rights. Because of local conditions, they often find it convenient to cross each other's land to get to parts of their own, but they readily give each other the necessary permission.[61] Charlie, on the other hand, intensely dislikes Betty, and wants to have nothing to do with her. The last thing he wants is to have duties toward her that impinge on his life. As an owner of property, though, Alf has the power to change Charlie's duties toward Betty. If Alf sells his property to Betty, Charlie now has nontrespass duties toward her that he never had; and in this case the duties impact his life in significant ways. This is not a marginal aspect of property rights. As Alan Ryan quite rightly points out, "the interesting thing about fully paid-up property rights . . . is that they allow the property owner to alter the status of others in ways he cannot physically control. . . ."[62]

Libertarians, of course, are not apt to refer to transfer as a power, but as a freedom to sell or dispose of goods.[63] To be sure, the power to alter the rights and duties of others does increase one's scope for action, and in this way does increase one's freedom, but surely this is not an element of negative liberty. It is much more akin to what is sometimes called "political liberty," or as Constant called it, the "liberty of the ancients"— where liberty consisted in the exercise of sovereign authority.[64] In a way, the right to private property makes each person a mini-sovereign, able to unilaterally alter the rights and duties of others.[65] A much closer parallel, though, is indicated by H. L. A. Hart's analysis of Bentham's doctrine of legal powers. Bentham distinguishes two different classes of legislation: the powers to legislate *de classibus* and *de singulis*.[66] The legislature

---

[60] See Alan R. White, *Rights* (Oxford: Clarendon Press, 1984), pp. 149–50; and Richard Flathman, *The Practice of Rights* (Cambridge: Cambridge University Press, 1976), pp. 51–58. It actually involves more than a power, requiring a meta-power: viz., "the ability to cause oneself and others to acquire or lose powers" (Thomson, *The Realm of Rights*, p. 58).

[61] Stephen Munzer alerts me that, if this is to be legally binding, the permission must be in writing to satisfy the Statute of Frauds, and must satisfy the legal criteria for valid servitudes.

[62] Alan Ryan, "Public and Private Property," in *Public and Private in Social Life* (*supra* note 6), p. 226.

[63] See, e.g., Rasmussen and Den Uyl, *Liberty and Nature* (*supra* note 52), p. 117.

[64] See Benjamin Constant, "The Liberty of the Ancients Compared with That of the Moderns," in *Benjamin Constant: Political Writings*, ed. and trans. Biancamaria Fontana (Cambridge: Cambridge University Press, 1988), p. 311.

[65] This, I think, is one of the reasons some see the right to private property as posing special problems for liberal theory. See Gaus and Lomasky, "Are Property Rights Problematic?" (*supra* note 11), pp. 495–500.

[66] H. L. A. Hart, "Legal Powers," in his *Essays on Bentham* (*supra* note 44), p. 203.

typically imposes rights and duties on general classes (*de classibus*); but it often remains unsettled precisely what individuals are included in a general class, thus the need for officials to "legislate" *de singulis*. The example analyzed by Bentham and Hart is a general act defining the rights and duties of judges; this general legislation needs to be supplemented by a power to appoint particular individuals to the class of judges, hence determining precisely what specific persons possess the rights and duties of the general class. Now the conveyance of property rights, as Hart remarks, "is in many respects analogous to the appointment of the new judge. . . . The old owner, we might say, appoints the transferee to the 'office' of owner of the property."[67] Though the "offices" allocated are very different, both the official and the property owner possess the power to distribute rights and duties, not just to the person selected to fill the "office," but also to those over whom that person will have rights. It is implausible to reduce all this to a claim of noninterference or negative freedom. A seller of property is not simply claiming a right to use his property without interference, or that he be allowed to hand it over to others without interference. He is claiming a right to alter the status of third parties.

This point, I think, is apt to be missed by confusing property with possession. A plausible argument runs thus: If Alf has a right to noninterference, and he possesses P, and if Betty has a right to noninterference, then when Alf hands P over to her, her right to noninterference protects her use of P. I think it does. If Betty is employing P in her ongoing activity, to take it away from her would violate the right to noninterference. However, as Kant recognized, there is no easy move from this right of continued possession to private property rights.[68]

> [I]f I am a holder of a thing (that is, physically connected to it), then anyone who touches it without my consent (for example, wrests an apple from my hand) affects and diminishes that which is internally mine (my freedom). . . . [T]he proposition concerning empirical possession does not extend beyond the right of the person with respect to himself.[69]

However, if Alf claims a right to private property, he claims that he has exclusive rights over P even when he in no way physically possesses it or when it is in no way a part of his activity. Consequently, this right cannot be derived from noninterference with his liberty and current posses-

---

[67] *Ibid.*, p. 208. He continues: "The differences are of course great."

[68] I have argued this point in more detail in my *Value and Justification*, pp. 407–20. Cf. Fressola, "Liberty and Property."

[69] Immanuel Kant, *The Metaphysical Elements of Justice*, trans. John Ladd (Indianapolis: Bobbs-Merrill, 1965), First Part, section 6, p. 57. See also Eric Mack, "Self-Ownership and the Right of Property," *The Monist*, vol. 73 (October 1990), pp. 530ff.

sions. What is required is justification of the very different claim " 'This external object is mine.' Through this, an obligation is imposed on everyone else to refrain from using the object, an obligation they would not have otherwise had."[70]

But, it may be objected, nothing about this is unique to property and transfer powers: the imposition of obligations on others is a feature of all genuine rights.[71] If Alf has a liberty right to ϕ, then at least one person has a duty to refrain from interfering with his ϕ-ing. Thus, rights, including freedom rights, impose obligations on others. Moreover, such rights also give us control over the lives of others insofar as they are waivable. If Alf has a waivable strict right to ϕ, he controls not only his own life, but an aspect of Betty's too; he can prohibit her from interfering, or allow her to, as he wishes. It would seem, then, that all rights, including freedom rights, impose obligations on others, and typically give us a degree of control over the lives of others. Just what makes the right of transfer different? As Bentham's notion of legislation *de singulis* suggests, the difference lies in the power to alter the distribution of rights in the community. A system of rights composed solely of rights to noninterference with full waivability would be static. Of course, the actions actually performed would constantly change as people made different decisions about how to exercise their rights; but the overall distribution of rights and duties would be invariant. However, when powers such as those involved in promising and property transfer are introduced, the distribution of rights and duties can change. And, crucially, when property transfer is involved, all parties whose duties are altered need not consent. As we saw earlier, Charlie can gain duties to Betty through a transaction to which only Alf and Betty consent. Admittedly, Charlie's total duties do not increase; what changes is the person to whom he owes them. This is what makes property transfer akin to legislation *de singulis* rather than *de classibus*. But it is also what gives property transfer something of the powers and spirit of an office and not simply a freedom.

C. *Property and claims*

Thus far, I have stressed the importance of transfer to liberal ownership. Another fundamental element of private property also fits badly with the "Property Rights Are Liberty Rights" thesis: viz., the extent to which property generates claim rights to benefits from others. As is well known, Feinberg employs the notion of a claim right for all rights, including the right to liberty.[72] In this sense, to say that Alf's right R to ϕ is a claim right is, essentially, to say that someone has a duty to at least not

---

[70] Kant, *Metaphysical Elements of Justice*, First Part, section 7, p. 62.

[71] See Gaus and Lomasky, "Are Property Rights Problematic?"

[72] See Joel Feinberg, *Social Philosophy* (Englewood Cliffs, NJ: Prentice-Hall, 1973), ch. 4. See also his "Duties, Rights, and Claims" (*supra* note 38), pp. 130–42.

interfere with his ϕ-ing, and that it is appropriate for Alf to insist on R or, typically at least, to choose to waive it. But of course, not all claims are claims to liberties.[73] Promises in particular generate a variety of claims that are not usefully understood as liberties.[74] When Betty promises Alf that she will go out with him, she grants him a claim on her. This claim facilitates Alf's planning, and increases his options. He can choose either to have dinner with her, which he has a claim on Betty to attend, or cancel out, and so release Betty from her promise. However, though Alf's claims on Betty certainly increase his options, it is misguided to say that they increase his negative liberty; he has gained a positive right over Betty to a performance on her part.[75] Central to property rights are such claim rights.[76] Rule (4) (from Section IIA) specifies a claim right to compensation for unjustified damage or use; the right to have debt repaid and, in general, rights involved in contracts, give one claims on others. In crucial respects the rights of contract just are promissory rights. Because such claim rights are not liberty rights, neither are liberal property rights.

D. The core/periphery analysis of rights

Throughout I have been emphasizing that the powers involved in transfer are not liberty rights; and neither, I have just argued, are the claim rights implied by rights to compensation and contracts. Because these are not liberties, I have insisted, the right to private property cannot be understood as simply a liberty right. However, it may be argued that all this has supposed too simple an analysis of a liberty right; a more sophisticated, core/periphery analysis of rights has recently been endorsed by several philosophers. In his explication of Bentham's account of liberty rights, Hart introduces the idea of a "protective perimeter." That is, the core of Alf's pure liberty to ϕ is that Alf is under no obligation to ϕ, nor is he under an obligation not to ϕ;[77] in itself, such a "naked" liberty does not impose obligations on others not to interfere with Alf's ϕ-ing. The standard example, given by Hart, is two people seeing a purse lying on the street: "each has a liberty so far as the law is concerned to

---

[73] As John Finnis points out, it is erroneous to understand a claim right as a protected Hohfeldian liberty. See Finnis, *Natural Law and Natural Rights* (Oxford: Clarendon Press, 1980), pp. 200–201.

[74] A. I. Melden focuses his analysis of rights on promises; see his *Rights and Persons* (*supra* note 50).

[75] On negative and positive rights, see Feinberg, *Social Philosophy*, pp. 59–60. Libertarians, of course, tend to be highly critical of basic positive rights. See Lomasky, *Persons, Rights, and the Moral Community* (*supra* note 6), pp. 94ff. On the increase of options and its relation to positive liberty, see Spector, *Autonomy and Rights* (*supra* note 59); and Richard Norman, *Free and Equal* (Oxford: Oxford University Press, 1987), chs. 2 and 3.

[76] White stresses the link between property rights and claims in his *Rights* (*supra* note 60), p. 131.

[77] Hart calls this the "bilateral character of liberty rights," which contrasts with Hohfeld's "unilateral" characterization of a liberty. See Hart, "Legal Rights" (*supra* note 44), pp. 166–67.

pick it up and each may prevent the other doing so if he can race him to the spot."[78] However, though this liberty does not itself impose duties, Alf's exercise of it is protected by a number of rights that do impose correlative obligations. Thus, Betty cannot shoot him or hit him over the head in an attempt to secure the purse; Hart calls this the "protective perimeter" of the naked liberty.

This idea of a right possessing a core and a perimeter can be extended. Most rights, Carl Wellman argues, are a complex structure of advantages:

> At the center of each right stands a defining core. This may be a single element, such as the creditor's claim to repayment, or more than one element, such as the speaker's liberty of speaking out on controversial issues together with his liberty of remaining silent on such issues. But if the core of a right is complex, the elements that make it up must be conceptually tied together or the total structure ceases to be a single right. This defining core specifies the essential content of the right. . . .
>
> Around the central core of any legal right is arranged a number of associated elements. Each associated element necessarily contributes, if respected, some sort of freedom or control concerning the exercise or enjoyment of the core to its possessor in the face of one or more second parties.[79]

Thus, for instance, it might be said that while the claim to be repaid is the core of a creditor's right, a liberty to waive this repayment is part of the periphery that gives the holder freedom to control this right.[80] Applying this analysis to property rights, it may be argued that the core of a property right is the freedom to use one's property and make choices concerning it, though the periphery concerns associated powers and claims. L. W. Sumner argues precisely this:

> The core of a liberty-right consists of a (full) liberty, while its periphery consists of further elements (especially claims, but also powers and immunities) whose function is to enhance and protect the exercise of the core liberty. The core of a claim-right, on the other hand, consists of a claim, while its periphery consists of further elements (especially powers, but also liberties and immunities) whose function is to enhance and protect the core claim. Examples of both varieties are abundant in legal systems. Liberty-rights, for instance, include the familiar liberties such as freedom of speech and association, as

[78] Ibid., pp. 171–72.
[79] Carl Wellman, Welfare Rights (Totowa, NJ: Rowman and Littlefield, 1982), pp. 14–15.
[80] Ibid., p. 15.

well as property rights, while claim-rights include the equally familiar welfare rights such as health care and education, as well as contractual rights.[81]

On this more sophisticated analysis, then, property rights are liberty rights even though their periphery contains powers and claims (e.g., to compensation).

In evaluating this proposal, we should note a difference between Hart's analysis of Bentham's "protective perimeter" and the core/periphery analysis of Wellman and Sumner. Hart was trying to show that "naked liberties," which do not themselves impose obligations of noninterference, are nevertheless of legal significance because their exercise is protected by other rights that are not themselves part of the liberty. Wellman's proposal, in contrast, has a more essentialist slant: in talking of complex rights, such as the right of property, we distinguish those elements of the right that form the essential core from those elements that are in the periphery. It is granted, for instance, that transfer involves a power that is part and parcel of the standard right of property; it is not another right that impacts on one's property rights.[82] The proposal, then, is that though transfer as a power is a constituent of the right to property, it is "peripheral" to it because it increases one's control over the core of the right.

It is hard to say how one justifies a claim that some part of a complex right is at the core while another is at the periphery. Such a claim would seem to depend on a prior justificatory argument: if one justifies property rights, say, on the basis of their liberty-enhancing elements, then it could be said that this is at the core of the right, and the other features are necessarily peripheral. And presumably the libertarian monist would want to say precisely this. If we assume a justificatory perspective, however, we immediately see that for classical liberals the defense of private property is intimately bound up with the defense of the market order. Whatever his other errors, C. B. Macpherson saw this clearly: the classical liberal defends essentially alienable property.[83] The market order not only supposes that people are free to use their property, or even give it away, but it depends fundamentally on the power to freely transfer property rights. Indeed, we should not forget that classical liberalism was crucially a doctrine endorsing free *trade*. If, then, we embrace a

---

[81] Sumner, *The Moral Foundation of Rights* (*supra* note 31), p. 77; see also p. 48. Sumner's "full liberty" is Bentham's "bilateral" liberty. See above, note 77.

[82] Note that on Sumner's analysis, contractual rights are not only different from property rights, but are rights of a different type.

[83] His classic work, of course, is C. B. Macpherson, *The Political Theory of Possessive Individualism* (Oxford: Clarendon Press, 1962). For a thorough analysis of Macpherson's arguments, see Kirk F. Koerner, *Liberalism and Its Critics* (London: Croom-Helm, 1985), ch. 2.

core/periphery analysis of property rights, classical liberals must place transfer at the very core of property.[84] Feudal property rights, allowing extensive exclusive use but regulating alienation and trade in numerous ways, were not liberal ownership without the peripheral elements; they were not liberal ownership at all.[85]

E. Is property required for freedom?

I conclude that the "Property Rights Are Liberty Rights" thesis is to be rejected. Another possibility, though, is that property and its crucial powers and claims are somehow necessary to, or derived from, a right to freedom. Call this the "Property Rights Are Required for Liberty Rights" thesis. Care needs to be exercised here; this idea easily leads to the instrumental view, according to which a regime of private property is, given a variety of social facts, instrumentally necessary for a free society (Section I). The proposal I wish to consider here is that property holding is in some way conceptually required for freedom. Hillel Steiner seeks to show precisely this.[86] Steiner adopts a rigorous conception of negative liberty, according to which "[a]n individual is unfree if, and only if, his doing any action is rendered impossible by the action of another individual. That is, the unfree individual is so because the particular action in question is *prevented* by another."[87] Steiner argues:

> All actions consist in some kind of motion: the passage of some body from one place to another, the displacement of some material substance from one portion of physical space to another. Interference by one individual's actions with another's occurs if and only if at least one of the material or spatial components of the one action is identical with one of the material or spatial components of the other action.[88]

We can immediately see how this makes exclusive use fundamental to liberty: "To be free to do *A* . . . entails that all the physical components of

---

[84] "[P]owers are at the heart of property rights" (Thomson, *The Realm of Rights*, p. 258). Cf. Sumner's view that only full liberties and claims are the core of rights (Sumner, *The Moral Foundation of Rights*, ch. 2, pp. 98ff.).

[85] See Adam Smith's remarks on feudal regulation in *The Wealth of Nations* (*supra* note 20), vol. 1, pp. 436ff.

[86] See also Jean Baechler, "Liberty, Property, and Equality," in *NOMOS XXII: Property* (*supra* note 5), pp. 269ff.

[87] Hillel Steiner, "Individual Liberty," *Proceedings of the Aristotelian Society*, vol. 75 (1975), p. 33.

[88] Hillel Steiner, "The Structure of a Set of Compossible Rights," *Journal of Philosophy*, vol. 74 (December 1977), p. 769. This view implies that "neither the making of threats nor that of offers constitutes a diminution of liberty" (Steiner, "Individual Liberty," p. 43).

doing A are (simultaneously) unoccupied and/or undisposed of by another."[89] Hence, only if a person is in exclusive possession of the physical components of his action is the individual free. Steiner concludes: "The statement that 'X is free to do A' entails that none of the physical components of doing A is possessed by an agent other than X. My theorem, then, is that *freedom is the personal possession of physical objects*."[90]

My interest here is whether a monistic libertarian could build on Steiner's analysis of freedom to defend the "Property Rights Are Required for Liberty" thesis, by claiming that property rights define a person's sphere of negative liberty.[91] For such a libertarian to successfully employ Steiner's analysis in this way, two further claims must be established: (i) that liberty rights require not simply de facto possession but titles to physical objects, and (ii) that the titles to objects *must* amount to liberal rights of ownership, again, including transfer. Let us grant (i).[92] The second claim, however, is problematic. To see the problem, we need to specify a little more carefully the conception of negative liberty being employed. As we shall see, two different interpretations are plausible, but let us begin with what I call *liberty as respected sovereignty* (RS):

RS: Alf's property rights define an area Ω, in which he has a right to act without interference; Alf is free to the extent Ω is not violated by others.

According to RS, one is free if one is not interfered with when acting within one's rights of exclusive use. On this view, the amount of freedom one possesses does not vary with the amount of one's property. One's current holdings define a baseline; if one is not interfered with when using one's holdings, one is free. The analogy here is to the external sovereignty of states; a state is free if it is not interfered with by others. Some states are large and rich, others are small and poor, but if their sovereignty is respected, they are all equally free.

If Ω is not violated, Alf's rightful freedom is not interfered with. Employing the moral-space analogy popular in discussions of property rights (as well as rights in general, see Section IV), we can say that Ω is Alf's personal sphere of authority, and his rights to freedom are respected

[89] Steiner, "Individual Liberty," p. 47.

[90] *Ibid.*, p. 48. See also Fressola, "Liberty and Property" (*supra* note 57), p. 317.

[91] Thus, I am not attributing the following views to Steiner. Steiner's main concern is about compossible sets of rights; I do not wish to deny that a system of property rights can be compossible in his sense.

[92] Steiner claims (i) in "The Structure of a Set of Compossible Rights," p. 770. Cf., however, Waldron's remark that "[l]iberty rights take us no further than the time of the performance of action," in Waldron, *The Right to Private Property* (*supra* note 47), p. 181.

if this sphere remains inviolate.[93] Thus, if Ω is inviolate, Alf's rights to freedom are perfectly met. Now suppose Alf wants to change the size of Ω, i.e., he wants to sell some of it to Betty. Is it necessarily a diminution of his rightful freedom to prevent this? I do not think so. Alf's right to noninterference (his right to freedom) is identical to Ω; if you violate Ω, Alf's rightful freedom is diminished, but you cannot violate Alf's rightful freedom so long as the boundaries of Ω remain inviolate. So a rule stating that "all current holdings are sacred and cannot be changed" need not violate Alf's rights to freedom because, *ex hypothesi*, Ω remains respected.

This conclusion can be challenged in at least two ways. First, it could be argued that preventing Alf from selling parts of Ω does violate his rightful freedom, because it limits what he can do with Ω.[94] But I really think this is confused. According to RS, Alf's freedom is defined by what he can do within the protected realm identified by his exclusive rights — his freedom is not defined by his ability to alter these rights. That is a different conception of freedom. Freedom as guaranteed noninterference to act within an area, and freedom as the power to expand (and contract) that area, are distinct ideas. This brings us to the second response: Might it not be argued that we have a right not only to noninterference within the "space" defined by our holdings, but a right to expand and contract our holdings? If freedom is noninterference, and property guarantees noninterference, then a liberal principle should be "the more freedom, the better." Since the more property a person has, the freer he is, a person should be able, in the interests of freedom, to expand his holdings.[95]

Although this reasoning seems persuasive, it requires another conception of freedom, one that poses deep difficulties for liberal theory. Crucial to RS is that it measures each person's freedom relative to his own holdings; if they are respected, he is free; if they are violated, he is not. This second objection, however, suggests that a person's freedom is to be measured by the *extent of his sovereignty* (*or holdings*). Call this ES:

> ES: Alf's property rights define an area Ω, in which he has a right to act without interference. Alf is free (i) to the extent Ω is not violated by others; and (ii) relative to the size of Ω, i.e., the larger Ω, the more free is Alf.

[93] Eric Mack thus describes the "organizing idea" of the "private property system: i.e., the idea of sanctioning expansion of personal spheres of authority so as to secure individuals inviolability in their respective life projects"; see Mack, "Self-Ownership and the Right of Property" (*supra* note 69), p. 536. Cf. the similar remark of Charles Reich: "Property draws a circle around the activities of each private individual or organization. Within that circle, the individual has a greater degree of freedom than without"; see Reich, "The New Property," *Yale Law Journal*, vol. 73 (1964), p. 771. On the expansion of the area of authority, see below, and Section IID on the expansion of *suum*.

[94] See Steiner, "The Structure of a Set of Compossible Rights," pp. 772–74.

[95] Notice here Mack's reference in note 93 to the *expansion* of the area of sovereignty.

In contrast to freedom as respected sovereignty, extent of sovereignty maintains that the greater one's area of sovereignty, the greater one's freedom. A person with extensive holdings is freer than one with few; he can act without interference across a broader range of areas. The analogy here, then, is to the distinction between large states, which have a greater scope for action and can do a great deal, and small poor ones who have a highly restricted area in which they can operate without interference.

Freedom as extent of sovereignty is inconsistent with the liberal ideal of equal liberty. Or, at least, it is inconsistent with the ideal of equal liberty conjoined with inequality of property.[96] According to ES, the distribution of holdings is also a distribution of rightful freedom. Embracing both ES and the liberal commitment to equal liberty drives us toward equalization of holdings.[97] Assuming, then, that a libertarian adopting ES does not wish to embrace radical egalitarianism, he must abandon the long-standing liberal commitment to equal liberty.[98] The liberal state could still be devoted to freedom, but its distribution would not be a fundamental liberal commitment. In a genuine and unflawed liberal state, some would be, literally, freedom-impoverished while others would be freedom-rich: there would be no commitment to equal liberty.

It may be insisted that this rests on a standard confusion: the libertarian upholds our equal liberty to acquire property, and it is this that renders the theory genuinely liberal. But remember that we are evaluating ES, according to which one's liberty varies with the extent of one's property. If we embrace ES, then an equal right to acquire property implies an equal right to acquire liberty. Thus, instead of being based on a right to equal liberty, an ES-based liberalism upholds a basic equal right to acquire liberty. In effect, this transforms liberalism into a political theory based solely on equality of opportunity: all are to possess an equal opportunity not only to acquire scarce positions and offices, but to acquire as much liberty as they can accumulate.[99]

Equal opportunity to acquire liberty is an inadequate articulation of the liberal ideal. As the liberal sees it, each individual has his own life to lead, and there is no reason why any citizen should accept less than the equal

[96] In this respect, ES shares a common feature with most accounts of positive liberty, viz., they undermine the idea that the liberal state is, first and foremost, based on a right to equal liberty.

[97] See Norman, *Free and Equal* (*supra* note 75), chs. 6 and 7; and Norman Daniels, "Equal Liberty and the Unequal Worth of Liberty," in Daniels, ed., *Reading Rawls* (Oxford: Blackwell, 1975), ch. 11.

[98] Amy Gutmann is quite right that a commitment to "systems of equal liberty and opportunity" has been a defining feature of the liberal state; see Gutmann, *Liberal Equality* (Cambridge: Cambridge University Press, 1980), p. 5. See also John Rawls, *A Theory of Justice* (Cambridge, MA: Harvard University Press, 1971), section 32, esp. p. 205n.

[99] The conception of equality of opportunity operative here would be even weaker than that which Rawls calls the "system of natural liberty," which supposes "a background of equal liberty" (Rawls, *A Theory of Justice*, p. 72).

basic liberties necessary to pursue a life of his own choosing. And this claim is not based simply on a prediction that equal rights will emerge as an equilibrium under conditions of open competition and negotiation. It is a moral claim. As Loren Lomasky puts it:

> Each project pursuer, whatever his projects may be, is fully on a par with every other project pursuer in having reason to value his own projects above the advancement of all others. And each is aware that every project pursuer has exactly the same reason personally to value his own project pursuit in virtue of its being his. None is rationally obliged to accept inferiority in protected moral space, and none can make good a claim to superiority. Even if equality of rights does not emerge as the equilibrium result within an actual community, it is nonetheless a *moral equilibrium* derived from reflection on the logical structure of practical reason.[100]

Even if it was the result of fair competition, for some to accept a restricted set of basic liberties would, as Lomasky says, amount to accepting an inferior moral position. It is in this way that an inequality of fundamental rights, especially liberty rights, indicates a lack of respect for some individuals.[101] If so, then liberalism is committed to a more robust conception of equal liberty rights than is consistent with an ES-based theory.

It may seem that this argument not only undermines an ES-based theory of freedom, but the very idea of liberal ownership itself. Consider: I have argued that a liberal state is committed to a principle of equal liberty, but liberalism is also supposedly committed to a system of private property, and in such a system, holdings will be unequal. But one person's property rights necessarily limit the liberty of others; consequently, an inequality of property rights necessarily involves an inequality of liberty. Thus, it seems, any regime of private property is incompatible with what I have called the basic liberal commitment to equal liberty.

Now it is certainly true that the property rights of Alf limit the freedom of Betty just because *all of Alf's rights* limit the freedom of others, including his rights to freedom.[102] Does this mean, then, that each and every inequality of rights entails an inequality of freedom that is inconsistent with the liberal commitment to equal liberty? For example, children have a duty to care for their aged parents, and it seems plausible that their parents have a right that they do so. Of course, those whose parents have

---

[100] Lomasky, *Persons, Rights, and the Moral Community* (*supra* note 6), p. 78. See also Alan Gewirth, *Reason and Morality* (Chicago: University of Chicago Press, 1978), pp. 127–28, 206ff.

[101] Cf. Rawls, *A Theory of Justice*, pp. 543–47; Benn, *A Theory of Freedom* (*supra* note 8), ch. 6; and Ronald Dworkin, "Liberalism," in his *A Matter of Principle* (Cambridge, MA: Harvard University Press, 1985), ch. 8.

[102] This claim is defended in Gaus and Lomasky, "Are Property Rights Problematic?" (*supra* note 11).

died are not encumbered by such a liberty-limiting duty; they are thus more free than are those who have elderly parents. More generally, our moral positions are not identical; each of us possesses a different array of duties (e.g., of gratitude, etc.) depending on our personal history and circumstances. But the inequality of freedom that is the reverse side of this inequality of duties does not undermine the liberal commitment to equal liberty, for this commitment is, clearly, to an equality of certain important freedoms—equal basic freedoms.[103] Consequently, an inequality of some freedoms—resulting from differential special duties or differential holdings—can be consistent with the basic liberal commitment to equal liberties. But this consistency cannot be obtained if liberty is itself defined by property, as ES proposes. If we accept ES, the only way to achieve any equality of liberty is through equalization of holdings.

IV. RIGHTS, MORAL SOVEREIGNTY, AND FREEDOM

I have argued (i) that some rights, such as the rights to bodily integrity and to freedom of religion, are not liberal property rights, and thus all rights are not liberal property rights; and (ii) that because powers of transfer and claims to benefits are essential to liberal property rights, liberal property rights are not a species of freedom rights. I believe, then, that a standard classical-liberal view, that liberty is a type of property, or property a type of liberty, is ultimately confused. However, this does not mean that property rights and freedom are not linked; they are, but through a more general link between rights and freedom.[104]

We have just seen how accounts of property rights and liberty sometimes employ the metaphor of a moral space. Rights in general are often described in the same way. A. John Simmons, for instance, says that Locke "suggests the idea of a right as a kind of moral control or sovereignty over a particular area of our lives, defining a moral space within which we are free to operate."[105] Along very similar lines, Lomasky holds that the core notion underlying basic rights "is that each person possesses a kind of sovereignty over his own life and that such sovereignty entails that he be accorded a zone of protected activity within which he is to be free from encroachment by others."[106]

[103] See Ronald Dworkin, *Taking Rights Seriously* (Cambridge, MA: Harvard University Press, 1978), ch. 12; and John Rawls, *Political Liberalism* (New York: Columbia University Press, 1993), pp. 294ff.

[104] Most likely, they are also linked through a version of the instrumental argument. See Section I.

[105] Simmons, *The Lockean Theory of Rights* (*supra* note 48), p. 92. Cf. Nozick, *Anarchy, State, and Utopia* (*supra* note 24), p. 57: "A line (or hyper-plane) circumscribes an area in moral space around an individual. Locke holds that this line is determined by an individual's natural rights, which limit the actions of others."

[106] Lomasky, *Persons, Rights, and the Moral Community*, p. 11. See also Machan, *Individuals and Their Rights* (*supra* note 6), pp. 27, 58, 128.

In two crucial senses, rights define a moral space that constitutes one's area of freedom or sovereignty. First, and most obviously, as we have seen rights are often waivable.[107] Over a wide range of rights, if Alf has a right to ϕ, Alf has a choice whether or not to ϕ; if he does choose to ϕ, his right will (at least) enjoin others from interfering with his ϕ-ing. Such rights secure Alf a normative control over ϕ-ing; it is up to him whether or not to ϕ, and if he does, others are not to interfere. Consequently, regarding such rights there is indeed an intimate link between rights, freedom, and moral sovereignty over aspects of one's life. This connection, though, applies just as much to claims to benefits as to liberty claims.[108] A waivable claim, for instance to a welfare benefit that one may or may not apply for, secures for the individual such normative control.[109]

More importantly, all rights—waivable or not—preserve an area of personal moral space by insulating some issues from public decisions and interference.[110] One's rights protect one's choices, resources, body, opportunities, and powers; in so doing they provide a strong presumption that government cannot redistribute these. They define what, in the extended sense of *suum* (Section IID), *belongs to one*, not in the sense that one has liberal ownership of it, but in the sense that it is not open to majoritarian or administrative interference or expropriation. In this way all rights are indeed propriety rights, defining "one's own"; [111] and hav-

---

[107] Contemporary analysts of rights tend to divide between advocates of the "will or choice theory of rights" and supporters of "interest theories" and the related "benefit theories." The former understand rights in terms of protected choices, while to the latter, rights are protections of morally important interests or benefits. I set this seemingly intractable debate aside; though there may be good reasons to reconstruct the concept of rights so as to fit one or the other model, it is quite clear that adopting either as the sole model requires some reconstruction. On the face of it, both models are useful in explicating rights. Simmons, for instance, says that Locke holds both a choice and benefit theory (Simmons, *The Lockean Theory of Rights*, p. 93). Munzer also suggests a combined theory in his *A Theory of Property* (*supra* note 23), p. 48. For a defense of the choice theory, see Robinson, Coval, and Smith, "The Logic of Rights" (*supra* note 43); Sumner, *The Moral Foundation of Rights* (*supra* note 31), pp. 98ff; and Hart, "Legal Rights" (*supra* note 44), pp. 171ff. For a defense of the interest theory, see Waldron, *The Right to Private Property* (*supra* note 47), pp. 87–105; on the benefit theory, see David Lyons, "Rights, Claimants, and Beneficiaries" (*supra* note 37), and Section IIB above.

[108] Thus, on a choice conception of rights, all rights, benefit rights as well as liberty rights, protect choices. See Sumner, *The Moral Foundation of Rights*, p. 49.

[109] In his almost classic essay, Martin Golding associated welfare rights with mandatory or nonwaivable rights; see Golding, "Towards a Theory of Human Rights," *The Monist*, vol. 52 (1968), pp. 540–48. Wellman, however, points to a number of counterexamples; see his *Welfare Rights* (*supra* note 79), pp. 22–23.

[110] See Ronald Dworkin, *Taking Rights Seriously*, ch. 7; and R. E. Ewin, *Liberty, Community, and Justice* (Totowa, NJ: Rowman and Littlefield, 1987). Cf. Joseph Raz, *The Morality of Freedom* (Oxford: Clarendon Press, 1986), pp. 256–57.

[111] As Buckle shows, seventeenth-century usage closely linked the ideas of *suum*, property, and what was properly one's own—"propriety"; see Buckle, *Natural Law and the Theory of Property* (*supra* note 47), pp. 172–73.

ing this assured space is fundamental to a free life.[112] However, there is no quick conceptual move from this basic truth about a regime of rights, to libertarianism. In "The New Property" — hardly a classic of libertarian thought — Charles Reich argued that transforming governmental largesse into rights that could be claimed as a matter of justice would secure islands of sovereignty immune from majoritarian interference.[113] Alf's right to, say, his taxi franchise or his social-security benefits secures to him an area of life not subject to administrative whim, and in that way secures his sovereignty. And Reich was surely correct about this.

Though the idea of one's moral space as what belongs to one (and thus is presumed to be off the political agenda) is fundamental to a regime of freedom, the metaphors of "moral space" and "sovereignty" easily lead away from classical liberalism and negative liberty. Suppose that one's moral space is the area of life over which one has sovereign authority, i.e., over which one has control. A person with extensive rights, including extensive property rights, would be sovereign over more areas of life. Further assume, as seems reasonable, that the larger one's protected space, the freer one is (the metaphor of rights as defining space suggests this).[114] But this leads quickly away from negative freedom. If we understand freedom in terms of one's area of moral control, one's area of control can be enhanced by providing one with resources as well as authority over other people. The most free person is the person who controls the most, i.e., is sovereign over the greatest area. Proponents of positive liberty may not hesitate about following this line of thought, but classical liberals must resist an analysis of freedom as essentially sovereignty over others. Freedom and authority are not that closely linked.

We can now see the similarity between "new liberal" monism based on positive liberty and classical-liberal monism. If enough is built into the concept of liberty, then all rights will be liberty rights, and all liberal commitments will end up being liberty commitments. That, though, is precisely the problem with positive liberty: the concept of liberty tends to gobble up all political values. The monistic classical liberal makes a very similar error: he typically employs a conception of property that gobbles

[112] Note that this same general idea has been used to describe rights in general, property rights, and rights of privacy. Stanley Benn, for instance, speaks of a "conception of privacy . . . closely bound to the liberal ideal. The totalitarian claims that everything a person is and does has significance for society at large. He sees the state as the self-conscious organization of civil society, existing for society's well-being. The public or political universe is all-inclusive: *all* roles are public. . . ." See Benn, *A Theory of Freedom* (*supra* note 8), p. 268. This is by no means to say that these three concepts are identical, but insofar as each identifies an area that is not subject to public interference or scrutiny, they all articulate requirements of a free life, and often are run together. For an analysis of the difference between property and privacy, see Munzer, *A Theory of Property* (*supra* note 23), pp. 46, 92, 95, 99. See also F. A. Hayek, *The Constitution of Liberty* (London: Routledge, 1960), p. 140.

[113] Reich, "The New Property" (*supra* note 93), pp. 771ff.

[114] Cf. the conception of freedom as extent of sovereignty in Section IIIE.

up all rights, no matter how little they have to do with liberal ownership. "Everything is what it is: liberty is liberty, not equality or fairness or justice or culture, or human happiness or a quiet conscience."[115] Nor, we might add, is it property. If we restrain these imperialistic conceptual impulses, we are led to a basic plurality of justificatory principles. Liberty, desert-based ownership, and the wrongfulness of harming others are all foundational to liberal justification.[116]

None of this undermines libertarianism. Not only have I not even considered instrumental arguments linking liberty with property (Section I), but there is no theoretical bar to classical liberalism's resting on plural foundations. Still, it is not without reason that so many libertarians have been attracted to a monistic theory. If all basic liberal rights are simply liberty rights, or simply property rights,[117] it seems that justified liberal principles may well ultimately be libertarian. However, if plural foundations are admitted, if liberals need draw not only on commitments to liberty, but also on, say, commitments to equality (at least to justify equal basic liberty rights), the wrongfulness of harm, and desert-based ownership, then it seems more difficult to rule out need or welfare as legitimate justificatory categories. After all, for all his stress on negative liberty, and his relentless criticism of positive liberty, Berlin is no libertarian:

> I do not wish to say that individual freedom is, even in the most liberal societies, the sole, or even the dominant, criterion of social action. We compel children to be educated, and we forbid public executions. These are certainly curbs to freedom. We justify them on the ground that ignorance, or a barbarian upbringing, or cruel pleasures and excitements are worse for us than the amount of restraint needed to repress them.[118]

Because values are both many and conflicting, Berlin insists, our devotion to one must limit our commitment to others. I have tried to show here that insofar as the classical liberal must reject identity monistic theses that, somehow, liberty and property are really one, he must acknowledge pluralism, and thus must acknowledge the possibility that liberty may be limited for the distinct value of property. However, this is not enough to establish Berlin's position. The possibility remains that harmony monism may be invoked to show that, though distinct, the demands of liberty and property never conflict. One monism down, but one (or two) to go.

Philosophy and Political Science, University of Minnesota, Duluth

[115] Berlin, "Two Concepts of Liberty" (*supra* note 9), p. 125.
[116] Or so I have argued; see my *Value and Justification*, ch. 8.
[117] Note that this is how Sumner defines libertarianism: "Libertarianism as a moral/political theory is based on the contention that natural rights are all liberty-rights (or property rights)" (Sumner, *The Moral Foundation of Rights*, p. 110).
[118] Berlin, "Two Concepts of Liberty," p. 169.

SELF-OWNERSHIP, AUTONOMY,
AND PROPERTY RIGHTS

By Alan Ryan

I. Preamble

Writers of very different persuasions have relied on arguments about self-ownership; in recent years, it is libertarians[1] who have rested their political theory on self-ownership, but Grotian authoritarianism rested on similar foundations, and, even though it matters a good deal that Hegel did not adopt a full-blown theory of self-ownership, so did Hegel's liberal-conservatism. Whether the high tide of the idea has passed it is hard to say. One testimony to its popularity was the fact that G. A. Cohen for a time thought that the doctrine of self-ownership was so powerful that an egalitarian like himself had to come to terms with it; but he has since changed his mind. I have tackled the topic of self-ownership glancingly elsewhere, but have not hitherto tried to pull together the observations I have made in passing on those occasions.[2] The view I have taken for granted and here defend is that self-ownership is not an illuminating notion—except in contexts that are unattractive to anyone of libertarian tastes.

Self-ownership is so intrinsically contestable a notion that appeals to it are rhetorically ill-advised. The simple, but to me decisive, point is that when argument turns from the discussion of an individual's rights of free agency to the discussion of the nature and extent of his "self-propriety," the terminology changes but no illumination results. Historically, it may well be true that "property" or "propriety" was an all-embracing term for rights of use and control, but once we have distinguished rights in general from property rights in particular, nothing is gained by reassimilating the larger class to the smaller. Thus, when A. John Simmons observes that Locke's account of a property in oneself just is an account of "the right to pursue our plans, to invest our actions and labors, to extend our sphere of rightful control (that which is private) into the world, and to alienate our rights in the pursuit of innocent projects," my reply is that we lose nothing if we restrict ourselves to talking of those rights and

---

[1] See, e.g., Robert Nozick, *Anarchy, State, and Utopia* (New York: Basic Books, 1974); Murray Rothbard, *The Ethics of Liberty* (Atlantic Highlands: Humanities Press, 1982); and David Lloyd-Thomas, *In Defense of Liberalism* (Oxford: Blackwell, 1988).

[2] See, e.g., my "Utility and Ownership," in *Utility and Rights*, ed. R. G. Frey (Oxford: Blackwell, 1982).

241

immunities and drop talk of "property."[3] My arguments for this conclusion are so simple that I am sure that those who talk of self-ownership
must know them well and are not moved by them for reasons I cannot
guess at. That remains to be seen, and what follows may at least provide
a fat target for counterattack. I advance historically on my subject, with
some observations on Hobbes, Locke, Kant, and Hegel, then say a little
about a circularity in Robert Nozick's employment of self-ownership conceptions in *Anarchy, State, and Utopia* and rebut David Lloyd-Thomas's
claim that liberalism is founded on self-ownership. I then sabotage myself
by suggesting one normative use of the idea of self-ownership that is
attractive in itself and makes some genuine use of the proprietary overtones of the idea. I end by showing that believers in the intimate connection between individual autonomy and the protection of private property
in its familiar sense need not be dismayed by what I say.

II. Some History: Locke

Libertarians, who are not enthusiasts for authority, nonetheless seem
to be comforted by the thought that John Locke founded private property
(in the common or garden-variety sense of ownership rights in objects,
services, and land) on each individual's prior possession of "a *Property* in
his own *Person*."[4] Our property in our own persons gives us a property
in our own actions, and these in turn give us a property in what we "mix"
our labor with. This property is a natural relationship, in the sense that
it suffices to establish a claim of natural right, in the absence of government and a system of positive law, and in the absence of any agreement
by other persons to acknowledge our rights over what we thus establish
a property in. This is all very familiar. Questions that spring to mind,
though often overlooked in the literature on Locke, include "What is the
extent of our property rights in external objects, and is this like or unlike
the extent of our rights in ourselves?" Another is whether Locke's idiom
of "a property" in ourselves is significant. My reply is that natural proprietorship is a very variable notion, and that we do not by natural acquisition secure "full, liberal ownership" in what we acquire, make, or settle.
In this, it is like our "ownership" of ourselves; for this also is something
other than full, liberal ownership.[5] Indeed, having "a property" in oneself is, if it is like anything in positive law, like having what an English-

---

[3] A. John Simmons, *The Lockean Theory of Rights* (Princeton: Princeton University Press,
1992), p. 261.

[4] John Locke, *Two Treatises of Government* (Cambridge: Cambridge University Press,
1969), *Second Treatise*, section 27.

[5] See Simmons, *Lockean Theory of Rights*, ch. 5; Jeremy Waldron, *The Right to Private
Property* (Oxford: Clarendon Press, 1988), ch. 6; and A. M. Honoré, "Ownership," in *Oxford Essays in Jurisprudence*, First Series, ed. A. G. Guest (Oxford: Clarendon Press, 1962),
pp. 108–41.

man would recognize as a "repairing lease," that is, a leasehold interest which grants rights of occupancy and enjoyment as extensive as those that the freehold owner would have, and allows one to sell the unexpired portion of one's lease, but imposes at the same time the requirement that we keep up the property and hand it back in as good condition as we received it. This analogy has to be handled delicately, of course; since in the long run we are all dead, it is not our bodies that we can expect to hand back in good shape. It is that more elusive entity, our "person," that we have an indefinite care for, and our bodies are to be used properly in its service.

Establishing this case should be done more slowly than I shall do it,[6] but the starting point of an adequate interpretation of Locke's meaning begins with the general principle that human beings have only those rights in themselves or over anything else that are required to enable them to achieve the purposes for which God established the world and created them. This does not mean that our rights are not for our benefit; since God created us to flourish according to the potentialities he planted in us, there is no conflict between our benefit and His purposes. The secular analogue to such a principle is equally persuasive: rights are proportioned to the purposes they serve, and authority over persons and power over things are two important kinds of rights that are so proportioned. Lockean rights are intellectually engrossing because one of their purposes in his account is so clearly continuous with the purposes appealed to in modern accounts, and one is so clearly discontinuous. Rights are, as they are in modern legal theory, barriers against invasion and assault by other men; but their positive role is to allow us to fulfill the duties of self-development, husbandry of the world, and the preservation of all mankind as much as may be—duties that God lays upon us. That we cannot have more than a leasehold interest in ourselves is clearly stated by Locke himself: "[M]en being all the workmanship of one omnipotent and infinitely wise Maker—all the servants of one sovereign Master, sent into the world by his order, and about his business—they are his, whose workmanship they are, made to last during his, not one another's pleasure."[7]

The view that God's ownership of us results from his having created us has led many commentators to offer a "creationist" account of ownership in general. The thought is that we create our own personality, express it in our actions, and so create what we appropriate. A creationist account causes, as Locke knew, an obvious difficulty, namely that parents seem to secure over their children the same property rights that God has over us. Murray Rothbard, indeed, bites the bullet and says that parents do own their children. He contrives, however, on successive pages both

---

[6] I feel happier about going too fast here because of the excellence of Simmons, *Lockean Theory of Rights*, ch. 5.

[7] Locke, *Two Treatises of Government, Second Treatise*, section 6.

to claim that "the parental ownership is not absolute, but of a 'trustee' or guardianship kind" and that "the parent should have the legal right not to feed the child, i.e., to allow it to die."[8] Such a view seems to be driven by the wish to insist that all rights are negative rights, that the child has the right not to be killed by his or her parent, but nothing more, and it is a view with little to be said for it. Locke's way out of these straits is not wholly satisfactory; he variously appeals to the fact that children are conceived only as byproducts of the slaking of our sexual passions, and that our inability to say how they are created means that we cannot have over them the sort of proprietorship that we have over our other creations.[9]

Neither of these arguments has much to be said for it; if I inadvertently painted a masterpiece, that would not impugn my ownership of it, and the fact that I cannot explain how corn, when planted, produces plants that produce more corn than I planted, does not impugn my ownership of the plants and their produce. Two arguments that work rather better do so only by invoking differences between divine making and our own. One is the claim that if mixing our labor with something gave us outright freehold ownership of it, on the strength of our creation of what was owned, we would have to be able to create something *ex nihilo* in the way God does. We cannot. Strictly, we never create; we rearrange elements in the world, and set the causal agency of the world in motion.[10] This argument will achieve the desired result, however, only if we also invoke another crucial distinction — between persons and other objects in the world. For this argument threatens to impugn the cases of acquisition that Locke explicitly defends; even in the case of the corn we have planted, we have not created the new corn; if our labor is sufficient to give us property rights in one case and not in the other, we have to explain the difference between the two cases. A second argument does that. It makes the crucial element in the human being the human being's possession of a soul. Into us, though into nothing else apparently, God has put a soul, and entities with souls are unownable.

Believing that Locke held this view in just this form is rendered more difficult by the fact that he acknowledged situations in which we could enslave other persons; most people think of slaves as very much owned by their masters. Locke was ready to accept that someone who had behaved badly enough to forfeit life, liberty, and possessions might be offered the lesser of two evils in the form of servitude rather than death. But it is far from clear that Locke supposes anyone becomes the "owner"

[8] Rothbard, *Ethics of Liberty*, pp. 99, 100.

[9] Locke, *Two Treatises of Government, First Treatise*, sections 52–54; and Simmons, *Lockean Theory of Rights*, pp. 180–81.

[10] See also Immanuel Kant, *The Metaphysical Elements of Justice*, trans. John Ladd (Indianapolis: Library of Liberal Arts, 1965), for a repudiation of arguments linking ownership to creation.

of the slave, let alone just what form of servile status he has in mind. The passage where the discussion occurs suggests that he has in mind only the situation of a captive on the battlefield whose life we spare so long as he serves us as a slave. "[H]aving by his fault forfeited his life by some act that deserves death, he to whom he has forfeited it may (when he has him in his power) delay to take it, and make use of him to his own service; and he does him no injury by it."[11] Where there is any agreement between them, the state of slavery ceases: "[I]f once compact enter between them, and make an agreement for a limited power on the one side, and obedience on the other, the state of war and slavery ceases as long as the compact endures." That all agreement confers only limited authority follows from the principle that "no man can by agreement pass over to another that which he hath not in himself, a power over his own life."[12] When a government allows a criminal his life in exchange for labor as a drudge, this is not slavery in the conventional sense, but penal servitude. The difference between penal servitude and slavery as it is generally known — say, in the form practiced in the southern United States before they revolted against the federal government — is obvious enough: a Lockean miscreant loses his own "self-owned" status, but does nothing to impair his descendants' status. His offspring are as free as ever, and the children he begets in servitude are as free as anyone else's children. This is the proper understanding of "inalienable" rights; as the Virginia Declaration of Rights put it, men "have certain inherent rights, of which, when they enter into a state of society, they cannot by any compact deprive or divest their posterity. . . ."[13]

The only reason for dwelling on Locke in this fashion is that it becomes increasingly clear that Locke's conception of self-ownership, that is, of our property in our own persons, relies not at all on what recent writers take to be the proprietary overtones of the idea. We are, if owned, owned by God; we are, most importantly, not owned by anyone else, and even when we have submitted to government, we do not become the government's property. While Locke is occasionally ready to equate "despotic" authority over another human being with something like ownership — though more usually it is merely such power as may be exercised over those who have lost their property in themselves — he is careful to distinguish political authority and ownership much as Aristotle had done long before. Nor is the invocation of Aristotle accidental. Aristotle drew the distinction between proprietorship and political authority without any suggestion that property rights themselves were "absolute." Aristotle did not think that they could be exercised at the arbitrary will of the owner,

---

[11] Locke, *Two Treatises of Government, Second Treatise*, section 23.

[12] *Ibid.*, section 24.

[13] The Virginia Declaration of Rights, reprinted in D. G. Ritchie, *Natural Rights* (London: Macmillan, 1893), pp. 287–89.

and Locke for the most part followed him. The instrumental character of property rights set limits on what was a legitimate exercise of those rights. Of course, it was still the case that the proprietary relationship was one in which the thing owned was owned for the benefit of the owner, and in which the thing owned had no "say" in that use, which was why slaves could be thought of as animated tools rather than persons.

In limiting the ability of a self-owning individual to alienate himself wholesale, Locke was doing two things that had recently been challenged. Though Hugo Grotius's conception of natural law was founded on the right of self-preservation, our property in ourselves could be alienated in the same way as other forms of property; we might sell ourselves into slavery to secure our survival, and in the process sell our descendants into slavery too. This was not out of line with the Roman law understanding of the *patria potestas*, where the male head of a household had the right to sell his children into slavery, and where there was no doubt that his family was within his *ius* and thus legally part of his property; nor was it out of line with the ancient institution of debt-slavery. We flinch from the obvious implication of this, that a head of a household might take what financial advantage he could from his children, but Roman society did not. It is not in any case so very long since English law recognized the wardship of an heiress as a valuable piece of property.

Grotius's view was not quite Thomas Hobbes's, though the consequences were much the same. Hobbes hoped to put us under the authority of as absolute a government as any envisaged by Grotius, but did not talk of us as either owning ourselves or as transferring ownership in ourselves to anyone else when we made a political compact with them. It is unlikely that this was out of any fastidiousness about distinguishing personal rights and property rights or distinguishing ownership from political authority. Hobbes had, however, committed himself to the view that in the state of nature there was no propriety, no distinction of mine and thine, so there was nothing to be said for explaining subordination as a species of transfer of ownership. Perhaps, too, he was aware that even given his observation that tyranny was but "monarchy misliked," his readers would wish to distinguish between allegiance to an absolute monarch and slavery.

Locke denied outright that the authority of fathers (and mothers) over their children amounted to ownership of them; it was an authority exercised as a trust for the children's benefit rather than the parents'. Locke's argument consorts with his picture of the state of nature as an orderly, law-governed condition, occasionally interrupted by the greedy or the violent; that is, he is fastidious about making distinctions analogous to those the law and everyday morality make in a settled political society. Hobbes was disinclined to draw distinctions outside a social setting in which those distinctions stood a reasonable chance of being observed and of shaping our conduct. In his universe, there was nothing to be made of a notion of self-ownership since it added nothing to the thought that we have a natural right of self-preservation. Hobbes bleakly points out that this right must extend to a right even to one another's bodies; in conditions where stable ownership is unknown, talk of self-ownership would make no sense either.

Secondly, however, Locke was resisting any suggestion that biblical authority could be appealed to in aid of the thought that ownership or any other sort of right could be exercised merely at will. Agreeing that God had made a donation of the earth to Adam, Locke was at pains to insist that this was on terms; indeed, initially those terms were such as to exclude anything but a vegetarian existence. The inferior animals were included in the donation only after the Flood. Modern writers who talk of self-ownership do so in order to emphasize the existence of a sphere in which we may act exactly as we choose; the point has been deftly made by Jan Narveson in just such terms. What exactly Locke had in mind by a property in our own persons is so open to debate that I would not pretend that my remarks have settled the matter; but Locke's purpose at any rate — the restriction of the realm of arbitrary action — was plainly the reverse of what Narveson takes to be the point of asserting self-ownership.[14] By the same token, it was the reverse of what Hobbes and Grotius had sanctioned.

III. First Conclusions

The point I am urging about self-ownership is simple, but decisive. It is part of the everyday experience of all of us that ownership of anything is a two-edged business. We may be entitled to use what we own for our own purposes, but the purposes we have will also be influenced by our ownership of it. The usual experience of owning something is not that of being sovereign over something we may abandon at a moment's notice, but of being tied to its fate by a network of social and often legal ties. Try abandoning your car on the New Jersey Turnpike with a note disclaiming ownership of it; try, even, leaving your yard to grow whatever random collection of weeds, grasses, and wildflowers North American nature is inspired to create. Locke's conception of a property in ourselves is closer to everyday experience than the idealized picture of Nozick's *Anarchy, State, and Utopia* or Narveson's *The Libertarian Idea*.[15] In Locke's duty-permeated universe, talk of property in our own persons is the

[14] Jan Narveson, "Libertarianism, Postlibertarianism, and the Welfare State," *Critical Review*, vol. 6, no. 1 (Winter 1992), p. 73: "Calling for property in oneself simply is calling for being allowed to do as one pleases. . . ."

[15] Jan Narveson, *The Libertarian Idea* (Philadelphia: Temple University Press, 1989); for Nozick, see note 1 above.

reverse of libertarian; since the notion of a person is, as he says, a foren-
sic one, we are in the domain of the parable of the talents. We each have
a life to look after, and will in due course be called to account for how
well we have done with it.

If this is right, we can see one reason why talk of self-ownership may
be misguided. Those who so talk presume an agreement on what ownership entails that does not exist. When we try to get agreement, the concept of ownership plays no part in the discussion. The question "What
kind of ownership in oneself do we possess?" dissolves into the question
"What rights over ourselves do we have, how do they relate to the duties
we owe, and to whom do we owe these duties?" It is only on the
assumption that all talk of ownership is talk of full, liberal ownership that
talk of self-ownership favors one moral position; and it does so by begging every serious question at issue. One illustration of this point is the
case of abortion. Not only in common political argument, but in such
famous essays as Judith Jarvis Thomson's "A Defense of Abortion," it is
taken for granted that "Whose body is it?" frames a question that only
needs to be answered "Yours" to yield a decisive answer to the question
whether a mother may abort a fetus.[16] In fact, it leaves everything to be
fought for. In a world that took teleological conceptions of the world seriously, and used those conceptions to explain why we must take property
rights seriously too, one might think that a mother's body was meant as
a safe haven for growing babies. This would yield the thought that it was
indeed the mother's body, but contrary to Thomson it would also yield
the thought that what that entailed was her duty to do whatever she
could to bring a healthy baby to term.

Different moral theories of ownership would naturally yield other conclusions. A Godwinian conception of property, if that is not a contradiction in terms, would yield wholly indeterminate results; if the baby was
likely to turn out a benefactor of the human race, it would be the mother's
duty to persist to term, and if the baby was likely to be a menace to the
human race, it would be her duty to abort.[17] To call the mother's person,
body, capacities, and desires "hers" would, in a Godwinian universe,
only gesture at the person whose decisions would have the effects we are
interested in. What rights over that person and body she had would be
just what we had to discuss in the terms offered us by Godwin's *Enquiry
concerning Political Justice*. It would be tedious to spell this out exhaus-
tively; the general point is obvious enough: that assuming that our rights
over ourselves—bodies and capacities alike—are well described as "prop-

[16] Judith Jarvis Thomson, "A Defense of Abortion," *Philosophy and Public Affairs*, vol. 1
(1971), pp. 47-66.
[17] I do not believe that Godwin ever discussed such a suggestion, but it is a fair extrapolation from his discussion of Archbishop Fenelon; see William Godwin, *Enquiry concerning Political Justice*, ed. Keith Codell Carter (Oxford: Clarendon Press, 1971), pp. 70-71.

erty" only leads to arguments about what conception of "property" to adopt, and how far to press genuinely proprietary interests against others when the crunch comes.

Anyone who has lectured on Thomson's wonderful essay knows that it trades on intuitions that many readers do not share; evicting a trespasser who will face certain death at the hands of a howling mob is not universally thought to be one of the rights that comes with ownership of a piece of property, and even the wretched violinist of her essay who needs such lengthy use of our blood supply might in many people's eyes have some entitlement to it — the crucial issue being not whose blood it is so much as considerations that would vary case by case: whether he is a wonderfully good violinist, whether I am engaged in humanitarian work such that looking after him would mean the death of many others, whether he will recover and not need such assistance again, and how easy it is to compensate me for my sacrifice.

That suggests that merely appealing to self-ownership leads to no determinate conclusions about what rights and duties we actually have, only to a debate in which we recast whatever ideas we have on that topic into the language of proprietorship. Historically, talk of a property in ourselves did not serve libertarian ends. As we have seen, Locke writes in such terms to show that individual rights, whether over ourselves or over others, are limited by the purposes they are instituted to serve, while Hobbes and Grotius allow us complete power over ourselves only in order to allow us to transfer that power to an absolutist government. Still, one might want to say that we are driven to think in such terms, for a reason that I have not yet mentioned. Thus far, "self-ownership" has been treated as if it embraced only questions about who has the authority to decide what we shall do, and within what range their authority lies. I have not yet allowed the concept of autonomy to do any work at all, other than in the residual sense of accepting that Lockean and Hobbesian persons in the state of nature are autonomous in the weak sense that they are self-directing, absent a settled legal authority that can direct them according to law. Hobbesian persons are in other respects never self-directing: they do not (or logically cannot) prescribe laws to themselves; they only uncover theorems pertaining to their self-preservation; and they never have more freedom of action than a stream coursing unimpeded down its bed. Lockean persons are more complicatedly situated, but here, too, there is no suggestion that self-direction is of any moral interest independently of its role in Christian worship. To be directed by reason, by the "candle of the Lord," and by the laws of nature, is highly desirable. That we choose to be so guided for ourselves is desirable because God wants the worship of willing believers, not a compelled and merely outward faith. There the argument stops. Locke has no positive interest in the human will; taming it is a substantial part of education, and

the notion of autonomy I am now about to introduce is not something he
would have thought acceptable.

IV. Some More History: Kant, Hegel, and Self-Direction

One attractive argument for the inevitability of some conception of self-
ownership is that when any of us act, we use our bodies. We can only
walk by moving our legs, swinging our arms, ingesting oxygen into these
lungs, and so on. To act is to invest our bodies with our intentions, purposes, or wills. We do this without thinking of our rights in the matter,
but in doing it we presume our rights over the otherwise inert stuff of our
body. This is Hegel's argument in his *Elements of the Philosophy of Right*,
and it has a certain plausibility to it.[18] One might turn this positive
defense upside down and ask, in a formula that joins Locke and Kant:
How could anything in the world come to be owned if persons could not
appropriate it? And how could they appropriate it if they had no right to
use their hands to grasp, their legs to walk to where what they needed
was to be had, and so on? How could property in externals begin unless
a previous property in the not-exactly-external of one's body existed?

Kant in fact embraced a different branch of the same line of thought.
If we ask why questions about self-ownership arise in this philosophical
form—they are hardly the stuff of everyday legal inquiry, even if they
blend into matters that are more nearly the stuff of non-everyday legal
inquiry—a plausible answer is that it is part of an inquiry into the way in
which the world becomes subject to intelligence and reason, is given
meaning and sense, and is brought into commerce with the human
race.[19] Both Kant and Hegel take it for granted that we are driven to use
the world—our bodies and things external to us therein included—for
largely utilitarian reasons. Both go on to say that this prompting serves
more importantly as the natural starting point of a process whose rationale is not adequately described by merely referring to the starting point.
Kant argues that the world is brought into human commerce by being
appropriated; this achieves two crucial things, neither of them a matter
of simple welfare: one is the education of the individual who works on
what he acquires to transform it and make it useful to himself and others; the second is a network of legal obligations and rights that itself
needs sustaining by a legal system and an adequate political order.

By indirect means, we are driven into governing ourselves in a lawful
community, governed by rules of justice that achieve an external political order without in any way infringing on our internal freedom. This is
required because there are some things that cannot be made objects of a

[18] G. W. F. Hegel, *Elements of the Philosophy of Right*, ed. Allen W. Wood, trans. H. B. Nis-
bet (Cambridge: Cambridge University Press, 1991), section 48, p. 79.
[19] Kant, *The Metaphysical Elements of Justice*, pp. 60–67.

proprietary relationship, namely those things closest to our personality, such as religious faith, moral agency, and conscience. It is Hegel rather than Kant who explains that the idea of being able to part with all aspects of our personality is incoherent because it depends for its legitimacy on just that feature of ourselves it proposes to see extinguished. Nonetheless, it is hard to escape the thought that Kant must have had a similar argument in mind. It is perhaps the strongest argument for the usefulness of some conception of self-ownership or other that when we act to bind ourselves by promising or by making a gift to others, we rely on the recognition of a power of disposal of ourselves and our abilities that is analogous to that which we rely on when making a disposal of property in the usual sense.

In Hegel's *Elements of the Philosophy of Right*, the derivation of the right of property follows the path just sketched. The concept of a person, claims Hegel, appears first and most primitively in the aspect of an owner; it is not clear why, but one can perhaps put together some reasons. One lies in the very notion of "abstract right," the title of the section of *Elements of the Philosophy of Right* concerned with property; even though what we own is usually some specific object with highly specific qualities, our relationship to it is abstract in the sense that all we need assert when challenged is "It's mine." A counter-claim may impugn our personhood in some simple way, such as "But you're a slave yourself" or "You're only twelve"; otherwise, it must impugn the pedigree of our claim, and do so in a rather small number of ways—"It already belonged to Jones" or "You did not find it, you stole it." Discussion on the merits is what is in general ruled out by claims of ownership and their rebuttals. Of course, in any actual legal system, matters are immensely more complex; one who is bankrupt is allowed to go on owning his tools, his bed, and a few other personal possessions, but cannot acquire new debts— how far is his personality diminished?

The Hegelian account of proprietorship, however, neatly demonstrates both the plausibility and the limitations of arguments to and from self-ownership. For Hegel treats ownership as one feature of the process whereby will and reason come to infuse the merely external. This makes our relationship to ourselves both proprietary and not. It is proprietary in the sense that what gives our bodies life is the fact that we are in some sense "in possession" of them. Yet it is not proprietary just because our bodies are also us. If you strike me sharply on the nose, you cannot escape the charge of assault by observing that you had an urge to punch a nose, but no urge at all to injure a person. This is one of the many things that explains the artificiality of discussing such things as the wrong you do me when you tread on my foot as matters of "trespass" or "boundary crossing." The concept of personal identity is notoriously slippery, and one would wish not to rely too heavily on an unanalyzed understanding of it to make the point, but Hegel is surely right to suggest that the owner/owned distinction breaks down in such cases.

What drives the discussion of ownership in Hegel is, as it is in Kant, the distinction between (1) the utilitarian promptings that drive us to use the things around us along with our ability to put them to use, and (2) the rational goal of the institutions that result from this use. The goal is to give value and meaning to a world that would otherwise lack it; it takes on our values and our meaning when we take it into ownership. We ourselves do not need to be given sense and meaning in that way; we are the source of the sense and meaning of mere matter, not ourselves empty vessels waiting to have meaning given to us. This is one of the reasons for Hegel's elaborate discussion of the ways we come to take possession of things. We may simply grasp them: this is, you might say, the purest assertion of our will to make them instruments of our purposes. We may work on them: this is, you might say, the more elaborate effort to permeate things with our purpose. Lastly, we may simply mark them as ours: but here, where we rely on conventional signs of ownership—using these signs to secure others' recognition of our special claims upon the objects so marked—we do not so much rely on the way one human will controls one or a few external objects as rely on the way a whole culture, once equipped with law, can bring the whole external world into such a relation with the whole human world.[20]

This, however, suggests something of a reversal in what we might think was the natural interpretation of such "will-based" accounts. They seem at first sight to glorify the will, to emphasize the individual's absolute sovereignty over mere external stuff. On further analysis, we find that Hegel's treatment of the individual relies on a thought that remains covert in the section on abstract right in Elements of the Philosophy of Right, but becomes increasingly important thereafter. This is the thought that the individual, and thus the individual will, is essentially a social creation. It is only for this reason that the natural fact that in walking, eating, drinking, we display a sort of possession of our bodies by using them, can have any moral import. This, however, also suggests that the self that is respected when we respect its possession is a self already shaped by social training and its moral and intellectual results. The results are thus anything but libertarian. The possessory image of the self turns out to be one that relies on the world to shape the self by way of our ownership of parts of the world, not one that implies domination by whim. This is not an argument against autonomy, however, though it is an argument for a particular conception of autonomy. Hegel's account of property was an account of its role in our attempt to secure rational freedom. Freedom, for Hegel, had to be determinate, not mere indeterminacy; hence, it had to

[20] Hegel, Elements of the Philosophy of Right, sections 54–58, pp. 84–88.

be autonomy, since it had to be lawful, but the law had to be self-generated, not externally imposed.

Both Kant and Hegel thought that property ownership was essential to autonomy. For Kant, this has political implications of a very direct and somewhat alarming kind. Nonowners become what he called "passive citizens," that is, they were not to be admitted to the suffrage, even though they were to be treated in other respects like all other citizens under the rule of law. Since they had no property, they were forced to sell their services to others, and in so doing they became dependents. Quite why their "time" was not a property in the required sense, it is hard to tell, although there is something to be said for the thought that what we really do when we sell only unskilled labor is sell nothing, but rather put ourselves at the disposal of another person's will for a time. We temporarily sell ourselves into dependency. This view perhaps owes something to another of Kant's insights. When considering why Western European countries had developed so much more swiftly than Asiatic societies in which princes lived more magnificently than Western kings, while their subjects lived far worse than Western peasants, Kant offered the thought that artisans in the West had had something of their own to sell, while a craftsman in the Orient was simply taken into the princely household as a dependent. It is not implausible that this did provide the Western artisan with an incentive to develop his skills and to produce new things for an impersonal market, where his Eastern counterpart would have had no incentive to do anything but what his employer for the moment set out for him. Kant was capable of recognizing that skills could erode the difference between merely selling one's time to others and the ownership of property. A person who recognized himself as possessing a skill had a something that could be developed, improved, and turned to new ends.

Mastery of a skill had, plausibly, the same good effects on the "thing" mastered, and on the person whose skill it was, as did the owning and husbanding of any other natural resource. One of the ways in which Kant was genuinely a "bourgeois" thinker was his elevation of this form of "property" to an equal political and moral standing with the landed property of the Prussian gentry and aristocracy. One of the ways in which Hegel built on Kant was in balancing this thought against another: that the double-edged aspect of property, its ability to hold a person in place as well as providing him with scope for individual freedom, could justify both the entails (limits on alienability) that Kant had complained of (for Kant, they diminished the number of property owners; for Hegel, they secured a traditional landed gentry's position, and therefore its political role) and the activities of the professional and mercantile middle classes, especially if these latter were organized in guilds and corporations rather than operating in a wholly unorganized fashion.

It is time to reinforce a moral drawn above before ending with some thoughts on more modern versions of these arguments. The obvious moral is that any talk of self-ownership is parasitic on whatever conception of proprietorship the speaker has in mind; if stewardship, then it will be the stewardship of our abilities that will be emphasized, and if some other view of ownership, then a correspondingly different emphasis will emerge. The second moral is that the naive question "If I am the owner of myself, then who is the owner and who is owned?" reappears in writers such as Kant and Hegel who stress the need to preserve the distinction between the agent as owner and the thing owned. We may, on this view, engage ourselves to work for wages, but not sell ourselves into slavery—since that would extinguish the owner whose ownership was the ground of the transaction. To decide where the line falls between those things we may do and those we may not, requires an inquiry into the essential and inessential features of personality that the concept of ownership as such does not help us with.

V. More Conclusions

I move briefly to three further tasks. The first is to illustrate the claims made above with an examination of Nozick's employment of the idea of self-ownership in *Anarchy, State, and Utopia*, the second to say a little about one nonlibertarian, nonliberal view of self-ownership, and the third to acknowledge that a stress on the role of private property in sustaining individual autonomy may survive a great deal of skepticism about self-ownership. Although Nozick and Rothbard disagree very sharply over the legitimacy of the state, both start with the same idea of individual self-ownership. Both argue for it effectively by dismissing alternatives; if we do not own ourselves, others must have part-ownership of us, and we are the partial slaves of other people. The somewhat feeble-sounding alternative that proprietary notions are just out of place in this context is not given a hearing, partly because there seems to be little interest on the part of either Nozick or Rothbard in the question of whether property rights are in any way peculiar or worth distinguishing as a particular kind of right among all the various kinds of rights we may want to categorize. But there are legal systems in which some things are explicitly declared to be impossible to own. Wild animals that lack an *anima revertendi* are not objects of ownership in Roman law. Nearer our target, the bodies of deceased persons are not owned in the English common law; persons who are entitled to possess them may do so for one reason only, and that is to secure their burial. Strictly speaking, the "resurrection men" who took newly buried corpses from their graves and sold them to medical students in need of corpses for dissection were not committing a theft, and the students were not in receipt of stolen goods. It is therefore not an absurdity to suggest that whatever rights we have over ourselves are not properly described as self-ownership.

This does not settle the matter. It is open to anyone to propose to revise our everyday habits of speech in these matters. The counter to such a proposal is that there are some distinctions ordinarily drawn that we do not want to give up, and that the purposes for which the revision is offered can be handled well enough in other ways. Thus, Nozick, like Rothbard, relies heavily on the thought that we are our own owners to dismiss the law's current penalization of victimless crimes. Since our bodies are ours, we may do what we choose with them; in particular, we may allow other people to derive whatever sort of sexual pleasure they like from them, so long as they do it on terms we agree to. We may, by the same token, inhale intoxicants and narcotics; these are our lungs, and over them we are rightly sovereign.

There are many situations in which we cheerfully accept this kind of argument; if I decide to dye my hair bright blue, I may say that it's my hair that I'm dyeing in the course of holding that it's no one else's business what color I choose to have my hair. Or if I choose altruistically to give blood even though I know I shall certainly faint as a result, I may say that it's my blood to give if I choose. It is not always the argument one reaches for; I may say that it's none of your business what color my hair is, or that it doesn't harm you, so you have no standing to complain of it; and I may say only that it's me that giving blood will damage, not you. These considerations seem not to rest on thoughts about property, though they rest on ideas about how we distribute powers of control, and of course one of the effects of property rules is to do that too.

The reason I stress these cases is that Nozick attacks several theories of distributive justice by claiming that they allow other people to intervene forcibly in determining what happens with my body. Applying John Rawls's maximin theory of justice[21] to marriage might involve us in pairing off the most attractive man and the least attractive woman, and vice versa, in the attempt to give the least advantaged person in the marital allocation as good an outcome as possible. To the extent that the example has any rhetorical force, and it plainly has some, it is because we regard marriage as something that involves a particularly intimate engagement of ourselves and our bodies; such sentiments clearly argue against the compulsory allocation of spouses. However, Nozick has no right to trade on such sentiments. Having committed himself to a view of self-ownership that allows us to commit suicide for as good or bad reasons as those that might lead us to discard an old fountain pen or a decaying Cadillac convertible, he has opened the gate to the enemy.

They can say: If all that is at stake is ownership, we are unmoved. Property is exactly what we do not mind redistributing; it is external to

---

[21] John Rawls, *A Theory of Justice* (Cambridge, MA: Harvard University Press, 1971).

the choosing self, something appropriately treated in simple means-end ways. If that is what you think decisions about marriage are like, why flinch from applying Rawls's conception of justice to them? The same is true of the identification of taxation with forced labor. One can readily concede that taxation is a forced something—perhaps a forced "contribution"—and remain unmoved by Nozick's argument. The reason is simple enough. To be forced to give up some part of the salary an employer is willing to pay me for my services is perhaps painful; but it is not deeply implicated in my inner life. This is why in countries such as *ancien régime* France, where the *corvée*, or system of compulsory labor on the roads, existed, those who were liable to it protested against real forced labor though they readily admitted that taxes would be needed to replace it, and understood that they might have to pay them. What is wrong with forced labor is that it involves the direct control over *me* that free agents resent.

It is not an accident that imposts arouse increasing resentment as they go up a scale from the financial impost of the taxation of salaries and purchases, to the taking of particular objects such as livestock or a portion of the crops we have just harvested, and on to forced labor. Any argument that equates all of them is rhetorically counterproductive. The general point, then, is that the rhetoric of self-ownership is self-destructive because it first relies on the ordinary understanding of property to argue that since our bodies are our property, we (but not other people) may do anything we like with and to them—which is not the ordinary view—and then relies on the ordinary view of our relationships with our bodies to argue that since our bodies are property, we must extend to all property the tenderness that we extend to rights of bodily integrity, privacy, and the like.

At the risk of flogging a dead horse, let me extend the argument one last time to another author. David Lloyd-Thomas's *In Defense of Liberalism* defends an interesting self-ownership doctrine—interesting not least because he combines a consequentialist defense of rights with an unusual view of what consequences are to count. The crucial consequence that Lloyd-Thomas says we should use to structure our view of rights is the contribution of those rights to our increased understanding of what is truly of value; Lloyd-Thomas's book is even more unusual in ending with a frank admission that the culture of Western society has, if anything, deteriorated over the past two centuries—so that we may well be less in touch with what is truly of value than we once were—and that his defense of liberalism is in the process of being falsified. My interest is limited to one feature of the account. Lloyd-Thomas defends the idea that we should be assigned ownership of ourselves; this repudiates the usual view of natural law according to which we perceive that people have rights of self-ownership. His reason for talking of ownership at all is one that I sympathize with; he argues that it is rights of control that matter to liberal theory.[22]

But the clarity of his account exposes the weakness of the argument. To know what ownership of ourselves he wishes to confer on each of us, he must first decide what rights of control will serve his consequentialist purposes; but this is to reverse any thought that our rights must be derived from our property in ourselves. This reverses the usual order. When we see someone riding a bicycle and ask whether he is entitled to ride it, he may reply that he owns it and can ride it whenever he likes, thus resting his rights of control on his ownership. We may wonder whether he owns it, and discover that he does not, and that his right to ride it rests on his having been lent it by the owner, but there, too, the owner's right to lend it is a function of his ownership, not a redescription of it. For the notion of self-ownership to do any real work for Lloyd-Thomas, we ought to deduce our rights from our self-ownership, not merely bundle up such rights of control as we believe in, in order to label the composite "self-ownership."

My second observation fulfills my earlier promise to commit self-sabotage. Among the several alternatives to a view such as Narveson's cited above, to the effect that talk of self-ownership is all about acting as we choose, one is the claim that we ought indeed to think, if not of ourselves, at any rate of our aptitudes and characters, as possessions — not in order to emphasize the right to do as we please with them, but in order to emphasize a duty to learn how to do with them what is pleasing to others. This is what we get a rather bleak account of in Locke's educational writings, and a more playful account of in Max Stirner's *The Ego and His Own*. [23] Here, too, what we get out of self-ownership will depend on the goals we suppose it is to serve. If the notion of friendship is placed at the center of our social thought, and we get away from the obsessive concern with rights vis-à-vis the state that has marked orthodox political theory for the past three centuries, we might find a use for the idea of self-ownership in the doctrine that our duty is to make ourselves attractive to others, so as to enhance sociability and friendship. Most of my earlier strictures against supposing that the concept of ownership will play a very large role in all this apply here, too, but one might say in defense of the introduction of the concept in this context that after a long period in which such talk has emphasized rights against others, there is some rhetorical value in showing that this is not the only emphasis that talk of self-ownership will bear.

The thought that self-ownership might play a fruitful role in a social and political theory that emphasizes friendship stems from two things.

[22] Lloyd-Thomas, *In Defense of Liberalism*, pp. 8–10.

[23] Max Stirner, *The Ego and His Own* [1844], ed. John Carroll (New York: Harper and Row, 1969).

The first is that friendship has much to do with giving—our time, attention, affectionate interest, along with the use of our bicycles, garden tools, and hair dryers—and what isn't mine I cannot exactly give to anyone else. The second is that ownership is universally seen to be socially useful as a way of allocating responsibility and identifying what anyone in particular is responsible for cultivating. This applies to our agreeable qualities; the noxious weeds of envy, ill-temper, disaffection, and idleness that make us justly disliked are ours to root out, in the same way that liveliness and openness and cheerfulness are ours to cultivate. Such a view makes some real use of the metaphor of self-cultivation and self-ownership, and so far as I can see, breaks away from the usual disputes. Indeed, given his emphasis on our duty to pursue what is truly of value, Lloyd-Thomas would have done better to have argued that his sort of liberalism rests on self-ownership not in order to stress rights of control but in order to stress the duties of development to which such rights are instrumental.

Lastly, then, I have to emphasize that my skepticism about talk of self-ownership does nothing to diminish the importance of the argument between libertarians and their opponents about the bases of autonomy, and the role of private property in the usual sense in maintaining a free society. It does, of course, entail skepticism about the amount of argumentative benefit the parties to that discussion will get from talking about self-ownership. But many other arguments remain. The best arguments for the importance of private property in sustaining individual autonomy are familiar psychological arguments about the need for people to have a control over things of all kinds—and ties of responsibility to them—that will induce in them both a sense of their own powers and a sense of the possibility of their development. It seems to me doubtful that a society built in the way envisaged in Nozick's *Anarchy, State, and Utopia* will be best-suited to this task, but it is absolutely clear that command economies have been strikingly ill-suited to it. Some system of private property rights in external things, and a legal system that encourages us to think of our talents and abilities as assets to be developed, is evidently needed—as well as many somewhat mysterious and hard-to-manipulate cultural stimuli. On this point, liberals, conservatives, and (some) libertarians are likely to be agreed. It is perhaps a properly uncontentious point to end on.

Politics, Princeton University

AN UNEASY CASE AGAINST PROPERTY RIGHTS IN BODY PARTS*

By Stephen R. Munzer

I. Introduction

This essay deals with property rights in body parts that can be exchanged in a market. The inquiry arises in the following context. With some exceptions, the laws of many countries permit only the donation, not the sale, of body parts. Yet for some years there has existed a shortage of body parts for transplantation and other medical uses. It might then appear that if more sales were legally permitted, the supply of body parts would increase, because people would have more incentive to sell than they currently have to donate. To allow sales is to recognize property rights in body parts. To allow sales, however, makes body parts into "commodities"—that is, things that can be bought and sold in a market. And some view it as morally objectionable to treat body parts as commodities.

I present a qualified case against property rights in body parts that are transferable in a market. As used here, the term "body parts" includes any organs, tissues, fluids, cells, or genetic material on the contours of or within the human body, or removed from it, except for waste products such as urine and feces. The qualified case rests on a Kantian argument concerning human dignity. But the case is uneasy. There is no swift transition from the mere existence of a market in body parts to a sound objection in terms of commodities and Kantian dignity.

Instead, there is a complicated route strewn with difficulties. Here is a map. Section II explains why this topic is controversial. Section III clarifies why, from a Kantian point of view, sales of body parts are sometimes inappropriate. Section IV describes three different ways of offending Kantian dignity. Section V then shows how to avoid the fallacy of division—a logical error that a Kantian perspective may seem prone to commit. Section VI shows how the analysis applies to the widely differ-

* For help with this essay I am indebted to Richard L. Abel, Ellen Brostrom, Evan Caminker, David Copp, Ralph A. DeSena, David Dolinko, John Martin Fischer, Gary Gleb, Mark F. Grady, Rebecca Gudeman, Kenneth L. Karst, M. B. E. Smith, and James Tully. I also owe debts to the other contributors to this volume, to its editors, to my colleagues and seminar students, to members of the Law and Philosophy Discussion Group, and to the participants in the W. G. Hart Legal Workshop in London in July 1993. I am thankful for a fellowship from the National Endowment for the Humanities and financial support from the Academic Senate and the Dean's Fund at the University of California, Los Angeles.

259

ent participants in a market for body parts. Section VII investigates the effects of the language of the market on persons, and addresses the impact on them of assigning monetary values to body parts in tort contexts. Finally, Section VIII summarizes my uneasy case. Since I cannot exclude the possibility of other or less difficult arguments, this article offers only *an uneasy* case against property rights in body parts.

I do not offer knockdown arguments for bold conclusions. I do contend that it is morally objectionable for persons to sell their body parts if they offend dignity by transferring them for a reason that is not strong enough in light of the nature of the parts sold. Furthermore, it is morally objectionable to participate in a market for body parts, as (say) a buyer or broker, if by doing so one offends the dignity of oneself or others. Lastly, it is morally objectionable for a market in body parts to exist if its workings offend the dignity of enough participants in the market. These contentions raise a moral objection based on dignity rather than the existence of a moral objection all things considered. That an action or institution is morally objectionable does not entail that one lacks a moral right to do it or participate in it, or that the state or others have a moral right to interfere with the action or institution. I state these qualified results here so that readers who cannot abide any but the most dramatic conclusions will see what is coming and lay this essay aside with the least expenditure of time.

In a previous, inadequate approach to property and persons in *A Theory of Property*, I touched on this topic only sufficiently to question the view that to speak of property rights in the body is to treat persons as "things" or "commodities." I also argued that it is unconvincing to hold that property-talk somehow demeans people by undercutting their autonomy.[1]

This approach is inadequate because, *inter alia*, I did not consider whether people might have property rights in various *parts* of their bodies, and, if they do, which parts and which rights those might be. In a recent essay I identified three different Kantian arguments against property rights in body parts,[2] but I did not develop a promising reconstructed version of one of these arguments. Hence there is much unfinished business so far as I am concerned. This essay is an effort to remedy some of the shortcomings of my previous discussions. Since whole bodies and their uses raise somewhat different (though related) issues, I do not take up such matters as slavery, indentured servitude, baby-selling, prostitution, surrogate motherhood, or the market for labor.

---

[1] Stephen R. Munzer, *A Theory of Property* (Cambridge: Cambridge University Press, 1990), pp. 55–56.

[2] Stephen R. Munzer, "Kant and Property Rights in Body Parts," *Canadian Journal of Law and Jurisprudence*, vol. 6, no. 2 (July 1993), pp. 319–41.

II. Why This Topic Is Controversial

The topic of property rights in body parts is controversial mainly because people differ over whether rights of this sort are appropriate at all. True enough, related issues also inspire debate. People discuss whether less money should be spent on transplants and more on other forms of medical care. They also argue over whether the supply of transplantable cadaveric organs could best be increased by conscripting decedents' organs, presuming decedents' consent to donate, or requiring medical personnel to ask decedents' families to donate the organs of the dead. But the controversy over sales exhibits the sharpest political lines. Some proponents of a market for body parts are scholars of law and economics and tend to come from the political right. Some opponents are Marxists or feminists or philosophers who emphasize the ethics of virtue; they frequently hail from the political left. Still, the controversy is not a knee-jerk drawing of political lines. Each group offers arguments for its position that merit examination. Space allows no thorough examination, but this section does sketch, and comment critically on, some leading arguments of each side.

Proponents hold that a market would increase the supply of transplantable organs and tissues. Given the current shortage of such organs and tissues, any mechanism that would increase supply is surely a reason for recognizing transferable property rights in body parts. Some advocate a market that would allow *inter vivos* sales — that is, transfers for value while the seller is alive.[3] They are not arguing for the right to sell a part essential to one's life or personal identity, such as the sale of one's brain. Yet they are proposing more than just a market for blood, semen, ova, hair, placentas, or diseased organs removed during surgery — the sale of which many readers may accept. Debate centers chiefly on organs that are nonvital but whose surgical removal involves significant risk or causes morbidity — such as the sale of a cornea, a kidney, or skin.

Other proponents advocate a market for the transfer of body parts at death. The literature contains at least two different proposals for a futures market in organs to be removed at death. Lloyd R. Cohen envisions a contract that would provide a fairly large amount — say, $5,000 per major organ — for each usable body part that can be removed upon the seller's death. Payment is contingent on the seller's supplying one or more usable

---

[3] See, for example, Richard Michael Boyce, "Organ Transplantation Crisis: Should the Deficit Be Eliminated Through Inter Vivos Sales?" *Akron Law Review*, vol. 17, no. 2 (Fall 1983), pp. 283–302; Marvin Brams, "Transplantable Human Organs: Should Their Sale Be Authorized by State Statutes?" *American Journal of Law & Medicine*, vol. 3, no. 2 (Summer 1977), pp. 183–95; Keith N. Hylton, "The Law and Economics of Organ Procurement," *Law & Policy*, vol. 12, no. 3 (July 1990), pp. 197–224; and Clifton Perry, "Human Organs and the Open Market," *Ethics*, vol. 91, no. 1 (October 1980), pp. 63–71.

body parts, and would go to the seller's estate.[4] Henry Hansmann imagines a contract that would offer a modest noncontingent annual payment — say, $30 — to the seller in return for such usable parts, if any, as he or she has at death. The money would go directly to the seller each year, but the amount would be heavily discounted because of the chance that the seller might die with no usable parts or in circumstances where any usable parts could not be removed in time.[5]

Common to both present sales and futures contracts are the following standard concerns. The supply of donated (free) organs may decrease. Sold organs may be inferior to donated organs. If the "market" operates only on the supply side, the total cost of transplants will rise, even though one avoids objections to using the market for allocating organs to recipients. If one has a full-fledged market on both the supply and demand sides, then one may get the result that only the poor will sell and only the rich will buy organs. This result will transpose existing inequalities in the distribution of income and wealth into new inequalities in the opportunity for an extended healthy life.

Yet even if one could subdue these concerns, there remains an underlying resistance to the moral appropriateness of a market for body parts. Hansmann traces the resistance to anxieties about "commodification." Since he can make only limited sense of this notion, he surmises that moral resistance stems from a kind of stubborn psychological inertia.[6]

Hansmann's analysis misses the mark. Consequences are not the heart of the matter. Today most countries bar voluntary indentured servitude, which was a common practice some centuries ago, even though it is easy to structure an adequate market for voluntarily selling oneself into service. The ban derives from the well-founded belief that if people turn themselves into commodities, the humanity of everyone — both master and indentured servant — declines. A similar concern lurks in the moral resistance to markets in body parts. Though a futures market is not the most worrisome type of market, it is by no means free from risks to a sense of common humanity.

If opponents of a market for body parts have a single term for what is wrong at the core with such a market, it is "commodification." This is the objection expressed by such widely different figures as Ruth F. Chadwick, Leon R. Kass, and Margaret Jane Radin. The objection takes various forms. Chadwick and Kass voice concerns about markets in body parts, but they lack any elaborate account of either property or commodification. Radin has an elaborate account of both, but her main concerns are with topics other than property rights in body parts. Together these scholars

[4] Lloyd R. Cohen, "Increasing the Supply of Transplant Organs: The Virtues of a Futures Market," *George Washington Law Review*, vol. 58, no. 1 (November 1989), pp. 1–51.

[5] Henry Hansmann, "The Economics and Ethics of Markets for Human Organs," *Journal of Health Politics, Policy, and Law*, vol. 14, no. 1 (Spring 1989), pp. 57–85.

[6] *Ibid.*, pp. 74–78.

give reasons for not recognizing property rights in body parts, though it remains to be seen how strong these reasons are.

I hope not to be rude in going over quickly the work of Chadwick and Kass. Chadwick opposes the sale of body parts on the ground that it interferes with a duty, owed to oneself and to others, to promote the flourishing of human beings.[7] Although she mentions the unattractive consequences of selling body parts,[8] her principal appeal is to an apparently nonconsequentialist notion of human flourishing. Regrettably, she does not articulate this notion clearly. Kass is even less clear. He agonizes over the "propriety" of selling organs.[9] He discusses "commodification" briefly.[10] Yet he does not advance a strong argument against a market in body parts.

I shall devote more space to Radin's work. My reservations about property rights in body parts have something in common with her recent invocation of Kant.[11] She deserves credit for highlighting some connections between property and persons and for illuminating such topics as prostitution, surrogate motherhood, and the selling of babies. But some features of her general approach cloud more than they clarify. Specifically, it is unclear how the positions and distinctions upon which she insists are superior to those that she rejects and how her account of "facts" permits her to compare her views with those of others. Moreover, her invocation of Kant is vague and undeveloped. I shall explain.

Radin argues that various connections exist between property and "personhood." By "personhood" she means, roughly, a developed and enduring healthy character structure in a human being. To achieve and maintain personhood in this sense, human beings need some control over resources in the external environment in the form of property rights. These rights fall into two classes. First are *fungible* property rights. These are held instrumentally. Second are *personal* property rights. These are "bound up with a person."[12] She sometimes calls them "property for personhood."[13] Personal property gives rise to a stronger moral claim than does fungible property.[14] In Radin's estimation, utilitarianism cannot account for this difference in moral strength. Instead, one needs a

---

[7] Ruth F. Chadwick, "The Market for Bodily Parts: Kant and Duties to Oneself," *Journal of Applied Philosophy*, vol. 6, no. 2 (1989), pp. 129–39.

[8] *Ibid.*, p. 137 ("one undesirable consequence . . ." and "dire consequences for society's values . . .").

[9] Leon R. Kass, "Organs for Sale? Propriety, Property, and the Price of Progress," *The Public Interest*, no. 107 (Spring 1992), pp. 65–86.

[10] *Ibid.*, pp. 81–83.

[11] Margaret Jane Radin, "Reflections on Objectification," *Southern California Law Review*, vol. 65, no. 1 (November 1991), pp. 341–54; see esp. pp. 345, 347, 351.

[12] Margaret Jane Radin, "Property and Personhood," *Stanford Law Review*, vol. 34, no. 5 (May 1982), pp. 957–1015, at p. 960.

[13] *Ibid.*, p. 960.

[14] *Ibid.*, p. 978.

nonutilitarian moral theory—in her first major article on property, Radin draws mainly on Hegel—to explain and justify the difference.[15] One can ignore some subtleties in Radin's general theory—for instance, how a ring can be fungible property for a jeweler but personal property for someone who wears it, and how to deal with unhealthy ("fetishist") attachments to property.[16] For now observe that she offers a nonconsequentialist argument in behalf of property for personhood.[17]

In a second major article on property, Radin presents her account of property and personhood in a somewhat different, and somewhat variable, terminology.[18] The various new terms include "thing," "object," "human flourishing," and, especially, "commodity" and cognates such as "commodification." So far as body parts are concerned, the thought seems to be that human beings and various parts of their bodies have a worth that is beyond the market. The "personhood" of human beings requires that human beings as a whole, and various parts of them, be nontransferable or at most transferable with severe restrictions. To allow the exercise of certain property rights in body parts would undermine personhood. Thus, human beings would tumble from a level that reflects their true, nonmarket worth to a level on which they are commodities.

Stripped to essentials, her central claims are that only some items should be salable, that neither "economic analysis" nor "traditional liberalism" convincingly tells us which, and that a conception of "human flourishing"[19] does tell us. These claims relate especially to prostitution, baby-selling, and surrogate motherhood,[20] though occasionally she refers to such parts of the body as human organs, kidneys, hair, blood, fetal tissue, and genetic material (sperm or ova).[21] In arguing for these claims, she remarks that whatever is inalienable is a "thing,"[22] but adds that to talk about "things" is to subscribe to the "subject/object dichotomy"—a "dichotomy" that she wishes to relinquish.[23] Also, she rejects

---

[15] *Ibid.*, pp. 971–78, 984–1013. I leave aside the question of whether a sophisticated rule utilitarian could draw a similar distinction. For a powerful interpretation and development of Hegel's views on property, see Jeremy Waldron, *The Right to Private Property* (Oxford: Clarendon Press, 1988), ch. 10.

[16] See Radin, "Property and Personhood," pp. 968–70, 987–88.

[17] For a different account of the interconnections between persons and property, and varied justificatory arguments for property based on different conceptions of persons, see Munzer, *A Theory of Property*, chs. 3–11.

[18] Margaret Jane Radin, "Market-Inalienability," *Harvard Law Review*, vol. 100, no. 8 (June 1987), pp. 1849–1937. For change in her views over time, see Margaret Jane Radin, "Lacking a Transformative Social Theory: A Response," *Stanford Law Review*, vol. 45, no. 2 (January 1993), pp. 409–24; see esp. pp. 422–24.

[19] Radin, "Market-Inalienability," pp. 1851, 1859–1909, 1936.

[20] *Ibid.*, pp. 1921–36.

[21] Radin, "Property and Personhood," p. 966; Radin, "Market-Inalienability," p. 1924 n. 261; and Radin, "Reflections on Objectification," pp. 342, 347, 351.

[22] Radin, "Market-Inalienability," p. 1852 n. 11.

[23] *Ibid.*, pp. 1852 n. 11, 1909 and n. 222.

a "metaphysical bright line" between "what is inside us" and "a mind-independent reality outside us."[24] "Facts are theory-dependent and value-dependent."[25]

My worries are these. First, her conception of property rights in body parts seems open to doubt. She writes:

> We have an intuition that property necessarily refers to something in the outside world, separate from oneself. . . . This intuition makes it seem appropriate to call parts of the body property only after they have been removed from the system.[26]

The intuition seems to be mistaken. If one could validly contract to sell blood or a kidney and receive money from the buyer, then the blood or kidney, even while it is in the body of the seller, would seem to be property. Of course, I can contract today to sell one thousand shares of stock a month hence, even though I do not yet own the shares. So some contracts do not logically presuppose that one has existing property rights in the thing to be sold. But when the thing sold is already part of one's body, it seems natural, if contracts to sell body parts are allowed, to regard one as having a property right in that part before its removal. Further, if Radin rejects the distinction between subjects and objects, and the line between what is inside us and outside us, these rejections seem inconsistent with the passage just quoted. They also threaten the intelligibility of her "intuition" about property in parts of the body.

Second, her rejection of certain distinctions or "dichotomies" undermines her central claims. She writes:

> If the person/thing distinction is not a sharp divide, neither is inalienability/alienability. There will be a gray area between the two, and hence the outer contours of both personhood and inalienabilities based on personhood will remain contested.[27]

If one accepts this passage at face value, the line between "personal" and nonpersonal items, upon which Radin insists, seems every bit as blurry as the line between persons and things in the external world, which she rejects. It is then unclear why one should prefer Radin's general theory of market-inalienability to, say, the efforts of "liberals" or "pluralists" to delineate the market realm from the nonmarket realm on the basis of a distinction between persons and things.[28] It is, moreover, unclear how

---

[24] *Ibid.*, p. 1897. But see *ibid.*, p. 1909 n. 222.
[25] *Ibid.*, p. 1882.
[26] Radin, "Property and Personhood," p. 966 (footnote omitted).
[27] Radin, "Market-Inalienability," p. 1897 (footnote omitted).
[28] Cf. *ibid.*, p. 1897 n. 179.

she can later appeal to Kant,[29] for he makes a sharp distinction between persons, who have dignity, and things, which have only a price.[30]

Third, if "[f]acts are theory-dependent and value-dependent,"[31] and if language reflects these dependencies, it is unclear what language Radin can use to compare the respective merits of her own position with that of, say, economic analysis or traditional liberalism. Perhaps one can eliminate the problem by excising Radin's reflections on the nature of facts. In any event, her own position, invoking as it does a vague account of human flourishing, seems to rest heavily on her own intuitions.[32]

Finally, there is a need to explicate and examine Kant with some care. In a recent effort, Radin states that "when we use the term objectification [of which commodification is one form] pejoratively, as in 'objectification of persons', we mean, roughly, 'what Kant would not want us to do'."[33] This statement helps little unless one knows what Kant wants and whether he has good reasons for wanting it.

III. A KANTIAN STARTING POINT

The works of Kant suggest several arguments against property rights in human body parts. One of them—the argument from dignity—runs as follows. Human beings have dignity (*Würde*). Dignity is an unconditioned and incomparable worth. Entities with dignity differ sharply from entities that have a price on a market.[34] If human beings had property rights in body parts and exercised those rights, they would treat parts of their bodies in ways that conflict with their dignity. They would move from the level of entities with dignity to the level of things with a price.

This argument, as just presented, is entirely too sketchy to be convincing. To fill it in, one must at least (1) unpack Kant's understanding of dignity, (2) explain his account of persons and their bodies, (3) clarify so far as possible the difference between sales and donations, and (4) articulate preliminarily the connection between selling a body part and being vulnerable to moral objection. I intend the resulting argument to be broadly Kantian in spirit. I do not claim that Kant scholars will find it faultless, or that it is consistent with everything that Kant says.

1. Persons have dignity just in virtue of being human.[35] This dignity is

---

[29] Radin, "Reflections on Objectification," pp. 345, 347, 351.

[30] In fact, Radin, "Market-Inalienability," pp. 1891–94, 1896–98, criticizes Kant for distinguishing between persons and things.

[31] *Ibid.*, p. 1882.

[32] *Ibid.*, pp. 1903–9, 1937.

[33] Radin, "Reflections on Objectification," p. 345 (footnote omitted).

[34] Immanuel Kant, *Groundwork of the Metaphysic of Morals* [1785], trans. H. J. Paton as *The Moral Law* (London: Hutchinson University Library, 1948), pp. 96–97.

[35] See, for example, *ibid.*, pp. 96–97; Immanuel Kant, *The Metaphysics of Morals* [1797], trans. Mary Gregor (Cambridge: Cambridge University Press, 1991), pp. 216–17, 230–31, 254–55.

not lost even if a person acts immorally.[36] Moreover, dignity is "uncon-ditioned"[37] — that is, it does not depend on needs, consequences, or other contingent facts. Dignity is also an "incomparable worth," for it is "exalted above all price" and "admits of no equivalent."[38] Thus, one cannot counterbalance an offense against dignity by any increase in price. Dignity is therefore priceless.[39]

Dignity is an attribute not mainly of isolated individuals but of persons as "ends in themselves"[40] who are members of a "kingdom of ends."[41] Persons so understood belong to a moral community in which dignity and autonomy must be ascribed to every rational person with a will. Accordingly, the construction of a legal system for these persons must observe the dignity of each individual.[42]

Let us now join these reflections on dignity with the idea of moral and legal rights. I suggest that Kant's understanding of dignity proceeds from an effort to wrestle with the question of how we must reciprocally recog-nize individuals in a moral and legal order that affords them equal rights. His answer is that we must ascribe to them the attribute of dignity if a practice of universal equal rights is to make sense. This attribute is tran-scendentally necessary. That is, ascribing dignity to oneself and others is a necessary condition of the possibility of universal equal rights.

Kant's use of the notion of dignity rests on an innovative reaction to predecessors in the history of political theory.[43] One tradition identifies dignity with honor. Under an ethic of honor, only some persons have dignity. Other persons, who belong to lower orders of moral attainment or of society, lack dignity in the sense of honor, and do not have moral rights equal to those who possess honor. Kant's move, following Pufen-dorf, is to redefine "dignity" in such a way that all persons have it just in virtue of being human. Accordingly, they are all bearers of equal moral and legal rights.[44]

[36] See, for example, Immanuel Kant, *Lectures on Ethics* [1775–80], trans. Louis Infield and foreword by Lewis White Beck (Indianapolis and Cambridge: Hackett, 1963), pp. 196–97.

[37] Kant, *Groundwork of the Metaphysic of Morals*, p. 97.

[38] *Ibid.*, pp. 96, 97.

[39] For a sensitive exposition and use of Kant's views on dignity, see Thomas E. Hill, Jr., *Dignity and Practical Reason in Kant's Ethical Theory* (Ithaca and London: Cornell University Press, 1992), pp. 10, 47–50, 56, 166–67, 178, 202–17, 246–47.

[40] Kant, *Groundwork of the Metaphysic of Morals*, pp. 97–98.

[41] *Ibid.*, pp. 98–100.

[42] See Hill, *Dignity and Practical Reason in Kant's Ethical Theory*, pp. 178, 208–9, 246–47, as well as Hill's general treatment of the "kingdom of ends" on pp. 58–66.

[43] James Tully suggested to me this way of looking at Kant's position.

[44] See Samuel Pufendorf, *De Jure Naturae et Gentium Libri Octo* (*The Law of Nature and Na-tions in Eight Books*) [1672], vol. 1, Latin text of 1688; vol. 2, trans. C. H. and W. A. Oldfather (Oxford: Clarendon Press, and London: Humphrey Milford, 1934), bk. 3, ch. 2, sections 1–9. Pufendorf almost always uses the terms *aequalitas, aequalitas naturalis, aequalitas juris* ("equal-ity," "natural equality," "equality of right") rather than *dignatio* ("dignity"). See also Peter Berger, "On the Obsolescence of the Concept of Honor," in *Revisions: Changing Perspectives in Moral Philosophy*, ed. Stanley Hauerwas and Alasdair MacIntyre (Notre Dame and Lon-

Kant is also reacting to a different tradition, represented by Hobbes, that identifies dignity with price. More precisely, Hobbes separates both "worth" and "dignity" from "honor." Honor he associates with power. Worth is the value of a person as set by his or her price, and dignity is that person's value as set by the commonwealth. In terms of the contrast with Kant, it is what Hobbes technically calls "worth" that is more relevant, and Hobbes insists that "as in other things, so in men, not the seller, but the buyer determines the Price."[45] Kant responds in effect that Hobbes, while he eschews the older honor-ethic, cuts off the branch on which he is sitting. One cannot achieve universal equal moral rights if one appeals only to worth in Hobbes's sense and if persons can have different values or "prices" on the market. Hence, Kant redefines dignity so that, as against Hobbes, it differs from price, and so that, as against the aristocratic ethic of honor, it undergirds universal equal moral and legal rights.

2. If these remarks help to explain Kant's understanding of dignity, they do little to elucidate the complicated, and not terribly clear, account of body parts, whole bodies, selves, and persons on which the argument seems to rest. Although Kant often makes stronger statements,[46] his deepest objection, I think, is only to property rights in *some* body parts as defined in my introduction. He comments that the "body is part of the self; in its *togetherness* with the self it constitutes the person."[47] He also appears to distinguish between body parts that are organs, such as kidneys or testicles, and body parts that are not organs or otherwise integral to the functioning of the body, such as hair.[48] His emphasis, then, is on the integration or "togetherness" of the various parts that make up a human person. And the core of his protest is against the sale of any part that is integral to the normal biological functioning of that person.[49]

One way to develop this Kantian argument is to distinguish between isolated sales and frequent exchanges in a market. Kant would have concern about both. Even isolated transactions could offend the dignity of the few individuals involved. Yet frequent exchanges pose a graver risk to the dignity of many individuals. If a market is an arrangement in which sell-

don: University of Notre Dame Press, 1983), pp. 172–81; Charles Taylor, *Sources of the Self: The Making of the Modern Identity* (Cambridge, MA: Harvard University Press, 1989), pp. 16, 20, 23, 25, 44, 65, 83–84, 94, 152–55, 214, 285, 365, 450; and James Tully, "Introduction," in Samuel Pufendorf, *On the Duty of Man and Citizen According to Natural Law* [1673], ed. James Tully and trans. Michael Silverthorne (Cambridge: Cambridge University Press, 1991), p. xxvi.

[45] Thomas Hobbes, *Leviathan* [1651], ed. W. G. Pogson Smith (Oxford: Clarendon Press, 1909), pt. 1, ch. 10, p. 67. Actually, a willing buyer and a willing seller would jointly determine the price.

[46] Munzer, "Kant and Property Rights in Body Parts" (*supra* note 2) surveys the stronger pronouncements and suggests ways of using Kant's general moral theory to soften them.

[47] Kant, *Lectures on Ethics*, p. 166 (emphasis added); cf. *ibid.*, pp. 147–48.

[48] Kant, *The Metaphysics of Morals*, p. 219.

[49] For a more careful textual reconstruction of this and other Kantian arguments, see Munzer, "Kant and Property Rights in Body Parts."

ers and buyers make exchanges, and if commodities are items that can be bought and sold in a market, then a market for those body parts integral to normal biological functioning, such as kidneys, would be quite worrisome for Kant. Specifically, the existence of such a market could transform attitudes that human beings have toward themselves and others. They might come to think of one another not so much as moral agents with inherent dignity, but more as repositories of organs, tissues, and other bodily substances. They might dwell heavily on the price that healthy organs would fetch on the market. In sum, a Kantian argument from dignity raises, at least prima facie, a concern about body parts as "commodities" that are exchangeable in a market.

3. But now it is necessary to clarify the difference between sales and donations. Ordinarily, it is easy to distinguish between them. Sales are transfers for value received in return. Donations are gratuitous transfers. An arrangement for donating body parts is not a market, and does not make body parts into commodities.

Yet sometimes the line between sales and donations can be fuzzy. Suppose that A needs bone marrow and B needs a kidney. Their tissues are compatible. A agrees to transfer one of her kidneys to B. B agrees to transfer some of his bone marrow to A. Does it make a difference whether these transfers are characterized as "mutual donations" or "mutual sales"?

It does, but the line can be hard to draw. Sometimes one can draw it. If each says that he or she will transfer even if the other does not, and if one has good grounds for believing both, then the transfers are mutual donations. No commodities are in play and no moral objections arise. But suppose that B realizes that it is harder to find histocompatible bone marrow than kidneys and surmises that he may be able to obtain a kidney elsewhere. B then agrees to the mutual transfer with A only if A pays B $20,000. Here the transfers are mutual sales — or at least the transfer from B to A is a sale. Here at least the bone marrow is a commodity, and one can debate whether B's action is morally objectionable. Differently, suppose that neither A nor B requests any cash, but each says that he or she will transfer only if the other does. Here it is hard to make a uniquely convincing case for either the label "mutual donations" or the label "mutual sales." Perhaps "barter" is apt. It is also harder to assess the morality of the motives and actions of A and B.

4. Yet even if the line between sales and donations is clear enough, it is necessary to articulate the connection between selling a body part and being vulnerable to moral objection. Recall that the core Kantian protest involves, in effect, two strands: selling body parts and losing body parts needed for normal biological functioning. A thought experiment can separate these strands and force consideration of what it is about *selling* that might be objectionable. Imagine that in the distant future artificial organs and other body parts are plentiful. Only a small subgroup of humans needs natural organs as replacements for organs that have become dis-

eased or injured. A member of the larger group sells various natural organs to members of the subgroup, and immediately receives artificial organs in risk-free surgical procedures. He makes money in these transactions because the price for his natural organs far exceeds the cost of the artificial replacements and the surgeries. Hence, in this hypothetical example, the strand of losing a body part necessary to healthy functioning drops out as a pertinent consideration.

What, then, might be objectionable about selling as such? It will not do to say that the hypothetical seller should get a job rather than sell natural organs for a living. The seller may well be leading a shallow life and not fulfilling the possibilities of a genuinely human existence. Even if that is so, the objection appears to be, not to selling as such, but rather to leading a shallow and unfulfilling life. Nor will it do to say, in the case of some organs or body parts, that they are so bound up with the seller's personal identity that they should not be sold. Examples of such organs or parts might include the brain, face, genitals, hands, tongue, and larynx. Once again, if there is a sound objection, it relates, not to selling as such, but to the transfer of intensely personal parts of the body.

A better answer invokes the *strength of the reason* for selling the organ or body part. Getting money is a superficial reason for transferring a body part, at least when the seller has morally unproblematic ways of earning a decent living. Compare Kant's remark that it is objectionable "to have oneself castrated in order to get an easier livelihood as a singer."[50] Kant's thought here may be that if a somewhat less easy livelihood is still possible, one does violence to the humanity in one's person by becoming a castrato. The hypothetical seller's reason differs from deeper or nobler reasons, such as donating an organ to save the life of a member of the subgroup. Furthermore, receiving money would be an especially superficial reason for transferring an intensely personal part of the seller's body. For such parts, the reason could be deeper if the recipient were the seller's identical twin, though here donating betokens a nobler class of reasons and associated motives than selling.[51] It is, of course, possible for a reason for donating a body part also to be insufficiently strong.

Lest the earlier comments on Radin seem overly severe, I wish to identify some common ground here between her position and my reconstruction of Kant. Radin's conception of human flourishing is vague partly because for her it functions as a "pragmatic" framework or heuristic device for working out practical solutions to philosophical problems that arise in particular social contexts.[52] My Kantian reconstruction empha-

---

[50] Kant, *The Metaphysics of Morals*, p. 219.

[51] Russell Scott, *The Body as Property* (New York: Viking Press, 1981), pp. 222–23, mentions a testicle transplant between identical twins.

[52] Radin, "Market-Inalienability" (*supra* note 18), pp. 1903–9; Radin, "Lacking a Transformative Social Theory: A Response" (*supra* note 18), pp. 409–10 and n. 2, 414 and n. 18, 422 n. 43.

sizes that the moral assessment of selling body parts has to take into account the nature of the part sold and the seller's reasons for selling it. Moreover, I have suggested elsewhere that a Kantian conception of a life lived in accordance with his duties of virtue could be a fragment of a larger understanding of human flourishing.[53] And were one to think of dignity not so much as a transcendentally necessary attribute in a Kantian vein, but as a social and cultural attribute constituted by the relations among persons understood along Hegelian lines, some of the pragmatic and contextual aspects of the present argument would stand out more sharply. I do not wish to stretch the point. Sharp differences in approach exist between Radin and me. Still, Radin and I share some concerns about the effect of some market transactions on a well-lived human life in society.

As a first approximation, then, selling a body part might be morally objectionable if the strength of the reason for selling is insufficient in relation to the nature of the part sold. This preliminary result should be understood against the background of the following points. First, money is just a medium of exchange. Thus, receiving money in return for a body part is not inherently or always morally objectionable. One has to look at the reason for which the seller wants the money. Second, even if selling is morally objectionable, it does not follow that the seller lacks a moral right to sell. Here, as in other situations, persons sometimes have a moral right to do what is morally wrong, objectionable, base, ignoble, or degrading.[54] Third, it is logically possible for an entity to have both a dignity-value and a market-value.[55] Nevertheless, it may not be psychologically possible for someone to think of an entity as simultaneously having both and still retain the attitudes typically exhibited toward entities regarded as possessing dignity. And there can be a kind of social split-mindedness if many regard some persons — e.g., women or children — as simultaneously having both kinds of value.[56] Fourth, even if a body part is salable and hence is a commodity, it does not follow that the body part is *only* a commodity. Fifth, this preliminary result has nothing to do with some familiar Marxian themes. The result does not suppose that anyone is exploiting the seller. Neither does it rest on the idea that exchange-value swamps or undercuts use-value. For instance, if kidneys can be bought and sold, then they have an exchange-value. But this fact does not interfere with their use-value, for sold kidneys, if successfully

---

[53] Munzer, "Kant and Property Rights in Body Parts," p. 10 and n. 17.

[54] See Jeremy Waldron, "A Right to Do Wrong," *Ethics*, vol. 92 (October 1981), pp. 21–39.

[55] Kant seems to oscillate on this point. In one passage he says that "everything has either a price or a dignity." Kant, *Groundwork of the Metaphysic of Morals*, p. 96 (emphasis omitted). In another work he writes that man regarded as a natural being can have a "price" even while, regarded as a "person," he has a "dignity." Kant, *The Metaphysics of Morals*, p. 230 (emphasis omitted).

[56] Cf. Michael Walzer, *Spheres of Justice: A Defense of Pluralism and Equality* (New York: Basic Books, 1983), ch. 4.

transplanted, will perform the same functions in the recipients that they did in the sellers. Sixth, so far only a possible objection to selling body parts has emerged. Lacking at the moment is any account of how buying body parts or the existence of a market for body parts could offend dignity.

IV. THREE WAYS OF OFFENDING DIGNITY

The Kantian starting point has not got us far. It proposes a definitional connection between a market for body parts and a view of body parts as commodities. It suggests that the lack of a sufficiently strong reason is what can make selling body parts morally objectionable. And it introduces some speculative worries about the impact of a market for body parts on dignity. Yet the previous section does not explain how this market, or participating in it, can offend dignity. Providing such an explanation is the next order of business.

I shall describe three ways of offending dignity by buying or selling body parts. The classification is consistent with but does not stem from Kant's writings. The first way affronts, insults, or demeans dignity. The offense is direct. The second and third ways degrade the sense of dignity. Here the offenses are indirect. They relate proximally to the sense of dignity and only distally to dignity itself. I shall elaborate.

The first way of offending dignity occurs if and only if an action affronts, insults, or demeans dignity, but does not reduce it. Kantian dignity, it will be recalled, is an unconditioned and incomparable moral worth that all persons have just in virtue of being human. It relates to a transcendentally necessary attribute of human beings. Consequently, this first offense against dignity does not reduce the worth of a person. It cannot do so. Unless the action kills the victim, or produces a mental disintegration that destroys the victim's capacity to act as a rational moral agent, the victim will survive as a person. And were the victim destroyed as a person, the dignity would be destroyed rather than merely reduced.

This first offense against dignity is significant because it is a specially disrespectful form of treatment. If one commits the offense against oneself, one exhibits a disregard for one's own inherent worth. However, I do not agree with those passages in Kant that suggest, for example, that by engaging in prostitution or selling oneself, one "jettison[s] [one's] person" and becomes a "thing" or a worm.[57] These actions, even if they are morally wrong, do not have a once-for-all effect. If others commit this offense against a person, indignation and resentment are appropriate. Suppose, for example, that a shop foreman upbraids a female employee, calls her a "typical stupid woman," and screams that her job "should be

[57] Kant, *Lectures on Ethics*, p. 124. But see *ibid.*, pp. 196–97.

done by a man." The employee is entitled to protest and rebuke the wrongdoer and defiantly to reaffirm her worth in the face of such treatment.[58] It is a tricky matter to say what sort of intention is necessary to offend dignity in this first way. The verb "affront" suggests that the intention selects dignity as its target. The verbs "insult" and "demean" probably require some less selective or precise intention to offend dignity.

Explaining the second and third offenses against dignity requires a pair of additional concepts. One is the *sense of dignity*: an awareness of unconditioned and incomparable worth. This awareness is connected to Kant's understanding of self-respect, which I take to be a sense of inner moral worth that comes from acting on principles rationally derived from the moral law.[59] Unlike dignity, the sense of dignity is partly subjective, since it rests on a person's awareness of his or her moral worth. Furthermore, unlike dignity, the sense of dignity is susceptible of being reduced.

The possibility of a reduced sense of dignity brings into play the other concept: *degradation*. Elsewhere I have suggested that degradation is treating someone or something in such a way as to reduce, or to attempt to reduce, him, her, or it to a lower level or degree.[60] There are many sorts of degradation. In the present context, a lower level or degree of sense of dignity is meant. So the thought is that to recognize and exercise property rights in body parts might sometimes be to lower a person's sense of dignity.

With these two concepts in hand, I return to the remaining offenses against dignity. The second way of offending dignity occurs if and only if an action has, and is intended to have, the outcome of degrading someone's sense of dignity. For instance, if an organ broker in a Third World country intended to make a prospective seller of a kidney feel of lesser moral worth, and if the broker succeeded, the broker would have degraded the prospective seller's sense of dignity. Of course, those who deal in body parts may not have such refined intentions as to undermine a person's sense of moral worth. They are more likely to intend to make money by dealing in organs. But whenever the appropriate intention is present, and the intended outcome is achieved, the second offense against dignity arises.

The third way of offending dignity occurs if and only if an action has, but is not intended to have, the outcome of degrading someone's sense of dignity. Here the person who degrades does not intend to lower a person's awareness of moral worth, but lowers it through some lapse, fault, mistake, misjudgment, or the like. Suppose that you are a medical

---

[58] See Jean Hampton, "Forgiveness, Resentment, and Hatred," in Jeffrie G. Murphy and Jean Hampton, *Forgiveness and Mercy* (Cambridge: Cambridge University Press, 1988), pp. 35–87. Her chapter offers a fuller discussion of the varieties of human worth than can be attempted here.

[59] See Munzer, "Kant and Property Rights in Body Parts," pp. 10–12.

[60] *Ibid.*, p. 4.

worker. Through insensitivity, you treat me as a repository of organs and tissues to be sold on the market. I am fragile and my sense of dignity declines. You have offended dignity in this last way.

The relevance to morality of this threefold classification of offenses against dignity is as follows. From the standpoint of consequences, the last two offenses are more serious than the first. From the perspective of the appraisal of intentions, the first two offenses are more serious than the third. Of course, the third offense may still exhibit a kind of moral fault that is distinct from consequences. It can be blameworthy to have allowed oneself to develop, say, the insensitivity to treat others badly without intending to lower their sense of dignity.

Some might argue that the first offense does not amount to much. This "no harm, no foul" approach might work for basketball, but it is not in order here. If I have an unconditioned and incomparable worth, and if you insult that worth by treating me as a repository of body parts, you have offended my dignity even if I have the strength to resist your impositions. I suspect that the root appeal of arguments couched in terms of dignity and the sense of dignity is not to consequences. Rather, it is to the moral inappropriateness of treating human beings in a way that does not comport with their equal moral worth in a community of moral agents.

The general payoff of this section is that participating in a market for body parts can sometimes undercut the distinction between dignity and price, and thus sometimes undermine the practice of mutual recognition as equal rights-bearing citizens. To appreciate this general point, one should, however, attend to the three different ways in which buying and selling body parts can offend dignity. Otherwise, one can fall into using such words as "demeaning" or "degrading" without noticing that they can apply to different situations requiring careful discrimination. In contrast to the previous section, we now have a tentative explanation of how market activities in addition to selling might sometimes offend dignity.

To prevent misunderstanding I should offer these points about the argument thus far. First, offenses against dignity, as understood here, are offenses against the dignity of particular persons—whether sellers, buyers, brokers, or other participants in a market for body parts. They are not offenses against an abstract or general dignity that floats as a brooding omnipresence in a Kantian sky. Second, that the sense of dignity is in some measure subjective requires no apology. Evidently, it can be tricky to discover the extent to which the second and third offenses reduce a person's sense of dignity. Still, an inquiry of this sort is no more troubling than that in any moral position that recommends beneficence or contains a principle against harm. In all such cases one has to discern the existence and extent of an impact on one person of the actions of others. I am not claiming that all persons who buy or sell body parts have negative subjective reactions that one can call reductions in their sense of dignity.

V. The Fallacy of Division

Any sound argument against property rights in body parts that uses a concept of dignity must avoid the fallacy of division. Those who commit this fallacy make the mistake of arguing that what is true of a whole must also be true of its parts. In the present context, the fallacy comes up in this way. Human beings have dignity. Human beings can also suffer offenses against dignity in three different ways. But it is fallacious to argue that, in consequence, human body parts have dignity or can suffer offenses against dignity. Similarly, even if a living human being has an unconditioned and incomparable worth, it does not follow that parts of that human being's body do. And even if persons lack property rights in themselves or their whole bodies, it does not follow that they lack property rights in their body parts or that those parts are not commodities.

Now some may respond that no serious thinker could be tempted by such obviously faulty reasoning. But Kant is a serious thinker, and some passages suggest that he succumbed to this temptation. For example, he writes that a man "is not entitled to sell a limb, not even one of his teeth." Part of his argument for this position is that "a person cannot be a property and so cannot be a thing which can be owned, for it is impossible to be a person and a thing, the proprietor and the property."[61] But even if persons cannot have property rights in the whole of their persons or their whole bodies, it hardly follows that they lack property rights in parts of their bodies. The quoted passages do not reflect Kant's best or considered thinking on this topic. Still, they indicate that this sort of logical blunder can attract a sober and intelligent, if momentarily unwary, philosopher.

To avoid the fallacy of division, one or both of two related strategies might be pursued. The *integration strategy* insists on the unified organization of the various body parts, of widely different kinds, that make up a living human being. The broadly Kantian view sketched in Section III exemplifies this strategy. Pursuing the matter in this way suggests a gradient of concerns about body parts as commodities. The concern is less serious for hair and for replenishable fluids such as blood and semen. It is more serious for a single paired but nonrenewable organ such as a kidney. And it is more serious still for single nonrenewable organs such as the heart, liver, or pancreas. This gradient of seriousness is an attractive consequence of the integration strategy.

The *derived-status strategy* invokes the fact that the various body parts are, or were, parts of a living human being and can have more or less personal connections with that human being. The status of the part has something to do with the status of the whole and its role in the whole. A gradient of appropriateness of treatment as a commodity suggests

[61] Kant, *Lectures on Ethics*, p. 165. See also Munzer, "Kant and Property Rights in Body Parts," pp. 7, 8–10.

itself, and concern about the ultimate use of the part is relevant. Here are some examples. If sold blood is used for transfusion, the concern is minimal. But if sold blood is used as a movie prop in place of so-called technicolor blood, the concern rises. If sold skin becomes a graft for a burn victim, the concern is minimal for cadaveric flesh but rises for skin supplied by a living person. And if sold skin is used for upholstery, the concern is great indeed. Differently, a sold kidney raises fewer concerns about appropriateness, because the function of a kidney is not especially personal. Concerns rise in the case of a sold testicle because (*inter alia*) any child conceived through it will have the genetic makeup of the seller rather than the recipient. If, fancifully, one could, while alive, sell one's face with the transfer to take effect at death, concern would be great, because one's face is intensely personal. This gradient of appropriateness of treatment is an appealing consequence of the derived-status strategy.

The latter strategy may seem problematic for two reasons. First, degrading uses are not confined to human beings or human body parts. For instance, one could degrade an original painting by Rembrandt by urinating on it or using it as a dart board. One is then no longer treating it in a way appropriate to a work of art. Now I agree that various objects can suffer degradation. And Section IV observes that there are many sorts of degradation. Still, my argument in no way requires that *only* body parts or persons be vulnerable to degradation. But persons alone are susceptible of the sort of degradation that involves a reduction in the sense of dignity.

Second, the derived-status strategy reflects concern about specific uses rather than treating body parts as commodities. Thus, it would also be objectionable to use *donated* blood as a movie prop or *donated* skin as upholstery. Now I agree that such uses of donated body parts are objectionable. All the same, I wish to argue that there is something particularly objectionable about *selling* body parts for uses of these sorts. The argument rests on a point made in Section III — namely, that sometimes receiving money in return for a body part is an insufficiently strong reason for selling, especially when the part sold is to be used in an inappropriate way. Hence, a special concern arises when body parts both suffer degrading uses and are commodities. It is, though, in no wise a feature of my argument that *only* sold body parts can be put to degrading uses.

I do not claim that obtaining money is always a frivolous, trivial, superficial, or shallow reason for transferring a body part. Modest need can be reason enough for selling blood or semen. And dire need can justify the sale of other body parts. There are reports of a vast market in kidneys and maybe even eyes and skin from the Persian Gulf to China.[62] The sellers are the desperately poor. The ultimate recipients are affluent patients with

---

[62] See, for example, Charles P. Wallace, "For Sale: The Poor's Body Parts," *Los Angeles Times*, August 27, 1992, p. A1.

renal or corneal disease or severe burns. These transactions can involve an offense against dignity. Yet it does not follow that, all things considered, the desperately poor lack ample justification for the sales. Writ large, a market in body parts may be prima facie objectionable, but on balance barring such a market may not be justified. Doubtless some redistribution of income and wealth is the most effective way to restore hope. Yet, short of that, sellers should recognize that they are worth *incommensurably more* than the amount their body parts would bring on the market. They are human beings with an unconditioned and incomparable worth. This self-recognition is a reason for holding on to a sense of dignity in the face of assaults on their struggle to live.

VI. Participants in a Market for Body Parts

In First World countries sales of blood and semen occur. In Third World countries there are reports of the poor selling organs such as kidneys for transplantation into the bodies of wealthy nationals or foreigners. But rarely do sellers deal directly with the recipients of their body parts. Hence, a realistic appraisal of body parts as commodities and the occurrence of offenses against dignity should distinguish the following questions: (1) How are sellers affected? (2) How are transplant recipients affected? (3) How are intermediaries affected? (4) How are nonparticipants affected? (5) Does it make a difference what sort of market is operating?

Even if sellers experience a lowering of their sense of dignity, transplant recipients will likely react quite differently. For one thing, they may not know whether the transplanted organ comes from a cadaveric donor or from a living seller. Even if they know that it comes from a living seller, recipients may not see *themselves* as reducible to the market worth of their body parts. If they are well-to-do, the need to sell an organ for, say, decent housing probably will never arise. Of course, one could say that knowledge of a market for organs dehumanizes both the seller and the ultimate consumer. Marx once made a similar claim about alienation. He believed that both the worker and the capitalist suffered, in different ways, from alienation in a capitalist society.[63]

The reactions of intermediaries—transplant surgeons, nurses, tissue typers, transplant coordinators, organ brokers—are much more difficult to gauge. The difficulty comes partly from their varied roles and how much they know. Perhaps organ brokers are most at risk of thinking of human worth as reducible to the market value of body parts. Even if that is so, their thinking may extend only to those whom they regard as

[63] Karl Marx, *Economic and Philosophic Manuscripts of 1844*, ed. Dirk J. Struik (New York: International Publishers, 1964), p. 119. Cf. Munzer, *A Theory of Property* (*supra* note 1), pp. 158, 177–78.

potential suppliers of organs. They may not see themselves or their friends as reducible to the worth of their parts. Once again, Marx's point about a dehumanizing effect on all comes to the fore. The existence of such an effect will be easier to declare than to document.

Nonparticipants may experience little effect, especially if they are much more numerous than sellers, recipients, and intermediaries. Consider sex. Most people are neither prostitutes nor customers nor pimps. It is unclear that the availability of sex for money leads most people to view sexual intercourse in a commercialized way. It may, however, lead some to do so or to view women differently from the way in which they otherwise would.

As to type of market, notice that up to this point attention has centered on sales by way of present transfers from living donors. Futures markets of the sort advocated by Cohen and Hansmann present less risk of eroding a nonmarket sense of human worth. Whether decedents' estates receive a large payment for a usable organ, or whether people receive small installment payments during life, the removal of organs only upon death might blunt the reactions of sellers, recipients, and intermediaries. Reactions may be more intense if transactions in a secondary market are well publicized. Imagine a commodities report that concludes: "In Chicago futures trading, human livers were steady today, and hearts rebounded after a morning sell-off, while corneas closed at $1,000 even." In short, depending on participants' intentions and the effects on others, there is a risk of offenses against dignity, but it will require analytical skill and empirical information to say how much of each kind actually occurs.

I have been surprised by the objection that the argument thus far licenses an assault on free speech. The thought behind the objection seems to be that a market in body parts could cause harm. The harm could be offenses against dignity and such staples as preference-dissatisfaction and interference with rights conceived along libertarian lines. The harm caused could be a reason for limiting freedom of speech and of the press. For instance, it might be said that the state could justifiably bar publication of a book that advocates the sale of body parts.

I respond that one would have to argue in much greater detail than I am prepared to do here to justify any such limits on free speech. No doubt some harm might come from merely advocating a market in body parts. Yet the basic structure of society might reasonably endorse a principle of free speech that is powerful enough to permit advocating such a market. Compare slavery. A society might bar slavery but establish free speech. The right of free speech might include the right to advocate a social change that would introduce slavery. Thus, I do not here wish to go down the road, as some do with racist speech or hate-speech, of arguing that the harm (if any) springing from the mere advocacy of a market in body parts justifies restrictions on free speech.

VII. Monetization and the Language of the Market

The fanciful commodities report described in the previous section raises a sticky issue for the case against property rights in body parts: If these parts are commodities, will the language of the market affect the way in which people view themselves and others, so as to insult dignity and impair the sense of dignity? Some might think that an affirmative answer has to be correct, for if people think of *body parts* as things that can be bought and sold in the market, surely they will view *themselves and others* as things that can be bought and sold. The italicized phrases underscore that this reasoning is faulty because it commits the fallacy of composition, which is the reverse of the fallacy of division. Even so, it hardly follows that people might not see themselves and others differently—for example, in ways that evidence a lowering of a sense of dignity. Whether they see themselves and others differently becomes a largely empirical question about the effects of the language of the market.

I must separate at once my concern with the language of the market from the currently fashionable interest in so-called economic rhetoric.[64] The latter deals mostly with terminology employed by professional economists. The key idea is that economic terminology often employs metaphors or images that, so it is claimed, subtly encourage certain ways of looking at things. Examples include "demand curves," "business cycles," "elasticity of supply," "velocity of money," "human capital," "Walrasian auctioneer," and, of course, "invisible hand." The language of the market and economic rhetoric do not capture entirely different collections of terms. For example, the words "commodity" and "market" appear both in the language of the market and in economic rhetoric. But I do not think that the terminology of professional economists rapidly permeates new areas of popular thinking, and in any case I doubt that it is a prime factor in degradation of any kind associated with the salability of body parts. Thus, for my purposes, I need only such everyday terms as "property," "property rights," "commodity," "money," "price," and "market."

The question now becomes whether the language of the market, as applied to body parts, plays any role in offenses against dignity. So far as the last two offenses (which require a lowering in the sense of dignity) are concerned, the issue is very much an empirical one. It is hard to locate solid evidence on this issue. The situation is somewhat different with the first offense precisely because it does not require the existence of undesirable effects. Empirical evidence is, though, still relevant to this offense, because one must establish that treatment has occurred that affronts, insults, or demeans dignity.

---

[64] See, for example, Arjo Klammer, Donald N. McCloskey, and Robert M. Solow, eds., *The Consequences of Economic Rhetoric* (Cambridge: Cambridge University Press, 1988).

Among the terms in the language of the market is the word "money," and it is useful to explore some connections between the assignment of monetary values to body parts (monetization) and the existence of a market in which these parts are commodities. Distinguish two propositions: (1) All commodities are monetized items. (2) All monetized items are commodities. I suspect that the first proposition is false. One can imagine rudimentary barter economies in which there is no common currency. This case may involve commodities because items are exchanged in a market. But the absence of a common currency suggests that these commodities are not monetized or even monetizable. I also suspect that the second proposition is false. Doubtless almost all monetized items are in fact commodities. Still, some ways of assigning monetary values do not seem to involve or create commodities. Here I shall consider, as examples dealing with the loss of body parts, Anglo-Saxon bots, workers' compensation schedules, tort damages, and negotiated tort settlements. I shall also discuss a recent pertinent addition to the academic literature on torts.

One can debate whether Anglo-Saxon law distinguished between tort and crime or between intentional and unintentional torts. It is undebatable that it paid a great deal of attention to bots (compensation or amends)—"bote" or "gebete" in Anglo-Saxon—for the loss of body parts. King Æthelberht of Kent issued the earliest laws (about 600 A.D.) that have been preserved. Roughly thirty-eight out of a total of ninety sections deal with body parts.[65] The laws list bots for striking off an ear (12 shillings), for striking out an eye (50 shillings), for striking off thumbs or fingers (3 to 20 shillings), as well as for breaking bones or disfiguring a face (3 to 20 shillings).[66] As a much later example, the laws of King Alfred of Wessex (about 889–893 A.D.) devote approximately thirty-three out of a total of seventy-seven sections to body parts.[67] They give a somewhat revised schedule—for instance, 30 shillings for an ear, 66 shillings $6\frac{1}{3}$ pence for an eye knocked out (reduced by one-third if the eye remains in the socket but the man cannot see with it), and so on.[68] Though the detail of these laws may surprise contemporary readers, these bots existed in an age when there was comparatively little trade in a modern sense. Bots do not much support a claim that parts of the body were treated as commodities. In the familiar and useful categories of Guido Calabresi and A. Douglas Melamed, the "entitlements" of Anglo-Saxons to various body parts are protected not by "property rules," under which seller and buyer voluntarily agree on a price for the seller's entitlement, but by "liability

---

[65] "The Laws of Æthelberht," cap. 34–72, in *The Laws of the Earliest English Kings*, ed. and trans. F. L. Attenborough (Cambridge: Cambridge University Press, 1922), pp. 8–15.

[66] *Ibid.*, cap. 37, 40, 43–50, 54, 56, 65–66, pp. 8–13.

[67] "The Laws of Alfred," cap. 44–77, in *ibid.*, pp. 86–93.

[68] *Ibid.*, cap. 46–47, pp. 86–87. The standard text for Anglo-Saxon laws from 600 A.D. until the Norman Conquest in 1066 A.D. remains F. Liebermann, *Die Gesetze der Angelsachsen*, 3 vols. (Halle am Saale: Max Niemeyer, 1903–16).

rules," under which the holder of the entitlement receives a collectively determined amount.[69] The language of the bot, though it monetizes, does not appear to be the language of the market.

Likewise, contemporary workers' compensation schedules sometimes monetize body parts, but do not make them into commodities. The New York statute, for example, provides for payment to employees of two-thirds of their average weekly wages as follows:

Member lost	Number of weeks' compensation	Member lost	Number of weeks' compensation
a. Arm	312	g. First finger	46
b. Leg	288	h. Great toe	38
c. Hand	244	i. Second finger	30
d. Foot	205	j. Third finger	25
e. Eye	160	k. Toe other than great toe	16
f. Thumb	75	l. Fourth finger	15[70]

Again, liability rules rather than property rules protect entitlements to these body parts. Hence, if a commodity is something that can be bought and sold in a market, then despite monetization the body parts are not commodities.

Tort damages present an interesting case. Whereas the property lawyer is apt to think of transferability of body parts and whole bodies as the hallmark of property rights in the body, the tort lawyer might think of compensation for bodily injuries and wrongful death as that hallmark. Moreover, if an injury that causes the loss of an eye or limb, or that impairs their normal functioning, is compensable, and if insurance companies and the personal injury plaintiffs' and defense bar have monetary schedules ("jury sheets") for such injuries, then some may claim not only that body parts are "property" in some sense but also that they are "commodities" as defined in my introduction. I need not deny the former claim. After all, property encompasses a bundle of rights, and a power to seek and a claim-right to obtain damages are part of the bundle. But I deny the latter claim. Jury sheets only facilitate a prediction of the damages that a jury might award in the case at bar. They do not bind opposing counsel. Either or both may prefer to try the case to a jury verdict. If they do try it, the damages awarded are collectively determined compensation *ex post*. Hence, they represent the operation of a liability rule. No property rule operates here to make body parts into commodities.

[69] Guido Calabresi and A. Douglas Melamed, "Property Rules, Liability Rules, and Inalienability: One View of the Cathedral," *Harvard Law Review*, vol. 85, no. 6 (April 1972), pp. 1089–1128.

[70] Workers' Compensation Law, in *McKinney's Consolidated Laws of New York Annotated* (St. Paul, MN: West, 1993), Book 64, section 15(3), pp. 5–6.

Negotiated tort settlements are a somewhat different matter. Suppose that a plaintiff has lost a hand due to the negligent operation of a machine by the defendant. The parties, their lawyers, and the insurance company may agree both on the existence of liability and on the amount of damages. Here monetization results in a commodity precisely because a property rule has come into play and there is a voluntary agreement on a dollar amount.

Still, the commodity is not the body part—the severed hand—but rather the tort claim. Only if the plaintiff releases the defendant from any further liability will the defendant pay the amount specified in the settlement. In settling tort suits insurers do not thereby purchase body parts. Furthermore, observe that the possibility of a negotiated settlement is parasitic on the existence of the tort system. In consequence, the relevant property rules presuppose a web of liability rules. Hence, in turn, the possibility that the tort claim might be a commodity rests on the possibility that the claim might turn out not to be a commodity at all. Observe also that personal-injury claims, unlike most contract claims, are rarely transferable. Thus, no secondary market exists in which tort claims are exchanged or have a monetary value prior to a negotiated settlement. And settlements would extinguish the claims.

To take stock: Many words make up the language of the market. The empirical effects of the use of this language are largely unknown. Furthermore, although the market lexicon includes "commodity" and "money," not all monetized items are commodities. For example, Anglo-Saxon bots, workers' compensation schedules, and tort damages for lost body parts involve monetary values but not commodities. Negotiated tort settlements for lost body parts do involve commodities, but the commodities are tort claims rather than body parts. In none of these examples does one encounter the sort of market that is most likely to offend dignity—namely, a market in which body parts are sold for transplantation into others.

I wish now to show how these reflections on property and torts link up with an important item in the literature on torts. In a thoughtful and instructive essay, Richard L. Abel criticizes the Anglo-American law of torts. His central negative claim is that this area of the law goes wrong by producing "a commodity—a tort—which has exchange value in both the state-created market (the court) and the dependent markets it engenders (negotiated settlements)."[71] He elaborates this claim in terms of the need for a moral judgment of the defendant's behavior, the victim's need for compensation, and the encouragement of safety precautions. He also offers a positive claim regarding the ways in which tort law should undergo reform. Neither claim directly addresses whether there should

[71] Richard L. Abel, "A Critique of Torts," *UCLA Law Review*, vol. 37, no. 5 (June 1990), pp. 785–831, at p. 790 (footnote omitted).

be a market in body parts. Nevertheless, some conflicts exist between the course of Abel's argument and my own.

In light of this section, Abel's negative claim confuses monetization with commodification, and fails to distinguish between liability rules and property rules. If one eliminates these mistakes, one will see that "the state-created market (the court)" is not a market at all. It does not even mimic a market. It is an arrangement for applying liability rules, and liability rules generate no commodities. Negotiated settlements do involve a market, for they rest on the application of property rules, and they do create commodities, though it is tort claims rather than body parts that they make into commodities.

Abel's negative claim may also rest on a further mistake. The mistake lies in assimilating all state-created constitutive rules to a single type. Regulative rules require or forbid independently existing behavior. Constitutive rules, such as the rules of games, set up as well as regulate new sorts of behavior. The new behavior — e.g., castling in chess — would not be possible without the rules. Abel seems to suppose that all state-created constitutive rules, at least in the relevant area of the law, create a market. In fact, these legal rules create both a market and a scheme for compensation. Insofar as they set up a market, they can make tort claims, but not body parts, into commodities. Insofar as they erect a compensatory scheme, they cannot do either.

Of course, one could always define "commodity" broadly enough to include both. Yet I suspect that the rhetorical force of Abel's negative claim comes from assimilating all existing tort-related recoveries to a market model, because that seems to make personal injuries and lost body parts into "commodities" in *my* sense, which in turn makes the law of torts appear to be a crass tool of capitalism. The appearance, however, trades on a confusion between my standard sense and Abel's expanded sense of "commodity." In one passage Abel seems aware of this point.[72] Yet the essay as a whole minimizes it. Abel shows that "commodification" is more common in the law of torts than some might suppose. It occurs not only in negotiated settlements but also in "risk premiums" (compensation *ex ante*), in the form of higher wages, for work that poses danger to life and limb.[73] Still, Abel does not show that "commodification" is the ubiquitous phenomenon that he claims. In any event, it is not body parts that become commodities. Even in the case of risk premiums, employers do not wish to purchase body parts, but rather their employees' willingness to run certain risks.

[72] *Ibid.*, pp. 808–9 (footnote omitted):

> Economists cannot tell us the value of bodily integrity, emotional well-being, or life because these are not defined by the market. The costs of accidents can only be determined collectively — after the fact by a judge or jury, or before by a legislature or regulatory agency.

[73] *Ibid.*, pp. 790, 820.

The net result is that gaps exist in Abel's argument that the tort system is objectionable. Compensation *ex post* is monetizing. However, that monetizing body parts *can* have negative effects does not establish that it is the same thing as treating these parts as commodities. Both guns and knives can be used to kill, but that fact does not make guns and knives identical. In any case, one still needs psychological evidence that monetizing — or that the tort system as Abel understands it — in fact produces some of the adverse effects that treating something as a commodity might. It might be possible to fill in these gaps in his argument without prejudice to the argument in this essay.

VIII. The Uneasy Case Summarized

This essay contains a sufficiently intricate argument to be worth a summary. The argument starts from the Kantian premise that all human beings have dignity. Dignity is an unconditioned and incomparable worth. Human actions can offend dignity in at least three ways. They can do so directly by affronting, insulting, or demeaning the moral status of a human being. They can also do so indirectly by degrading, either intentionally or unintentionally, the sense of dignity of a human being. Offenses against dignity can be committed either by those whose dignity is offended, or by others, or by both.

Because Kantian dignity differs sharply from having a price on the market, sales of anything possessing such dignity may seem, at least prima facie, to be morally objectionable. Still, it is logically possible for an entity to have both a dignity-value and a market-value. Hence, the argument is not that having dignity precludes having a price on the market, or that exchange-value swamps use-value, or that if something can be bought and sold in a market it is *only* a commodity. Rather, the argument is that if an entity has dignity, then treating that entity or some part of it as a commodity is morally objectionable if the treatment offends dignity.

One now comes to the issue of *when* treating an entity having dignity in certain ways is morally objectionable. To grapple with this issue, we need to distinguish between whole persons and body parts. Most will readily agree that treating a *whole person* as a commodity — for example, as a slave to be bought and sold — offends dignity and thus is morally objectionable. But they might resist the claim that treating a *body part* as a commodity offends dignity. They might urge that any such claim rests on an illegitimate whole-to-part reasoning — the fallacy of division. This essay accepts that the fallacy of division really is a fallacy. And it rejects the idea that body parts *themselves* have dignity in Kant's sense.

How, then, can treating a *body part* as a commodity offend the dignity of a *person*? An answer lies in the pursuit of two complementary strategies. The integration strategy points to the fact that the unified organization of body parts, of various kinds, makes up a living human being. This strategy marks out a gradient of concerns about body parts as commodities. The derived-status strategy emphasizes that the status of any given body part is a function of the status of the whole organism and the role of that part in the whole. This strategy suggests a gradient of appropriate uses of body parts. Together these strategies keep one from falling into a blundering whole-to-part reasoning, while still enabling one to see how treating body parts as commodities *can* offend a person's dignity.

These strategies and gradients have theoretical implications. The implications vary among the participants in a market for body parts and the effects of the market on the participants' sense of dignity. It is morally objectionable for persons to sell their body parts if they offend dignity by selling for a reason that is insufficiently strong relative to the characteristics of the parts sold. It is also morally objectionable for others, such as buyers and brokers, to participate in a market for body parts if by doing so they offend the dignity of sellers or themselves. To say that these actions are "morally objectionable" is not to say that the agents have no moral right to do them, or that the state or other persons have a moral right to interfere with the agents. Finally, it is morally objectionable for a market in body parts to exist if its operation offends the dignity of enough participants in the market. This last implication is fragile. It is difficult to say how many participants are "enough." And even if such a market were morally objectionable on grounds of offense against dignity, it would hardly follow that people have no right to participate in the market, or that the state or other persons have a right to interfere with the market.

The practical payoff of these strategies and gradients is as follows. Worries about offenses against dignity are least serious if one sells body parts that are replenishable or naturally shed and whose removal involves virtually no risk. Examples include hair, blood, and, aside from specifically religious objections, sperm. The worries are not much more serious in the case of replenishable or naturally shed body parts whose removal involves some minor risk to the seller. Examples are ova and bone marrow. One reason that these last examples carry at least some extra concern is that, because of the risk and pain involved, financial considerations may exert more pressure than is desirable on the decision to sell.

Practical worries about offenses to dignity increase with the *inter vivos* sale of nonreplenishable solid organs, such as a kidney or a cornea, for transplantation. Removing the organ involves some risk to the seller — especially in countries where the rate of mortality or morbidity is high. Even if the surgical removal is completely successful, a person with one remaining kidney has a slightly lower life expectancy than a person with two, and a person with one remaining intact eyeball has poorer vision than a person with two. Given these risks and consequences, only financial exigency is likely to spur someone to sell. Accordingly, the prospect of offenses against dignity, in any of the three forms described, looms larger than with sales of blood, sperm, ova, or even bone marrow.

So far as futures contracts are concerned, the practical worries occupy some intermediate level of concern. Financial urgency plays almost no role here. The payment is contingent and deferred under Cohen's proposal. And it is modest under Hansmann's plan. The principal anxiety here relates to the existence and public character of a secondary market in futures contracts. If one hears commodities reports of the sort imagined near the end of Section VI, one can worry that this sort of language of the market might distort the way in which people view themselves and others. They might tend to see persons as repositories of body parts with a market worth rather than as entities with a Kantian dignity.

As I noted in the introduction, this case against property rights in body parts is uneasy. One reason is the difficulty in clarifying what is objectionable about selling as such. A second reason is that a market in body parts has varied participants as well as many who do not participate at all. Hence, the extralinguistic effects on them will vary significantly. Yet another reason is that our understanding of the effects of the language of the market, *for this sort of market*, is sketchy. There is, then, no rapid and cogent move from the mere existence of a market in body parts to a sound objection, in terms of commodities and Kantian dignity, to that market.

Law, University of California, Los Angeles

INDEX

Abel, Richard, 282–84
Aboriginal law, and common law, 174, 176–80
Aboriginal peoples, 153–56, 170–71; governments of, 163–65, 176–79; Locke's view of, 158–65
Abortion, 189 n. 21, 248–49
Administrative agencies, 206–7
Adverse possession, 33
Agency, 131
Agriculture, advantages of, 160–61
Air, rights in, 54–55
Air travel, 61
Animals, ownership of, 34, 36, 39–40, 47–48, 51–52, 148, 254
Appropriation. *See* Original acquisition
Aristotle, 245–46
Autonomy, 137–38, 249–54, 258

Balance of power, 115
Bargaining, 7, 97–99
Bargains, self-enforcing, 107
Barry, Brian, 88–89, 122
Benn, Stanley, 239 n. 112
Bentham, Jeremy, 226–28
Berlin, Isaiah, 210–11, 240
Blackstone, William, 20, 22 n. 10, 31–32
Blame, 131–32
Body parts, rights in, 259–86 *passim*. *See also* Organ donations; Rights, to one's body
Boundary disputes, 36–37
Broadcast spectrum, rights to, 21, 27
Buchanan, James, 95 n. 35, 101, 104, 117–18, 120–22, 221 n. 46
Buckle, Stephen, 221–22, 224, 238 n. 111
Bulkley, John, 165
Bush, Winston, 4

Campbell v. Hall, 172
Canadian Charter of Rights and Freedoms, 173
Chadwick, Ruth, 262–63
Chapman, John W., 210
Children, rights of, 243–44, 246
Civil society, 187, 191–92
Claims, 128 n. 7, 228, 281–83
Classical liberalism, 210–11, 231–32, 239–40; and monism, 224–25
Coase, Ronald, 31
Coercion, 108–10, 150–52

Cohen, G. A., 241
Cohen, Lloyd, 261–62, 278
Coleman, Jules, 96–102, 107–8, 110–115
Collective-action problems, 4–6, 101, 138, 192. *See also* Free-rider problem
Commerce, 59–60. *See also* Exchange
Commerce clause, 39, 200 n. 52
Committee system, in Congress, 203–5
Commodification, of body parts, 259, 262–64, 269–71, 277, 280–83
Common law, 14–15 n. 24, 31, 49 n. 19, 154, 169–76; and aboriginal law, 164, 174, 176–80
Common property, 21–22, 27–31, 36–37; versus private, 50–57
Commons, 38–39, 46–50, 59; management of, 52–53, 55–56, 58
Communes, 55–57
Communitarianism, 168–69
Communities, 134
Compensation, 124–25, 128, 136–37; for bodily injury, 280–84
Congress, 202–6, 220
Consent, 214
Constitution, U.S., 37, 193–202
Constitutional design, 192–202
Contracts, 8, 190 n. 23
Cooperation, 113–14
Coordination problems, 4–6, 101, 138, 192
Copyright, 60
Corfield v. Coryell, 38–39
Crimes, victimless, 255
Culpability, 131
Custom, 57–58

Dawkins, Richard, 12 n. 19
Degradation, 273, 276
Democracy, 200
Demsetz, Harold, 34, 51–52
Desert, 82–83, 90
Dignity: Kant's view of, 266–72, 275, 284; offenses against, 260, 272–75, 284–85
Distribution. *See* Justice, distributive; Wealth
Due process, 200–201 n. 53
Duties, 128, 133
Dworkin, Ronald, 128 n. 7

Ellickson, Robert, 11–12, 52–57, 59
Endangered species, 47–48
Engels, Friedrich, 19, 77 n. 24